1,000,000 Books

are available to read at

www.ForgottenBooks.com

Read online
Download PDF
Purchase in print

ISBN 978-1-330-98278-5
PIBN 10129636

This book is a reproduction of an important historical work. Forgotten Books uses state-of-the-art technology to digitally reconstruct the work, preserving the original format whilst repairing imperfections present in the aged copy. In rare cases, an imperfection in the original, such as a blemish or missing page, may be replicated in our edition. We do, however, repair the vast majority of imperfections successfully; any imperfections that remain are intentionally left to preserve the state of such historical works.

Forgotten Books is a registered trademark of FB &c Ltd.
Copyright © 2018 FB &c Ltd.
FB &c Ltd, Dalton House, 60 Windsor Avenue, London, SW19 2RR.
Company number 08720141. Registered in England and Wales.

For support please visit www.forgottenbooks.com

1 MONTH OF FREE READING

at

www.ForgottenBooks.com

By purchasing this book you are eligible for one month membership to ForgottenBooks.com, giving you unlimited access to our entire collection of over 1,000,000 titles via our web site and mobile apps.

To claim your free month visit:

www.forgottenbooks.com/free129636

* Offer is valid for 45 days from date of purchase. Terms and conditions apply.

English
Français
Deutsche
Italiano
Español
Português

www.forgottenbooks.com

Mythology Photography **Fiction**
Fishing Christianity **Art** Cooking
Essays Buddhism Freemasonry
Medicine **Biology** Music **Ancient Egypt** Evolution Carpentry Physics
Dance Geology **Mathematics** Fitness
Shakespeare **Folklore** Yoga Marketing
Confidence Immortality Biographies
Poetry **Psychology** Witchcraft
Electronics Chemistry History **Law**
Accounting **Philosophy** Anthropology
Alchemy Drama Quantum Mechanics
Atheism Sexual Health **Ancient History**
Entrepreneurship Languages Sport
Paleontology Needlework Islam
Metaphysics Investment Archaeology
Parenting Statistics Criminology
Motivational

ST. ANGELA

(POLLARD & MOSS, PUBLISHERS. N.Y.)

AND

THE URSULINES.

BY

REV. BERNARD O'REILLY, L.D. (LAVAL),

AUTHOR OF "HEROIC WOMEN OF THE BIBLE, AND THE CHURCH;" "THE MIRROR OF TRUE
WOMANHOOD;" "TRUE MEN AS WE NEED THEM;" "A LIFE OF PIUS IX.," ETC.

"... *Never* ...
De ...

W... a ... and sweating as the ... ;
O mate of Poverty! O Pearl unpriced!"
W. H. MYERS

NEW YORK:
POLLARD & MOSS, PUBLISHERS,
47 JOHN STREET.

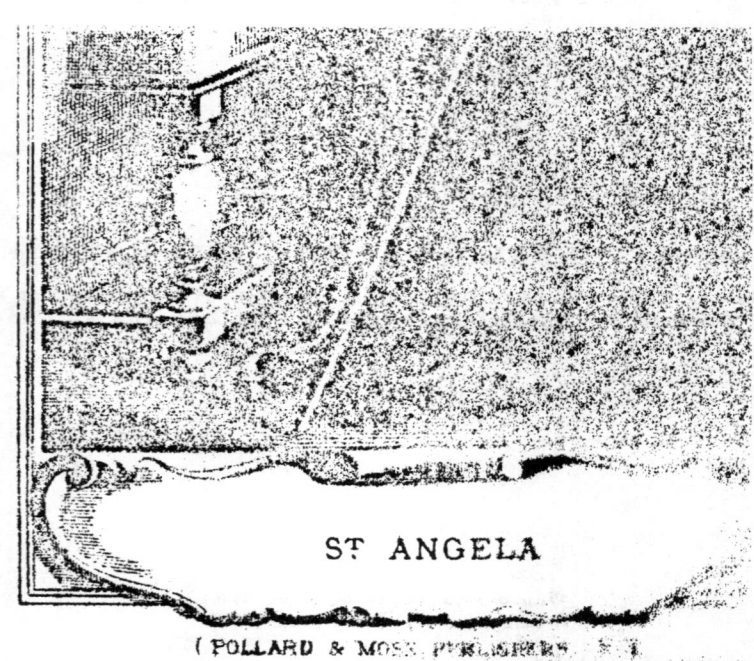

ST ANGELA

(POLLARD & MOSS PUBLISHERS)

AND

THE URSULINES.

BY

REV. BERNARD O'REILLY, L.D. (LAVAL),

AUTHOR OF "HEROIC WOMEN OF THE BIBLE, AND THE CHURCH;" "THE MIRROR OF TRUE WOMANHOOD;" "TRUE MEN AS WE NEED THEM;" "A LIFE OF PIUS IX.," ETC.

". . . Never may thy sainted name
Be thought or written save with soul aflame,
Nor spoken openly, nor breathed apart
Without a stir and swelling of the heart;—
O mate of Poverty! O Pearl unpriced!"
                              W. H. MYERS

NEW YORK:
POLLARD & MOSS, PUBLISHERS,
47 JOHN STREET.
1880.

Entered, according to Act of Congress, in the year 1880, by the
URSULINE SISTERS,
(*Ursuline Convent, East Morrisania, New York,*)
In the Office of the Librarian of Congress, at Washington, D. C.

THE AUTHOR'S PREFACE.

THE book here offered to the public was undertaken at a time when the author was busy on other most important and more attractive matter. Several heads of religious orders of women had written to him expressing the wish that he would undertake to prepare lives of their respective founders. Two of them were especially urgent in their request.

Thereupon it was thought that a series of biographies, entitled "Modern Apostles of Female Education," might be of no little interest and advantage to our numerous teaching Orders and their pupils, as well as to the general public. At any rate, out of this conception grew ST. ANGELA MERICI AND THE URSULINES. Who knows but, all imperfect as it is, it may inspire other writers, both more zealous and more competent, to continue the series, and show how so many noble rivals and auxiliaries in this glorious apostleship of female education sprung up around the daughters of St. Angela?

In the following narrative the author has taken for his principal guide the Jesuit Salvatori, who, writing in Italy, and having ready at his hand both the local traditions and the most approved histories of St. Angela and her Order, has left us a Life incomparably better than any of those which preceded it.

Even Salvatori's book, however, does not explain at all, or explains but unsatisfactorily, the long delays which occurred between the vision in which Angela was commanded to found in Brescia a society of religious women, and the foundation itself, a few years only before her death. This long interval, in the existing popular biographies of the Saint, is filled up—if indeed it can be said to be filled at all—with but few interesting incidents. How far the present Life has succeeded, both in explaining these delays and varying the monotony of these intervening years, is left to the reader to judge.

The first half of the manuscript was in the hands of the publisher and printer, when a kind Quebec friend sent the author the first volume of Abbé Postel's *Histoire de Sainte Angèle Mérici et de l'Ordre des Ursulines*. Though this able and interesting book came too late to help the author amid the confused and conflicting dates and statements of St. Angela's historians, it was no small satisfaction to see that Abbé Postel had taken pains, and not without success, to explain the obstacles met with and overcome at length in founding the Company of St. Ursula.

If, in some respects, the arrangement followed in the present Life of St. Angela differs from the Italian or French biographies, it need only be said that the author has consulted principally the best interests of American readers. To them, he firmly trusts, the sketch here submitted of the life and labors of the Holy Maid of Desenzano will prove attractive, edifying, and instructive.

NEW YORK, *April* 2, 1880.

NOTE.—The reader unacquainted with the language and customs of Italy, may be surprised that the names of some of the Lady-Directresses should be written one way on page 231, and quite a different way on pages 182 and 183. All are scrupulously written, in both places, as they are given by Father Salvatori, who, in the orthography of pages 182 and 183 follows the general rules of classical Italian, and in giving the "Testament" of St. Angela, conforms to the local idiom of Brescia, used by the Saint.

TO

THE URSULINE COMMUNITY OF MORRISANIA, NEW YORK CITY,

WHOSE GENEROUS LOVE FOR THEIR GLORIOUS PARENT,

Saint Angela Merici,

HAS LED TO THE WRITING OF THIS BOOK,

IT IS NOW OFFERED IN ACKNOWLEDGMENT OF THEIR SELF-SACRIFICING
PIETY AND ZEAL, WITH THE FERVENT PRAYER THAT THEY
MAY EVER BE, IN SPIRIT AND PRACTICE,

THE TRUE DAUGHTERS OF SO ANGELIC A MOTHER;

THAT EVERY ONE OF THE YOUNG SOULS TRAINED BY THEM MAY PROVE
THE LIGHT AND JOY OF HER HOME IN THE WORLD; AND THAT
THEIR INSTITUTION, EVER GROWING IN FERVOR AND EX-
CELLENCE, MAY, LIKE THE SACRED TREE OF INDIA,
COVER THE LAND FAR AND WIDE WITH
ITS OFFSHOOTS.

THE AUTHOR.

TABLE OF CONTENTS.

	PAGE
ARCHIEPISCOPAL APPROBATION	iii
DEDICATION	v
AUTHOR'S PREFACE	vii

CHAPTER I.

INTRODUCTORY: SUPERNATURAL ATMOSPHERE OF ITALIAN HOME-LIFE IN THE FIFTEENTH AND SIXTEENTH CENTURIES.

Supernatural Sanctity, how Prevalent among all Classes of Italian Society 1-2
Italian Saints contemporary with the Parents of Angela Merici..... 3
Living Saints of Upper Italy about 1474......................... 4
B. Caterina da Palanza.. 4
B. Maddalena Panatieri.. 4
St. Cajetan of Tiene and his Mother............................ 4
St. Jerome Emiliani... 5
B. Margaret of Ravenna.. 6
Influence of Women in Cultivating this Abundant Growth of Sanctity... 7
Saints Living in 1540, at the Date of Angela Merici's death........ 7, 8
In Rome, Ignatius Loyola, Francis Xavier, Philip Neri; elsewhere, Charles Borromeo, Michael Ghisleri (St. Pius V.), Francis Borgia, St. Camillo de Lellis, St. Felix Cantalici, St. Andrew Avellino, BB. Paul of Arezzo, Alexander Sauli, and Benedict Filadelf..... 8, 9
Uncanonized Saints; how numerous 9, 10
Saintly Personages not the Rare and Gigantic Flowers of Equatorial Regions; but the Sweet and Modest Flowers which Thrive in every Land... 10, 11
Angela Merici and her Sister's early Virtues as Compared with some Holy Contemporaries... 12
St. Veronica of Milan and her Parents; a Poor Peasant Family.. 12-14
Their Ideal of Christian Holiness as Familiar to the People of Upper Italy, as the Way of Cultivating the Vine.................... 15

CONTENTS.

The noble Catharine Fieschi-Adorno of Genoa; her Married Life; her Life in the Cloister; her beautiful Writings.............15–19
The Transforming Love of Christ Crucified in St. Ignatius, St. Francis Xavier, St. Francis of Assisi........................20–22
The last named Saint and the Stigmata; the Fire and Light which Enwrapped Monte Alvernia..................................... 23
This Sacred Fire Burning Brightly at the Birth of Angela Merici..25–27

CHAPTER II.

BIRTH AND PARENTAGE OF ANGELA MERICI.

The Lake of Garda and the town of Desenzano..................28, 29
The Merici and Biancosi... 30
Spiritual Influences Surrounding the Home of the Merici.........31, 32
The Observantines of St. Francis................................ 33
The Merici, Ardent Admirers of Heroic Sanctity.................. 33
Uncommon Pains taken by Angela's Parents to Cultivate the Love of Heroic Piety in their Children.......................... 33
Nightly Reading in common of the Lives of the Saints............ 33
Angela's Early Admiration of these Heroic Men and Women........ 34
Her Early Efforts at Imitation of Them.......................... 34
Her Beauty in Childhood; her Generosity, Wisdom, and Self-control. 34
How she Resented being Complimented on her Beautiful Hair....... 35
Her Parents Encourage while Controlling the Ascetic Fervor of Angela and her Sister...36, 37
A Happy and Blessed Home.......................................37, 38

CHAPTER III.

ANGELA'S FIRST BITTER TRIALS.

Why her First Communion was Delayed; Concourse of Circumstances which were Unfavorable to Frequent Communion and Confession in the Italy of those Days........................39, 40
Divine Economy of the Eucharistic Sacrament and Sacrifice........ 41
Angela's Merici's Intense Happiness at the Table of the Lamb...... 42
Growth of Angela in Spiritual Loveliness; the Bright and Pure Atmosphere of her Home; Precautions taken to Shield the Soul of Girlhood from the Knowledge of Evil........................ 43

	PAGE
Angela's Early Vow of Virginity not the Result of Temptation; but Inspired by the Love of Perfection	44, 45
She Loses her Father in her Fifteenth Year	46
She Devotes herself to her Widowed Mother	47
Her Sister becomes her Guide in Spirituality	47
Their Pious Remembrance of their Father's Soul	48
Her Sister Dies Suddenly within the Year after her Father's Death	50
How both Girls had Grown in Supernatural Perfection during these years: the Mystery of Life in the natural and supernatural Worlds	52, 53
Vision in which Angela beholds her Deceased Sister among the Blessed; She is Bidden to Persevere in the Better Way	54
Effect of such Miraculous Visions on Chosen Souls like Angela's	55

CHAPTER IV.

UTTER DESOLATION.

The Vision sent to Angela probably helped to Prepare her Mother for Death	57
Signora Merici Sickens and Dies in less than a Year after her daughter	58
Secret Purpose of Providence in these trials	59
The Girl of Seventeen and her Brother taken to Salò by their Uncle Biancosi	60
Magnificent Situation of Salò; Enchanting Scenery of the Lake Shore Northward of Salò	61, 62
Interior Trials which assail Angela at this Period; she and her Brother Resolve to lead the Life of Hermits in the mountains	63–66
They Leave Salò Secretly; but are Brought Back	67
Angela even then Popularly Designated as "a Little Saint from Paradise;" the two Orphans held up by Parents as models for all Children	69
Angela Loses her Brother in her Twenty-second Year	69

CHAPTER V.

BACK IN THE OLD HOME.

She is Welcomed by her Townspeople and finds a Companion, who takes her Sister's place	72

CONTENTS.

	PAGE
The Process by which God perfects Chosen Souls in detachment from all things	73
She Loses her Adopted Sister	73
Young Persons of her own Age drawn to Angela	73
The Vision at Brudazzo, in which Angela beholds a Company of Saintly Virgins; and is Commanded to Found one like it in Brescia	75, 76
Increase of Fervor caused by this Second Vision	77
To become a frequent Communicant she joins the Tertiary Order of St. Francis	77
Angela Merici may be justly called the Seraph of Christian Schools	77
Why St. Francis of Assisi is called the "Seraphic."	77
Protestant Testimony to the Genuineness of his Seraphic Spirit	78
A Pregnant Lesson for all the Christian Men of To-day	78

CHAPTER VI.

THE PATERNAL HOME IN DESENZANO CONTINUES TO BE ANGELA'S SCHOOL.

How Angela Spent Seventeen Years in the Home of her Childhood	79
Grateful Testimony borne by her Fellow-Citizens	79
Her House a School for Young and Old	80
Imperious Circumstances which rendered Impracticable the Founding of a New Order in Brescia	81
Her Saintly Influence over her Young Countrywomen	82
Why Angela could not in Desenzano open a School for Children like Our Schools of To-day	82
Printing was then only in its Infancy	82
What High and Low learned in Angela's School	83
The Noble Family of the Patengoli from Brescia cultivate Angela's acquaintance	83
They desire to have her Reside in Brescia	84
Situation of Brescia; Its History	85
Occupied by the French in 1512	85
Horrible Butchery of 22,000 Brescians by the French, under Gaston de Foix	86
The ruined City restored to Venice in 1516	86
Jerome Patengoli Loses suddenly his two Children	86

CONTENTS.

	PAGE
Angela Merici sent to Brescia by her Superiors	87
Her Delight in Visiting the Venerable Churches of the City	88
Her active Charity	88
The Ruinous Condition of Brescia forbids her thinking of Founding her Society	89
She is offered a Home by Antonio dei Romani	89
She visits the Tomb of B. Osanna Andreasi in Milan	90
Is Welcomed at Solferino by the Gonzagas	90
State of Upper Italy in 1522	92
Angela feels Impelled to Visit Jerusalem	93
Generous Provision made by Venice for Pilgrims to the Holy Land	93

CHAPTER VII.
LIGHT IN DARKNESS.

Founders of Religious Orders the passionate lovers of Christ Crucified	94
Ignatius Loyola a Pilgrim to Jerusalem in 1523	95
Angela Embarks for Palestine in May, 1524	97
She is suddenly struck Blind on the Way	97
Insists on Continuing her journey	97
Her Raptures in Jerusalem and Bethlehem	98
Memories which Enlighten her in Christ's Birth-place	100
St. Jerome, St. Paula, and her daughter Eustochium	101

CHAPTER VIII.
THE LIGHT INCREASING.

Return from Jerusalem through Rama	104
Angela recovers her Eyesight Miraculously	108
Dangers from Storms and Pirates	108, 109
Angelo esteemed, under God, the Pilgrims' Preserver	109
Admiration of the Venetians for her	111
She Escapes secretly from the City	112

CHAPTER IX.
WAITING AND WORKING.

Angela warmly Welcomed by the Brescians	113
New Obstacles to Angela's Designs	114, 115

	PAGE
She goes to Rome for the Jubilee of 1525	116
Explains her Vision to Pope Clement VII	118
Returns to Brescia	118
War-Clouds over Rome and Italy	119, 120

CHAPTER X.

INSUPERABLE OBSTACLES.

Charles V. and Francis I. distract and devastate Upper Italy	121
Brescia Paralyzed; Religious Improvement impossible	122
Angela's Self-Crucifixion amid these Calamities	123–126
She is more than ever the Guide and Comforter of all Classes	127
The Duke of Milan takes her for his Spiritual Guide	128
Angela is obliged to take Refuge in Cremona	129
She becomes the Public Comforter there	130, 131
Vigorous Intellectual and Moral Life of Upper Italy in those Days	132, 133
Angela taken Ill and at Death's Door	135
Her sudden Restoration to Perfect Health	136
She makes a Pilgrimage to the Sacred Hill of Varallo	137
Sudden Cessation of Hostilities	138

CHAPTER XI.

THE FOUNDATIONS AT LAST.

Vision of St. Ursula and her Companions	140
Delays enjoined on Angela by her Confessor	142
The first Twelve Ursulines	143
The high Aim Angela set before her Companions	144
Second Pilgrimage to Varallo	145
The Duke of Milan would have them stay in his Capital	146
Angela fixes her Abode near the Church of St. Afra	147
Increase of the Associates	150
Why Angela sought the Aid of noble Widow Ladies	151
How timely this Organization was for Italy	152
How Nature repairs Wounds and Losses in Tree and Flower; and how God repairs them in His Church	153, 154
Reforms by renovated Home-life and Education	155, 156

CHAPTER XII.

WHY ANGELA CALLED HER SISTERHOOD "THE COMPANY OF ST. URSULA."

PAGE

The Legends concerning St. Ursula and her Band of Virgin-Martyrs.. 157
The simple Historical Facts....................................... 158
The Popular Legends in Upper Italy............................. 159
St. Ursula and the Venetian Painters............................ 160
St. Ursula accepted as Patron Saint by the great Universities of Christendom... 161
Another Vision in which Angela is urged to hasten her Work...... 162
The Company of St. Ursula formally inaugurated................. 163
First Inauguration of the Society of Jesus....................... 164
Fundamental Conception of an Ursuline's Life.................... 165
Why Angela did not wish to Oblige her Maiden Sisters to make Religious Vows... 166
She excludes no Class of the Deserving........................... 167
Simple Dress of the Sisters....................................... 167
Their Charity and Humility....................................... 167
The wide Interest taken in them.................................. 168
The word "Company" suggestive of a Militant Life............... 169
The two Great Armies who contended for Souls in the Italy of the Sixteenth Century.. 169
Outlines of Angela's Organization................................ 170
How the Spirit of God directs Holy Men and Women..........171-174
The Nineteenth Century like the Sixteenth..................174, 175

CHAPTER XIII.

ANGELA'S WORK—THE CONSTITUTIONS OF THE COMPANY OF ST. URSULA.

Her Self-Crucifixion while drawing up the Constitutions of the Company... 176
The Cardinal-Bishop of Brescia approves them.................... 179
Angela is unanimously elected Superior-General.................. 181
Election of the other Officers.................................... 182
The Spiritual Directors of the new Company..................... 183
Was the Education of Young Girls the main purpose of Angela?.. 185

CONTENTS.

Testimony of the Holy See to the First Apostle of Female Education... 185–187
Testimony of St. Charles Borromeo.................................... 188
Brief Mention of Education in the Constitutions.................. 189
Angela wished to Educate in the Bosom of each Family.......... 190
Her Main Purpose to be Directed by Providence.................. 191

CHAPTER XIV.

THE LAST LABORS AND TRIALS—MOST BEAUTIFUL COUNSELS—THE STRONG WOMAN SETTING HER HOUSE IN ORDER.

Delay in Obtaining the Approbation of the Holy See............. 192
Opposition in Brescia to the Secular Dress of the Sisters........... 195
Angela's Persistence in Prayer and Austerities 197
Beginning of her Last Illness.. 199
She appoints a Mother-Vicar.. 199
Dictates her *Ricordi* and her spiritual "Testament"............... 199
Summons the Lady-Counselors to hear the *Ricordi* read............ 200
Admirable Counsels of the Dying Saint........................ 201–212

CHAPTER XV.

THE GATES AJAR—LOVE STRONG IN DEATH—THE PILGRIM AT REST.

The Spectacle presented by the Sick-room at St. Afra's............ 214
The disheartening Circumstances which color Angela's last Counsels to her Daughters.................................... 215
The Motherly Tenderness she enjoins toward her Sisters........... 217
Virtues which these are to Practice................................ 219
They are to Cherish above all Things the Honor of their Divine Spouse... 219
Ever-present Aid promised to them in Christ's Name............. 219
Angela sits up in her bed to repeat the last "Reminder".......... 220
Deep Impression made on all Present........................ 220, 221
Consternation in Brescia... 222
Her last Words to a few noble Friends............................ 223
Her scrupulous Care to prepare herself for Burial................. 224
She receives the Last Sacraments................................. 225
Her angelic Devotion.. 226, 227
Angela Merici's Mission.. 228

CONTENTS.

	PAGE
The Ursulines in Venice	345
" Genoa	345
" Parma	346
" Piacenza and Foligno	347
The Roman Ursulines	347
The Uncloistered Ursulines of SS. Rufina and Secunda	348
The Cloistered Ursulines of the Via Vittoria, founded by the Duchess of Modena	348
Vicissitudes of the Roman Ursulines	351-353
Existing Monasteries of Calvi, Stroncone, Sesto-Calende, Cannobio, Galliate, Omegna, Miasino, and Saluzzo	353
Fate of the Congregation of Brescia before and since the French Revolution	354
Swept away by the First Napoleon	355
Only a Single Monastery of Cloistered Nuns since 1827	355
The Primitive Ursulines of Brescia reviving under Pius IX	357-359

CHAPTER XXI.

THE URSULINES IN FRANCE—CONGREGATIONS OF AIX, BORDEAUX, PARIS, LYONS, AND TOULOUSE.

Frances de Bermond, of Avignon, the Angela Merici of France	360
The First French Ursuline Establishment at L'Isle, near Avignon	362
Frances de Bermond and Cardinal de Sourdis, of Bordeaux	363
The Cardinal visits Milan	364
He Chooses Frances de Cazères to Found the Ursulines of Bordeaux	365
The Ursulines of Bordeaux become a Congregation of Cloistered Nuns	366
Their Apostolic labors Described by Pope Paul V	369
The Ursulines of Paris; their beginnings	371
Blessed Mary of the Incarnation (Madame Acarie) and her cousin, Madame De Sainte Beuve	371, 372
The Parisian Ursulines become Cloistered	373, 374
Mother de Bermond Recalled from Paris to Aix	374
She Founds the Monastery of Lyons	377
Her Establishments wonderfully Multiplied	378
The Lyonnese Congregation accept the Cloister	379
Death of Mother de Bermond	379

	PAGE
The Congregation of Toulouse	380
The "Ladies of Mercy of St. Ursula"	381
Extraordinary Fervor of the Toulouse Ursulines	381, 382
Other Congregations in France	382

CHAPTER XXIII.

OFFSHOOTS OF THE FRENCH URSULINES THROUGHOUT THE GERMAN AND AUSTRIAN EMPIRES, CANADA, THE UNITED STATES, IRELAND AND ENGLAND.

Marvelous Fecundity of the Congregations of Bordeaux and Paris	384
Temporary Suppression of the Ursulines throughout Germany and the Low Countries by the French	384
"The May Laws"	385
Landshut and Breslau	385
The other Ursuline Schools of Austria-Hungary	385
The American Ursulines:	
Quebec and Three Rivers	386
New Orleans	387–389
The First Ursulines in New York Unsuccessful	389
The Ursulines of East Morrisania	389
The Ursulines of Boston	390
The Tragic Story of the Charlestown Convent	391
Archbishop Purcell and the Ursulines of the Western States	392
Nano Nagle and the Irish Ursulines	393
The Monastery of Black Rock and the Ursulines of South Carolina	394
The Monastery School of Valle-Crucis, near Columbia, cruelly Destroyed by Sherman's Army	395
The Ursulines in England: The Monastery of Upton, a Colony from Sittard in Limburg	395
The Abbé Lambertz and the "Independent Ursulines" of Belgium	396
The Conditions under which Religious Communities can prosper among Modern Peoples	396

CHAPTER XVI.

A SAINT'S TESTAMENT AND LEGACIES—A PEOPLE'S GRATITUDE AND VENERATION—INCORRUPTION LASTING THROUGH CENTURIES.

	PAGE
Angela's "Testament and Legacies" to her Daughters	230–240
Instinctive Veneration of true Sanctity by the Catholic Heart	240, 241
Extraordinary Affluence from City and Country	242
All proclaim her "Blessed"	243
Delay in her Burial	243
Veneration in all Ages for the Remains of the Saintly Dead	244
The Delay of Thirty Days most Providential	245
Prodigious Concourse of Pilgrims, and other Prodigies	245
The Holy Remains preserved Incorrupt	246
The Painters of Brescia at work around the Bier	247, 248
End of the Delay; the Solemn Entombment	248
Tributes to the Saintly Dead	248
A Scoffer Rebuked and Converted	250
Changes made in Angela's Tomb	251
Its Appearance and that of the Saint's Body in 1867	252–254

CHAPTER XVII.

THE "ODOR OF SANCTITY" AND POPULAR VENERATION—MIRACULOUS FAVORS OBTAINED—DELAYS IN ANGELA'S BEATIFICATION AND CANONIZATION.

The Good or Ill Odor diffused by every Christian's Life and Death	255
Flocks in Alpine Regions attracted to their Mountain Pasture by the Fragrance of Spring Flowers	255
The People of God drawn to the Shrines of his Saints by "the Sweet Odor" of Christlike Holiness	256, 257
The Popular Veneration toward Angela Merici	258–260
The Honors paid to her tacitly Sanctioned by the Holy See	261
This *Cultus* becomes Universal	262
First Judicial Proceedings toward Beatification	264
Delays in Rome caused by the Dissensions with Louis XIV	265
She is solemnly Beatified by Clement XIII	266
Translation of Blessed Angela's Remains	267
Appearance of the Body on this Occasion	267

Contrast between this Triumph of the Ursulines and the simultaneous Downfall of the Jesuits..................................269, 270
Proceedings for Blessed Angela's Canonization..................... 270
She is solemnly Canonized... 271

CHAPTER XVIII.
MIRACLES, AND VIRTUES AS MARVELOUS AS MIRACLES.

Irresistible Authority of Miracles..................................... 273
The Miracle-working Power to abide in the Church................. 274
The Three Great Miracles wrought by St. Angela, and accepted by the Congregation of Rites................................275-281
St. Angela's Heroic Virtues.. 282
    Her Prudence... 285
    Her Temperance.. 291
    Her Justice... 291
    Her Fortitude.. 291
    Her Supernatural Faith, Hope and Charity.................292-294

CHAPTER XIX.
ST. ANGELA'S CONSTITUTIONS.

They are her Principal Literary Production........................ 295
They breathe the Apostolic Spirit which passed into the Constitutions of the various Ursuline Congregations...................... 296
They deserve to be Preserved lovingly by Angela's Daughters...... 296
Text of the Constitutions... 297

CHAPTER XX.

THE URSULINES: THEIR VARIED FORTUNES IN ITALY — PRIMITIVE CONGREGATION OF BRESCIA—HOW THEY FARED IN MILAN—URSULINES OF VENICE, PARMA, PIACENZA, FOLIGNO, AND ROME.

Dangerous Controversy about the Dress of the Ursulines........... 337
The Ursulines in Desenzano and Salò................................ 339
    "   Cremona...................................... 341
    "   Milan.. 342
The Milanese Ursulines living in community and bound by vows... 344

LIFE OF ST. ANGELA MERICI.

CHAPTER I.

INTRODUCTORY.

It will help the readers of this book not a little toward understanding the edifying story it tells, if we make them acquainted not only with the beautiful country in which the heroine was born, but more especially still with the religious condition of the society among whom she was brought up. The flowers that bloom and the fruits that ripen in our gardens, as well as the harvests that grow in our fields, depend for their beauty, their fragrance, their excellence on the qualities of soil and atmosphere. Even so do the most heroic souls need for their growth and maturing the genial influences of earth and sky, the light and warmth of supernatural examples in the family home and the social world around it.

To persons who may wonder at the early love of prayer, holy solitude, bodily austerity, the aversion to all worldly honor and pleasure, and the constant yearning to be in all things like the Crucified,—displayed by Angela Merici and her sister, by their near neighbor Aloysius Gonzaga (though born many years afterward), and so many others of the same age, and country,—we can only say, that even so was the child Samuel visited early by the divine favor, that Jeremias was sanctified from his birth for the lifelong struggle with the corruptions of God's people, and the impiety of their princes, and John the Baptist anointed by the outpouring of the Holy Spirit.

The knowledge and love of Christ crucified, and of the glorious hosts cf his followers in the road of crucifixion, were a thing as natural and familiar to the children of all Christian households in the year of grace 1474, as was the glorious aspect of the earth around their homes. Sainted followers of Him who for us crowned His own head with earth's bitterest thorns, and drank in death to the dregs its bitterest cup of woe, had tenanted while living the wildest crags and mountain solitudes of Northern as well as of Central Italy: around their hermitages and their tombs, chapels and monasteries had been reared, shining from afar all over the land, as lights pointing out to the crowds in city and plain the way to Christ-like holiness.

Saintly men and women, whose names have been solemnly placed by the church on the catalogue of the Blessed, lived in every part of Italy, age after age,—saints of the cottage as well as of the palace, saints among the poorest classes as well as among the highest, shining amid the obscurity of the village hamlet in some retired valley of the Alps or the Apennines, as well as among the crowds and hustle and glitter of cities; honoring the throne of the sovereign or the seat of the bishop; saintly laymen, priests, and monks, sent,—not like the great Prophets of old,—from time to time, to thrill and rouse and raise the souls of a perverse, a slumbering, or a fallen generation; but succeeding each other, like the fair flowers of a southern clime that knows no winter, and in whose sunlight the beauteous buds of promise are evermore opening by the side of the golden fruit.

Such, most truly, was the Italy of the fifteenth and the sixteenth centuries, to both of which belongs the heroic life we are about to tell.

Let not the reader fancy for one moment that there is in this assertion anything approaching to exaggeration. A brief glance at a few only of the illustrious names thus honored and embalmed by the veneration of the people and the infallible judgment of the Church, will settle all doubts on this point, and encourage us to pursue our theme with increased fervor and confidence.

The parents of Angela Merici might, during their lifetime, have seen the persons or heard of the virtues of such holy personages as the Blessed Margaret of the Royal House of Savoy (died 1467), and her saintly kinsman, the Blessed Duke Amadeus (died 1472). Both had spread far and wide throughout Northern Italy the fame of their goodness and holiness. Venice was blessed at the same epoch in the possession of a great man and a great saint on the episcopal seat, Lawrence Giustiniani (died 1455), while Florence gloried in the learning and virtues of her own archbishop, St. Antonine. Filling the valleys of Southern Tyrol and Northern Venetia with the fruits of his apostolic zeal, lived Blessed Andrea Grego, born at Peschiera, on the picturesque shores of their own Lake Garda,—while they, like all the population of Northern Italy, had been thrilled and captivated by the eloquence and examples of such living saints as Vincent Ferrer, Francis of Paula, and Bernardine of Sienna. There were women, too, whose deeds of heroic sanctity were no less celebrated by the grateful veneration of their contemporaries: the Blessed

Serafina D'Urbino, duchess of Pesaro (died 1478), St. Catherine of Bologna (died 1462), St. Louisa Albertone, whom all Rome worshiped, and that other Roman lady, even greater than she, Francesca Ponziani, or "St. Frances of Rome," as the capital of the Christian world in its gratitude delights to call her.

But, without searching other parts of Italy for the illustrious names of saintly men and women, who shone all over it during th middle of the fifteenth century, let us see what a galaxy of saints shed lustre on the immediate neighborhood of that same Lake of Garda, just at the very time Angela Merici was born (1474). The Blessed Catarina de Palanza was making the mountain pilgrimage of Varese dear to the surrounding populations by the sweet virtues of her last years (died 1478). St. Veronica, a poor, illiterate peasant girl, was then the wonder of all Milan and its territory. Blessed Maddalena Panatieri was equally revered in the neighboring city of Vercelli; while in the diocese of Brescia, at Orzinovi, was just blooming into perfect womanhood and perfect holiness the Blessed Stefana Quinzani, and at Mantua the Blessed Osanna Andreasi, both destined to exercise so salutary an influence on Angela Merici's after-life.

Then, again, if we consider the great practical purpose to which Angela gave up her whole existence,—the succoring of needy souls by heroic devotedness,—we shall find public opinion in every Italian community actively alive to the imperative duty of instructing the ignorant, educating youth, and relieving every want of soul and body among the poor of Christ.

Four years after the birth of our saint, in 1478, to the princely family of Tiene, in the neighboring city of Vicenza, was born a son destined to found an order of apostolic men,— the Theatines. It is only necessary, however, to say what kind of a woman the mother of the future St. Gaetano de Tiene was, to open out to our readers a most beautiful prospect of the womanly excellence and supernatural piety that graced Italian home-life in the fifteenth century. Maria Porta, countess of Tiene, was, like the Blessed Margaret of Savoy, and St. Jane, Queen of France, her contemporaries, a woman guided solely by the Spirit of God, a true Christian woman, who fulfilled perfectly every duty of wife, mother, and mistress of a household, while giving to God and to the needy everything which heart and hand could give. Like the mother of the great St. Francis of Assisi, before the birth of her boy, she had a secret presentiment that her child was destined to be a close follower of the Divine Babe of Bethlehem. She wished that like Him, her son should be born in a stable, and to a stable she went to give birth to her first born, and would have him placed in a manger, thereby consecrating him to poverty and self-sacrifice. How such a mother would rear her boy, and direct his thoughts and aspirations to all that was most heroic and most generous, we need not inform the reader. Besides, the most authentic testimony in all modern history is there, in the story of the life of St. Gaetano and the solemn acts of his canonization, to show what Christian education meant in the truly Christian ages.

That same territory of Venice,—though sadly fallen away both from its pristine Christian fervor and its ancient supremacy on the seas,—produced about the same time another glorious scion, worthy of the proudest days of patrician virtue. This was to be a devoted friend of Gaetano de Tiene and Angela Merici. He is still dear to the homeless and the orphan as St. Jerome Emiliani. Descended of the best nobility of Venice, a soldier while yet in boyhood, in spite of his mother's entreaties and tears, Jerome plunged headlong into the excitement and licentiousness of warfare, was taken prisoner while bravely defending his trust, and found amid the horrors of his captivity, the light which showed him the depth of his own guilt, the vanity of the fame for which he thirsted, and the glory of serving Him, "whom to serve is to reign." Thenceforward his life became one of expiation, self-crucifixion, and boundless devotion to the cause of charity and Christian education.

While Jerome Emiliani was still in his cradle, and Angela Merici was blooming into her lovely girlhood, a poor peasant girl born near Ravenna, stricken with blindness in infancy, and grown to womanhood amid a succession of trials and sufferings so unceasing and so fearful, that one is reminded of holy Job in the extremity of his affliction,—was also chastened and perfected like Job by the very extremity of ill. The bitterest portion of the deep cup she had to drain till she was long past the season of youth, came from the persecutions of those who should have been her protectors. But blessed Margaret's angelic patience and sweet humility disarmed her detractors and made of them her friends and disciples. Her bed of suffering became the chair from which she taught supernatural wisdom. City and country folk soon thronged to gaze upon the weak sufferer, to learn from her lips and her life the secrets of holiness, and to reform their own conduct on the model of one who was the living image of the Crucified.

They united,—the choice souls among them, at least,—to form a society called the "Confraternity of the Good Jesus," for which she drew up rules. Three hundred of the most distinguished citizens of Ravenna and its vicinity, thus bound themselves to holiness of life, and the practice of heroic charity. The Blessed Margaret died on January 23rd, 1505. Her influence, however, was to effect a still greater good after her death. Among her disciples was a holy widow, now known among God's saints as the Blessed Gentile Pianella, the wife of a tradesman. She it is who converted a worldly priest into an apostle, and made of that priest, since so widely known as the Venerable Jerome Maluselli, the founder of the first body of Regular Clerks recognized by the Church, "The Regular Clerks of the Order of the Good Jesus." Thus the humble sodality established by the Blessed Margaret brought forth a religious order long blessed by the population of Northern and Central Italy; the humble shrub planted near the blind girl's grave, growing up into a lordly tree, and bearing fruits of salvation for the entire region.

The atmosphere of the Christian home in Italy,—and, through it, the social atmosphere of the great busy, warring world outside,—was filled with the sweet odor of Christ, even Christ crucified. It was, under God, due mostly to the influence of woman,—true mothers, wives, and maidens,—from whom men learned to be true and brave, and self-denying and self-sacrificing,—the love of all that was beautiful in God's world, and the practice of all that was heroic and ennobling in His religion.

Such were some of the life-giving influences which met Angela Merici in her native land and from her infancy. We have only pointed out a very few, to enable the reader to study the religious and social condition of Italy during the age of Christopher Columbus, and thus to form an intelligent and independent judgment on the beautiful civilization which the Church had been creating and fostering in spite of the constant and relentless hostility of the Powers of Evil.

Now, dear reader, only think of the magnificent array of living saints whom Angela Merici left behind her the year of her happy death. She breathed her last on January 27, 1540. In Rome, April 7th of the following year, Francis

Xavier tore himself away from the fatherly embrace of Ignatius Loyola, whom he loved with a love so pure and so deep, to travel on foot all the way to Lisbon, before sailing for the East Indies. We have thus named, in these great twin-souls, the parents of an army of apostles and saints, who had then begun to extend their labors to the needy souls of both hemispheres. But besides Xavier and Loyola, there lived at the death of Angela, a host of other saintly men and women, some only of whom have received the honors of canonization or beatification.

St. Teresa was then in her twenty-fifth year ; St. John of the Cross, Teresa's help-mate in the great work of religious reformation, was in his second ; St. Charles Borromeo, who was to consummate and crown the work of St. Angela, was in his fourth year, watched over, at Arona, amid the grand scenery of Lago Maggiore, by his pious mother, or kneeling with her at Brescia, among the pilgrims crowding to the lowly grave of that same Angela, or visiting with her the home in which the saint was born at Desenzano, on the sunny shores of the Lake of Garda. St. Philip Neri, in 1540, was in his twenty-sixth year, in the beautiful springtide of his holiness,—and the Dominican monk, Michael Ghisleri, destined afterward to save and to edify all christendom under the name of St. Pius V., was in his thirty-seventh year ; —Francis Borgia, Duke of Gandia, destined also to be the most efficient help-mate of St. Pius in the crusade which broke forever[1] the power and pride of the Mohammedan,—

---

[1] It is not generally known that St. Francis Borgia, then general of his society, was sent by St. Pius V., in conjunction with the papal legate, to exhort the kings of Spain and Portugal to unite their forces with those of Venice and the Holy See in order to crush the Turkish power. It was the last of the crusades. Borgia's saintly presence in the Spanish court, where he had formerly shone as the model of the Castilian nobility, obtained from Philip II. all that the Pope desired. And thus was organized the expedition which won the glorious victory of Lepanto, Oct. 7, 1570.

was in his thirtieth year, the envy and the model of Spain's nobility, as St. Thomas of Villanova, Archbishop of Valencia, was, at the same time, the model of her bishops and the father of her people. Indeed, Spain was, in that age, the wonder of christendom by the number of her saints. But we would fain not turn away the reader's attention from Italy. St. Camillo de Lellis, St. Felix Cantalicio, St. Serafino de Monte Granario, St. Andrew Avellino, the Blessed Paul of Arezzo, and Blessed Alexander Sauli, the Apostle of Corsica, the bosom friend and counsellor of St. Charles Borromeo, were all growing up to the full stature of Christ-like heroism, while Angela Merici was impatiently yearning to be at rest with Christ.

From the foot-hills of the Alps which overshadowed her home in Brescia, to the southernmost coast of Sicily, where lived, beautiful in soul and angelic in life, the Blessed Benedict of Filadelfo, a man of the much-despised negro race,— there was not a city, or a noted country place, in which some such saintly men or women, were not keeping before the eyes of the living generation the ideal virtues which are the soul of Christian life and the aim of all Christian generosity.

To be sure, only a few of the many souls who were thus foremost in the race of sanctity, have left names behind to be known and revered of all succeeding Christian ages. We of this barren nineteenth century, and denizens of a land unblessed by the splendor of a single sainted name, are apt to think that the God-like personages deserving of the honors of canonization resemble those rare and gigantic flowers[1] of the Brazilian forests, which cannot thrive or live on our barren northern soil, and beneath the illiberal and uncertain warmth of our sun. On the contrary, sanctity is like the

---

[1] The magnificent water-lily known as the *Victoria Regina*.

sweet and modest flowers which bloom and thrive in every land fit for the habitation of man—like the wheat and the corn which ripen best for man's uses amid the cooler plains and valleys and under the showery skies of the temperate zone. Ah, He who is the ever-present Sun of Righteousness, as He daily encircles the earth in the course of His Fatherly Providence, pours into our minds the light, and into our hearts the warmth, which move them to aim at Godlike excellence and enable them to attain it. His allwise, and untiring care of the souls which He constantly urges onward and upward to height above height of holiness and perfection—never fails to attemper, for the special measure of each dear soul's need, both the ardor of the surrounding atmosphere and the rigor of its severest colds, to govern for our souls' welfare every accident and event which may befall them here below. Dear to Him, and most dear, is the soul of the poor blind peasant girl of Ravenna, beset from infancy to womanhood and old age, with the bitterest trials which can assail the sensibilities of a heart born truly noble, or test the patience of the most heroic temper; most dear also that other poor servant-maid of Milan (St. Veronica), who found time, amid her own hard and manifold labors, to aid and comfort the weak of limb or of heart around her, and created from out the resources of her own poverty,—of her overrich charity and holiness, rather,—hospitals for the sick, and asylums for infirm old age, and orphaned infancy. Surely, most dear too, are such royal souls as Maria and Gaetano de Tiene, as Margaret and Amadeus of Savoy, as Ignatius Loyola and Francis Xavier and Francis Borgia, and that good shepherd who laid down his life for his sheep, Charles Borromeo,—to choose one holy bishop among many. Beautiful is the royal rose that is the pride of our gardens. but beautiful none the less are the thousand lowly flowerets that display their timid loveliness and shed their sweet fragrance in the secret places of hillside, valley, and forest— near the shady brook which steals through our meadows, or on the borders of some unknown lake in the wilderness. There is not one of these sweet and beauteous creatures but is the object of the great Creator's care,—daily visited by the beams of His sun in the heavens. Nor is there, among the thousands of obscure souls most dear to the God who is the lover of souls, the passionate lover of holiness,—a single one that is not the especial care and dear delight of His angels and Himself. Astronomy teaches us that the stars which are brightest in our firmament are not the largest in size, that the smallest visible to the naked eye are incomparably greater than those whose splendor charms us after sunset or before sunrise. Nay, it is no improbable conjecture, that our sun, surpassing as we know him to be in size, and transcendent in life-giving light and warmth to all the heavenly bodies near our earth, is nevertheless far surpassed in volume and splendor by myriads of stars placed beyond the reach of the naked eye, or of the instruments devised by science to aid the investigator.

So, there may be,—nay, there are doubtless,—in every age thousands of souls who delight in living for God alone, and whose sole aim and prayer is to die unknown to men, and to remain forever unknown to human fame. They are known on high in the great society of the Blessed,—where true glory is securely reserved for them,—that glory which consists in being praised eternally by God, and by His angels and saints.

They are known on earth, too, during their life-time,— though, it may be not widely known. Their influence, like that of our sweet and lowly flowers among the depths of the tangled forest, loads the atmosphere with a subtile fragrance which is felt and blessed by the traveler, though its cause remains unseen, hidden beneath the surrounding undergrowth. Sometimes, however, it so happens that God, whose holiness and power are glorified in His saints, will cause the name of these hidden creations of His grace to come forth into the full light of publicity long ages after they have passed away from earth, just as we see stars hitherto invisible emerge from the depths of space, and astonish by their brilliancy the skilled observers of every land.

It may, however, assist us greatly toward understanding the spirit which directed the aims and inspired the actions of Angela Merici and her sister, while as yet little more than children,—if we glance at the doings and sayings of one or two of the saintly women, whose names were household words in Northern Italy at the close of the fifteenth century, and whose lives were the frequent topic of conversation in Christian households. Two personages, taken from opposite social conditions, will serve our purpose admirably.

Here we have, in the first instance, a farmer of the poorest class of the Lombard peasantry a man whose unremitting toil barely enables him to ward off from his dear ones pinching want and the degradation to a family consequent on extreme poverty. In his poor household, however, as indeed among the peasant classes of Catholic countries in the ages of living faith, though book-learning there was none, there was, nevertheless, that lofty education of the soul, which religion never fails to give to all who are docile to her teaching and lovingly practice her precepts. Such a parent had St. Veronica of Milan. So well principled was he, and so much was he guided in all his actions by the fear of God, that, on the markets of Milan where he brought for sale the produce of his farm and home-industry, he would never allow purchasers to buy from him without fully acquainting them with the imperfections of what he sold. His was a poverty full of contentment and holy joy, privations and hard work being seasoned by a cheerfulness which no change of season or increase of adversity could ever cloud for a moment.

His daughter Veronica's temper and disposition partook of the brightness of this sunny home. Her parents trained her from her cradle to the most tender piety, and she became perforce the companion of all their toil and hardship even before she had ceased to be a child. The sons and daughters of Christian homes were early taught to have ever before their eyes as their model, the adorable Son of Mary—born to poverty, labor, obedience, and suffering. In His footsteps the little Veronica advanced rapidly in all grace and loveliness. She worked with incredible ardor, and, while helping her poor parents in every way her strength permitted, she cheered and charmed them by her childish joyousness, and her little loving industries. They had taught her to love prayer as a conversation with the invisible but ever-present Almighty Goodness, and her fervor in prayer even surpassed her ardor for work. In the house and in the field the child showed herself to be an angel without ever ceasing to be a child.

Her beautiful maidenhood was only the continuation of her gracious childhood; she shone on the neighbors as she did on her parents, as an angelic being sent on earth for some merciful purpose.

Both parents, indeed, much as they needed her, and greatly as their happiness depended on her dear companionship, felt as she grew up to be wise and holy beyond what they admired in the best people, that they must not think of earthly bridals for their Veronica. And still when she was old enough to choose her own path in life, there seemed to be an insuperable obstacle to the accomplishment of their and her dearest wishes. She felt drawn irresistibly toward the

Augustinian Sisterhood of St. Martha in Milan,—famed throughout the land for austerity of life. But she could not bring to them the usual dower; nor could she so much as read and write. She resolved to overcome this latter impediment, however; and so, while giving up her days to the necessary labor which the poverty of her family rendered imperative, she worked by night,—alone and in the greatest secrecy, to teach herself to read and write, and to educate herself in the beginnings of secular knowledge. Of course, she succeeded. But it is said of her that she had to contend with the most disheartening difficulties, such difficulties indeed, that one day our Blessed Lady consoled her by a vision. "Do not be cast down," the heavenly voice said to her. "Suffice it to you to know three things as the alphabet of spiritual knowledge: First, the purity of heart which ever aims at loving God above all things, and in only loving other things in conformity with His will; the second is, never to complain, never to show impatience at seeing the short-comings of others, but to bear with them sweetly and to pray for their correction; and the third is, to set apart each day a time for reading the divine book of the crucifix, and contemplating the sufferings of the Crucified." Three years of such discipline as this fitted our little maiden for her supernatural calling. She brought with her treasures of goodness and knowledge which made her the light and glory of the Sisterhood,—a wonder and a fruitful source of blessing to the city and territory of Milan. The little peasant girl became the guide and counsellor of the greatest and the most learned in Church and State, as well as the indefatigable providence and comforter of the poor. And she was all this because her constant study of Christ crucified transformed her into a living image of the Virgin-Mother who had, of all created beings, known Him best, loved Him most tenderly, and followed Him most closely, from the manger to the cross.

This ideal of Christian holiness was, then, as familiar to high and low in Milan, as were the practical methods used in the culture of the vine throughout the length and breadth of Lombardy. Every class of its people, from the earliest Christian ages, had known how to judge of supernatural goodness, how to appreciate the beauty of godliness, as infallibly as they could estimate the qualities of the grape, or the flavor of their wines.

Another holy member of the Augustinian order, living at the same time in Genoa, furnishes a further and still more striking illustration of the truth we are here endeavoring to inculcate. The Genoese saint, however, is a woman of the world, born in the highest rank, and educated as became her rank. Catherine Fieschi Adorno, by birth the daughter of a viceroy of Naples, by marriage the wife of one of Genoa's proudest patricians, had tasted of all the bitterness of wedded life, and felt all the emptiness of worldly greatness. In her father's house, and while still under the loving care of her Christian mother, Catherine had been just what St. Veronica was at the same age,—angelic in body and mind,—passionately devoted to Christ and His Blessed Mother, and finding her supreme delight in reading about His passion, or in contemplating objects of art which portrayed His sufferings. Though solely bent on consecrating herself to His service and that of His poor, she had to conform to the will of her family and become the wife of Giuliano Adorno, a scion of one of the most powerful families in the ancient republic. The ten years of her wedded life was a long martyrdom endured,—and not in vain,—for the purpose of winning to God the soul of her profligate husband. She had even relaxed the austerity of her life, and mingled for a while in the gay throng around her, in order the better to shield and to save her companion. This was a serious mistake, of which she afterward bitterly repented.

In 1474,—the very year of Angela Merici's birth, Catherine Adorno, then in her 27th year, took up the cross in earnest to follow her Lord and Master, Christ. Her whole life, from that moment, became one uninterrupted act of heroic devotion to the poor and suffering. So great was her austerity, so unearthly the life of crucifixion she led, that nothing short of a miracle could have enabled her to live at all, especially when one considers how unceasing and arduous her labors were. In the admirable writings which she has left us, there is a mine of spiritual knowledge inferior in wealth only to the works of the great St. Teresa. Among her works is a dialogue in three books, in which the speakers are the Body, the Soul, Self-love, the Intellect, and the Sacred Humanity of our Lord. The purpose of the writer is to point out clearly the path through which Grace led her from her own state of imperfection to the most elevated degree of spirituality. The conception as well as the execution of this charming treatise is worthy of the best age of Italian literature.

"I saw," she tells us in the beginning, "a Soul taking counsel with her Body. The Soul spoke first and said:

"Body mine, God hath created me to love and enjoy bliss, and I am desirous of seeking where I can satisfy my yearning; and I also wish that you would quietly follow me, inasmuch as my contentment would contribute to your own. We shall go forth into the world, and wherever I find any good that delights me, I shall forthwith enjoy it. Even so shall you do with what thing soever pleaseth you, and when either of us finds anything still better, then shall we both be free to possess ourselves of it.

"Although," replied the Body, "I cannot help doing your pleasure, I perceive, notwithstanding, that you cannot have what you will without me. If, therefore, we are to journey together pleasantly, let us come to some understanding that may prevent all future jars."

And so they agree to take Self-love with them, to be an impartial umpire, should any difference of opinion arise. They are to go their own way, and seek their own pleasure, each a week in its turn,—beginning with the Soul, who is the nobler of the two.

"The Soul then said to herself : I who am pure and stainless, shall begin by considering how I was created and how many other benefits I owe to my Creator. I acknowledge that I was made for such unspeakable blissfulness, and raised to so sublime a dignity, that I almost surpass the angelic orders, seeing that I am a spiritual being of a nature almost divine, and drawn so powerfully to meditate upon divine things, and then to feed upon the very bread of angels. I am, of my nature, invisible to fleshly eyes, and therefore seek my food and my delight in things unseen ; since for this was I created. In this I find my peace, and this contemplation is my only need ; and from this food I draw the strength which lifts me up to heaven, and enables me to put the world beneath my feet. Wherefore, during this entire week, I shall make of such contemplation my sole sustenance. Of other food I have no need or care : let who needs it feed upon it !"

Of course the Body is not satisfied with such ethereal diet as this, while Self-love, who ever inclines toward the enjoyment of the good things in this world, is as ill content as the Body. The latter's turn has now come.

"This is my week !" the Body exclaims. "Therefore come thou with me, O Soul, that I may show thee how many things God hath created for my use. See the heavens above us and the earth around and beneath us, with all their splendid array. See the sea with its swarms of fish, and the air with its flocks of birds. And then consider the kingdoms that cover the face of the globe, with their various principalities, provinces, cities, the dignities possessed by both church and state; the hoarded treasures of wealth, and the refined pleasures which wealth commands,—music and harmony, banquets with their varied delicacies,—all destined for my sustenance and pleasure, and all capable of affording innocent enjoyment, without offence to the Creator. Thou didst not introduce me into thy invisible country, as I have now shown thee mine. Nevertheless, as I cannot enjoy all these things created for me, unless thou condescend to help to taste them and take delight in them,—I must remind thee that thou art greatly indebted to me for all these varied sources of joy, and that thou must not soar away above this earth and leave me on it without my own necessary nourishment. Besides, my concern also is that thou shouldst secure thy salvation for the life to come, because my lot is inseparable from thine. Thou must not fancy, then, that I am asking thee to do what is contrary to reason or sinful before God."

Self-love, to whom the Body appeals, decides that the Soul must yield and come down from its long contemplation, shorten its vigils and fasts, and not distress its companion by unnecessary privations. The soul, in its endeavors to satisfy both its fellow-travellers, is drawn by them, step by step, into the full enjoyment of what each requires, and then, by an easy transition, into sinful excess. From the degradation, the servitude, the guilt, and the remorse of this condition she is delivered by the divine light, which shows her, on the one hand, her own miserable plight, and, on the other, the only road to liberty and salvation,—the subjecting both her companions to the iron yoke of her own will. Then begin a series of heroic struggles against sensuality, and all the downward inclinations and affections of our poor nature. The allegorical veil which St. Catherine throws over the facts she recites, scarcely conceals her own real history in her progress upward to the sublimest heights of spiritual perfection. We see, in succession, the rigorous bodily austerities by which sensuality was overcome. The Body is told by his imperious companion, that he must be content to endure the bitterest privations, to give a willing aid even in doing the things most repugnant to sense,—with the prospect of enjoying, after the final victory is won, the blissful fruits of a peace which no sensual revolt may disturb and in which both Body and Soul shall be the docile instruments of the Spirit of God. We see, beneath the transparent veil of the allegory, Catherine learning the practice of the highest forms of prayer and contemplation, and then giving herself up, in the hospitals of Genoa, while serving the poor and the sick, to the most heroic acts of mortification and self-abasement. Wherever nature showed resistance and repugnance, there Catherine overcame it instantly and conquered it once for all.

The Spirit of God, under whose guidance she wrote, inspired her to leave us in substance the same practical doctrine, which, some twenty years later, He dictated to Ignatius Loyola in the Cavern of Manresa. The worldly-minded Soul is, at first, flooded with that supernal light which enables her to see clearly the end for which she was created, and the sweet, powerful, and ever-present means divinely provided for her to reach her sublime destiny. In this light, she perceives how far she has wandered away from the right road, and what a horrible misuse she has made of God's graces. The disorder of her conduct, the sinfulness of her life, her own moral deformity in God's sight, dawn upon her by degrees, while her own sense of guilt, of shame, of horror, and of grief, increases from hour to hour. At this point, Christ Crucified is set before her,—as the victim and price which God demanded for sin,—for her sins in particular,—and she understands, while kneeling at His feet, how infinite is the love which brought the Incarnate God to such a death,—and how horrible the ingratitude which has only repaid Him by forgetfulness and repeated transgression.

The Crucifix—Christ Crucified—is thenceforward the Book from which the Soul learns; its light is the only one which teaches her the measure of what she must do to expiate the past and to make herself most Christ-like in the future.

Comparing her sinful self, as she has made herself by the misuse of all God's best gifts,—with her crucified Lord and Love, and with what He wished her to be,—she sets about *reforming* her whole life. She has now but one rule of action: to conform herself absolutely, immediately, and forever to the Divine Will. All else is indifferent to her. Here, again,—the Book of the Crucifix sheds its steady light on her way. He who came down from Heaven to reform the world and to teach it by His own example how to conform in all things most perfectly to that Will which yearns solely for our sanctification,—now walks before the Soul from the Manger to the Cross. It is the Royal Road of divine generosity,—the light constantly increasing as the soul advances in the footsteps of the Master and Model, and with that light an ever-increasing fire warming the heart of the Christian to emulate the poverty, the self-renouncement, the humility, the obedience of the God-man,—who was obedient unto death, even the death of the Cross.

Here the doctrine of St. Ignatius is so identical with that of St. Catherine,—that one must see it is the teaching of the same Spirit. It is addressed especially to chosen souls who are called to renounce all things and follow Christ. The form in which St. Catherine puts it applies to the seclusion of the convent, the hospital, the school-room, or the hermit's cell. The steps by which the converted Soldier of Manresa leads the soul forward, are intended to lift apostolic men above every worldly repugnance and affection, till they become all athirst for the humiliations and sufferings of their crucified Master. To be more like Him, and thereby to glorify His Father more,—they will seek the Cross in all things.

The first stage on the road toward holiness,—that in which the soul purges away her own stains and conceives the intense desire to do something worthy of Christ crucified,—has been happily expressed by two Latin words, *Deformata reformare*,—" to reform (by penance) the deformity of one's conduct." The second stage, in which the soul, thus purified, proceeds further, under the guidance of Almighty grace, to follow Christ and become Christ-like in all things, has been expressed no less happily by *reformata conformare*,—the conforming Christ as a model to one's reformed life. Now, as nothing so confirms or strengthens a servant in generous fidelity toward his master as to suffer for him or to share his sufferings,—even so the meditation on Christ's passion and fellowship with Him in suffering and humiliation, marvellously strengthen the soul in heroic devotion: this is the meaning of the formula expressing the third stage in the "Spiritual Exercises" of St. Ignatius: *conformata confirmare*.

The transformed state of our Lord, after His resurrection, furnishes the fourth stage, expressed by the words, *confirmata transformare*. It is the condition of one in whom body and soul, thanks to the crucifixion of all sensuality and earthly affections, become the instrument of the Holy Spirit, living here below a life which seems an anticipation of the condition of the Blessed, enjoying a close and unbroken union with the Divine Majesty, transported beyond themselves and transformed by His love, and, like an overflowing vessel, pouring their over-abundance on all around them.

It was the condition of St. Paul, after having been taken up to Heaven, when he declared that he no longer lived, but that Christ it was who lived in him. It was that of St. Ignatius in the last years of his life, when the vision of the Divine Beauty became so habitual and overpowering, that his soul was flooded with ecstatic ardors. What else made Xavier, as he ran his giant race in India and Japan, to bare his burning bosom to the night air, exclaiming, "Not so much sweetness, O Lord! Not so much sweetness!" Or kept the eye of his soul so constantly fixed on the uncreated loveliness, that he was heard, as he hurried along the streets and highways, to cry out continually, "O most holy Trinity! most holy Trinity!" as if for him the veil of our mortality was withdrawn, and he was given to gaze upon the Sun of all blissfulness and eternal joy! Again,—to take from Italy another and more popular instance,—was not St. Francis of Assisi marked, while yet living on earth, with the sacred wounds of his Master, Christ? Did not the Crucified draw this passionate lover of the cross up to Himself by cords that reached and pierced hands and feet and heart through the transpierced side,—making him also drunk with the bittersweet of His passion-cup, and sending him forth, in the intoxication of the love which transformed him, to preach of that love to all men, even to the very beasts and birds that he met with?

"In this seraphic apparition," says the historian of his life,

"Christ spoke certain high and secret things to St. Francis, saying, 'Knowest thou what I have done to thee? I have given thee the stigmata which are the ensign of My passion, that thou mayest be my standard bearer.' And when the marvelous vision disappeared, upon the hands and feet of St. Francis the print of the nails began immediately to appear, as he had seen them in the body of Christ crucified. In like manner, on the right side appeared the image of an unhealed wound, as if made by a lance, still red and bleeding, from which drops of blood often flowed and stained the tunic of St. Francis. Although these sacred wounds impressed upon him by Christ, afterward gave great joy to his heart, yet they caused unspeakable pain to his body; so that, being constrained by necessity, he made choice of Brother Leo, for his great purity and simplicity, and suffered him to touch and dress his wounds on all days, except during the time from Thursday evening to Saturday morning, for then he would not by any human remedy mitigate the pain of Christ's passion, which he bore in his body, because at that time our Saviour Jesus Christ was taken and crucified and died for us."

Another account of this wonderful vision,—a vision commemorated in the Church of God by a solemn yearly festival, goes on to say: "Then did all the Monte Alvernia appear wrapped in intense fire, which illuminated all the mountains and valleys around, as it were the sun shining in his strength upon the earth, whence the shepherds who were watching their flocks in that country were filled with fear, as they themselves afterward told the brethren, affirming that this light had been visible on Monte Alvernia for upwards of an hour, and because of the brightness of that light, which shone through the windows of the inn where they were resting, muleteers who were travelling in the Romagna arose in haste, supposing that the sun had risen, and saddled and loaded their beasts; but as they journeyed on they saw that light disappear, and the visible sun arise."

Surely,—as generation of Christians succeeds to generation, and the great battle goes ever on of souls contending with the flesh, and the world, and the pride of worldly life, it is needful that the Spirit of God should raise up among us saintly men and women, to whom He gives this consecration of sanctity begotten of suffering and self-crucifixion, in order that they may thus become the standard-bearers of the Crucified, and call beneath their banner heroic souls fired with the generosity which animates themselves. Surely, too, the light of such examples, heaven sent as it is, will at least be understood and hailed with rapture and remembered lovingly by the poor toilers of the land. Listen to what a Protestant writes of Monte Alvernia,—the wild and lofty theatre of St. Francis' holy contemplation.

"La Vernia is one of the few religious shrines which have not been confiscated by the avarice of the Sardinian government. Fortunately it belonged to the Arte di Lana (woolen weavers) who conceded it to the Grand Dukes (of Florence); they in their turn made it over to the Municipality of Florence, who have defended their property. . . . Most beautiful are the forest walks behind the convent, fragrant with the memories of holy Franciscan monks. 'In these woods'—says Sir J Stephens—'St. Francis wandered in the society of Poverty, his wedded wife, relying for support on Him alone by whom the ravens are fed, and awakening the echoes of the mountains by his devout songs and ejaculations. Here, in the beech avenues, Brother James of Massa beheld in a vision all the Friars-Minor in the form of a tree, from whose branches the evil monks were shaken by storms into perdition, while the good monks were carried by the angels into life eternal. Here the venerable

Brother John of Fermo wandered, weeping and sighing in the restless search after divine love, till, when his patience was sufficiently tried, Christ the Blessed appeared to him in the forest-path, and with many precious words restored to him the gift of divine grace. And 'for a long time after, whenever Brother John followed the path in the forest where the blessed feet of Christ had passed, he saw the same wonderful light, and breathed the same sweet odor,' which had come to him with the vision of his Saviour.'"[1]

Let us not pass away from this sacred spot to follow Angela Merici in her career of self-sacrifice, without becoming more and more penetrated with the spirit of the place. The same Author,—though differing so widely with us in belief,—evidently lingers lovingly on these rugged summits along whose heights St. Francis, six hundred and fifty years ago, led his followers heavenward. "The whole of the way (upward along the steep ascent) is alive with the recollections of St. Francis. . . . It was in the woods which we pass through that he vanquished demons in conflict, during his first ascent, while his companions, overwhelmed with fatigue, had fallen asleep in the shade. Then, 'beating his breast, he sought after Jesus, the beloved of his soul, and having found Him at last, in the secret of his heart, now he spoke reverently to Him as his Lord, now he made answer to Him as his Judge, now he besought Him as his Father, now he conversed with Him as his friend. On that night, and in that wood, his companions awaking and listening to him, heard him with many tears and cries implore the divine mercy in behalf of sinners.' Leaving the wood we enter upon the steeper and hotter path of the ascent, where,

---

[1] Hare, Cities of Northern and Central Italy, vol. iii., pp. 234, 239-41.

'The next morning his companions, knowing that he was too weak to walk, went to a poor laborer of the country, and prayed him, for the love of God, to lend his ass to Brother Francis, their father, for he was not able to travel on foot. Then that good man made ready the ass, and with great reverence caused St. Francis to mount thereon. And when they had gone forward a little, the peasant said to St. Francis— 'Tell me, art thou Brother Francis of Assisi?'— And St. Francis answered, 'Yes.'— 'Take heed, then,' said the peasant, 'that thou be in truth as good as all men account thee; for many have great faith in thee. And therefore I admonish thee to be no other than what the people take thee for.' And when St. Francis heard these words, he was not angry at being thus admonished by a peasant, but instantly dismounting from the ass, he knelt upon the ground before that poor man; and, kissing his feet, humbly thanked him for that his charitable admonition.'"

Such divine examples had ever been the result of the teaching of the Church and the practice of the God-like virtues which followed that teaching. The disorders begotten of political revolutions and worldly passions, and the scandals that offended in every age the true Christian,—were the fruit of the world's teaching, and to be solely attributed to its spirit.

Certain it is that the fertile plains of Lombardy, the teeming territory of Venice, the valleys and mountains around the Lake of Garda, were as familiar with the soul-stirring narratives borrowed from the Life of St. Francis, as was beautiful Florence and the wild tracts surrounding Monte Alvernia, or Genoa the Magnificent, in the days of St. Catherine Fieschi Adorno. All these doctrines relating to supernatural sanctity, and all the heroic lives that illustrated them in the present age or in the glorious past, were as well known in the home of the Merici as they were in that of the noble Tiene at Vicenza, of the Gonzagas at Mantua and Castiglione, or the Borromeos at Arona.

CHAPTER II.

PIOUS PARENTS AND ANGELIC CHILDREN.

NORTHERN ITALY is singularly favored by nature in the fertility of its soil, its singularly healthful climate, the steep mountain-wall which protects its fields, on the north and west, against the cold winds which sweep over Switzerland and Tyrol, as well as the no less destructive blasts borne across the Mediterranean from the coast of Africa. But a no less singular feature of this privileged land are the series of most beautiful lakes which extend from Lake Orta, in the west, to the Lake of Garda in the east. These, inclosed as they are among the lofty foot-hills of the Alps, and running, all of them, in a northerly direction, from where they join the fertile uplands of Lombardy and Venetia, to the wild and sublime scenery of the great Alpine valleys, afford to the thrifty populations of the adjacent countries an easy means of intercourse and traffic. In our day every one of the larger lakes can boast of steamers on its bosom.

The largest, if not the most beautiful, of these great bodies of water, is the Lake of Garda, the Benacus of the Romans, fourteen miles broad from Desenzano to Peschiera, at its southern extremity, and thirty-seven miles long from the former place to the picturesque town of Riva in the north, where the lake penetrates for some miles into the Tyrolean mountains. Its clear blue waters, which are upward of a thousand feet in depth, teem with the most delicious fish, although, from the remotest times, its surface is subject to storms which vie in fury with those of the ocean.

It may be said to be shut in on all sides by lofty mountains or hills,—as around its southern end,—which slope away like an amphitheatre from the shore. It is, therefore, sheltered on all sides; and, thus protected from the rigors and changes of an Alpine climate,—its shores in springtide and summer resemble rather the environs of Naples than any other portion of Northern Italy. The peninsula of Sermione, which runs out for several miles into the lake where it is broadest, divides it into two equal parts, and is covered with olive groves and vineyards, with a noble medieval castle and Roman ruins at its lofty extremity, where once stood the luxurious residence of one of Rome's most famous poets. Another Roman poet, far greater than he[1], has again and again described the lovely country beheld from the declivities of Sermione. One has only to travel along the southwestern borders of the Lake from the foot of the Peninsula to Desenzano, and thence to the lovely town and magnificent bay of Salò, to find that his road lies beneath one endless citron grove, with hills covered with olives and vines, and fields of waving corn seen at intervals from the roadside.

All the day long, the precipitous walls of rock which close in upon the Lake toward the north, and the towering summits beyond them with their everlasting snows, the rich hilly country at the south, the many beautiful towns, hamlets, castles and villas, which gem both sides of this glorious expanse of water, and its own deep blue bosom, become to the eye one ever-changing and transcendently beautiful panor-

---

[1] Virgil, a native of the neighboring Mantua.

ama,—so beautiful indeed, at sunrise and sunset, that the spot has ever been a favorite resort of artists.

It is on these enchanted shores, in the town of Desenzano, nestling in the southwestern corner of the Lake, that Angela Merici first saw the light, on the twenty-first day of March, 1474, according to the most reliable authorities. Her father's name was Giovanni Tommaso (John Thomas) Merici; her mother's maiden name was Biancosi, from the neighboring town of Salò. Both families, at the time, were comfortable and respected proprietary farmers,—the Merici at least being registered among the burgesses of Brescia. Of the Biancosi, we can say that if they did not rank as nobles, they were even then held in great esteem, and received much additional lustre afterward from their matrimonial alliances with the noble families of Bertalozzi, the Counts Lanfranchi, and the Counts of Tracagno[1]. The Merici also, during the sixteenth century, were divided into several houses, acquiring no little fame from the achievements of some of their members who lived in Manerba della Riviera and in Solarolo. At the beginning of the present century some scions of this house still remain at Darso in the vale Camonica.

Angela was one of five children, of whom only an elder sister and a brother are mentioned by the biographers of our saint[2]. Certain it is that, whatever may have been the

---

[1] Salvatori.

[2] In the various biographies of this saint, which have come under our notice, there is a sad dearth of intelligence regarding not only her parents, but her brothers and sisters. Salvatori, who seems to have enjoyed the most ample sources of information, only mentions in detail the one brother and sister who play so important a part in Angela's early life. Of the two other children of John Merici no word is spoken,-- leaving the reader to conclude either that they had died before their parents, or that they were already married or settled in life, at the time of their father's death. Salvatori, however, says positively that John Merici died in his fortieth year,—a very youthful age at which to have two married children! A "Doctor Tracagno" is spoken

social position and the wealth of Giovanni Merici, that both he and his wife were fervent Christians, intent on preserving their children from all taint of evil, and on filling their tender souls with the love of all goodness.

In the preceding chapter we saw that several personages, since then honored by the Church as Saints, were living in the neighborhood of Desenzano,—persons who even then were the objects of universal reverence among all classes. St. Francis of Assisi also had visited the shores of Lake Garda, and stirred the hearts of its populations by his words of burning love and his angelic life. An entire island near the entrance to the bay of Salò had been given to him as a site for a monastery. He had accepted the gift, and planted there one of his colonies of saintly men, whose chants at evening song, at midnight, and at early dawn were wont for centuries to be borne over the waters, like voices from the angelic choirs, and the fragrance of whose unearthly self-denial was borne further all over the land than the perfumes of the citron groves of Salò and Maderno. It is still called the Isola dei Frati (the Friars' Island), though the new masters of modern Italy have driven out the sons of St. Francis, and the voice of matins or evening song no longer wakes the echoes of desolate island or shore. But the brown robes of the Franciscan monks, and the distant sounds of holy psalmody over the clear blue waters of her native lake, were things as familiar to Angela Merici in childhood or in girlhood, as the sights and sounds of her father's home. Her mother, moreover, had been brought up beneath the shadow of a church and convent of the Obser-

---

of during Angela's last illness as being her "nephew,"—therefore, her sister's son. But it is the Biancosi that are said to be allied to the Count of Tracagno. Was not the "nephew" a cousin rather?

vantines in her native town of Salò¹, as we shall see further on. We need not, therefore, wonder to learn that both Giovanni Merici and his wife were ardent admirers of the heroic men and women, who, in all ages, had been the devoted followers of Christ and His Blessed Mother. Hence the custom which these excellent people observed in their household, of reading daily a portion of some edifying book, particularly the Lives of the Saints. Both parents must have taken uncommon pains to develop deep religious principles and generous sentiments of piety in the souls of their children from the first dawn of reason. That this labor of love should have been most assiduously performed by the mother, especially in a family blessed with a father so truly enlightened as John Merici, we are prepared to expect. But the biographers of our Saint dwell with such peculiar emphasis on the great share he had in forming her mind and heart, as well as those of his other children, that one is at a loss to account for it otherwise than by admitting that he was singularly careful

---

[1] The Franciscans, or "Order of Friars Minor," in England "Gray Friars," comprised during the lifetime of the holy founder (1182-1226), three distinct, though not independent, orders;—the order proper of Friars Minor or Minorites (1208); the "Order of Poor Ladies," or "of St. Clare" (1212), known in the English speaking world as "Poor Clares;" and the Third Order, or "Order of Penitents," (1221), for persons of both sexes living in the world. The rigorous enforcement of the rule of poverty established by the Seraphic Saint of Assisi, was bitterly and obstinately opposed by the man next in authority to himself, Brother Elias of Cortona, whom Francis had made his vicar-general. The strife between this man, his followers in the order, and those who would not admit of any mitigation of the rule, saddened the last years of the meek and gentle Saint. After his death, it led to a lamentable strife, renewed with increased violence each time a new superior-general was to be elected,—till, in 1517, Pope Leo X. sanctioned the division of the Minorites into two independent societies, bestowing the name of *Observantines* on those who clung to the observance of the primitive rule of the poor St. Francis, and the denomination of *Conventuals* on those who clung to a mitigated rule,—the title of Minister-General of the whole Order of Friars Minor remaining with the head of the Observantines, as well as the quality of lawful successor of St. Francis.—Happy had it been for the Church that religious orders had preserved the pristine spirit of religious fervor and holy poverty which distinguished their beginnings!

to train his dear ones to a full knowledge of the beauty of holiness, and to inflame their souls with a holy desire to emulate the unearthly goodness of the Saints. His love and piety must, therefore, have been above those of most fathers.

He appears to have made it a rule to have all his children, the youngest as well as the oldest, around him each evening when he performed his family devotions, and prefaced them by the pious reading alluded to. Parents are only doing God's dearest work, when they are thus sowing the tender souls of their young children with the seeds of supernatural truth, and the early love of Himself and His Saints. And He aids them mightily in the doing. We remember how Anna, the mother of the great and saintly Samuel, prevailed over God by prayer, and so taught her boy by word and example, that, when brought to the Temple and given up to its service, while yet little more than a nursling, the child Samuel already found his delight in conversing with God. He had been taught how near to us is that most loving and most sweet Presence, how near to our eyes the veiled Countenance, and how near to our lips the Heart, in which all-sufficient love is ever planning our welfare. Even in childhood Samuel was favored with the direct communications of the Divine Will, —and all through his long and eventful life he never ceased to be the man of prayer, crying to the Lord for hours together in favor of his erring people and that people's faithless ruler.

Everything told us of the childhood and girlhood of Angela Merici forces us to believe, that the same gracious Voice which had made itself so familiar to the little Samuel, was also wont to speak to her heart in these wondrously gentle but powerful tones. He is Creator, and best knows, dwelling as He does in the very centre of our being, how to move sweetly but irresistibly the springs of life within us, by the simple touch of His almighty hand, or by one word from His lips. And so, chosen as Angela was to be the parent of so wide-spread and great-souled a family, everything which reminded her of God or of God's most privileged friends and servants, attracted her attention powerfully even during these years of her precocious childhood. She would listen with a rapt look to the marvelously beautiful stories read to her from the most authentic sources, about Christ and His Mother, and the army of Saints who had shed such glory on her own native Italy, as well as on the other countries of Christendom. The knowledge of God and the things of God, enters as easily into the soul of innocent and holy childhood, as the light enters into the healthy eye. The one imprints indelibly on the understanding, the memory, and the imagination, the great truths of Religion, and the great facts embodying the lives of her apostles and martyrs,—just as the other conveys to the soul the sensible images of the beautiful world around us.

There seemed to be in the angelic child's eagerness for religious instruction, and in the absorbed attention with which she listened to her parents' words, a something preternatural. They remarked it then, and so did others. But when these pious exercises were over, nature resumed its sway, and the child was the child again, returning to her playmates and the amusements of her age with all the zest of childhood.

She was a singularly beautiful child, fair-haired, with a brilliant complexion, a light and graceful figure, sweet-tempered and low-voiced, and gifted in an eminent degree with that loving nature, which is ever ready to sacrifice itself to the good and comfort of others; endowed, too, with uncommon penetration, and that precious faculty of self-control so inestimably precious to those who are to have the government of others. All these qualities of mind and heart shone forth in the child, and were developed in her by the sunny atmosphere of her parents' home, as well as by the providential circumstances in which she grew up to womanhood[1].

She was not a vain child, conscious of her personal attractions, and seeking either the admiration or the notice of others. Even with all her childish ways and predilections, she was too seriously bent on imitating to the utmost of her power the heroic abnegation of the holy men and women of whose lives she heard so much, that it never entered her mind to seek to be admired, or praised, or petted, because of her beauty, her grace, or her wit.

In her tenth year occurred an incident which reveals the strength of her character and the bent of her inclinations. Playing one day with girls of her own age, one of them caressing her beautiful hair, could not help saying, that this alone would be sure to bring her a crowd of admirers. The little maid, instead of taking this as a compliment, resented it as an insult. She had already resolved to belong to God alone, and to live as lived the Blessed Osanna Andreasi at Mantua, the Blessed Stefana Quinzani at Soncino, St. Veronica at Milan, or St. Catherine at Genoa. The fame of these holy women, and of many others who were then living in Northern Italy, was the subject of daily comment on the shores of the Lake of Garda, thrilling the souls of the aged with regret for lost opportunities, and moving those of the young to ardent desires of emulation.

Even the youngest, like Angela, who constantly heard these reports, or who, not unfrequently, were brought by

---

[1] Father Salvatori thus speaks of her in her tenth year: *Giunta però all' età di dicci anni diedi una più luminosa riprova di questo parziale suo affetto. Quanto liberale la grazia co' suoi doni, altrettanto le si mostrava la natura. Avvenente di volto, leggiadra di portamento, e sopra tutto di una chioma così bionde e gentile, che nominata veniva per un esemplare di rara bellezza, Ella però niente invanita di questo, anzi neppur sospettando, che veruno a lei pensasse, viveva a se ed alle sue divozioni.*

their parents to visit these great servants of God,—perfectly understood, that who would imitate their saintly examples, must not only put away all thoughts of vanity and self-indulgence, but lead a life of retirement, prayer, and self-crucifixion. This both Angela and her elder sister had laid to heart, even before the former had reached her tenth year. When, therefore,—for the first time, most likely,—the child was surprised and shocked at being praised for her comeliness, and told that her beautiful hair was sure to win her many admirers, her first thought was to cut off her hair. Then, as she could not do this without the consent of her mother, she bethought her of destroying its color by some horrid mixture. This she continued to use secretly, and even went so far as to apply the same mixture to her face in order to spoil her complexion. But this spirit and these tendencies became manifest in Angela even before her tenth year. The precocious intelligence which enabled her to understand and enjoy intensely the reading of the Lives of the Saints while yet scarcely emerged from infancy, was accompanied by a fervent desire to imitate them. Nor did her pious parents discountenance their child's purpose. On the contrary, they encouraged her love for prayer, the delight she took in spending a long time before the altar in the neighboring church, and her wish to perform certain acts of abstinence and self-denial in imitation of what they read to her or told her of the men and women revered as the highest models of goodness.

Her sister, a few years older than herself, and one of her brothers,—probably the only surviving children of their family,—shared this fervent spirit of early generosity. Indeed, the sister, both on account of her age and her superior wisdom, became the little Angela's confidant, counsellor, companion, and guide in all the plans which she formed and put into practice for her advancement in piety. Just, as in the next century, we see St. Teresa and her little brother playing at saints and hermits in their father's home in Avila, and even stealing away secretly to go to convert the Moors or receive at their hands the crown of martyrdom, even so,—though apparently in a more serious and rational manner,—our two little sisters at Desenzano, seized every opportunity to imitate the solitary life, the long vigils, prayers, and fasts of the Saints they read of. Angela would even steal out of her bed by night, when her sister was fast asleep, and kneel in prayer till her strength gave way. These practices and the little industries practised by the child to mortify her appetite for food, went so far as to affect her health perceptibly. The watchful eye of her mother had no sooner detected this change in her appearance, than she divined the cause. So both parents agreed to check these childish excesses.

Angela submitted, though sorely against her will, and not without being occasionally carried away by the powerful instincts which led her to seek every opportunity of self-denial and self-infliction. The older girl yielded more implicitly to the parental guidance. Nevertheless, John Merici and his wife were far too enlightened and conscientious to thwart their youngest daughter's disposition, when they perceived that the spirit which prompted her to follow the most perfect way, was truly the Spirit of God. They observed her carefully, then; and once they became convinced that the hand of God was guiding their darling towards the sublime heights of holiness,—they bestowed their care in developing every quality of mind and heart which would fit her to be a perfect instrument of the Divine purpose in its own good time.

And so in this blessed and happy home the three children grew up, as all children will where parents do their full duty lovingly; where the fear of God and the desire to please the Divine Majesty in all things, is the foremost law of life in the Christian home; where that home is blessed, if not with wealth, at least with abundance of all earthly comforts, where the family is held in universal esteem, and the beautiful and bountiful earth is in harmony with the peace and love and goodness that reign around the family hearth. .

Assuredly, the home of the Merici at Desenzano was singularly privileged in all these respects. Nor was that of the Biancosi, near at hand in the far more beautiful town of Salò, less blessed by the bounty of nature or the gracious gifts of the Spirit. Indeed Salò, possessing as it did a church and monastery of the Observantines, enjoyed many religious advantages above Desenzano. And thus, it is not unlikely that Angela, as well as her brother and sister, were often induced by their piety as well as by their affection for their noble uncle and his family, to make the short journey between the two towns,—a journey which, even in our day, no one can make in Spring or Summer or Autumn, without fancying, as they skirt the magnificent lake, between groves of lemon-trees, or beneath a continuous canopy of overhanging vines, while the air is loaded with the most delicious perfumes and vocal with the songs of birds;—that the land they are in is almost an earthly paradise.

CHAPTER III.

ANGELA'S FIRST BITTER TRIALS.

Favored of nature as we know this part of Italy to be, we know it to be still more privileged in the incomparable religious and intellectual advantages which it has enjoyed during so many centuries. And yet,—even in the time of John Merici,—a concourse of fatal circumstances had brought about, even in the bosom of the most pious families, such a neglect of the most life-giving sacraments as might be taken for a want of faith. We know that one of the chief aims of St. Ignatius Loyola, St. Francis Xavier, and their companions, while evangelizing Northern and Central Italy, from 1537 to 1540, was to re-establish the practice of frequent confession and communion, which had declined in nearly every country of Christendom. The entire fifteenth century, as well as the fourteenth, had been filled by continual wars, as well as by religious disturbances. The great schism in the Church, known as the Western Schism, had only terminated in November, 1417, by the election of Pope Martin V., and the resignation of the other claimant to the title. But the political passions which had induced the European sovereigns and statesmen to create the schism and to perpetuate it, as well as the worldly spirit which their joint efforts had sought for centuries to introduce into the government of the Church itself, continued to be active forces of evil long after 1417.

War after war, like billows on a storm-lashed coast,—swept over Italy, over its northern and central provinces in particular, so that scarcely a single generation knew what peace, repose, or security meant. And, in these times, war implied spoliation, pitiless destruction, the oppression and harrowing of the weak and defenceless, the blotting out in a single season of all the fairest fruits of religion, piety, culture, and civilization produced by the labor of ages.

We all know that nothing can grow on the shore unceasingly beaten by the ocean surge, and that no harvest will ripen on the field continually torn by the plow and the harrow, or daily ravaged by the wild herds of the forest, or desolated again and again by earthquake, fire, and storm. So is it with the home-life of any people, even the most civilized, and the most religious: its deepest beliefs are torn up by the roots, or weakened by religious division, strife and scandal; its most hallowed customs and cherished virtues are omitted, or forgotten, and cease to be a necessary source of strength or consolation, when the political or social whirlwind is abroad, and when there is no rest to the earth from evil.

When we are told, therefore, that Angela Merici was in her thirteenth year, and had not yet made her first Communion, we are tempted to question the faith or the piety of her parents. And yet they were both unquestionably pious and faithful in no ordinary degree. The subsequent years of her life were to be a calamitous period for her native land and religion. She,—the angelic maiden of Desenzano,—and many such as she, were destined to be the chosen instruments of renovation. The very hunger and thirst her young soul had to endure in its long yearning for the divine Eucharistic food, were to help her afterward to provide for others the means of more frequent refection.

At any rate, while the girl was yearning for the great happiness of receiving the Lord of her soul in His divinest gift, an accidental inquiry of the rector of her parish informed him of the fact that she had not till then been numbered among his communicants. Her extraordinary virtue was, of course, well known to him, unless, indeed, that he was one recently appointed to the pastoral office, and was therefore inspired to repair the neglect of others. He fixed a day for Angela's happiness; and happiness it surely was for her, such as she had not known or conceived of before.

The Eucharistic Sacrifice is to the Christian world a perpetual reminder of what Infinite Love could do to save the soul and win the heart of man. The Eucharistic Banquet accompanying that Sacrifice is the pledge and foretaste of the eternal fruition which that incomparable Love purchased for its own. On the very day when He rose from the grave, we see how intent He is on imparting to every one of the disciples who clung to Him, though with never so uncertain a faith, the sweet consolation of His presence. Two of them are traveling toward the hamlet of Emmaus, near Jerusalem, where their residence was, or where they received hospitality during the Paschal festivities. He suddenly joins them on the road, instructs them on the truth of His resurrection, and opens the eyes of their soul that they may see the truth clearly. Then they arrive at their destination, and, as it is growing late, press their unknown instructor to tarry with them for the night. He accedes in part to their request, and takes His seat at their table, blesses and breaks the bread set before them, and gives it to them,—as He had done to the Twelve on the eve of His passion. "And their eyes were opened and they knew Him: and He vanished out of their sight. And they said one to the other, Was not our heart burning within us whilst He spoke in the way, and opened to us the Scriptures?"[1]

He never ceases to come to us "in the way," as we journey toward eternity amid the doubts, the uncertainties, the weariness, the manifold dangers and difficulties of our road here below. His grace it is that "opens" and makes plain to us the whole plan of divine love and mercy as revealed in the Scriptures. They are full of Him, and He takes away the veil that we may see Him clearly, fulfilling in His own person all the gracious offices of Redeemer. But it is in the Eucharistic banquet that He comes to us to apply, literally, to our souls all the merits, all the saving and sanctifying efficacy of His passion, by bestowing on us, in that Bread, HIMSELF. The true Elisæus not only restores us to life by the touch of His pierced hands and feet, but is ever near to us "in the way," to bless and break and give that Bread, and to warm our hearts with the divine virtue that issues from His own, as the light and warmth pour forth from the unclouded noonday sun.

Blessed are the pure of heart! To them is it given to say, —while that Sacramental Presence lasts, "Was not our heart burning within us, whilst He spoke in the way?"

Even so was it with the angelic maiden of Desenzano. What words the Divine Guest spoke to that soul, it were needless to inquire. He has said: "I am come to cast fire on the earth, and what will I, but that it be kindled?"[2] Angela Merici was to kindle that sacred flame in many a soul. Her own, therefore, was to be a furnace of living fire. Indeed such is the rule of our God's supernatural providence. For it is not solely, or even principally, of the spirits whom

---

[1] St. Luke xxiv., 31, 32. [2] St. Luke xii. 49.

He appoints to guard mankind, and to minister to their wants, that it has been said: "Who makest Thy angels spirits, and Thy ministers a burning fire."[1] This applies much more to the saintly men and women whom the Divine Majesty selects and employs to enlighten and inflame the souls of a blind and cold-hearted generation. We know from the unanimous testimony of all who beheld Angela at that period, that her fervor of spirit was increased to an incredible degree by her first Communion.

Thenceforward her chief delight for many a year was to remain in prayer in the Church, kneeling before the Mercy Seat, and conversing sweetly with the Veiled Majesty ever present there. A time was to come,—when a still far greater delight to her should be to set other souls aflame with the divine fire which burned within her own, and which was fed continually by her loving familiarity with that adorable Presence.

Meanwhile, the girl of thirteen, wise as she was, spotless as she was, and devoted to her admirable parents and the performance of all her home-duties, was to grow still further in all maidenly virtue and spiritual loveliness beneath the eyes of these parents.

We should be greatly in error, were we to imagine that the home of the Merici was an austere and joyless home, or that any one of their children was either condemned or allowed to lead therein the life of a recluse. The brightest and most joyous abodes are those of truly Christian parents, whose souls are lifted and lighted up by the consciousness of the divine friendship. There are mothers who make it one of their chief cares to make the cup of delight they daily prepare for their children as deep and full as they can, pre-

---

[1] Ps. ciii. 4.

cisely because the happiness they enjoy with their dear ones is most innocent, and because they are careful to keep away from these guileless souls even the remotest thought of evil in their home amusements and pleasures.

It is because the biographers of St. Angela have all agreed in representing her parents as both blessed with abundant means and remarkable for their enlightened piety, while all their children are described as true children of God,—that we are justified in believing that the interior of their home was ever as sunny as the aspect of nature around it. To preserve childhood and youth from the least stain of sin, it is necessary, first of all, to cultivate in the soul the love of all that is good and beautiful, for His dear sake, who has made this world so bright only to remind His children of the Eternal Home; and next, to preserve these innocent souls not only from the contact of evil, but from all knowledge and all thought of it.

While perusing some of the published Lives of the Saint, one would be led, wrongly, we believe, to think that Angela, not only when budding into womanhood, but during the tender years of her childhood, had a full knowledge of moral evil, and was surrounded by companions of her own age who were not unacquainted with evil. The most angelic souls known to us among the Saints,—such as an Aloysius Gonzaga, a Stanislaus Kostka, a Berchmans, a Rose of Lima, or a Marianna de Paredes, were enamored from childhood of a life of retirement, prayer, and self-crucifixion, although utterly unacquainted with moral evil. The very thought of sin would fill them with fear and horror; but that did not arise from either a practical knowledge of it, or any mental conception of its nature that could leave a foul impression on the fancy. These angels of earth would recoil from the thought of anything sinful, as one would from the touch of a red-hot iron. But this instinctive horror in the soul is one of the fruits produced by the abiding presence therein of the Holy Spirit. When it is, therefore, said of St. Angela, that she made an early vow to consecrate herself to God alone, and that she afflicted her tender body by fasting and other austerities, we must not think of her as doing so to expiate sins that she had committed, or to preserve herself from the stain of a moral corruption of which she had any notion. In the towns and hamlets of Northern Italy in the fifteenth century, as well as in those of Spain, or indeed of any other country in Christendom, young people of both sexes grew up beneath a watchful mother's care as unconscious of moral wrong, as ignorant of the existence of evil in their neighborhood, as is the child unborn. Nay, we know it to be so in the very midst of the nineteenth century, in the midst of the great Babylon of the New World, with all the multiplied means of information produced by our modern cravings for knowledge of every kind. God owes it to Himself and to us, that, while the world around us is solely occupied in gratifying sensuality, and ministering to the most unhallowed passions and appetites, the Christian home should be still a nursery of virgin souls, from which His angels are careful to ward off every evil influence.

So our little maiden, after the great event of her first Communion was seen to advance rapidly in self-control, and in these habits of devotion to the needs and comforts of others, which are the very source of all peace and happiness in home-life, as well as the most essential requisite of community-life in Religious houses.

John Merici was now approaching his fortieth year. He must have been a most happy husband and parent. Indeed all Desenzano and its neighborhood esteemed both parents most blessed in the two angelic girls and the modest and manly boy who vied with each other in serving God generously, and in honoring father and mother The restraint which the parents had formerly imposed on the pious fervor of their little girls, had been removed as these grew up and gave proof of ripe wisdom and solid piety. So, just as the proud father had delighted to read to his little flock, in their childhood, the history of the most heroic souls, even so did he now pride himself in being their associate in their every pious practice and act of charity.

We are in the year 1489. Angela was now fifteen, her sister being, probably, some two or three years older. They were at this time the companions of their mother, repaying her in a thousand ways for all her loving care of them. Their sincere and well-tried piety,—indeed the neighbors gave it a higher name,—dispensed her from the anxious watchfulness so needful at this age. Both girls seemed bent on seeking heavenly bridals; and if the position of their parents, their own beauty and rare qualities, did ever bring suitors for their hand, no mention is made of the fact in authentic history. Nor is it said that their parents sought any establishment for them. It may be that the report had gone abroad,—one warranted by the Christian customs of these ages,—that both Angela and her sister had "chosen the better part," and vowed themselves to the Virginal Life so much honored in the Church, and so fruitful in heroic sanctity and charity. Be that as it may, in that year began for Angela a series of extraordinary trials, which were to search cruelly every depth of her heart, to chasten her soul for the Divine purpose, and to loosen every tie that bound her to the dear home of her parents.

A malignant fever suddenly carried off her father, overwhelming his family with grief. To Angela, more even than to her brother and sister, this loss was irreparable.

For her father seems to have taken especial care in training her, as if he had a presentiment of the glorious life-work for which she was destined. But with the forgetfulness of self which was so beautiful a feature in her character, the orphaned girl devoted herself to the task of consoling her remaining parent. To a widowed mother's heart nothing is so sweet, in the first period of her bereavement, as the endearments and companionship of daughters of the age of Angela and her sister. And so both girls gave themselves up entirely to the sacred duty of sustaining and consoling their mother. Religion, speaking through such pure and loving hearts as theirs, must have had a double power to raise and cheer the poor mourner. From what we shall soon have to relate, however, it would appear, that, although resigned to the Divine Will in the loss of her husband, Signora Merici never rallied completely from the prostration caused by this unexpected death. Where two souls are as thoroughly united by the exalted love which the Sacrament of Matrimony bestows on the sinless and the deserving, the death of either only causes the other left behind to yearn unceasingly for the day of eternal reunion. And so the Christian mother, with her love and her hopes fixed on that eternal world where there would be no separation, endeavored to fulfill both a mother's and a father's place in the desolate home. We are not told how old her son was at this time, or how far she could rely upon him to attend to the care of their property. That he was entirely worthy of his parents and sisters, we shall see presently. Perhaps he was the youngest of his family, and thus the least able to relieve the widow of her load of care.

She was to be soon still further tried. Angela, after the death of her excellent father, looked up to her sister for the counsel and guidance she had ever found in him. It was not a rare thing in those times,—filled as monasteries were with the daughters of the wealthiest and most noble,—for girls who felt themselves called to the Virginal Life to remain at home, bound only by such vows as members of the Third Order of St. Francis or St. Dominic were allowed to make, discharging most perfectly all the duties of their place in the family, and distinguished only by their devotion to the suffering poor and their avoidance of all worldly pleasures and amusements. Frequently also in families, especially of the rank held by the Merici and Biancosi, the parents themselves belonged to the Third Order, and united heart and soul with their daughters in the fervent though quiet pursuit of spiritual perfection. We have, indeed, no proof that either John Merici or his wife had bound themselves by any such religious obligations as these. Yet it is apparent from the details left by their youngest daughter's biographers, that they encouraged their children, as these advanced towards womanhood, to make of their home so much of a cloister as the performance of all neighborly charities and the fulfillment of their own home-duties permitted.

Angela and her sister, in this their first sorrow, would naturally be united and more fervent than ever in the pursuit of the great purpose of their lives,—the attainment of holiness. Their beloved parent had gone before them to the Judgment Seat; and their own deepest faith and most hallowed affections impelled them frequently to kneel in spirit at the feet of the Judge and implore Him to give speedy rest to the father who had labored so much for them. Of course, a Christian mother and wife, such as Merici's loved companion, would find her sweetest consolation in joining her daughters,—all her three children, rather,—in these supplications. We have only to remember the words left on record by one of the greatest Saints of Northern Italy, some thousand years before their day, to understand how the

Catholic heart follows its dead with tenderest solicitude into the awful regions of the eternal world unseen. St Ambrose thus speaks of the soul of Theodosius the Great, to whom he had been so wise, so stern, so loving a guide:

"Give rest to Thy servant Theodosius, that rest which Thou hast prepared for Thy Saints. Let his soul return to [Thee] whence it came: where it cannot feel the sting of death, and where he shall know that death itself is not the end of our natural existence, but of our sinfulness. Him have I loved, and him shall I follow to 'the land of the living;' nor will I forsake him, till my tears and prayers shall place him where his merits call him, within 'the holy mountain of the Lord;'—where there is life without end, where there is neither decay nor contagion, nor wailing, nor sorrow, nor companionship with the sepulchre;—but the true land of the living, where 'this mortal (body) must put on immortality, and this corruptible must put on incorruption.'"[1]

A disciple of St. Ambrose, and greater even than his master, St. Augustine, thus speaks of his own mother, St. Monica, who had also been a devout listener at the feet of the holy Archbishop of Milan:

"I then, O my praise and my life, Thou God of my heart, putting aside for a little her good deeds, for which I joyfully give thanks to Thee, do now beseech Thee for the sins of my mother. Hearken unto me, through that Medicine of our wounds, Who hung upon the tree, and Who, sitting at Thy right hand, 'maketh intercession for us.' . . . To this sacrament of our ransom did Thy handmaid bind her soul by the bond of faith. Let none separate her from Thy protection!"[2]

The death of their worshipped one, therefore, only made mother and children enter in spirit, not into the gloom of

---

[1] St. Ambrose, *De Obitu Theodosii.*   [2] St. Augustine, "Confessions," b. ix.; c. ii.

the Valley of Death, but into the blissful presence of the Lord of Life, the merciful Father of men and angels, in His own bright and glorious City on high. We Catholics mourn not as do those for whom death is the end of all things. Our grief is tempered with holy joy at the thought of the eternal rest and the unfading crown, which our dear departed have already obtained; and if we mourn or pray, or beseech the intercession of others in favor of the dear one gone to judgment, it is only to obtain from the Divine Victim of Calvary a more speedy application of His cleansing blood to the precious soul. So our tears are not tears of unalloyed bitterness, nor our mourning unmixed with joy at the prospect faith opens to us of heavenly glory and repose.

God, who knew what fresh trials were at hand for the mother and her orphans, thus drew them more powerfully and more closely to Himself. This sense of nearness to Him, given at certain seasons to the souls He loves best, is, in the judgment of the great masters of spiritual life, a warning to prepare for new crosses. The afflicted mother, who now leaned so much for support on her two angelic daughters, and who derived so much sweetness and strength from the devotional exercises they preformed in common, had no sooner begun to resume her former active share in the household duties, than she was alarmed at seeing her oldest child sicken and pine. Her husband had been snatched away by a malignant fever. We are not told what was the nature of the disease which carried off the daughter. At any rate, within the year, the Angel of Death paid his second visit to the home of the Merici, bearing away with him this time Angela's twin soul. He had given no warning of his approach, not even allowing time for the administration of the last sacraments. Such a sudden visitation must have added greatly to the grief both of Angela and her mother, had they not known how pure, unselfish, and devoted to all goodness was the young life thus cut short in its opening promise. To the poor mother, whose heart had, most probably, as we have seen already, been sorely tried by the death of two other children, and who had not yet recovered from the cruel blow inflicted by the loss of her husband, this last bereavement was overwhelming. Perfectly as she may have acquiesced in the inscrutable wisdom of the Father, her gentle and loving spirit sank beneath this additional load of suffering. Thenceforward she only continued to droop and waste away slowly till the end came for her also.

Meanwhile Angela, on whom now devolved the care of the family and household, as well as the superintendence of her parents' property, gave proof of her heroic qualities of soul. She felt like one who had set foot on a difficult mountain road, and over which she must needs travel, but who is all of a sudden forsaken by guides and companions, and left alone in the night to pursue her journey amid pitfalls and precipices.

At this critical period of her life is made manifest the maturity of all these womanly virtues which had been steadily growing and ripening in the maiden's soul among all the blissful peace and sunshine of her dear father's home. A hasty and superficial perusal of the story of her early life thus far, might impress one with the notion that Angela had been a little wayward as well as eccentric in her girlish piety, often seeking to satisfy her bent for long prayer and austerity at the expense of filial obedience. The child, for most readers, would thus wear a somewhat unamiable aspect. And yet she was, invariably, the loving, dutiful, unselfish, bright, and winsome child, who seemed to draw from her frequent and familiar intercourse with God and the angelic world, only an increase of devotion to the need, the comfort, the pleasure, and the happiness of her idolized parents and her sister and brother.

We have said "frequent and familiar intercourse;" for, in truth, the Spirit who guided that privileged soul, exercised on its movements a control which was, in a measure, beyond her will. Was it not an imperious impulsion of the Spirit of grace that urged John the Baptist, while yet a child, to seek the solitudes between Juttah, his native place, and the Dead Sea? Was it not the same divine impulse which he obeyed in choosing for his clothing the rude camel-hair tunic, as worn by Elias and Elisæus, and for his food the wild-honey and locusts which these desolate hilly regions supply?

Both Giovanni Merici and his wife understood, after a very little while, that their fair-haired darling was under the spell of a Spirit who would be obeyed. The wise and prudent father no longer thwarted his child's determination; he was content to direct her in the divinely-appointed path, and to share with her and his oldest daughter the "honey from the Rock," which they found in their devotional and penitential practices.

And so Angela had grown steadily, silently, in supernatural holiness, from early childhood to her sixteenth year; setting her heart on the one great aim of all God-like lives,—the honor of being allowed, in God's good time, to consecrate herself solemnly to her one Love and Lord, Christ Crucified. In the soul of child, maiden, and woman, this one thought and hope was the mighty force which gave purpose and shape to her whole life.

If there is in the unfolding of life so much of awful mystery, even in the instance of the oak on the hillside, advancing from the acorn to the tiny sapling, and from the sapling clinging to the sheltered corner of the crag to the mighty tree which has battled victoriously with the storms of centuries,—how much more so is the growth of the saintly soul, God's masterpiece in the moral world! This development of the highest energy, this progression in the beauty of highest goodness, in the grandeur of self-conquest, self-sacrifice, and boundless devotion to the glory of the Divine Majesty and the dearest interests of immortal souls,—is the special work attributed to the Holy Spirit. Man, even when most enlightened by Revealed Truth, can only note its outward manifestations, and thus describe its stages with more or less of hesitancy and obscurity. The secret of the oak's interior life, the mystery of God's working in the privileged souls of His Saints, remain for the world an unfathomable abyss.

St. Catherine of Genoa has left us a most beautiful allegory, which might be called the story of her own soul's progress from the first struggles with victorious sensuality to her sublime transformation into the likeness of the Crucified God of charity. More beautiful still, and more instructive, are the writings of St. Teresa; but how few among the most learned and the most spiritual are privileged to understand aright this mystic theology, so full of awful depths and impenetrable obscurity?

That Angela Merici had attained to an extraordinary degree of sanctity, even in her sixteenth year, is a fact for which we have good warrant in the acts of her canonization, solemnly attested as these were by the most credible witnesses, and after the most searching investigation.

The affliction caused her by the loss of her dear father, and the further grief arising from the death of her cherished sister, had, as we have seen, only made Angela increase in love and tenderness toward her mother. She had always been the angel of the household; every act and word of hers toward her dear ones, while crushed by these successive misfortunes, made them consider her as most truly an angel.

But the girl herself, while adoring the hand of God which thus chastened a family devoted to Him, was also made to know that every loved object taken away from her own clinging heart was an earthly tie removed, and a higher measure of liberty given to the soul. She could not divine as yet what work God would have her do. She only strove, with all the power of her soul, to make His will her own, and to render herself in every way worthy of His designs.

A fortnight after the death of her sister, while her mother's desolation was yet at its height, and her own grief was keenest, an incident occurred—one mentioned in detail in the Bull of canonization. It was harvest-time, and Angela, as we have said, had not only to superintend the household concerns, but those as well of the farm belonging to her family. This was situated about a mile and a half from Desenzano. Just as noontide was at hand Angela had set out for the fields bearing with her a basket with some refreshments for her workmen. She went along, her whole soul wrapped up in the thought of the dear companion so lately and so suddenly snatched away from her side. The remembrance of her having been cut off without any of the consolations so coveted by Christians at their last hour, was just then causing Angela the deepest anguish, and she was lifting her heart and her eyes to Heaven in fervent prayer for the repose of that dear soul, when lo! a most glorious vision opened upon her sight. The fields, the citron-groves, the clustering vines, all disappeared, and she beheld, as if she stood at the opened gate of Heaven, a multitude of angels and angelic maidens surrounding one who was evidently their Queen. Among the virgin train, when her eyes could bear to look attentively, she soon discovered her lost sister. Filled with an exstatic joy and a sweetness that no words can express, Angela stood rooted to the earth, forgetting all else in the world but that supernal glory a glimpse of which was afforded her, and that Blessed Mother to whose service she had given herself from infancy, and that sweet sister whose saintly life had been to her a perpetual exhortation to holiness. All at once she heard these words distinctly uttered from amid that shining throng: "Angela, only persevere in the path you are following, and you shall have a share with us in the glory you behold;" and then the vision disappeared.

The constant tradition among the people of Desenzano places the scene of this apparition on the Macchetto road, quite near a farm-house known as *Le Grezze*, which had belonged to the Merici for many generations, and which, at the beginning of this century, had become the property of the noble family Del Villio. There, Father Salvatori assures us, stood in his day a little chapel dedicated to St. Angela, and destined in all likelihood to perpetuate the memory of this miracle.

Such extraordinary favors bestowed on God's chosen servants, never excite in them a thought of self-love or self-complacency. They are only bestowed on the humble, impelling them to still greater humility, that is, to a higher degree of that greatness of soul which impels the Saints to undertake in the Divine Service things that appear impossible to worldly wisdom, things most repugnant to flesh and blood. A glimpse of the eternal glory, though only dimly discerned from afar, and a momentary vision of that Uncreated Perfection, though but seen through some sensible veil, has sufficed to transport these great souls beyond themselves, and to impart to them a boldness and a courage which nothing could appal.

A cold mass of iron, naturally inert and lifeless, when placed within an electric coil will acquire the force of a mighty magnet; it will then attract and lift up other iron masses, magnetizing them in its turn, and converting their newly acquired energies into unfailing sources of heat and light.[1] What extraordinary graces for her own soul's sanctification must not Angela have derived from this one brief vision of the blissful citizens of the heavenly Jerusalem? And what new power to electrify others with the love of heavenly things, and to raise them with herself above the attractions of earth and the pleasures of sense? These effects we shall see further on. There was one chief purpose which the Divine Goodness had in view by vouchsafing this favor to the devoted girl,—and that was to prepare her to bear the death of her mother.

---

[1] Our readers will be reminded that in the wonderful discovery of the Electric Light, which is now going to supersede gas,—artificial magnets are the great generating power, the great secret of economy as well, in this latest application of modern science to the wants of life.

CHAPTER IV.

UTTER DESOLATION.

THE vision just described had for its immediate purpose not only to console Angela in her great sorrow, and to fortify her against another approaching bereavement, but also to dispose her mother to meet death with resignation and holy joy. No doubt, though Angela was reticent about what she had beheld in speaking to all others, she would naturally communicate to her dear sorrowing parent the heavenly assurance just given her of her sister's most enviable lot. Nothing could so move and cheer the gentle sufferer, as this extraordinary favor bestowed on her remaining angel. It brought home to the heart of the widowed wife and mother the fact that her family was one most dear to God, and, therefore, marked with the seal of predestination, the seal of suffering. No Christian mother could have listened to the description of that glorified throng of angels and saints surrounding the Mother of the Redeemer, or dwelt in spirit on the picture of her own child among the blessed train of virgins, without feeling something of the ecstatic joy which flooded the soul of Angela, or wishing to be reunited to her dear ones in the Land of the Living.

One of the most trying incidents in the life of our Blessed Lady herself was, doubtless, the ascension of our Lord;—to see Him, her adored and only One, going up to the Eternal City of God, amid the exulting multitude of His delivered saints,—and to have to remain after Him on earth for many a long, weary year,—what a trial for the heart of such a Mother yearning for reunion with such a Son! To be sure, as our Second Eve had to watch over the infancy of the Church, and support it in its early and fearful struggle, just as she had nursed and reared Him whose mystic body the Church is, so she could but exult in the glorious exile thus appointed to her in the divine plan. Nevertheless, while accepting this mission which was to consummate her merit, our Blessed Mother's heart could not but follow with unutterable yearnings the ascending form of her Divine One. The beautiful picture sketched to her by Angela, of her lost darling clothed with immortality, and so near to Mary, once the Mother of Sorrows, now the Mother of Eternal Joys, of a necessity drew Signora Merici's desires heavenward. At any rate, not a very long time passed between the vision and the last illness and death of the good lady. It most probably occurred within the twelvemonth thereafter.[1]

If the sweet duties of daughterly love performed toward one's parents in a season of joy and peace, amid all the sunshine of a happy home, are sure to be most acceptable to God and most meritorious in His sight, how much more so are the ministrations of a daughter's love toward a widowed mother, when borne down by grief, and dying in her darkened home, with only two orphans left her of all her little flock of loved ones! We cannot help admiring the wonderful way in which Providence was moulding the soul and character of Angela by this quick succession of the bitterest trials.

---

[1] Father Salvatori says: "A year had scarcely passed,—indeed, according to some writers,—a year had not entirely passed since the death of the father and sister, when the mother also fell dangerously ill and died."

God, in forming a saint destined to be the parent of a countless line of pious and motherly educators of youth, surely purposed to form her heart to all the dearest and holiest affections. No one so needs a heart filled to overflowing with the deepest, purest, tenderest, and most unfailing motherly love as the Superior of one of these great schools which claim Angela Merici as foundress, protectress, and model. Even in a community of cloistered nuns, devoted to a purely contemplative life, the Superior's heart should always be a great motherly heart, with all its wealth of tenderness open to every member of her family of nuns. Communities of women,—nay, communities of men, as well,—should find in all who govern them not only the provident wisdom and watchfulness of a father, but the untiring and unfailing tenderness of a mother. Much more need is there of these divine qualities in the "teaching orders,"—when young people and tender children ought ever to find a father's love and a mother's tenderness in those who hold toward them a parent's place in the school-room and outside of it.

And now we can understand why Angela should have been so sorely tried in every one of her home-affections, and have had to practise perfectly all the duties of daughter, sister, and mistress of a household, even. Every fibre of that great womanly nature was to be tried and perfected and hallowed, in order to fit her to be the mother of an immortal race of women consecrated to the divine work of education.

It is, therefore, no imaginary picture that we form to ourselves, when we think of the holy maid of Desenzano proving to her sick and dying mother what she had been to her father and sister in their last extremity, the tenderest of nurses, the sweetest of comforters, a very angel of light amid the gathering shadows of death.

No girl of seventeen who reads this page, and who is still

blessed with the priceless treasure of a true mother's love,—but will be moved with pity and admiration in recalling that death-bed scene in the home of the Merici at Desenzano: the widow beholding with the eye of faith the heavens opened above her, and her dear ones among the shining multitude beckoning her to join them; the two orphans kneeling by their expiring parent,—the angelic girl forgetting all sense of grief and loss in her anxiety to fill the dying soul with the sentiments of ardent faith and hope and love,—unwilling to leave the spot for a moment, or bestow a thought on aught else till she has, in a manner, given up the precious spirit into the hands and heart of its Creator and Father. And then, when she knows she is motherless, opening her arms and her whole heart to her only remaining one, her brother,—who has now but her in the whole world.

There was another present there, the noble and pious brother of the dying lady, Biancosi, from Salò. His was a heart that could sympathize to the utmost with the two orphans. He was a perfect Christian, tenderly attached to his deceased sister and her husband, and one who thoroughly appreciated the supernatural beauty of his niece's soul. They had no sooner performed the last solemn duties to the dead, than this worthy man proposed to Angela and her brother to make his home at Salò their own, till such time as the latter would be able to take charge of his father's home and property at Desenzano. To this proposal Angela yielded a willing assent. Her old home was haunted by such sad memories, that a change may have been absolutely needful even for her bodily health. Besides, her uncle, who was a man of wealth, position, influence, and ability, now held a father's place toward her. She, therefore, placed herself and her brother under his guardianship.

We may pause a moment in our saddening narrative, to

bestow a rapid glance on the locality and neighborhood, in which some six years of our Saint's life were to be passed. Salò, with its magnificent bay, is about fourteen miles to the north of Desenzano, the road to it lying partly along the lake, but mostly across a rolling country, every foot of which is devoted to agricultural purposes. Even the crannies of the rocks on the steep hillside which you pass, are filled with olive-trees, the intelligent and indefatigable labor of the Italian husbandman having enabled him to create in these apparently useless and inaccessible rocks little terraces most solidly constructed and covered with rich earth, in which he plants his favorite tree, and shelters it from the keen winds descending from the Tyrolean Alps. Desenzano, with the neighboring towns of Gardone, Maderno, Toscolano, and Gargnano, present a most charming aspect from the deck of the steamer which daily coasts the glorious lake. Goethe thus writes of this portion of it: "The noble aspect of the water and of the adjacent shore of Brescia refreshed my very heart. . . No words can express the beauty of this richly inhabited spot."

From Desenzano to Salò, and for several leagues above it, the shores of the lake are fringed with lofty trellises, on which the grapevine hangs its rich clusters in autumn, and in springtide and summer are brilliant with roses of every hue. "Scarlet geraniums," says Hare, "cover the whole face of the houses, while large tufts of oleander wave their pink plumes near the water's edge." The whole country on this western shore, almost as far as the borders of Tyrol, besides its rich crops of corn, olives, and other valuable produce, seems to be covered with lemon and orange groves. They erect, with incalculable labor and a perseverance beyond all praise, gigantic terraces along the sides of hill and mountain, and there plant their lemon and orange trees, when all the space on the level has been filled up. It is wonderful to see with what intelligent industry they shield these precious trees from the inclemency of an Alpine winter. Massive pillars of brick are built up to the height of twenty feet from distance to distance along these terraces, as well as in the citron groves lower down, and on these strong beams are laid, with a covering that effectually protects the trees beneath in the coldest weather. These rows of huge white pillars, glistening in the sunshine amid the deep rich masses of the surrounding verdure, arrest the traveller's attention, and form a most striking feature in the ever-varying panorama along these enchanted shores.

Salò, like the neighboring towns of Maderno and Campione, nestles in these beautiful groves,—while standing like sentinels to guard the approach of her bay are a group of lovely islands, among which is the Isola del Frati, or "Friars' Island," mentioned above.[1] In the beautiful town itself there was an establishment of Friars Minor, devoted to the rigid rule of their founder, and much beloved by the people far and near. So Angela would be sure to find among them one of these wise and far-seeing men of God, whose counsel is so needful to souls climbing the rugged paths of spiritual perfection. The Biancosi mansion was, besides, a spacious and a comfortable one, as became the rank and wealth of its owner. Angela and her brother received a most warm welcome from their generous uncle's family, and the orphaned girl found herself perfectly free to devote herself to her devotional exercises, at the same time that she found in her uncle and his household not only the comfort of true-hearted sympathy and friendship, but the still greater comfort of companionship in her pursuit of holiness of life.

---

[1] Page 31.

Among her cousins one only, Bartolommeo, is mentioned afterward as having been Angela's guardian and fellow-pilgrim on a memorable occasion. He was probably younger than herself, and fell, like her brother, under the spell of her grace, her magnetic presence, and her preternatural goodness. As to the latter, he had been, in the old home at Desenzano, his sister's pupil in more than one way; and, if others looked upon her with an admiring reverence, he worshiped her as the embodiment of all that was most perfect in woman. She was all in all to him, and profited by his unlimited trust and affection to shield his soul from evil, and to teach it the unspeakable sweetness of serving the King of kings.

How long Angela was allowed to enjoy, in her new home at Salò, the retirement, the freedom from observation, and the repose of spirit rendered so necessary by the ordeal through which she had just passed, we are not informed with any precision. We know that this season of repose was followed by one of cruel and protracted interior trials. Just as our most loving Father permits storms to purify the atmosphere and cool the intolerable heat of summer, just as He makes the mountain-pine wax strong in the tempest, and allows the waters to overflow the earth in order to give fertility to the fields; even so does He allow evil spirits to assail with doubt and temptation the souls of His dearest ones, that they may come forth from the trial more chastened, more heroic, more fitted to the mighty work which He has appointed for them. The most terrible part of holy Job's agony was not the loss of fortune, possessions, home, and children, nor even the fearful and most disgusting leprosy that made him an object of loathing to his servants, his friends, his own wife, but even to himself. The bitterest portion of his deep and bitter cup was to hear his wife and his dearest friends arraign not only his own innocence, but the goodness and justice of God, and to find involuntary shadows of doubt and diffidence arise to cloud his own soul, like hideous forms of darkness and despair that stand between the righteous soul and the bright sun of its life,—God's countenance.

It is not unlikely that, with all her extraordinary gifts, being of a good family, most beautiful, and mistress of her own hand, she became an object of attraction to the world around her, and was eagerly sought for by the young of both sexes. In the very best Christian families,—and there are very many such, even in our own day and country,—children who are brought up to manhood and womanhood not only without having ever stained their baptismal garment, but utterly unconscious of the nature of sin, are by their very innocence and absolute purity of soul irresistibly attractive to those of their own age and disposition.

That Angela, arrived at the age of seventeen and eighteen, should become even for the best and noblest youths of her native province of Brescia, an object of deep, ardent, and pure affection, was inevitable. It was natural, too, that her uncle and his family should have looked with favor on some at least of the most worthy and desirable suitors, and laid their proposals before his niece. To be sure, she had set her heart on other bridals, and had no thought of encouraging in her own heart, or in others, anything like earthly love, though never so exalted.

Without, therefore, going out of our way to find a cause for the interior struggle which she had to endure in the first year of her stay at Salò, we may account for it by these obvious circumstances, and put aside the suppositions and commentaries of some of her biographers. The first and highest purity is that of the soul,—the preservation of understanding, and memory, and imagination from the very remotest suggestion of evil. Parents, mothers particularly, know well how many such innocent souls there are ever in our midst, whose snowy whiteness has never been touched by the first thought of evil. This is God's fatherly providence over Christian society.

Looking at Angela and her dear brother's position with the eyes of worldly wisdom, one must feel convinced a speedy and honorable establishment was greatly to be desired for the sake of both. To a soul given wholly to other aspirations, this must have been repugnant. And yet God may have permitted this opportunity of a public and decided choice between a happy life in the world, and the virginal life to which she felt called, to have aroused a fierce struggle in her soul.

A struggle there was, indeed, in which her will never wavered. She employed the means which the saints always have recourse to in such trials, protracted prayer, greater vigilance over her thoughts and senses, and the frequent use of abstinence and other austerities. That the nature of her temptation was such as we have indicated, is further proved by the fact of her having taken her brother into her confidence. The spiritual education of this precious soul had been one of her chief cares since they had come to live in Salò. As if some prophetic instinct had warned her that he, too, like his oldest sister, was to be cut off in the first flower of his youth, Angela hastened to develop in him all the beautiful virtues which render holy youth so lovely in sight of God and men. He proved an apt scholar under one whom he trusted so thoroughly, and worshipped with such a tender reverence.

Salò with its citron groves, the Lake of Garda with its sublime scenery, her uncle's mansion with its comforts and its distractions, the visits of her friends and acquaintances, the attractions of the gay and pleasant social world around her,—all this was to the spiritual sense of the holy maiden full of secret and formidable danger. She conceived the notion of leading among the labyrinth of secluded valleys which radiate on every side around her native lake, a life of utter seclusion, such as had been led by the ancient hermits in Asia Minor, Palestine, and Egypt; such also as had been led by many of the most illustrious saints of her own Italy. This project was communicated to her brother; and he not only approved it, but declared he would be his darling sister's associate and protector in this pious undertaking.

Both had often heard and read of the twin sister and brother, St. Scholastica and St. Benedict, the great parents of monastic life in Western Christendom. The sister, while yet a girl of tender age, had left the home of her patrician father, to live in solitude and poverty of all things. Her young brother, at the age of fourteen, frightened by the corruption which he beheld around him, and fearing his own weakness to resist temptation, resolved to do what his sister had done, and buried himself for years among the wild and inaccessible crags of Subiaco. Later, when both Subiaco and Monte Cassino swarmed with the *élite* of the Christian youth of Rome, emulous of Benedict's heroic virtue, Scholastica, with her nuns, wished to be near her brother's voice, and to be governed by his rule. History has preserved the story of the imperishable friendship of these twin-souls, and of their holy rivalry in the divine service. To this brother and sister, as, indeed, to Angela and her brother, on the present occasion, could be well applied the words of St. Paulus of Nola, addressed to his wife, St. Theresia, when they had left their immense possessions, to retire into the desert and follow Christ in humility and poverty.

"Come, my faithful companion, let us put on our armor

for this new warfare. O thou whom God hath given to sustain my weak courage, thy love and care must moderate my rashness, and comfort me when downcast. Let us be to each other a model of holiness of life. Be thou the guardian angel of thy protector, and thus pay me back my care of thee. Raise me up when I fall, and let me lighten thy load when it bears thee down. Let us have but one mind, and let one spirit sustain both our souls!"[1]

Within their own time a holy woman had transformed the mountain of Varese into a paradise of piety and holiness: could not they find in the neighborhood of the beautiful lake some unfrequented summit where they might sanctify themselves beneath the eye of God, and unknown to the world of wealth and fashion? Such was the thought and the purpose which took possession of them. And so, leaving their uncle's house in the greatest secrecy, and striking into the least frequented paths, they betook themselves toward the neighboring mountains. They were but little, if at all, acquainted with the country beyond Salò, and so must, perforce, often make inquiries, thus arousing the curiosity of the peasants they met with.

The uncle had no sooner missed them than messengers were despatched in all directions, and the fugitives were brought back to Salò. Biancosi made no reproaches. He perfectly understood the reasons which they alleged for their departure. Sincerely pious as he was, he did not dream of turning either of the two orphans away from the path toward which the

---

[1] Tu modo, fida comes, mecum isti accingere pugnæ,
Quam Deus infirmo præbuit auxilium.
Sollicita elatum cohibe, solare dolentem;
Exemplum vitæ simus uterque piæ.
Custos esto tui custodis, mutua redde;
Erige labentem, surge levantis ope.
Ut caro non eadem tantum, sed mens quoque nobis
Una sit, atque duos spiritus unus alat.

divine voice called them. But the age in which he lived, and the condition of the country, were far from being favorable to such designs as their hasty fervor had contemplated. Venice was at war with France, and French troops overran the Peninsula from the Alps to Sicily, while the Italian princes and republics were espousing, some the side of Charles VIII., and some that of Spain. A few years later, the entire province of Brescia was held by the French, and the beautiful city itself was ruthlessly burned by these lawless invaders.

No—these were not the times when the mountain solitudes of the Alps or of the Appennines could be with impunity converted into a safe retreat for hermits,—especially those of Angela's tender years and sex.

Biancosi gently told the shamefaced fugitives that his house should be a safe retreat for them, in which they might be perfectly free to seclude themselves as much as they pleased, and practise the virtues to which they aspired. Only, he said, they must pledge themselves not to commit a second time the rash act of withdrawing from his home in a way that would expose themselves to much danger, and himself and his family to unmerited suspicions. The promise was readily given and most faithfully kept.

Wherefore, resigning herself to what she considered to be the will of Providence, Angela made the best use of her present opportunities. For the time being Salò and its neighborhood remained undisturbed by the approach of hostile armies; and amid the peace and security of their seclusion, both sister and brother advanced rapidly in the science of the saints.

Indeed, as Salvatori assures us, so great was the admiration with which the people far and wide regarded the beautiful girl, so tried by sorrow, so angelic in life, so ready to devote her entire energy to the service of the needy or the suffering, that she was universally designated as "the Holy Maiden," or "the little Saint from Paradise."[1] Parents held her and her brother up to their children as models of that close union of hearts which should ever exist between persons so nearly related to each other. Indeed as Angela had been the model daughter, so was she now the model sister. She had succeeded in making her dear one a model youth, adorned with all the natural and supernatural graces of the true Christian man. Was she proud of the accomplished brother, who looked up to her with such a grateful sense of dependence? Was there in the love which bound the two orphans together anything which seemed to Angela to savor too much of mere human affection? We know not. But at this very period, when both had arrived at the full flower of their blameless youth, death came to the door of the Biancosi mansion in Salò, just as he had repeatedly visited the Merici home at Desenzano, and Angela beheld her brother taken away from her, just as her parents and their other children had been so mysteriously snatched away.

She was now all alone in the world. It was indeed true, that her cherished companion had died as he had lived,— like a true child of God, relinquishing earth and its hopes without a murmur, and solicitous only about the fatherless and motherless girl whom he left all alone to face the dreary way before her. This cost the dying youth a bitter pang. But she, who had been his sweet instructress and guide, would not have him think of her; God, their most loving Father, would be her unfailing stay, and He and His blissful

---

[1] Menando dunque in mezzo al secolo una vita non pur da Religiosi, ma da Serafini si resero l'ammirazione di tutto il paese; ed Angela in ispecie non veniva più comunemente chiamata, che col glorioso soprannome di "Vergine di Cristo," e "Santa del Paradiso."

eternity must fill the soul of her dear one in his last hour.

Still, when all was ended, and he had been laid to his early rest, a feeling of utter desolation swept over the brave girl's wearied spirit. The transcendent merit of such great souls as Angela's, does not consist in being without or above these deep and holy natural sentiments which are harrowed by the successive loss of father, mother, brothers and sisters, and crushed at finding the home so full of dear faces and loved voices yesterday, all empty, silent, and dark to-day. Holy souls feel deeply, more deeply even than the imperfect, because they are less taken up with self, and that they look upon all these hallowed home affections as the creations of the loving hand of the Almighty Parent.

But saintly and heroic souls are wont to see the Divine Will in all these afflictions which befall the best Christian, and desolate the most virtuous homes. Angela had long learned to see that Fatherly Hand in the special providence which ruled events in her own family. She had from childhood practiced herself to "walk before that Adorable Majesty and therein find perfection." She found in this constant sense of nearness to Him, in the consciousness of His unfailing presence to her soul, her perfect happiness as well. There is so thin a partition-wall between the Christian soul and that only real world, the unseen and eternal, in which live and reign and exult Christ and His saints.

Doubtless Angela had related to her dying brother, as she had to their mother previously, the glorious vision sent to cheer and encourage them all, while still at Desenzano. She had been training him to set his young heart on that other life and that blissful world where her own holiest affections dwelt. And so he had died, with the light of eternal day dawning brightly on him. When he was gone, her spirit followed him. Her "conversation,"—the daily and hourly thoughts and aims and aspirations of her soul,—were "in Heaven;" God was now all in all to her.

It is probable that her brother while living was able to superintend, together with his uncle Biancosi, the homestead and family estate at Desenzano. All this devolved, after his death, on Angela. She was then in her twenty-second year. Wherefore, after having enjoyed for six years the cordial hospitality of her uncle, and profited by his fatherly care and large-minded piety, to make wonderful progress in holiness, she resolved to return to the dear home in which she was born. The chief motive which induced her to take this step was that she had found, in a girl of her own age and rank, one fitted by her spotless life, rare piety, and ripe wisdom. to fill the place of her lost sister and companion. The design of both the one and the other appears to have been to lead in the retirement of Angela's home a life of spiritual perfection,—guided by such rules as the Bishop of Brescia might give them, and directed by some experienced priest among the local clergy.

In all this there was One who was guiding Angela's soul in His own wonderful way, and preparing her, by all the experience thus acquired, to be the enlightened teacher of others,—the mother of a countless family.

CHAPTER V.

BACK IN THE OLD HOME.

We need not dwell on the joy with which Angela's return was hailed not only by such of her kinsfolk as lived in Desenzano, but by the townspeople. Her presence in Salò had been esteemed a blessing by all classes alike; and her departure looked upon almost as a calamity. What projects Angela and her new companion may have entertained about their own future, have not been revealed to us. They lived, in their privacy, as if they were bound by religious vows, and the sweet fragrance of their fervor increased daily, and with it the veneration of their fellow-citizens. Their seclusion, however, not being a cloister, the poor, the sick, and the ignorant far and near soon learned to know and bless the two devoted ladies.

Was this companionship deemed by Angela to be a compensation for the loss of all those who had once made that dear home so unspeakably happy for her? . . . At any rate God soon put an end to it. As the dark shadow of this new affliction closed around her, the tried girl, had her soul not been taught to read the divine counsels in a supernatural light, might have been tempted to think that her love and trust seemed to blight and kill every one that was dear to her.

The truth is, that the Divine Majesty will use for its holiest and most merciful designs toward mankind only instruments which will become perfectly united with the Hand that works with them. Such close union manifestly supposes a detachment from all earthly affections. So, while we are perusing this first portion of the Life of St. Angela, we can admire how the Divine Workman prepares and fashions this chosen instrument of one of His most gracious purposes. It will thus become apparent why the inestimable favor of a saintly death removes from Angela's path every one of her best beloved, that so she might look up to God alone, and place her trust and her affections in the All-mighty and All-sufficient. This brings us to another wonderful incident in the career of the Holy Maid of Desenzano.

The exemplary life led by herself and her late companion, the singular union in them of a most active and tender charity, and of a spirit which was utterly unworldly and self-sacrificing without being repulsive in its austerity, had drawn to them the hearts of the young persons of their own sex in the town and neighborhood. Angela's heroic fortitude under misfortune, her beauty, her sympathetic address,—and that unseen but irresistible charm exercised by holiness on all who approach it, led these young girls to seek the home of the Merici. And Angela, who had as yet no settled plan about her own future, welcomed her old friends and playmates with the winning grace that distinguished her manner toward others. She encouraged them to join her in many of her devotional exercises, and deeds of beneficence, and shared as well in their innocent amusements and recreations. It was a wise thing to go with them in their pleasant road as far as she could, in order the more safely to lead them into her own. About a month after the loss of her last dear companion, these good girls had planned a little excursion into some one of the lovely sites around Desenzano, most probably for the purpose of turning Angela's mind away from the sad thoughts which seemed to oppress her. They had stopped in a beautiful shady spot called Brudazzo, not far from the main road to Salò. Angela, whose soul was not so much affected by the death of her friend as perplexed by the uncertainties of her future, was making it a matter of continual meditation how she must choose for herself in order to obey the Divine Will. Indeed, that will had not as yet declared itself to her. So far her effort had been to follow undeviatingly the light vouchsafed her, to refuse to the promptings of the Spirit of grace no sacrifice which she thought He demanded of her.

The sublime regions of holiness contained, she knew, fields of activity that lay wide apart, and heights above heights of varied and glorious excellence. The road over which the Spirit of God had led her so far, had been like the easy ascent from the populous plains of Lombardy up to the foot-hills of the Alps around her native lake. From the sunny vine-clad slopes on which she was about to kneel in prayer at Brudazzo, the acclivities just around Salò arose so steeply that they shut out all objects beyond. Yet she was well aware how many intermediate mountain masses stood between Monte San Bartolommeo and the snow-clad summits visible from her native town,—the crests nearest heaven, on which rested the last glories of the setting sun and the first illumined by his morning beams,—the cold and shining ice slopes, accessible only to the daring and practised few. Was it not so with these arduous heights of sanctity, visible to the multitudes down below in the plain, approached and climbed only by those who surrendered their souls to the Spirit of God?

Angela had left her companions to enjoy themselves beneath the shade, and, retiring to a remote corner of the vineyard, she knelt in prayer. She besought with tears the Divine Goodness to put an end to her perplexities, to show her the road which He would have her to follow, to enlighten her as to the means that she must choose to carry out His designs, and to grant her the strength to follow out the path of His will without faltering or turning aside. Her whole soul went up in this great heart-cry for light and strength, and her tears flowed copiously.

All at once she was dazzled by a flood of light, the heavens were opened above her, and from the bright portals on high a luminous ladder descended, resting on the earth. Down the steps came trooping a multitude of holy maidens clothed in flowing vestments and bearing, each, a royal crown. They approached her in beautiful array, chanting divinely the hymns of the Heavenly Jerusalem, while two shining ranks of angelic spirits formed an escort to them, swelling with their voices the chorus of song from the maiden-train. Angela, transported beyond herself by the sight of this heavenly multitude and these divine harmonies, was suddenly thrilled by the appearance of the dear companion so lately taken from her. "Angela," the well-known voice said, "know thou that our Lord hath sent thee this vision, to inform thee that before thy death thou shalt found in Brescia a society like this: such is His injunction to thee." And the shining procession reascended into Heaven.[1]

Here was a prompt answer to Angela's prayers, leaving her full of peace and courage. Her spiritual director, after listening to her account of this marvelous occurrence, declared that it could not be an illusion, and that she was justified in accepting the injunction conveyed to her as a clear manifestation of the Divine will. That she knew on this occasion,

---
[1] Salvatori, c. iii., p. 16.

and from circumstances not mentioned in the authentic relation of this incident, her vocation to be the educator of her sex, is what we can gather from her own conduct. She forthwith began to prepare herself for the work of teaching, by seizing every opportunity offered her to gather children and young people around her. Indeed so well did she succeed in this, and so fruitful became her endeavors and those of such as volunteered to aid her, that her fame as an instructress spread rapidly all over the province.

Let us bear in mind that the year in which the divine purpose was revealed to Angela was that in which St. Francis Xavier was born, Ignatius de Loyola being then in his sixth year; it was also the very year that beheld Vasco da Gama sailing around the Cape of Good Hope, and discovering the East Indies; while on that same year, Christopher Columbus, returned from his second voyage to America, was contending in Spain with opposition of every kind before starting on his third expedition to that Western World which he yearned to subject to the Cross. We who know what a glorious share Ignatius and Xavier, with their zealous progeny of apostolic men, were to have in evangelizing the two worlds thus laid open to the religion and civilization of Christendom, cannot forget that the daughters of St. Angela have shared with them on almost every field in both hemispheres, the apostleship of education. We must, therefore, plainly see the hand of God in the beginning of the great work inaugurated at Desenzano and Brescia, just as we recognize it in the conversion and long preparation of Ignatius de Loyola for his appointed task. Before the end of this book, we shall see the societies founded by the Maid of Desenzano and the heroic Spanish soldier growing side by side in Italy, and thence extending their branches to other countries.

This second vision sent to Angela so opportunely, filled her with extraordinary fervor. The increase of spiritual strength which she invariably derived from approaching the Table of the Lamb, caused her to desire to receive the divine Bread more frequently, nay, daily,—if she were only permitted to do so. This, however, was a privilege rarely, if ever, granted in that age, to secular persons. And her insatiable yearning for this "Daily Bread," led her to take one more step in the road toward monastic life. The Third Order of St. Francis numbered in the diocese of Brescia, as in every diocese of Western Europe, many persons of both sexes and of every rank in society. Angela, while at Salò, had entertained a wish to become a member of this Order, but was dissuaded from her purpose by her uncle Biancosi, who did not like to encourage in his orphaned niece, at so early an age, a design which he might have praised in his own daughter.

It was in the Franciscan habit that she was buried, and in it that her body was found clothed when her grave was opened by order of the Congregation of Rites during the proceedings for her beatification. Among the many holy women who claim as their spiritual parent the seraphic Monk of Monte Alvernia, few, if any, deserve more than Sister Angela Merici the gratitude of Christian homes; she may be justly called the seraph of Female Schools[1].

---

[1] It may not be out of place to give you, dear reader, some of the reasons why St. Francis is called the "Seraphic," and why the same epithet has been given as a title to his order. Seraphs are among the angelic spirits who ever gaze upon the face of God, and become all aglow with the fire of His love, those who are considered to burn with the divinest flame. They have so superior a knowledge of Him and His abyssal perfections, that they resemble Him most closely. As they know Him and love Him better than their fellows, so do they know and love in Him all created beings,—seeing His perfections mirrored in them, and conceiving even the irrational and inanimate creation to be instinct with the Creator's love and to send forth its voice evermore in His praise.

A writer well known on both sides of the Atlantic, and whose bitter anti-Catholic prejudices are equally well known,—thus speaks of the seraphic spirit of St. Francis:

"It was here (on Mount Alvernia) that St. Francis learned the tongues of the beasts and birds, and preached them sermons. Stretched for hours motionless on the bare

This act of receiving publicly the habit of the Third Order she considered to be her solemn betrothal to the God of her soul. She could not contain her exstatic joy on this occasion, nor prevent the sweet tears which would overflow from the pure depths of that virginal heart. Thenceforth she was Christ's,—she wholly belonged to Him and to the little ones of His flock. Thenceforward, deeming that she had as yet done nothing for her Lord and Love, she began to run forward in the road of sanctity,—in the practice of humility, self-sacrifice, and entire devotion to the good of others.

---

rocks, colored like them, and rough like them in his brown peasant's serge, he prayed and meditated, saw the vision of Christ crucified, and planned his Order to regenerate a vicious age. So still he lay, so long, so like a stone, so gentle were his eyes, so kind and low his voice, that the mice nibbled bread crumbs from his wallet, lizards ran over him, and larks sang to him in the air. Here, too, in these long solitary vigils, the Spirit of God came upon him, and the spirit of Nature was even as God's Spirit, and he sang:—'Laudato sia Dio mio Signore, con tutte le creature, specialmente messer la frate sole; per suor luna, e per le stelle; per frate vento, e per l'aire e' nuvolo, e sereno, e ogni tempo.' Half the value of this hymn would be lost were we to forget how it was written, in what solitudes and mountains far from men, or to ticket it with some cold word like Pantheism. Pantheism it is not, but the acknowledgment of that brotherhood, beneath the love of God, by which the sun, moon and stars, and wind and air and cloud, and clearness and all weather and all creatures, are bound together, with the soul of man. Here is a sentence of the 'Imitation of Christ,' which throws some light upon the hymn of St. Francis by explaining the value of natural beauty for monks who spent their lives in studying death: 'If thy heart were right, then would every creature be to thee a mirror of life, and a book of holy doctrine. There is no creature so small and vile that does not show forth the goodness of God.' With this sentence bound about their foreheads, walked Fra Angelico (a Dominican) and St. Francis. To men like them the mountains, the valleys, and the skies, and all that they contained, were full of deep significance. . . The whole world was a pageant of God's glory, a poem to His goodness. Their chastened senses, pure hearts, and simple wills, were as wings by which they soared above the things of earth, and sent the music of their souls aloft with every other creature in the symphony of praise. . . We, who have lost sight of the invisible world, who set our affections more on things of earth, fancy that because these monks despised the world, and did not write about its landscapes, therefore they were dead to its beauty."—*Cornhill Magazine*, vol. xiv.

CHAPTER VI.

THE HOME IN DESENZANO CONTINUES TO BE SISTER ANGELA'S SCHOOL.

As she now wore the religious habit, she was admitted to the privilege so ardently coveted of frequent Communion. Her happiness was so great that with the independence and privacy she enjoyed in her own home at Desenzano, as well as the continual opportunities she sought and obtained of teaching, instructing, and doing all manner of good to those around her, she might well believe that she was in God's hand, doing the good He wished her to do, and in the only sphere she could do it in for some time.

Desenzano, Salò, and the surrounding districts long continued to cherish a grateful memory of the years between 1497 and 1516. For during this long period of preparation and expectancy did imperious circumstances force Angela Merici to remain beneath the shelter of the home in which she was born and reared. It was the peculiar feature of her beautiful life that it was to bloom and bear its fruit on the native soil, so that the eyes which had beheld it in its springtide, should watch its growth until its blessed maturity.

And, as her grateful fellow-citizens ever gladly testified, most beautiful was that life, as well as most holy, most lovable appeared to all who approached her that saintliness which shone forth in her bearing, her speech, her womanly gentleness and grace, and that exquisite tact which knew so well how to find the fitting words for each one's need, and to do the right thing at the happiest moment. Her life was one of retirement and prayer and secret austerity, but not one of seclusion, or of unamiable and unapproachable rigor. She had to remain in the world, attending to her own worldly concerns, dealing with men and women whose spirit was oppressed with material cares, and whose hearts were bruised and bleeding from the wrongs inflicted by the world: they came to her because she was unworldly, because she was heavenly-minded, because a healing virtue went forth from her, filling the very atmosphere of her home, and felt in the touch of her hand, the sound of her gentle voice, and the unearthly light that beamed from the pure depths of her eyes.

The highest and the oldest sought her in their troubles and sorrows, young as she was, because there was a wisdom in her counsels and consolations that was not the slow growth of age; and many a man who had come to consult Sister Angela about his temporal concerns was moved to lay bare the wounds of his soul, and bore away with him a firm resolve to live a little for eternity. Many a woman whose life had been wasted till the hour she crossed the threshold of the Merici, and crossed it too impelled by curiosity, went away changed in heart, after having looked upon the face of a living saint.

As to the young people of her own sex, they were irresistibly drawn to Angela, all submitting to the charm of her manner and won by the kind and pleasant words which she knew so well how to say to each one,—though the few only among the most fervent had courage to imitate the extreme austerity of life revealed to her intimate friends. Still, as it happened later in Brescia, so did it befall at Desenzano and, in a certain measure, at Salò, women of every class adopted both a more modest and a far less costly style of dress,—through the silent eloquence of Angela's example.

There is no mention in authentic history of Angela's having opened a school during her stay at Desenzano, any more than during her long residence at Brescia. Nor was she, while sheltered at her parents' home, the superior in any sense of a community of women. Indeed there was no such community in existence. Not before the year 1530, as we shall see in its place, was the saint able to lay the foundations of anything like a congregation, or even a community.

Distracted by fierce civil dissensions as all Upper Italy was during the early part of the sixteenth century, with Lombardy and Venetia overrun again and again by the hostile armies of France and Spain; and most unfavorable as were the times not only for the peace of monastic life, but more especially still for the founding of new monastic orders,— Providence gave to Angela's aims and efforts a direction singularly in keeping with the needs and circumstances of her age. It was the complaint of men who would not reform their own evil lives, that Religion sadly needed reform; the saying of priests and monks to whom the fulfillment of their own solemn obligations had become an intolerable burthen, that Religious Orders were in a deplorable state of degeneracy, while many men in authority, influenced by these outcries, had openly set their face against the admission by the Church of any sort of new monastic institutions.

It was, then, a special inspiration of Providence that led Angela Merici, even after this last vision, to remain in her own home while wearing the monastic habit, and honoring the Religious profession by a most saintly life. His spirit it was, assuredly, which made her counsel the maidens who were drawn to her, and strove to imitate her, to live in the world beneath the protection of the parental roof,—presenting to the disordered and pleasure-seeking society around them the forcible argument of their blameless conduct and active charities. Angela and her associates were to be everywhere along the most frequented paths of daily life in town and country, like so many guides stationed, whose very angelic mien and unearthly virtues, were to proclaim to the passing crowd that Heaven was to be won by violence and that Christian men and women were born to something beside the present life's bodily wants, or pleasures, or vanities. Their mission was to leaven the masses in the great cities, especially with the living faith and the heroic piety springing from it, so sorely needed by the times.

This view of their immediate providential purpose,—for on the foundations laid by Angela was to be erected after her death the glorious superstructure dimly foreshown to her, but never beheld by the living saint,—will enable us to understand her long preparatory labors and trials.

If Angela did not open a school for children in her home at Desenzano, it is none the less certain that she was most zealous in procuring their being taught the elements of the Christian doctrine, first of all, and then, so far as she might, the first elements of secular knowledge. Books were very rare and very dear in those days,—printing being as yet but in its infancy,—and the cost of procuring either manuscripts or printed works was entirely above the means of the lower classes. This dearth of books, however, was to be remedied to a very great extent before the end of the sixteenth century, and with the enormously increased facilities for learning and for teaching afforded by the printing-press, the zeal of the Institute of St. Angela in promoting education was to keep a constant pace.

All this, and much more than this, should be kept in mind when comparing our age and country with the Italy of the fifteenth and sixteenth centuries. People who are resolved to find fault and condemn blindly, will shut their eyes to the wrong and injustice of such comparisons and the sweeping censures pronounced by fanaticism or prejudice.

Meanwhile, although the home of the Merici at Desenzano was converted neither into a convent nor into a school of secular learning, it continued to be none the less a daily resort for learners in the far higher knowledge of the things of God. As we have stated above, the highest as well as the lowliest in the land were impelled by the needs of their own soul, much more than by a laudable curiosity, to look upon the face of a living saint, to feel themselves lifted up toward God by the near presence of the angelic maiden, or to receive from her the rules for the amendment and direction of their lives in conformity with the spirit of the Gospel.

One noble family, in particular, formed during this period a warm and generous attachment for Angela, which was to influence her after-life in no ordinary degree. These were the Patengoli of Brescia. Jerome and Caterina Patengoli had a country-seat at Patengo, a hamlet not far from Desenzano, and there they were wont to spend some months every year. They had watched the growth of Angela's reputation, and, feeling a lively interest in one so tried by misfortune and so universally revered, they made of their stay at Patengo an opportunity for cultivating a nearer acquaintance. All that they saw and heard themselves of her untiring charity and zeal among her townsfolk, ceased to excite their wonder when they were admitted to her privacy, and privileged to witness the absolute poverty in which she chose to live, her rigorous abstinence, and her insatiable thirst for prayer. What, however, convinced them most of her sanctity, was not only the unhesitating promptness with which she tore herself away either from her rapt contemplation before the altar, or from her private devotions at home, to be at the beck of all who needed her, or called upon her, but the beautiful cheerfulness with which she met, at all times and in every place, the persons who thus intruded upon her occupations.

From the sweetest joys of her converse with the Divine Majesty, she was ever ready to pass to the presence of the poorest stranger. She worshiped Christ in the persons of His poor, she beheld God in the souls of all His children, and found no difficulty in forsaking the sweets of spiritual communion with Him on the Altar or in her oratory for the still sweeter occupation of ministering to Him in the persons of the bodily or spiritually needy. Her incredible austerities did not apparently impair her strength; most certainly they did not sour her temper; while the hours spent alone with God only made her more radiant toward all those who came to interrupt her.

All this the Patengoli saw with increasing admiration, year after year, with an increasing desire also to have such a treasure with them or near them in the beautiful, busy, and populous Brescia. They had prevailed on Angela to spend a few days with them at Patengo, and the intimacy springing from this visit so filled them with veneration for their visitor, that they resolved to try every possible means to have her in Brescia. Their desire was to have its fulfillment later, and in a way which they as well as their happy children little dreamed of then.

As the name of Brescia is so closely interwoven with the events of our heroine's history, as to cause her to be designated sometimes as "Angela of Brescia," it may be well to know something of the city in which were laid the foundations of the Order of St. Ursula, and which was for twenty-four years the home of its foundress.

It is situated among the spurs of the Venetian Alps, about fifteen miles to the northwest of Desenzano, in a position which commands a magnificent prospect, ranging over the upper hilly region of Lombardy, as well as the glorious plain below, the garden of Europe, and destined by God to be the blissful abode of peace and plenty and religion. Brescia,— the Roman Brixia,—was famous, powerful, and prosperous at the beginning of the Christian era, and looked up to as the parent of such neighboring cities as Verona. At the birth of Angela it was the capital of one of the most beautiful provinces of the Venetian Republic, distinguished not only for the highly cultivated country which surrounded it, but for its iron works, its manufactories of arms, and its love of the fine arts.

In 1512 it fell into the hands of the French, who made themselves so odious to the inhabitants that they rose like one man, attempted in vain to storm the citadel in which there was a French garrison, tore down the Fleur-de-Lys, and hung out from the battlements the standard of St. Mark. Thereupon Gaston de Foix returned with 12,000 men, the flower of the French army, and demanded the instant and unconditional submission of the city, threatening that unless it surrendered the population should be pitilessly exterminated. The citizens, thus placed between the combined attacks of the garrison from within and such a superior force from without, preferred the issue of combat. They were overcome, and De Foix,—of whose chivalry we have read such exaggerated accounts,—carried out his inhuman threat. Bayard, who was wounded in the assault, tells us in his memoirs that 22,000 persons of every age and sex were butchered by the victorious soldiery![1] It was not to be expected that Desenzano and Salò would be quite free from the intrusion and exactions of these hordes, as much to be dreaded as the Mohammedan fleets and armies which threatened the Mediterranean sea-coast. Still no mention is made by any of the historians of Angela of these terrible events.

Not only were such massacres perpetrated by Christians on their fellow-Christians, but the city itself was fired in every part, and for many days pillage, murder, and licentiousness reigned without control.

Brescia never recovered either her former population, or her wealth, or her industrial activity. She remained beneath the yoke of the foreigner till 1616,—when, as we shall see presently, Angela was induced to take up her abode there.

It is only after remembering calamities like this, falling with such crushing force upon her native land and its people, that one sees how utterly hopeless it must seem to the devoted girl, as well as to her most enlightened and energetic counsellors, to found anything like a religious order,—or even to lead, amid the successive invasions of a foreign army, a life of undisturbed religious seclusion.

While their beautiful city was beginning to rise from its ashes, and men's souls were despairing of ever again binding up or healing permanently the cruel wounds inflicted by the unchristian generals of the Most Christian King, Jerome and Caterina Patengoli, saw, within the space of a few months, both of their promising children taken from them by death,—the victims, most likely, of the terrible fevers or fatal en-

---

[1] Bayard's account of this memorable assault is, of course, as favorable as possible to the beseigers. Other writers, perhaps not very much inclined to favor the French, give a much higher figure. According to these 7,000 of the defenders were slain in the heat of battle, and 46,000 of both sexes and of every age and condition were ruthlessly slain.

demics that follow in the track of war, and break out with such fearful violence within a fortified city, the gutters of whose streets, for several days, ran with the blood of fifty thousand slain! The year 1516 gave peace to Brescia, and the French flag disappeared from her walls. But there was utter desolation in the home of the Patengoli.

The afflicted parents would fain have Angela with them, knowing as they did that she would be a comforting angel. Nor were her presence and ministrations needed by them alone. There was not a family within the walls of Brescia who did not then mourn the loss of their dearest and best, as well as the utter ruin of their fortunes. So, if Angela wished to reap a rich harvest of charity and devotion, no time was more propitious than the present condition of Brescia; no more favorable opportunity could she ever have of endearing herself to a people who were already sufficiently acquainted with the fame of her blameless life.

The Patengoli did not address themselves directly to Angela. They were convinced she would do nothing without the orders of her Franciscan Superiors at Lonato. Therefore not a moment was lost in obtaining from these a positive command to Angela to proceed to Brescia and take up her residence with Jerome Patengoli. She obeyed without a moment's hesitation, and proved to be all that her friends and the entire city expected,—an angel of God in their midst. Many and unceasing as were the demands upon her time and strength, she was equal to all. Her whole soul went out to the multitude of her afflicted fellow-citizens and countrymen.

It was also the first time that she had lived in a populous city; and, in Brescia, much as the houses of private citizens had suffered even where the fire had not swept away everything, the churches and religious institutions had escaped with comparatively slight injury. The beautiful churches,—beautiful especially in their numerous works of Christian art, were to Angela a source of perpetual delight. There everything in the sacred edifice spoke to her soul. The monuments recalling the devoted lives and heroic death of the saints who had made Brescia illustrious among Christians, or who had been honored by the special veneration of the citizens; the works of painting and sculpture which kept alive before the mind and heart of the people, the glorious history of the great men and women who had died bearing witness to the divinity of the Christian faith, or had honored it with deeds of supernatural sanctity or had been the apostles of the truth to the surrounding countries;—all these made a deep impression on a soul so open to all the sublimest impulses and inspirations of grace. So, once she had consoled the Patengoli, she gave herself up to the numerous works of charity which awaited her on every side. When not in the hospitals, or visiting the sick poor, or preparing for death some poor needy soul, she was sure to be found before some favorite shrine or altar in the Cathedral or St. Afra, rapt in prayer, and lost to all sense of what was passing around her. It sufficed, however, to say one word to her about some urgent errand of mercy or neighborly kindness, to see her rise from her knees, and set out with face all aglow with the divine fire within to perform what was asked of her.

At length her friends, as she thought, needed her presence no longer; Brescia was also busy in repairing the evils of war and foreign occupation. What had been spared by the enemy of the largest fortunes was, it was thought, barely sufficient to meet the wants of the owners, the requirements of reviving industry, and the assistance needed by the impoverished condition of local institutions. No one thought or could reasonably think of creating new ones amid the ruin and bankruptcy of the present.

Angela, therefore, deeming these conjunctures most unfavorable to her cherished design, was about to return to Desenzano, when Providence interfered, and enabled her to prolong her stay in Brescia.

Among the many distinguished persons whose veneration she had won in that city was a wealthy merchant named Antonio dei Romani, who insisted on Angela's remaining in the present field of labor, offering her in his own spacious mansion a room remote from all noise and interference, and securing, besides, the authorization of her Franciscan Superiors. This did away with every objection which Angela could have toward prolonging her stay in Brescia. Indeed it was her own wish to continue there her fruitful labors among all classes, especially among the young people of her own sex, very many of whom were in the habit of coming to her for spiritual instruction and comfort. And thus, although she fancied, in her extreme diffidence of her own powers and influence, that there was no near prospect of her establishing such a congregation as the last vision foreshadowed,—she nevertheless felt instinctively that she was meanwhile doing a preparatory work by continuing her present labors.

In these tentative efforts the years passed slowly by, much to Angela's disappointment. Her soul was full of what she could not help considering to be her life-work, the one thing which the Divine Majesty had set apart for her to accomplish. It had been her wish, soon after the prophetic vision at Brudazzo, to consult the Blessed Osanna Andreasi, then near the close of her saintly career in Mantua. Such a holy personage, with the supernatural lights vouchsafed her, could reassure the inexperienced girl on the reality of her vision, and best counsel her concerning the best means for carrying it out.

What Angela could not do before 1505,—the date of Osanna's death,—she resolved to do in 1522, when she had permanently fixed her abode in Brescia. She went to Mantua, to pray at the shrine of this great servant of God,—hoping that the intercession of a saint in Heaven would procure for her the light she had so often yearned to get from her lips while living. Several of the Brescian ladies, who looked up to Angela as their guide, resolved to accompany her; and they all set out under the protection of the good Antonio dei Romani. Angela could scarcely tear herself away from the tomb of the Blessed Osanna. After spending a long time in prayer before it, says Salvatori, "she threw both her arms round the tomb-stone, kissing it again and again with the tenderest devotion, shedding sweet tears of joy, and filling all present with the like devout sentiments." On her return she passed by Solferino, where Prince Luigi de Gonzaga, lord of Castiglione, and a near relative of Federigo Gonzaga, the reigning sovereign of Mantua, happened to be then residing with his wife.[1] Both Luigi and his wife had heard much of Angela, and were anxious to make the personal acquaintance of one whose reputation was so widespread. They were both solidly pious; and their desire was not prompted by mere curiosity. Nor was Angela's visit one dictated by mere courtesy or

---

[1] This Luigi (Latin, *Aloysius*), was grandfather to St. Aloysius Gonzaga, who was named after him. Solferino is quite near the little town of Castiglione, where the saint was born. Both towns are situated in a hilly but richly cultivated country, Solferino,—now a straggling hamlet with ruins of the Castle of the Gonzagas,—crowning a bold eminence, about ten miles south of Desenzano. The terrible battle of Solferino was fought on June 24, 1859, between the Austrians on the one side, and the allied French and Piedmontese, on the other. The Piedmontese army extended its lines almost to Desenzano, the fiercest struggle taking place near Rivaltella, on the very shores of the Lake of Garda.

any other worldly motive. She had a mission of charity to perform. One of her own kinsmen, and a subject of the Gonzagas, had incurred the penalty of banishment and forfeiture of all his possessions, by some treasonable act. The audience which she solicited was granted at once; and after presenting her petition for mercy, and conversing for a considerable time with both sovereigns, she was sent on her way rejoicing. These visits were so designed by Providence as to secure Angela and her Congregation powerful friends in the day of need.

The day of action, so long wished and prayed for by the humble pilgrim was to be deferred for some ten years more. Even while Angela and her companions were on their way homeward to Brescia, the war clouds which had so often within the generation then living deluged Upper Italy with blood, were gathering once more above the Alps. The contest between Francis I. and the Emperor Charles V., which had already been so disastrous to Italy, was to continue for five years more to ruin all the best interests of Religion and society,—till, in 1527, all Christendom was to be startled by seeing a French renegade with an army of heretics and cut-throats under the imperial banner of Spain, besiege Rome, sack and plunder it during two entire months, and hold Pope Clement VII. a prisoner in Castle Santangelo!

The Gonzagas, all through these heart-sickening wars, had been pre-eminent in patriotism and military skill.

Their aim,—like that of every Pontiff who ascended the papal throne, was to rid Italy of foreign domination. Unfortunately both France and Spain claimed as their heirlooms the Kingdom of Naples at the south of the Peninsula and the Duchy of Milan, at the north. Between these two great powers all the Italian princes divided their allegiance, often changing sides as suited their own selfish policy, or as the victory happened to declare for King or for Emperor. The reigning sovereign of Mantua in 1522 was Frederic (Federigo), who helped to drive the French under Bonnivet back across the Alps in 1524, and was for that and other heroic services created Duke of Mantua in 1530. His father, Gian-Francesco (John-Francis), was one of Italy's greatest captains, and again and again worsted the armies of the French Kings, Charles VIII. and Louis XII.

Can we wonder that this beautiful country,—like a harvest-field devastated year after year in the season of the ripening grain,—should have borne no fruit or comfort to the husbandman? Or that Angela Merici, though burdened with the divine injunction to found a religious order, should have deferred, as each year dawned upon her with its terrors and uncertainties, the fulfillment of her cherished purpose, till at length her soul grew sick with the interminable and unavoidable delays?

Such indeed were the dark prospects of all Upper Italy when she re-entered the gates of Brescia in the year of grace 1522. This city, as well as Verona, had been under the Venetian rule since 1516. It had been the last dream of Pope Leo X. before his death (December 1, 1821), to unite the Italian princes in a solid league, so as to expel both the French and the Spaniards from the Peninsula. He therefore joined hands with the Emperor Charles V. to drive out the French from Upper Italy, purposing afterward to force the Spaniards to relinquish their hold on Naples and Sicily. Venice came, in this struggle, to the support of France, and exposed her own territory to be overrun by the Spanish and German troops, as it happened after the expulsion of the French. Through the whole of 1522, therefore, Brescia and its territory were either held by the Spanish forces or subject to be overrun by their victorious bands. The next year, indeed, Venice gave up the French for the Spanish alliance. But in 1523 Francis I. had a splendid army of 30,000 men in Upper Italy, and another sanguinary struggle began on the same field so often laid waste during these sad years, and around the same beleaguered cities for whose citizens there seemed no prospect of lasting peace or solid prosperity.

To one of Angela Merici's heroic and self-sacrificing temper, there was abundant opportunity for the display of her characteristic virtues in a city like Brescia. Still while thus reaping a rich harvest of merit and gratitude before God and men, her forty-sixth year had come and gone, and she saw not when she might begin the great work enjoined on her and to be consummated in this same city of Brescia.

Just then she felt impelled to visit Palestine, not only for the purpose of reverently treading in the foot-prints of the Master on the land privileged to behold Him in the flesh, but to obtain from Him, on the spot where He had shed His blood for mankind, the grace of seeing clearly what His will was with regard to her appointed life-work, and how she was to accomplish it. Her own Venice was still the mistress of the Adriatic; nor had the Mohammedan as yet overthrown her supremacy on the Mediterranean. Though sadly fallen away from her pristine power and her pristine piety,—for Angela while yet in her early womanhood beheld all Europe in arms against Venice, to the shame of the Christian name,— the grand old Republic still prided herself on protecting on sea or land all who felt inspired to visit Jerusalem and the other holy places. Yearly, in the beginning of May, one of her noblest ships, commanded by a Venetian senator, was placed at the disposal of the pilgrims of every nationality. And in that which was to sail in the spring of 1524, Angela resolved, if possible, to take passage to Palestine.

CHAPTER VII.

LIGHT IN DARKNESS.

Religious Orders to be long-lived and fruitful in holiness must be Christ-like in their members. Hence it is that we find the great men and women, who have been instrumental in founding these Orders carried beyond themselves by a passionate love for the Crucified and for His Cross. Their humility lay not only in the practice of the most extreme poverty, but in the endurance of the most abject humiliations and the bitterest bodily pains, in order to bear a closer resemblance to their Divine Model. Convinced that in the Cross of Christ lay the virtue by which the proud and sensual and selfish world around them could be lifted above earth, could be saved and sanctified, they sought in all things to be like Him,—destitute of all earthly comfort and goods, despised and held as most vile, nailed with Him to the bitter wood of shame, and treated like the worst of outcasts and criminals.

We know that during the years 1523 and 1524 Angela practiced a poverty and an habitual self-crucifixion, the bare thought of which would appal our cowardly delicacy. There happened to pass through Venetia in the summer of the former year, and while Angela was on her way to Mantua, a noble Spanish soldier, on his way to the Holy Land, whose

Christ-like poverty, humility, and sanctity of life, left a heavenly odor behind it wherever he passed.

He too had been chosen to found a mighty religious society, and his soul, like that of the Maid of Desenzano,—was tried by seemingly inexplicable delays, and prepared by wonderful experiences. From Genoa, where he landed first on the shores of Italy, he traveled on foot to Rome, braving the dangers and outrages to be met with in a country covered with hostile armies and afflicted with the plague. In Rome he astonished and edified all who beheld him,—although they knew not how highly born was the poor way-worn mendicant on whom they bestowed their alms, while admiring the preternatural light that shone through his pallid and noble features. Back through Central Italy he painfully dragged himself dividing among the poor the gold given him to pay his way to Palestine, begging his bread from door to door, arriving in Venice, utterly exhausted and unknown, and, after worshiping the God of his soul in the glorious temple dedicated to St. Mark, sinking to sleep on the pavement outside, beneath the shadow of some of the porticoes around the magnificent square.

In his splendid palace, near at hand, Senator Marco Trevisan, illustrious alike for his descent, his learning, and his piety,—one destined later (1553) to fill the highest office in the Republic,—is warned in his sleep to seek and care for the houseless pilgrim. From Jerusalem, where Ignatius de Loyola would have fain dwelt forever, feeding near the Sepulchre of Christ the fire which burned within his heart,— he is forced to return, his hope unfulfilled, and the yearnings of his great love unsatisfied in all save in the cruel sufferings he had to endure. In January, 1524, he lands at Venice and knocks at the gate of the Trevisan palace, clad in "a short thin coat and an open vest of black cloth, very ragged at the shoulders, with pantaloons of some coarse material, that reached no lower than the knees, leaving his legs quite bare. His sufferings had been great, for the cold was extreme, and there were frequent falls of snow." [1]

Had Angela heard of the passage of this noble pilgrim through Venice and Upper Italy both in the preceding summer, and during the winter months of 1524? We have no grounds for affirming it positively. Nevertheless, it is anything but unlikely that the name and fame of the heroic Spaniard should have reached Mantua and Brescia. What happened during her own pilgrimage was noised far and near, as we shall presently see. And the saintly virtues of Ignatius Loyola produced a no less profound impression.

Be that as it may,—the Love of the Crucified drew to Jerusalem both these great souls. To all Christians, indeed, ever since the birth of Christendom, Jerusalem became of all places the dearest and most sacred. It was for all who truly loved the Redeemer, as it is still,—the home of the soul.

Bartolommeo Biancosi, one of Angela's cousins from Salò, had also longed to visit Jerusalem.

Happening to visit her in Brescia about this time, he became acquainted with her project and asked to be her companion on this pilgrimage. He was young, however, and had never traveled, and was but ill-fitted to be the guide and protector of his cousin during so long a voyage, and amid the serious dangers to be met with on sea and land. From this perplexity they were both relieved by Antonio dei Romani, who offered to be himself their guide to Palestine and back. To make sure of there being no delay to their setting out in the spring of 1524, Romani went him-

---

[1] Stewart Rose, "Ignatius Loyola and the Early Jesuits," p. 64; 2d ed., London, 1871.

self beforehand to Venice, and found the flag displayed, which the Republic every year hung out as a signal for the Pilgrims. So he sent word to Angela to lose no time in joining him at Venice.

Angela forthwith, on the 1st of May, repaired to Salò; and both she and Bartolommeo set out on horseback for Venice. They arrived in that city on the 25th, after having encountered more than one mortal peril. On the 25th, which happened that year to be the Feast of Corpus Christi, they all partook early of the Divine Bread vouchsafed to pilgrims here below, and embarked on the vessel set apart for the yearly pilgrimage, under the command of the Venetian Senator Luigi Giustiniani.

It fared well with our pilgrims during the whole of their voyage down the Adriatic, and until their arrival at the port of Canea, in the Isle of Crete (or Candia), when without any previous warning or indisposition, Angela was suddenly stricken with total blindness. Thereupon both Romani and Biancosi bethought them seriously of returning to Venice, taking it as an indication of the Divine Will that their dear companion was thus disabled from seeing the Holy Places, and the direct object of their journey was frustrated. Not so Angela: she could, indeed, she said, well believe that this sudden affliction had befallen her in punishment of her sins. Still, although unworthy of seeing with her own eyes the places where her adored Lord had labored and suffered for her sake, she would only prove to Him both her gratitude and reverence by touching them with her hands and her lips.

Her friends were too manly and too Christian, not to be moved by such reasons as these. So, without further objection, they pursued their voyage all together, Angela's cheerfulness and courage under this sudden visitation only serving to increase still more the veneration in which she was held by them, and by the entire ship's company.

She was received with much honor by the Franciscan Monks in Jerusalem, to whom had been intrusted the guardianship of the Holy Places, and the duty of providing for stranger pilgrims arriving in the city. She wore her Franciscan habit; and the testimony of her fellow-travelers, her own gentle and saintly bearing, as well as her present helplessness, rendered her an object of ten-fold respect and sympathy to the devoted monks.[1] She found hospitality with her Sister Nuns of the Third Order of St. Francis on Mount Sion.

Angela was more fortunate than had been Ignatius Loyola, who was not allowed to visit any of the Holy Places outside of Jerusalem, and in Jerusalem itself was treated with unaccountable harshness both by the Turks and by his fellow-Christians. He was compensated for the blows received and for his peremptory dismissal from Palestine, by a vision in which he beheld our Lord Himself, and which filled him with unspeakable joy.

Unspeakable also was the consolation experienced by Angela, as they led her by the hand from place to place. What happy concourse of circumstances enabled her fellow-pilgrims and herself to visit Bethlehem, has not been told by her historians. She deemed it an unspeakable privilege to be permitted to kneel and adore the Incarnate Word on the very spot where He first blessed His Virgin-

---

[1] There exists a formal testimony to the veneration with which Angela was regarded in Palestine, from Father John di Calorra, a Franciscan of the strict observance. In his "Chronological History of the Province of Syria and of the Holy Land of Jerusalem," (*Storia Cronologica della Provincia di Siria e Terra Santa di Gerusalemme.*) Venice, 1694, book v. ch. 27,—he goes on to say: "At that same time another servant of God shed a great lustre in Jerusalem on the Monastery of the Nuns of the Third Order situated on Mount Sion; her name was St. Angela of Desenzano."

Mother with the joys of maternity. Angela, guided as she assuredly was by the Spirit of God, could contemplate with the eyes of her soul the scene of that nativity, as it had occurred so many centuries before: the Mother and her Babe and their devoted guardian, Joseph, cast out at the midnight hour from the homes and hearts of their kinsfolk; the Messiah born in a wayside cavern, laid after His birth in the poor, cold crib; that Mother and her companion,— the first companions and followers of the King of souls,— kneeling in rapturous adoration of this infinite self-abasement, divining, though dimly, the mighty mysteries of the career began in the Manger only to end on the Cross of shame. What mattered it that Angela had to be led by the hand, like a child in infancy, as she approached Bethlehem, climbed its hillside road, and entered the church constructed by early Christian piety above the cavern in which the Light of the World first shone from the crib upon the eyes of his Mother? Hers was a soul long habituated to the loving practice of the poverty, the self-abasement, and self-sacrificing charity taught by the Babe of Bethlehem. From her childhood Angela had been in spirit and truth the faithful companion of Mary and Joseph in that glorious path which leads to Calvary. And here she was on the very soil which their feet had trodden. Here they had knelt by the crib, the two first worshipers of God made man,—His most faithful and loved imitators,—the two most lovingly watchful over Him and His interests while on earth,—and the two most devoted to Him and His Church in Heaven. Here Mary and Joseph had beheld the splendors which shone above the hills of Bethlehem on the ever-memorable night of the Nativity, as if Heaven and its glories were nearer to our earth,—and here they, too, we may well believe, heard the voices of the Angelic multitude singing "Glory to God in the highest," while the celestial harmonies sounded in vain for all but the two lonely worshipers by the crib and the poor simple-souled shepherds in the wilderness. Here Mary's motherly heart was thrilled by the arrival of these poor "watchers on the wold," flocking to the roadside cavern to do homage to the new-born God of the poor. Alas, and here too were to begin the terrors of that same motherly heart and Joseph's agony of solicitude, when they had, at the midnight hour, to "take the infant" and fly in hot haste across the western mountains to the sea-coast and to Egypt, in order to escape old Herod's pitiless sword.

For Angela,—nay, for her fellow-pilgrims from Italy,—how eloquent of devotion to the Infant Christ were the tombs shown them within the vast Church of St. Mary,—those of St. Jerome and his two noble disciples in self-abnegation, St. Paula and her daughter Eustochium, and that other great Italian, St. Eusebius of Cremona, from Angela's own native hills, who had sold his patrimonial estates to cast his lot with Jerome,—and spread the knowledge and love of the Incarnate God, from Bethlehem and Jerusalem as a centre to the uttermost boundaries of Asia! Not unworthy of the living faith which inspired her countrywomen in the fourth century, was the fervor of the holy Maid of Desenzano. Her soul, while kneeling near Christ's own birthplace, was flooded with light, enabling her to discern the height and depth of the mystery of condescension consummated there. The poor sightless eyes overflowed with a constant and sweet stream of tears, while her whole heart went out to the Divine Babe cast with His Mother, at His entrance into our cold world, like a ewe with her lamb, forgotten in the storm and the darkness, and left to perish by the roadside.

This abjection, this utter destitution of all human sympathy and earthly comfort, it was which touched the stern soul of

Jerome had moulded it to such exquisite tenderness toward Christ and His suffering poor. This too it was that fired the hearts of the noble Paula and her daughters, inspiring them with a love of poverty so passionate, that their deeds even at this distance move our souls to generosity, and their words are like coals of living fire, taken from the altar of the Lamb and inflaming the reader to heroic love of Christ and His Mother.[1]

---

[1] Paula was still young when, after the death of her husband, she betook herself to Bethlehem with her daughter Eustochium, and founded at her own expense two monasteries, one for women, which she governed herself, and another for men under the direction of St. Jerome. There both ladies lived and labored till their death, another Paula, the granddaughter of the foundress having come to join them in the full flower of her youth.

We may judge of the boundless generosity of this great-souled woman by the following answer to St. Jerome, who was trying to restrain her from ruinous almsgiving. "I have but one wish," she said, "and that is to die a beggar, so poor that I cannot leave one penny to my daughter, and that I must be buried in a winding cloth bestowed on me through charity. Should I ever be reduced to become a beggar, I shall find plenty of people to give me alms; but should I refuse the poor man who now solicits my aid, and should he perish of want in consequence, who will be responsible for his death, if not I?" She did indeed die without, literally, possessing one cent,—nay, heavily in debt for the maintenance of a host of the neediest poor.

Nor must we, in the midst of a calculating generation whose hearts are narrowed by the perpetual seeking of self and self-interest, and whose minds are being gradually poisoned by the scientific materialism propagated by printing press and professor's chair, and lecturer's platform,—think that this sublime love of the God of Bethlehem and of His poverty, had extinguished in the souls of these ardent followers of His any of the natural and hallowed home-affections which He enjoined and consecrated by His own example. Listen, rather, to the words of the eloquent author of "The Monks of the West," and judge for yourself, dear reader:

" One likes to know that these most austere Christians, these Roman ladies, possessed of so high a courage in combatting their own inclinations, cherished in their hearts a deep spring of tenderness, and clung fervently to the domestic ties which they did not sever in devoting their lives to God. Motherly love and filial piety still overflowed in these brave hearts During the funeral service of Plesilla, her oldest daughter, Paula, could not repress her grief, and fell into a swoon so deadly, that her life was in danger. St. Jerome found it necessary in order to reconcile her with the Divine Will, to write her an eloquent letter, in which he made use of authority and persuasion, convincing her that her excessive grief scandalized the heathen, and redounded to the dishonor of the Church and the monastic profession.

" When, twenty years later (404), Paula herself died in her monastery of Bethlehem,

If Angela's soul was so deeply moved by contact with the sacred soil of Bethlehem; if the vivid light vouchsafed to the interior sense more than compensated the loss of her eyesight, how much more powerful must have been her emotions as they led her, in Jerusalem itself, along every stage which the Man of Sorrows followed during his passion? how much more abundant the clear knowledge imparted to her concerning these unfathomed depths of the Infinite Love?

It is certain that while kneeling in the Garden of Gethsemane, and on Mount Calvary, and again by the side of the Holy Sepulchre, Angela could not contain herself. Her love and compassion for the Divine Sufferer broke forth in great heart-cries, which melted all who heard them. Little cared she then, absorbed as she was in the contemplation of all these realities of incomprehensible mercy, for the darkness which had fallen so suddenly on her bodily sense. She only yearned, she only craved to be made more and more like to the Master.

She was permitted again and again to revisit the theatre of our Lord's sufferings, each time with a sensible increase of fervor and comfort,—praying all the while that He for whom alone she wished to live, labor, suffer, and die, would en-

---

Eustochium after nursing her mother in her last illness with the most indefatigable assiduity, had to run from her death-bed to the grotto in which the Saviour was born, and, prostrate there, to beseech Him with tears and ardent supplications to grant her the grace of dying then and there and to be buried with her parent, St. Jerome had again to interfere, in order to combat this natural weakness, and to remove the orphaned nun from her saintly mother's remains. These were desposited in a tomb in the rock alongside the Cavern of the Nativity ; and on this tomb Jerome engraved an epitaph of which this is a translation:

"*Here reposes* PAULA *the daughter of the Scipios and Paulus Æmilius, descended from the Gracchi and Agamemnon: She was the first of the Senatorial order to forsake her family, Rome her birthplace, her fortune, and her children, in order to lead a life of poverty in Bethlehem, near Thy crib, O Christ, where the Wise Men worshipped in Thee both Man and God.*"—Montalembert, " Monks of the West," vol. i., pp. 176, 177.

lighten her and guide her surely in all things relating to the work He would have her accomplish for His glory.

And so, unconscious herself of the veneration with which she was regarded by all who approached her in Jerusalem,—by the Franciscan monks and nuns as well as by her fellow-pilgrims,—she had at length to tear herself away from a place in which she would fain have dwelt forever. But feeble, blind, and helpless as she was, and utterly unworthy as she deemed herself, she knew that she was not called to labor there. Her field of action and trial lay in her native land,—in Brescia. And, like Paul, after he had been stricken blind on the road to Damascus,—she allowed herself to be led by the hand, anxious only to do the Divine Will, and to allow not one particle of the grace from on high to fall useless on her soul and her life.

CHAPTER VIII.

THE LIGHT INCREASING.

OUR pilgrims had left Venice in the end of May; the month of September was far advanced when they turned their backs on the Holy City. It would appear, that they took the road which leads northward to Er-râm (the Ramah of the Bible), and thence towards the west, across the lofty range on which stood Mizpah and Gibeah of Saul, through the broad Suleiman Valley to Lydda and Jaffa. We say "it would appear;" for the pilgrims were forced to remain "eight entire days" shut up in Rama through fear of a band of brigands who were lying in wait for travelers in the mountain passes. The marauders, either wearied by this long delay, or thinking that the caravan of pilgrims had taken the more southern road through Ramleh, disappeared, and left Angela and her companions free to continue their journey to the coast. We must not imagine that Italian pilgrims of the sixteenth century were so unfamiliar with the topography of Palestine, or so unacquainted with the great events connected with each memorable place they passed on their way to and from the Holy City, as to find in these enforced delays, and in such a spot as Rama, anything but most abundant food for mind and heart.

Rama, the birth-place of Samuel, and his home while controlling the destinies of Israel, was identified from the earliest Christian ages with the highest mountain-summit near Jerusalem, now known as Neby-Samweel (the Tomb of Samuel). It is mentioned by St. Jerome,—who lived so long in Palestine,—as being situated "near Gabaa (Gibeah of Saul) at the seventh milestone from Jerusalem." Around the summits of Neby-Samweel and Gabaa are Beth-Horon, Gilgal, and Mizpah. In Gabaa Saul was anointed king by Samuel; from Beth-Horon Josue commanded the sun to stand still; Mizpah was the great watch-tower and stronghold of Israel in all the national struggles. There Samuel called the nation together to confess their sins to Jehovah, as a preliminary to their being freed from the yoke of the Philistines; there too Saul's previous selection by God and his consecration by Samuel were ratified by the solemn choice of the assembled people. It was with Bethel and Gilgal one of the three holy cities where Samuel successively held his sessions as Judge of Israel. And at Gabaa the Ark of the Covenant abode before its translation to Jerusalem.

The first Crusaders were well acquainted with the claims of these and other memorable places in the veneration of the Christian world. They may have been sometimes misled as to the fixing of certain localities; they were always right as to the feeling which prompted their acts of piety and generosity. They built a beautiful church around the tomb of Samuel at Ramah, and erected a monastery near it,—just as they graced the traditional tombs of Rachel near Bethlehem, and those of Abraham and Sara at Hebron, with similar structures. What they did in Bethlehem itself, in Jerusalem, at Nazareth, and elsewhere, is too well known to require anything but the merest allusion.

Near the remains of the great Prophet-Judge of Israel,

then, Angela and her companions were forced to remain for an entire week. She and they were too well informed in Sacred History not to profit by their stay in a place so full of the most thrilling memories. They could, indeed, from the dominating crest of Neby-Samweel, take in from horizon to horizon every scene consecrated by the visible display of God's power and mercy Desolate and barren as the boundless panorama of hills to the east and south appeared under the late September sun,—they knew how beauteous and blooming the land was when Josue's conquering hosts first swept over it. But Angela's soul needed not the aid of the outward sense, to know what feet had trodden these mountains and valleys, and how near God had once been, in His loving protection to the privileged race who possessed them. She was in the home where Anna with tears and prayers had obtained from the Lord and Giver of life the birth of her blessed boy Samuel; and here too it was that she reared him so tenderly and so holily, forming him to that love of prayer and habitual sense of the divine Presence, which were to be the great features of his character and the potent weapons of his glorious administration. On this same spot the devoted mother,—even when her boy had been given up to the service of Jehovah,—yearly wrought for him with her own hands the Nazarite robes which Samuel wore before the Lord.

Angela, who would have gladly travelled on her knees through the length and breadth of the Holy Land, and whose heart had poured itself forth in such rapturous adoration in Bethlehem and Jerusalem, was also destined to be the mother of a long line of indefatigable workers in Christ's chosen vineyard. She had seen the beautiful places of Italy laid waste by contending hosts, and all promise of a spiritual harvest destroyed by the evil passions of men. Oh, if she could only save Christian homes in her own dear native land from the utter desolation threatened by interminable strife and the scandals which ever follow swift and strong on the heels of strife! If she could only sow in the souls of the young of her own sex, all over warring, convulsed, and divided Christendom, the supernatural faith and practical virtues which would be compensation for the moral ruin she was forced to contemplate! She felt the conviction growing stronger in her soul every day she spent on that sacred soil, treading in the footsteps of the Master and Shepherd of souls,—that the family she was destined to found was to be instrumental in repairing the ruins of the present, and preparing a new and faithful generation to Christ. And, if she clung with regret to those hilltops, so often illumed by the splendors of God's revelation to man, she was also impelled to hasten homeward to begin in earnest the great work allotted to her.

The pilgrims pursued their journey without molestation, embarked at Joppa, and, after touching at Cyprus, where some of the merchant pilgrims took in a stock of wares, they once more made sail for Canea in the Isle of Candia. They made but a brief stay in this port, which painfully recalled to Angela the loss of her sight; but brief as it was, it was marked by a miracle that raised her still higher in the esteem of her fellow-travellers, and was soon noised abroad all over Upper Italy. In one of the churches of Canea was an image of our Crucified Saviour, which had been made by the Divine Goodness the instrument of many wonderful cures; and Angela happening to hear of it, was suddenly inspired to go to the spot, and there implore of Him the restoration of her eyesight. Her companions resolved to accompany her in a body, headed by Monsignor Paola della Puglia, private chamberlain to the Pope, and who had joined their band in Jerusalem. Angela, when she was led to the foot of the venerated image, lifted her soul to Him whose Sepulchre she had so lately visited, and in whose presence she evermore dwelt by day and by night. "My Lord and my Saviour,"—she prayed,—" were my life to be spent in solitude and employed solely in procuring my own sanctification, it would be of no account to remain thus in darkness all my days. But Thou hast made known to me that I was to devote myself to the salvation of others, and this blindness renders me helpless even for my own need. If it be, therefore, to Thy glory and the furthering of Thy interests that I should recover my sight, do Thou, O Lord, restore it to Thy handmaid. If I can serve Thee equally in this my helplessness, then, dear Lord, let me continue blind to my dying day"

Scarcely had she ended this short and fervent prayer, when she cried out that she could see; and the astonished assistants flocked around her to congratulate her and to join their thanksgiving with hers. How her trusting and generous friends Romani and Biancosi now felt rewarded for their fidelity to her, their compliance with her wishes, and the pious care with which they had watched over her every footstep during this long and perilous journey! There was but little time left for congratulations, however, as the pilgrims' ship had to set sail that very day,—the 4th of October, 1524. The Governor of Candia embarked with them this time, and two other merchant ships with rich cargoes. Many passengers,—among whom were several noble Venetians,—sailed in company with them. Scarcely, however, had they reached the Ionian Sea, between Sicily and the Morea, when all three vessels were assailed by one of those sudden and furious storms so frequent and so fatal in that part of the Mediterranean. During three entire days and nights they were at the mercy of the winds and waves; the two vessels which had left Canea with them foundered beneath their eyes, perishing with all on board, while the pilgrims' ship was only preserved by what all her company believed to be a visible interposition of Providence.

And their preservation, under God, they were unanimous in attributing to the holy Maid of Desenzano. From the very first appearance of danger, they all turned to her as to the one person whose prayers could help to save them. She was so calm, so retiring, so humble, and prayerful in the midst of the elemental uproar and the general consternation. From the first also she bade them, with a serene and smiling countenance to put their trust in Him who rules the storm and the whirlwind. She remained in almost uninterrupted prayer, while the hurricane grew in violence, appearing in the midst of frightened crew and passengers, when, at the end of the third day, they beheld the other ships going down before their eyes,—to exhort them to do their duty by their own ship, while trusting themselves absolutely to the divine protection.

For six other days and nights they continued to drive helplessly before the wind, fearful all this time lest the storm should drive them on the coast of Africa into the hands of the Tunisian or Algerine pirates. This fate would have been a worse calamity than either death or shipwreck. But Angela bade them have no fear.

At length the wind fell and the sun reappeared, but only to show them how very near they were to the haunts of the Mohammedan corsairs. The ship's head was forthwith turned toward the coast of Albania, which they soon reached, anchoring in the bay of Durazzo, where the Venetian flag still waved proudly. A Turkish fleet had also taken refuge there from the recent storm, and this incident was not without its danger to them. The Turks were for the moment the strongest on sea, and resolved to pursue and capture the pilgrims' ship. But even in this extremity Angela's prophetic voice encouraged them, when they had refitted and taken in the necessary supplies, to set sail with all secrecy and expedition, promising them a favorable wind and a happy termination to their journey.

They did not hesitate to obey her, and the issue turned out as she had predicted. They arrived safely at Citta Nova, on the coast of Istria, opposite to Venice, and thence leisurely continued their voyage to the end.

One may easily conceive how dear all these occurrences had rendered Angela to the entire ship's company, and with what veneration they spoke of her on their landing at Venice. The arrival of the pilgrims' ship, like its departure, was always an occasion of great solemnity in the beautiful city. No one who joined the pilgrims in solemn procession to the High Altar of St. Mark's but was shown the gentle Tertiary of St. Francis, who had been stricken so suddenly with blindness on the voyage and had been so suddenly cured; whose presence had been to all of her fellow-passengers a pledge of safety amid the storm and the shipwreck, and whose angelic modesty, exceeding austerity of life, sweet and unoffensive piety, and superior wisdom had been from first to last their admiration and their model. She, meanwhile, utterly unconscious of all but the one overwhelming sense of gratitude to the Fatherly Providence which was guiding her in all her ways, passed up the Grand Canal with its crowd of barges and gondolas and the joyous multitude who from both sides saluted the returning pilgrims, passed up the glorious square of St. Mark's to the shining portals of the incomparable Cathedral, and into the crowded aisles within, intent only on kneeling before the Mercy Seat, and pouring forth there the full tide of her love and thanksgiving.

She soon stole away from the thronged church and the busy streets to take refuge with her Franciscan sisters in the Convent of the Holy Sepulchre.

She had been, nevertheless, the cynosure of all eyes on that day,—and the public veneration much more even than the public curiosity followed her to the hospitable retreat which the Franciscans provided for pilgrims to the Holy Land. Fallen, as Venice was in the year of grace 1524, both from her proud eminence as a political power and from the simple-minded piety of her most glorious days,—she had not yet ceased to value the glory of possessing one saintly man or woman born on her soil, above the wealth of the East or the homage of the West. Even on the night of Angela's arrival from Palestine, it was a subject of discussion among her merchant-princes as well as among her population of seamen and soldiers how they might best retain in their city one who was so manifestly the favorite of Heaven. In her native town of Desenzano, as well as in Brescia, Angela had shone as the indefatigable friend of the suffering poor, and as the wise and zealous guide of the young persons of her own sex who sought to emulate her charity, or her extraordinary self-abnegation. There were in Venice magnificent institutions devoted to the varied purposes of Christian beneficence; and there were also among all classes of her citizens very many young souls who, while they found no encouragement to enter the monastic profession, were still desirous of serving in the world the poor of Christ, and sanctifying their own souls by a life of self-crucifixion.

It was suggested to the magistrates of the Republic,— probably by Senator Giustiniani, who had headed the pilgrimage to the Holy Land,—that Angela Merici would be the very best person to whom could be given the general superintendence of these great charitable institutions. She, wearing as she did the Franciscan habit, would encourage others of her own sex to embrace a similar mode of life, and thus Venice would possess a body of holy women living in the world an unwordly life, rendering active piety attractive and admirable by their own daily virtues, and ministering faithfully to the bodily and spiritual needs of the laboring population of a great commercial metropolis.

They approached Angela with a proposition to this effect. This was assailing her by her weak side,—the prospect of a field of labor far wider, and a harvest of good incomparably greater than Brescia could present even during a long period of peace and security. And what prospect was there in that same autumn in 1524, that Brescia, still occupied by a Spanish garrison, with the French armies even then returning across the Alps into Upper Italy,—should be otherwise than it had been for half a century,—like a low-lying peninsula between two adverse tides, forever inundated by the raging waters, and offering scarcely a safe foothold for man or beast amid the hostile elements?

Still Angela's soul, during the six months of her eventful pilgrimage, had become more than ever impressed with the distinct conviction, that the Divine Voice had appointed Brescia as her field of future labor. And from obedience to its direction, no temptation of an apparently greater good could divert her. She answered those who thus honored her by making this proposal, with the gentle modesty and womanly tact which ever marked her intercourse with men of the world. It would seem that they did not understand her as giving them a peremptory refusal. For Angela, fearing that the public authorities might interfere to detain her in Venice, persuaded Romani and Biancosi to leave the city with her that same night, and to take the direct road to Brescia.

CHAPTER IX.

WAITING AND WORKING.

ANGELA and her two companions arrived in Brescia on the 25th of November. She was warmly welcomed by those who were thenceforward to consider themselves her fellow-citizens, both because her father and the Merici family had long been inscribed among the free burgesses of the place, and because her own many devoted services, her gentle virtues, and the shining light of her holy life, had made her most dear to the entire city. There was another reason; she had more than once declared that God Himself willed her to do a great work there.

A great work she had, indeed, already achieved among them during the period of Brescia's most terrible calamities. This, however, the citizens looked upon as only the pledge of a mightier performance. They had not favored her pilgrimage to the Holy Land. Antonio dei Romani did not win many compliments for his volunteering to be Angela's guide on so distant a journey, at a most troublous epoch, and when his own city sadly needed the presence of every man and woman who could help to build up wide-spread ruin, and bind up wounds that seemed beyond all healing,—save only from the All-healing hand of the Creator.

It might thus seem that the circumstances amid which

Sister Angela entered this ancient city,[1] were most propitious to her project. It was far otherwise, however; just when Angela was preparing for her departure to Jerusalem, the French invading army under Bonnivet and Bayard were driven back to France through the valleys of upper Piedmont,—the latter heroic soldier, who had lain wounded in Brescia during the horrible assault and massacre of 1512,— perishing on the battle-field. But the retiring wave of invasion was to return more impetuous and terrible than ever before Angela re-entered Brescia on that memorable 25th of November. All through the winter months, Francis I. poured his troops into the Milanese; and on the 24th day of February, 1525, the hostile armies of France and Spain with their respective Italian allies, met near Pavia, the French being utterly defeated, and their king remaining a prisoner in the hands of the Imperialists. Pope Adrian VI., who had suc-

---

[1] Catullus (died B. C. 47), who was a native of the neighboring city of Verona, calls Brescia the parent-city. This ill-starred place was again bombarded by the Austrians under Marshal Haynau in 1849. "The view from the castle (citadel) of Brescia, is indeed a noble one. And it is not a mere noble view; it is a view on which the characteristic history of Italy is legibly written. . . . With a single glance of the eye we look down on a crowd of cities, each of which was once an independent commonwealth, with its name and place in history. On one side are the spurs of the Alps on which we are standing, reminding us that there is a land beyond, from which the Emperors came down to demand the crowns of Italy and Rome. To the far East we get a glimpse of smaller hills on the same horizon, suggesting that the natural ramparts of Verona are not beyond our sight. But to the south the eye ranges over the boundless plains of Lombardy, spreading like a sea, with a tall tower here and there, like the mast of a solitary vessel. Each of these towers marks a city, a city which once ranked alongside of princes, a city making war and peace, and containing within its walls the full life of a nation. The map seems to show that one of them is the mighty tower of Placenzia, and that another is the yet mightier tower of Cremona, the fellow-worker of Brescia in the great work of restoring Milan. . . We have vividly brought home to us how near the great cities of Northern Italy lie to the Alpine barrier, the barrier which was so often found helpless to shelter them against the Northern invader. We think of all the conquerors who have crossed the mountains from Hannibal to our own day. . . From such a point we may well run over the shifting fates of the land before us from Brennus to either Bonaparte."—*Freeman.*

ceeded Leo X., had persuaded the Republic of Venice to become the ally of Spain, after having been long faithful to France. But Adrian, who was a Spanish subject, only governed the Church during twenty months; and his successor Clement VII., who was an Italian, reversed Adrian's policy, separated from Spain, and allied himself with France. Therefore, after the disaster of Pavia, the Pope was left defenceless.

It was the year of jubilee, nevertheless; and Christians not only from all parts of Italy but from every country in Christendom were preparing to visit Rome, in spite of the armies and bands of marauders who watched the passes of the Alps and beset every road within Italy itself. In the universal alarm, distress and uncertainty, Angela could not think of establishing a congregation. Sooth to say, she did not see her way clearly as to the precise object and form of the society she contemplated.

What better,—in this unsettled condition of public affairs as well as of her own plans,—could she do, than go to the Shrine of the Holy Apostles, and seek there not only an increase of light for her own mind, but the direction of the great and wise men who ruled the councils of the Holy See? Her own countryman,—the noble and saint-like Cajetan de Tiene, now a cardinal, had been one of the most trusted counselors of Pope Adrian VI. While she had been on her way to Palestine, in June, 1524, Cajetan and Cardinal Caraffa had obtained from Adrian the approbation of a new order of Regular Priests, thenceforward known as "Theatines." Would not the holy Cardinal of Tiene enlighten and assist her in her perplexity?

To Rome she therefore went, accompanied by several pious ladies and gentlemen of Brescia, to whom her presence on the journey was considered to be a sure pledge of the divine protection. Among her companions were two excellent priests and Antonio dei Romani, whose veneration for Angela would not permit him to trust her to the guardianship of strangers. There was, for the Brescians and for all who were still subject to the sway of Venice, a special motive for being present in Rome during the solemnities of the Jubilee. The Pope had declared his intention to beatify, during the month of May, Laurence Justinian (Giustiniani), patriarch of Venice, who died in 1455, one of the most heroic souls who ever graced the priesthood of the Christian Church,— the boast and pride of the grand old Republic in her decline.

His near relative had been Angela's protector during her memorable pilgrimage to Jerusalem, and he together with the most distinguished members of his illustrious family, and the Duke of Venice, Andrea Gritti, were to represent Venice at Rome on the solemn occasion. Thus the great Republic had a particular interest in securing the safety of all those of her children who visited Rome in this year of Jubilee. And so,—although a terrible pestilence was prevalent all over the Peninsula,—all who gloried in the name of Venice and revered the name of her saintly archbishop, braved every danger and obstacle in order to visit the Eternal City. And,—in very truth,—the Venetians and Upper Italians formed the majority of the comparatively small concourse of pilgrims. So unsettled and threatening was the aspect of public affairs, and so deadly were the ravages of the plague, which seemed sent on the land to complete the fearful destruction wrought by war!

Angela, as was her wont, lived during the entire journey on what she could get by begging from door to door. No entreaties of Romani or her other fellow-pilgrims could induce her to change her ordinary mode of life. She forgot, while in the capital of the Christian world, everything but the one great purpose for which she had journeyed thither,—

the obtaining in its fulness the grace of the Jubilee, the heart-satisfaction found by the true Christian in visiting the most venerable sanctuaries in Christendom, the delight felt in proclaiming by her every act and word, while near the shrines of the Holy Apostles, her allegiance to the See of Peter at a time when others were revolting against it,— and then the crowning grace of knowing more clearly the Divine Will in her own regard and the courage to fulfill it perfectly.

The fervor with which she visited the churches of Rome was scarcely inferior to that which had so much edified her companions in Jerusalem. Indeed her reputation had preceded her. The princesses of the Gonzaga family from Mantua and Castiglione were residing temporarily in Rome, and they, like many others from Northern Italy, were loud in their praise of Sister Angela's saintly virtues. Monsignor della Puglia, who had learned to revere her in Palestine, and on the journey homeward, soon renewed his acquaintance with her. To the Holy Father he had more than once spoken of her as a living saint, relating how she had miraculously recovered her eyesight in Candia, and how all the ship's company attributed to her prayers their preservation from shipwreck and their escape from the Turkish fleet. To Angela herself he had shown every possible mark of respect during her stay in Rome, and to perfect her satisfaction he obtained for her a private audience with Clement VII.

Angela was too sincerely humble not to feel the deepest gratitude for this favor, and too forgetful of self to feel disconcerted in presence of the Vicar of Christ. She was too familiar with Him in His sacramental presence, and in the sweet and uninterrupted communion of prayer and contemplation,—to feel abashed when she knelt before His representative. The Holy Father spoke to her with extraordinary kindness, and at great length, questioning her closely on her manner of life and her projects for the future. Her answers confirmed the high estimate he had been led to form of her modesty, her disinterestedness, her devotion to the poor, and her singular tact and discretion. He expressed the wish that she would remain in Rome, promising to further to the utmost her zeal for all good works. He even offered to give her the direction of any one of the charitable institutions that she might prefer.

This compelled the honorable daughter of St. Francis to lay open to the Holy Father the history of her soul,—her visions and the distinct command to establish in Brescia a society of religious women. Everything which he heard from her and saw in her, convinced Clement that the hand of God was there. Without however,—as is the wont of the Holy See,—expressing any opinion on the truth of the visions themselves, His Holiness encouraged her to persevere in her manner of life, and dismissed her with his blessing.

Father Salvatori adds that, when she had left, the Pope reproved his chamberlain for his lack of discernment, telling him that there were in Angela much higher qualities than he had described, and that it would be a great privilege to keep her in Rome.

Alas for Rome and for the Pope! Ere twice a twelvemonth had passed, the walls of the Eternal City would be scaled by the German Lutheran bands of the murderous Frundsperg, fighting under the imperial standard of Spain, and led on by the French Duke of Bourbon! To the shame of the clergy and people of Rome one of their own noblest families,—the Colonna,—were but too zealous within Rome's walls to introduce the sacrilegious assailants! And for two whole months every Church in Rome was to run with blood, every monastery and private dwelling-house to be the prey of a brutal soldiery, while Pope Clement was to look on, helpless and forsaken by the whole world, a prisoner within the castle of S. Angelo! "Never perhaps," says the Protestant historian Sismondi, "in the history of the world was a great capital city given over to a more atrocious abuse of victory; never was a powerful army made up of such ferocious soldiers, or freed from every restraint of discipline; and never did the prince in whose name the army fought manifest so utter an indifference to the calamities endured by the vanquished. . . . Every dwelling resounded with the shrieks and wailings of the wretched inhabitants, who were put to the torture; the squares before the churches were strewn with altar furniture, relics, and all manner of sacred objects, which the soldiers cast into the streets after having torn off the gold and silver ornaments. The German Lutherans, uniting fanaticism with their greed of spoil, vied with each other in showing their contempt for the worship of the Roman Church, and in profaning the very things which would have been respected by the nations they called heathen." "The Goths," says Gibbon,—" evacuated Rome, at the end of six days; but Rome continued to be during nine whole months the victim of the Imperialists,—and every day and hour during this time was marked by some abominable act of ferocity, licentiousness or rapine. The authority of Alaric knew how to impose limits to the licentiousness of the barbarous multitude who hailed him as fellow-soldier or chief; but the death of the Duke of Bourbon in scaling the walls, left without chief or restraint or discipline an army composed of Italians, Germans and Spaniards." The prince of Orange, who assumed the command after the fall of Bourbon, had too many theological passions to gratify to allow him to put a stop to murder and rapine and sacrilege.

We dare not venture on the details of this fearful picture. If Angela's eyes, when they rested for the last time on the throne of St.' Peter and the spires and battlements of Rome, had been illumined with a prophetic light to see the black storm which was gathering in the heavens, or if her ears could have heard from afar the tramp of Bourbon and Leyva's impious legions,—how dark for her would have appeared the summer skies of her beloved Italy, and how cursed the teeming earth which was condemned to bear the tread of these monsters!

As it was, she turned her steps homeward, rejoicing that to the Vicar of Christ had been disclosed the inmost secrets of her soul and the most cherished aims of her life,—that his voice had commended them and his hand blessed them. The plague was to be the dread avenger of blood and sacrilege and robbery. Of the thirty thousand barbarians who glutted all their evil passions in the City of the Holy Martyrs, in the home of the common Father of Christians, but a small remnant was destined to revisit their native land. The pestilence was waiting for the spoilers and their spoil along every road and pathway from Rome to the Alps and the straits of Sicily.

CHAPTER X.

INEVITABLE OBSTACLES.

THE political and social condition of Brescia,—indeed, of the whole of Upper Italy,—during the autumn of 1525, and throughout the next five years, was such as to render the execution of Angela's project hopeless and impossible. Pope Clement VII did not wish to see the Emperor Charles V. attain to universal domination in Christendom. Charles had treated Francis I., during the latter's imprisonment at Madrid with intolerable harshness,—imposing on him as one of the only conditions on which he could regain his liberty, the dismemberment of his kingdom. This was a stipulation to which the captive monarch could not lawfully agree, and to which, in order to recover his freedom, he gave a fraudulent assent. The partition of the French monarchy thus left Charles not only rightful sovereign of Spain and its newly discovered transatlantic empire, but the lord paramount of all Germany and the Low Countries, the sole undisputed arbiter of Italy, where he possessed Milan and the kingdoms of Naples and Sicily,—the master indeed of all Western Europe, with the exception of England. Even Henry VIII. of England deserted the overruling Spanish monarch and sided with the French King, with whom were now allied the Pope, Venice, Florence, and Fráncesco II. of Milan.

Francis I. was liberated from prison in March, 1526, and lost not a moment in rousing his people to revenge. The stipulation made with Charles V. was repudiated by the French nation, and powerful armies were again sent in hot haste into Upper Italy. These were destined to defeat, proving helpless to withstand the imperial forces under Bourbon and Frundsperg. And so all Lombardy and Venetia continued to be the battle-field on which France, Spain, and Germany contended for European supremacy and the possession of Italy's most beautiful provinces! Alas for the cities which lay, like Brescia, nearest to the Alps and to the great highways across this mighty mountain-barrier! What could Angela do when she reëntered once more the hospitable mansion of Antonio dei Romani? The whole city and the surrounding districts were agitated by the most alarming rumors. Industry of every kind was paralyzed, nor amid the perpetual fears and tumults of war, was any leisure left for the cultivation of the sweet Christian virtues, any more than for the study of the arts of peace. Men's minds were unsettled by these ever-recurring conflicts between Christian princes, in which all the most sacred precepts of religion, and all the most inviolable rights of humanity were utterly disregarded,—while religion herself, by her being dragged perforce as a party into all these unhallowed quarrels, incurred the aversion or the contempt of friends and foes.

The only remedy to these crying and seemingly interminable ills, lay in fostering with redoubled care all the home-sanctities of the Christian family, in the increase of regularity and fervor in the Religious orders and the clergy. This was Angela's aim all through the long darkness and desolation of these sad years. She did not, however, attempt to exhort others to the practice of any one virtue with which she had not previously made herself familiar. On her return from Rome, and when the whole atmosphere of Upper Italy was aflame with the preparations for the impending war, the humble daughter of St. Francis, acting under the inspiration of that unearthly wisdom which is the sure guide of souls, began to increase not only her private austerities but her long and prayerful vigils. She said to the truly pious souls who were bound to her by friendship, and who looked up to her for counsel, what she was ever saying to herself,—that the divine wrath could only be turned away from sinful Italy, and the woes of the Church be ended, only by the blood and tears and incessant supplications of all the true children of God. Without ceasing any of her charitable labors for the sick and the poor of Brescia,—indeed, while increasing them,—she led, from the Autumn of 1525, a life of uninterrupted penitential rigor and continual pleading with the Divine Mercy. Still, although she constantly exhorted others to fast and pray for the peace of their common country, for the prosperity of the Church, and the relief of the Holy Father,—there were but very, very few of her most intimate acquaintances who were allowed to witness the extremity to which Angela carried her austerities and her perseverance in prayer.

We have only to recall how St. Teresa and St. John of the Cross made their lives one of continual and fearful self-crucifixion, while laboring to restore the pristine purity and fervor of the Carmelite Order in Christendom, as well as to atone to the Divine Justice for the decrease of practical faith in Spanish society, and the loss of holiness in Spanish homes.

We remember also how St. Rose,—the first flower of American saintliness,—and her near relative, Marianna de Paredes, "The Lily of Quito," atoned by a life of appalling rigor for the sensuality of their countrywomen and the wrongs inflicted by Christians on the South American native races. But there is another Spanish-American saint, whose example can enable us still better to grasp the purpose and the spirit of Angela Merici's self-inflicted punishment and unceasing intercession with the Divine Majesty during these years of Italy's agony and of the Church's humiliation. The Blessed Peter Claver,—the Apostle of Cartagena in New Grenada,—had chosen as his special task to evangelize the numerous slave population of that city and province. It was no easy task to make the hearts of the slave-owners and slave-merchants pitiful towards their wretched thralls, or to win a way to the darkened souls and angry hearts of the poor, deeply-wronged Negroes themselves. How then did the man of God,—the most glorious specimen of Christian manhood who ever lived on American soil,—fit himself to appease the Majesty of Heaven offended by such monstrous inhumanity, and to win grace with both masters and slaves?

His life was, during half a century, one of continual and gigantic labors, sanctified by prayer and self-crucifixion. When he returned in the evening or late at night from his fearful toil on board the slave-ships, in the slave-pens on shore, or in the leprosy hospitals, he would only taste of the coarsest food he could find, mixing even that with ashes and bitter herbs. Besides while preaching, catechising, baptizing his catechumens, tending the sick and the dying, and discharging the manifold duties of his priestly office in a populous seaport and amid such a mass of spiritual distress and bodily suffering,—he was covered literally from head to foot with hair-cloth studded with sharp iron points and nails. The historians of his life almost terrify the reader by the mere unexaggerated description of his nightly flagellations and protracted vigils. And all this in an equatorial climate!

We may think what we please,—but if we believe that He who is the dear Father of our souls, THE MAN OF SORROWS, came to atone for a sinful world, to save and sanctify mankind, and to be our model, we must feel that Claver and Xavier, and Ignatius Loyola, and Teresa, and Angela Merici only copied the examples set them by the Master. He was born in a stable, brought up in the carpenter's shop, had no home of His own while fulfilling His public mission, spent whole nights watching and praying on the hill-tops after the superhuman toils of the day, and was scourged, crowned with thorns, laden with His own cross, and crucified between two thieves! There is the only Light for man or woman who would labor actively and successfully in helping to raise, to save, to sanctify the world around them in their own day and generation, as well as afterward.

So, dear reader, if you hear that the holy Maid of Desenzano, after having received the blessing of Christ's Vicar on herself and her designs, returns to disturbed and still half-ruined Brescia, only to pray more fervently, to weep more abundantly, to afflict her own body more assiduously than ever before,—you must know that it is because she sees that the scourge is heavier than ever before on her beloved native land, on God's people, on His Vicar, and on the Church; and that new and fearful perils are threatening the souls for whom Christ died. When Herod-Agrippa imprisoned St. Peter, in the infancy of the Church, all those who believed in Christ ceased not by night and day to make intercession to God for the shepherd of the whole flock.

What was not Angela's affliction, when she learned that the savage German legions of Frundsperg and the unscrupulous Spaniards of Leyva were led against Rome by the Duke of Bourbon? And what was not the bitterness, worse than death, which filled her soul, those of her friends, and all true Italians, on hearing of the sack of Rome, and the outrages heaped on the Holy Father?

Her penitential austerities were increased to what seemed an excessive degree during the calamitous months which beheld the Pontiff a prisoner in the castle S. Angelo, his soul tortured by the spectacle of the sufferings he could neither prevent nor alleviate, and equally humbled at seeing the savage invaders abetted by an auxiliary Italian force, led into Rome by one of Rome's chief dignitaries, and by the hypocrisy of the Spanish monarch, who caused his court to go in mourning for the misfortunes of the Holy Father while imposing the most oppressive conditions for his ransom.

Can we wonder that while the civilized world stood amazed and shame-faced at learning of such barbarities perpetrated in the capital of Christendom, that all good Christians should have covered themselves with sack-cloth and ashes, weeping for the sins that deserved such punishment, and looking with fearful eyes into the dark and angry future?

Even then Angela's health began to be seriously threatened, and her friends began to remonstrate with her, and to urge her to moderate what they deemed to be unwise if not sinful excesses. In truth, however, it was Angela's heart which suffered most, not her body. Loving the Church of Christ, as she did, with a love scarcely to be distinguished in degree from that which consumed her for Christ Himself,—it was impossible that the indignities heaped upon Christ's Vicar, and the unparalleled atrocities inflicted on all classes in the Eternal City, should not crush a heart so tender, so true, so faithful as Angela's. She would not, nevertheless, allow any one to express for her own sufferings or health anything approaching to sympathy. More than ever she sought all opportunities to be helpful to those around her. And, in truth, Brescia, desolated, distressed, and threatened as she was, afforded ample scope to the good Sister's indefatigable zeal. Ever since her return from Palestine, she was sought after, not only by the poor and sick, but more particularly by persons of the upper classes who needed consolation in their sufferings, or light in their spiritual difficulties. Nobles and plebeians, priests and laymen flocked to her for counsel and guidance. For,—often as we have spoken of the charm of her modest and gracious presence, and of the exquisite tact with which she suited her conversation to the quality, disposition, and need of those who sought her,—we are bound to say, after a careful perusal of her biographers that we have not given the reader any adequate conception of the wide and powerful influence exercised by her personal intercourse,—by her words even as much as by her saintly examples. Further on we shall speak more at length of the reforms which that influence effected in the private and public manners of the Brescians;— we can mention even here that the spell which she exercised on men's minds and hearts was felt even by the great artists of Brescia and its neighborhood.[1]

---

[1] We know,—we all know,—how much such painters as Titian and Tintoretto, Venetians both of them, have been exalted by John Ruskin, and bepraised by the second and third-hand critics who admire and imitate Ruskin. There are, however, at least three painters of the Venetian school far more deserving of the admiration and respect of all true lovers of art than either of these two great artists,—for great they assuredly are in many respects. Of these three the two brothers Giovanni and Gentile Bellini,— we do not wish to say more here than that they were truly Christian artists, and are likely to grow in reputation as the enlightened knowledge of art increases. But they were born nearer to Venice than the third,—who is a native of Brescia, a contemporary of St. Angela, and who labored in his native city beneath her eyes, and feeling the full influence of her teaching and examples.

This is Alessandro Bonvicino,—called Il Moretto (1500-1547), who died in the very springtide of his fame, and while all men were looking up to him as the successor of the Bellinis, destined to outstrip them in the loftiest qualities of the Christian painter. " He has," says Kügler, " a style of his own. He adhered at first closely to Titian's manner, but afterwards adopted much of the Roman school, and by this means formed a mode of

One notable instance of the veneration in which she was held by the most exalted personages, and of the trust reposed in her extraordinary wisdom, relates to the last Duke of Milan, the ill-starred Francesco (Sforza) II. During the irresistible ascendency of the Spanish power in Upper Italy, from 1525 to 1530, the Duke of Milan, who had been induced to side against the Imperialists, was exiled from his states. In 1528 he found a temporary refuge in Brescia, which was then held by the Venetians; and, impelled by some trouble of conscience, he wished to consult Angela. From the convent of the Hermits of St. Barnabas, where he had taken up his abode, he sent a respectful message to her begging her to visit him. She had too sincere a respect for his misfortunes as well as for his high rank, to hesitate a moment. It became evident to Angela, from the very beginning of her interview, that she had been sought for, not through any motive of worldly curiosity, but through the far higher one of obtaining spiritual consolation and guidance. The prince spoke of the disasters which had fallen upon his people and himself, as of a chastisement merited by the ingratitude of both toward God's most liberal Providence and intimated the resolution to consult principally the religious welfare of his subjects, whenever it pleased that same Providence to restore him to his capital. Angela's modest and well-timed answer spoke of the great spiritual profit to be derived from suffering and adversity, of the sweet peace which resignation to the Divine Will and a loving accept-

---

representation distinguished for a simple dignity, and tranquil grace and stateliness, which occasionally developed itself in compositions of the very highest character. In such cases he evinces so much beauty and purity in his motives, and so much nobility and sentiment in his characters, that it is unaccountable how this master should, till within the last few years, have obtained little more than a local celebrity. . . . Moretto was distinguished by a childlike piety: when painting the Holy Virgin, he is said to have prepared himself by prayer and fasting."

ance of the ills which befall even the best, with such fervent and touching eloquence, that her listener was deeply moved. There is such a power in the words of a saint!

From the account given by F. Salvatori, one would be led to believe that Francesco had opened his whole soul to his venerable visitor, laying bare before her whatever troubled his conscience, and requesting her advice as to his future conduct. At any rate, "he besought her to become his spiritual adviser, and to be his own protectress and the intercessor for his afflicted people near the Divine Majesty. Angela was filled with confusion at this request, and protested that she was only a poor sinner who could have no power with the most holy God. But the unfortunate sovereign renewed his importunity with such manifest fervor, that the good Sister was perforce obliged to promise that she would exert in his favor and that of his subjects all the influence she might have with the court of Heaven. And leaving him somewhat consoled, she withdrew."[1]

Brescia itself soon became an insecure abode for its own inhabitants, as well as for refugees. It was too near the valley of the Etsch (Adige) and Stelvio pass, the great highway by which the German Emperor kept pouring his troops into Lombardy and Venetia. The remnants of Frundsperg's sacrilegious bands had returned to their native country with spoils so rich, that others were easily found to replace them on Italian battle-fields. The French monarch, on the other hand, was, at the very least, as unscrupulous as his imperial antagonist, and just as regardless of all the most sacred rights of their common religion. In the autumn and winter of 1528 all Upper Italy became filled with the armies of these two unchristian sovereigns,—armies all the more

---

[1] Salvatori, p. 38.

dreaded by the wretched populations of city and country alike, that the treasury of both King and Emperor were absolutely empty, and their soldiers were only kept steady in the service by the unrestrained liberty of pillage and rapine. Under these circumstances Angela had no choice but to take refuge in Cremona, whither she was urged to go in all haste by her dearest and best friends. Among these were Augustine Gallo and Hippolyta, his widowed sister, both belonging to the old Brescian nobility, both as distinguished for their piety as for their rank, and who looked up to Angela as to one who was the living temple of the Spirit of God. Both became also instrumental in forwarding the foundation of our Saint's intended society, as we shall see. So they now besought her to fly with them before the advancing Imperialists had reached the immediate neighborhood of Brescia. She could not resist either their entreaties or the reasons with which they supported them, and, in September, 1529, she set out with Augustine Gallo and his sister, Jerome Patengoli and his wife, and our old acquaintance Romani. She was, however, the guest of Augustine Gallo, during the whole time of her stay in Cremona, where they took up their lodging in the *contrada* or street of S. Vittore.

This was the culminating point in the life of Sister Angela. Slowly the fame of her holiness, her unbounded charity, and her supernatural wisdom had spread from Desenzano to Brescia and Venice, to Palestine and to Rome. Her name and the praise of all her gentle virtues and great qualities were on the lips of the laboring and suffering poor; they were still more so on those of the wealthy and noble, of the most learned and most exalted in the Church and State. Duke Francesco Sforza, while still amid his court in Milan, had learned to revere her name from the most influential personages in his own dominions. His brief intercourse with her in Brescia had produced on the exiled sovereign an impression which influenced his aims, his sentiments, the whole of his private and public conduct ever afterward. In Cremona, he was again to be brought into contact with the lowly daughter of St. Francis, and he was anxious not only to profit himself by this providential nearness to one of God's living saints, but to make every one of the nobles who had followed him thither become for Sister Angela a special object of interest.

So, while the furious conflict between the hostile armies of Francis I. and Charles V. grew hourly fiercer around the walls of the ancient Celtic city,[1] and men's souls despaired more and more deeply of ever seeing their native land freed from the baneful presence of the invader,—Angela was enabled to open a school of spirituality and practical holiness for the benefit of the crowd of noble exiles who had taken refuge there. Augustine Gallo, who was the daily and hourly witness of all her actions, has testified that from earliest morning till night, his door was continually beseiged by persons of every class, impelled by the needs of their own souls to seek the help of the retiring and ever-humble woman. The most eminent members of the regular and secular clergy were to be seen among those who consulted the unlearned and modest Tertiary on the matters relating to their own conscience, or on the most profound difficulties of Scripture and theology. Men who had been for many years the spiritual guides of others were known to treasure as practical rules of perfection,—precious beyond all price,—the simple advice

---

[1] Cremona,—like Brescia and Verona,—was founded by the Celtic tribes who were in possession of all Northern Italy long before Rome came into existence. In the year 219 before Christ, it was made a Roman colony, and thenceforward its name became conspicuous in all the wars and revolutions of which Italy was the theatre.

of this poor, timid, shrinking girl, in whose every word there seemed to burn and shine the heavenly fire of charity and the light of the Holy Spirit. From Milan itself, sorely beset as it was by foreign armies, and from every part of its territory, people soon came thronging in to see one whose whole life was the "Following of Christ" in practice, and whose very appearance was the most eloquent of sermons.

The amount of good effected in the souls and lives of men by Angela's brief sojourn in Cremona was incredible. Sinners could not approach one so pure, so self-sacrificing, so far above the pride, the sensuality, the manifold self-seeking of the worldly crowd, without being touched by the light which revealed the hideousness of their own conduct while it showed so evidently the beauty of holiness. Good men were impelled to be better. Even the most generously devoted to the divine service, felt, as they looked upon her pale and radiant features and listened to her glowing words,—that they must strive to attain to that supreme degree of generosity, which refuses nothing that the Crucified demands, and is only satisfied in resembling Him in the extremity of His self-abasement.

It was one of God's greatest mercies to Italy, in that dreadful age of violence, lawlessness, and sacrilege,—that such souls as Angela were placed on high before the eyes of the warring, distracted, and despairing multitudes, to force men to see that God had not yet forsaken a guilty land, and that the blessed tree of Religion,—sadly scarred and shattered as trunk and branches were by the terrific storms which prevailed,—still bore the loveliest blossoms and the most perfect fruits of holiness.

Even in the year 1529 Cremona was overflowing with the rich intellectual life which the church had been sedulously fostering for so many ages. A whole school of illustrious painters,—for instance,—natives, all of them, of the city itself, were covering the forty-five churches of Cremona, as well as her monasteries, her palaces and municipal edifices, with paintings which are the admiration of artists in our own day.[1] We have no authentic record of the influence which Angela may have exercised on the minds and lives of these great Christian artists. But the traveler who in our times, after admiring the works of Il Moretto in Brescia, passes on to Cremona and pauses in wonder before its wealth of paintings, cannot help tracing to the same source the influences which guided the hands and inspired the souls of the contemporary painters of both cities. So Religion is ever the parent of holiness, just as holiness is the creator of all that is beautiful in life.

And what would have become of that land of Italy, so privileged in its natural and supernatural aspect,—amid the inevitable ruin and decay consequent upon a half-century of incessant warfare and the manifold disorders that war begets inside and outside every Christian home,—even the home of the cloister? What fate must befall us here, in this New World, in a land where we are free to create all that is best in private or public life and the institutions which express that

---

[1] The three brothers Giulio, Antonio, and Vincenzio Campi were natives of Cremona, as well as their cousin Bernardino. They, together with two other native artists, Boccaccio Boccaccino and Camillo Boccaccino, were contemporaries, laboring with a generous rivalry to make the city as beautiful as Milan, or Mantua, or Verona. The celebrated Bishop-Poet, Mario Girolamo Vida, was prior of the monastery of Canons of St. John Lateran near the church of St. Margherita, while Giulio Campi was painting there. So, sheltered beneath the wings of Religion, the Arts labored unceasingly to create masterpieces, while war in all its horrors was desolating the land. This was that same age when

"A Raphael painted, and a Vida sung:
Immortal Vida, on whose honored brow
The poet's bays and critic's ivy grow:
Cremona now shall ever boast thy name
As next in place to Mantua, next in fame."—*Pope.*

life, had we not in our midst holiness in the cloister and holiness at the family hearth,—keeping ever before the minds of young and old the highest models of moral heroism, while freedom all around us seems to become only the liberty to degenerate and degrade?

Holy souls, living in the silence and obscurity of their homes, —so often the poorest homes!—or amid the glare of public station,—are the germ-centres of that true life with which the All-wise God renovates the face of the earth after its longest wintry periods of desolation and seeming death. This thought consoles the Christian heart in the deep gloom which has settled in this nineteenth century over the face of long-tried Italy,—over France also, and over Spain, the once fertile nursery of saints and heroes.

The year 1529 was one of the saddest years which had ever dawned upon Italy. The straits to which the Holy See was reduced in its vain efforts to turn away the tide of devastating war from the Peninsula, and to bring about peace between the two great rival sovereigns,—were most deplorable. As we have already said, Angela, now in her fifty-fifth year, believed herself bound, in common with all good Christians, to appease the divine anger by fervent prayers and penitential austerities. Before leaving Brescia she had been most urgent in persuading her friends and acquaintances to join her in thus pleading with the Divine Majesty for the afflicted Church, and had increased to an extreme degree her long fasts and other self-chastisements. On her arrival in Cremona there was a visible alteration in her health. She did not, however, seem to heed it or even to be conscious of it, so great was her desire to enlist all who came to her in this union of prayers for the peace of Christendom, and so intense her zeal in promoting on every occasion purity and holiness of life in all who sought her intercourse. Her wasted frame seemed to be consumed by the interior fire of love for God and for all His best interests.

At length, while all Cremona was loudest in her praise, and all classes of its citizens were under the spell of her eloquence and examples, her strength gave way altogether, and she was brought to death's door. The progress of the fever was so rapid, that the physicians pronounced her case hopeless. Jerome Patengoli, her oldest friend among those who now were most devoted to her, took on himself to apprize her of her danger. She was prepared for it. Her poor opinion of her own worth and ability caused her to think that she was not a fit instrument for the work appointed to be done in Brescia. At the same time, the prospect of approaching death and of a speedy union with Him who was her sole absorbing love, filled her with unspeakable joy.

The sick-room presented a most touching scene. Augustine Gallo and his sister, Patengoli and his wife, Antonio dei Romani, the generous follower and guardian of Angela in her travels and charitable labors, together with the *élite* of the Cremona and Milanese nobility, flocked in alarm about what they considered to be the death-bed of the saint. She could not bear to see their tears or to listen to their regrets. Sitting upright on her poor couch, her face all radiant with an unearthly light, and her tongue touched with a seraphic fire, she discoursed to her assembled friends on the bliss of that eternal life into which she was about to enter. As if she already stood beneath the portals of the Everlasting City on high, and beheld all its glory with unveiled eyes, she described its citizens and its joys with a such a rapt eloquence, that all who heard her,—as they afterwards solemnly testified,—were carried beyond themselves with wonder and delight. It seemed to them that they were listening to one of the Seraphim sent to entertain them on the incomparable felicity of the Eternal Home.[1]

This extraordinary effort and the ecstatic joy with which the sufferer's soul overflowed, brought the fever to a crisis. No sooner had she done speaking than a change for the better was perceptible. Indeed,—so Father Salvatori remarks,—from that moment she appears to have been perfectly cured. If this sudden change added greatly to the joy and astonishment of her friends, it was to Angela herself only a subject of deep regret. She too had wished with St. Paul to be released from the body and at rest with Christ. She had already entered into the shadow of that ineffable and everlasting peace. And now she must again take up the burden of this life's cares! To her friend Patengoli, who seems to have withdrawn from the sick-room after discharging his painful message, she said, when he returned, that he surely meant to amuse himself in telling her she was going to die. But he called the physicians to support his assertion. And so Angela had nothing for it, but to resign herself, declaring that this new lease of life was given her in punishment for her sins.

All this had occurred during the autumn of 1529. Meanwhile, to all human forecast, the dreadful condition of Italian affairs was daily growing worse and worse, without, apparently, any hope of a cessation of these intolerable evils. Angela's sudden and almost miraculous recovery happened at the moment when Charles V. was in Piacenza concentrating the entire available resources of his army and his diplomacy in a final effort to crush the French power in Italy and to deal the Italian allies of Francis I.,—the Pope among them,—a blow so terrible, that they must accept the imperial domination as the inevitable decree of fate.

---

[1] Salvatori, p. 40.

Terror and despair seemed to possess even the most stout-hearted. Angela deemed this the proper time to exhort all those around her to assail the Divine Mercy by solemn supplications and pilgrimages to the most revered sanctuaries of Upper Italy. Among these was the Sacred Hill, near Varallo, in the province of Novara, and not far from the beautiful lake of Orta. Fifty chapels stationed at intervals along the hillside, and filled with life-like groups of statuary and fresco-paintings, represented the principal events in the life of our Saviour, especially the sufferings of His most bitter Passion. To all who visited this place the Sovereign Pontiffs had granted the same spiritual benefits attached to the pilgrimage of Jerusalem,—an inestimable benefit to the surrounding populations, who loved to throng to the hallowed spot, and learn as from the most eloquent pages of an ever-open book which all could read and understand,— the divine lessons taught by the Eternal Love incarnate.

Our old acquaintance Antonio dei Romani became also on this occasion the guide of Angela and her fellow-pilgrims. Passing by Crema and Lodi, they stopped at Loncino to visit the holy Dominican Nun, the Blessed Stefana dei Quinzani, who governed the monastery of St. Paul, which she had founded in that city. Angela had seen this saintly woman more than once; but she was at the present time, more than ever desirous to consult her, not only about her own spiritual advancement, but about the first practical steps to be taken toward establishing her contemplated society. What advice Angela received from her holy friend, has not been put on record. But in Varallo our saint appeared to enjoy over again the bitter sweet ecstacies of her visit to the holy places of Palestine. As if she was treading for a second time on the soil made sacred by the blood of the Redeemer, and assisting at the consummation of His labor of love on Calvary, she poured forth her whole soul in tears and ardent supplications, beseeching Him to give at length peace to Italy and to His Church. Her companions emulated her piety and patriotism, moved most powerfully by her example as well as by the eloquence of the place.

There is every reason to believe that our Lord was pleased to make known to His faithful handmaid that He had heard her prayers. For she went away from Varallo with a radiant countenance, a more buoyant step, and a more cheerful manner,—telling her companions and all who met her to rejoice,—that the Divine Goodness would soon give peace and rest to Italy.

And so it befell; for ere the winter had begun, there came glad rumors of a suspension of hostilities. And then all heard that Margaret of Austria and the mother of the French King had taken it on themselves to plead with their royal kinsfolk the cause of humanity and Christendom, and had concluded a treaty of pacification.

So Angela could go back to Cremona with a lighter heart, and pulses that beat more joyously. Brescia could now receive her in security, and allow her to consummate what had been the purpose of her entire existence.

CHAPTER XI.

THE FOUNDATIONS LAID AT LAST.

THE peace which Clement VII. accepted with all its intolerable conditions, meant only servitude for all Italy as well as servitude for the Church. It was imposed by dire necessity, and made all the more bitter and humiliating to the Pontiff and to every true Italian, that Charles V. insisted on receiving, in the first months of 1530, the imperial crown from the hands of Clement himself. It required a superhuman degree of magnanimity to comply with the demand of the pitiless and conscienceless autocrat. But, for the first time since the Papacy had created the glorious unity of Western Christendom, a freak of ill-fortune had made a King of Spain the lord paramount of continental Europe, while not one single sovereign was able or willing to oppose the arbitrary will of him who claimed the crown of Charlemagne only to undo the work of that heroic and most Christian ruler.[1]

While Clement VII., therefore, was preparing, in the bitterness of his soul, to crown the dark and hypocritical conqueror in Bologna, Angela Merici and her friends returned to

---

[1] It is but a very small consolation to the reader of history to learn that Charles V. ended his life in the same melancholy madness which had fallen on his mother, Joanna. The fits of remorse and wild asceticism which characterized his conduct in the monastery of St. Justo, may well have been prompted by the remembrance of such sacrileges as the sack of Rome.

Brescia, grateful that even a short breathing space was given to their grievously oppressed and long suffering country.

During her late stay in Brescia, she had been the guest of Antonio dei Romani, alternately perhaps, with Augustine Gallo. Now that she was resolved to give effect to her purpose of founding a religious society, she desired to have some little dwelling-house of her own, no matter how poor, in which she might be free to live with one or more companions, and to receive the visits of all who might have recourse to her for instruction and guidance. So, after yielding to the earnest entreaties of Gallo and his sister, and enjoying their hospitality for a short time, she made her abode in a poor house near the church of St. Barnabas.

She felt impelled by an interior voice to begin without delay to find companions for her great work. But the diffidence and fears begotten of her extreme humility made her still hesitate. She was unwilling to believe that one so weak and unworthy in every way as she deemed herself to be, could have been selected by the Divine Majesty for an undertaking of such importance. And so her dread of being a prey to some delusion, or of yielding to some hidden motive of pride and presumption, filled her with agony, whenever the thought of creating a congregation of religious women came before her in a practical shape.

Now it so happened, that while she had been deliberating whether she should go to Cremona with her friends and protectors, or stay in Brescia during the advance of the Imperialist forces, she had a dream which made a deep impression on her.

She beheld in her sleep the holy Virgin-Martyr of Cologne, St. Ursula, who exhorted her to begin at once to establish the society foreshown to her in Desenzano, and reproved her for her unwarrantable delays. This, as it would appear, was not the first time that St. Ursula had appeared to her, as we shall see further on And yet, though everything was in the most frightful state of commotion in Upper Italy during the summer and autumn of 1529, and though Angela did but yield to the counsels and solicitations of her wisest and best friends in forsaking Brescia for a time,—it afterward appeared evident that she might have safely remained in the threatened city, and begun at once the labor of laying the foundations of her long-meditated edifice. For it is now known that the first steps toward a reconciliation between the Pope and the Emperor took place during the month of June, while the treaty of peace between Charles and Francis was agreed upon almost at the time Angela was on her way to Cremona. To be sure, it was not to the advantage of either the French or the Imperialist commanders that the tidings of such peace or conciliation should be spread abroad. Neither generals nor soldiers had been paid for a long time, and they were allowed to pay themselves by plundering, each in their turn, the unfortunate Italians; and so, the armies continued, if not to fight, at least to pillage and devastate, for months after their respective sovereigns had made peace.

If, therefore, Angela might have shown more heroic faith in Providence, by heeding the words of warning and exhortation sent to her in this dream or vision, she on the other hand, would feel justified in listening to the counsels of those who bade her to fly from Brescia, and bide a more peaceful and propitious season for the beginning she contemplated.

Be that as it may, certain it is, that as soon as she had taken up her abode near the Church of St. Barnabas, she deemed it prudent to lay her intention before F. Serafino da Bologna, a member of the Augustinian Congregation,

Canons Regular of St. John Lateran,[1] who were at that time attached to the Venerable Church of S. Afra in that city. Father Serafino was himself a man not only of great learning and piety, but one of excessive prudence. For, knowing Angela, as he did, he thought it wise to submit one of her ripe age, judgment, and experience, to a long course of trials and delays. He bade her increase her fervent prayers, her vigils, and austerities, in order to obtain greater light from on high, and then, satisfied that his saintly penitent was not laboring under any spiritual illusion, he exhorted her to go on with what, he doubted not, was the work of God.

Her long sojourn in Brescia had made Angela thoroughly acquainted with all the persons of her own sex throughout the city. She had watched the growth, from childhood to womanhood, of most of its maidens, and had been instrumental in forming to all the practices of Christian life the souls of very many of them,—perhaps of most of them. They

---

[1] The establishment at St. John Lateran in Rome, of a body of priests living in community under the Rule of St. Augustine, took place, according to Cæsar Franciotti, under Pope St. Leo the Great, between the years 440 and 457. But Panvinio, in his history of the Lateran Basilica, says that this establishment was made in 495 by Pope St. Gelasius, who was himself a disciple of St. Augustine. These were the first " Canons Regular of St. John Lateran." A branch establishment bearing the same title was made about the same time in Lucca, by St Frigidian, the first bishop and apostle of that city, an Irishman, sent thither by the same Pope. The Roman establishment was broken up by Pope Boniface VIII. (1294-1303) after eight centuries of existence, and a body of secular priests placed in the monastery and at the head of the world-famed school of St. John Lateran. They too bore the title of their predecessors without claiming to follow the Rule of St. Augustine. The expelled monks, however, did not give up their rule, or their name, or their mode of living. For we find their successors and brethren living not only in Lucca but in Brescia during the 15th and 16th centuries. Pope Sixtus IV. (1471-1484), decreed that the monks bearing the title of " Canons Regular of St. John Lateran," although dispossessed of their monastery and church in Rome, should retain their ancient denomination and form one of the same congregation or order. They take precedence of all other Regular Orders. It is a house of this same Congregation that St. Angela found in Brescia, and to which F. Serafino da Bologna belonged.

all looked up to her as their model and guide in all that pertained to true womanly virtue. So,—when the proper time came, she could choose knowingly from among the very flower of the flock.

History has preserved the name of the first twelve maiden associates of Angela Merici;— they are: Simona Borni, Catherine and Dominica Dolce, sisters, Dorosilla Zinelli, Pellegrina Casali, Clara Gaffuri, Paula and Laura Peschieri, also sisters, Barbara Fontana, Clara Martinengo, Margaret dell'Olmo, and Maria Bartolletti.

Of these, Barbara Fontana became Angela's inseparable companion, sharing thenceforward with the latter, all the poverty and privations of what they called their home,— the scanty portion of fare begged from door to door and not doled out to the poor of Christ, the cold hearth on which a fire never glowed, the hard bench, on which they both sat by day reading to each other some holy book during the intervals of their long prayers, and on which, sitting upright with their backs to the wall, they allowed exhausted nature to snatch the only brief needful repose which they ever enjoyed,—and, with these exercises of prayer and praise, the rapturous fervor of spirit known only to those who take up their cross and follow Christ, and the overflowing consolations of His sweetness who is never outdone in generosity.

The remaining eleven continued to live with their parents, aiding these in the performance of their household duties, edifying all who beheld them by their active but unobtrusive piety. Two things distinguished every member of the little band; like their model and guide, Sister Angela, they made open profession of that virginal life, which Christ and His Mother had first honored, and which had ever after them continued to be in the Church the source of so many divine virtues and such fruitful self-sacrifice; and, besides, they sought every opportunity to teach and train the young, and to minister to the suffering and the needy.

Angela associated them to all her own devotional exercises, carefully forming their conscience, grounding them thoroughly in the principles and practice of that high spirituality which was the distinctive feature of her own character. Training them to emulate her own extreme poverty and self-crucifixion, she made them understand that bodily austerity and the most exalted purity of soul only prepared the Christian to approach the Divine Majesty in oral or mental prayer, while mental prayer itself was the furnace in which the soul was inflamed with supernatural charity toward God and the neighbor.

Self-denial and self-sacrifice, while seeking in all things the honor of that Adorable Majesty and His best interests in the education of youth and the salvation of souls,—such was the grand aim which she set before them, and which she pursued herself with a heroic single-mindedness beyond all praise. She was herself distinguished by a singular tact and a surety of judgment, ripened into preternatural wisdom by her constant intercourse with God, and the purity of purpose that guided her in all her actions. She prized exceedingly in those who sought to become her associates, these same sterling qualities of uprightness of purpose, excellence of judgment, natural sagacity and tact in dealing with others. She had no patience with pious fools. Her companions were destined to be apostles, who were to learn to make themselves all things to all men in order to win all souls to the divine service. This required practical wisdom and a sure judgment, the magnaminity which no trial and difficulty could appal, and that humility which leaves self in the hands of God as a passive and docile instrument for every one of His uses.

It was this absolute forgetfulness of self, united to a wonderful appreciation of the needs of the world around them, that earned for Sister Angela and her early associates the sweet name by which they were at first popularly known in Upper Italy,—"the Humble or Little Sisters," *Demisse.*

No sooner, therefore, had Angela made proof of the solid virtue and generous self-sacrificing humility of these her twelve apostles, than she resolved to go with them on a pilgrimage to the Holy Hill of Varallo, where she had received so much light and consolation in the autumn of 1529. It was now August, 1532; and as she could not lead her band of devoted maidens to Jerusalem, to make together their act of consecration to the Crucified on the very spot hallowed by His blood, she felt that the next best thing to do was to offer themselves to Him at Varallo, where the Christian heart of Italy had peopled the mountain side and summit with the most life-like representations of Christ's infinite love.

In this second visit to Varallo, Angela had also for her fellow-travellers and protectors her dear friends Augustine and Hippolyta Gallo. These noble personages looked upon Angela's religious family as their own, encouraging and fostering its timid beginnings by their devotion and generosity. In truth all that was noblest and best in Brescia shared the sentiments of Gallo and his sister toward the infant society. The pilgrims, who had found the chapels on the Holy Hill in an incomplete or ruinous condition three years before, were now delighted to see them repaired and completed. With so much ardor did the people and the artists who shared and interpreted their lively faith vie with each other in bringing to perfection one of the most glorious creations of Christian art!

Angela, remembering Jerusalem and Bethlehem the while, and knowing well that but few hours were left her of daylight to rear from its foundations the spiritual edifice, which was to be her life-work, besought the Divine Goodness with renewed fervor to grant herself an increase of light and energy with an increase in all holiness, and to shed on her companions the fulness of His Spirit.

From Varallo the little band went to Milan to venerate the relics of our Lord's passion so carefully treasured there. There again Angela was honored by a visit from the Duke, Francis II. He had asked her, while an exile and a fugitive, to act as a parent toward him, to counsel and direct him in all that pertained to his conscience. The unhappy prince appeared to have followed scrupulously, so far as the tyrannical force of adverse circumstances would permit him, the advice of the holy woman. He showed himself during the few remaining years of his life, a father to his people and an exemplary Christian in his private conduct. He thereby endeavored to repair the oppressive measures which had made the beginning of his reign so odious. Nor was the Duke satisfied with visiting Angela at her lowly lodgings in the city; he made all his courtiers pay her every possible mark of respect. Indeed all Milan was moved by the presence of the Saint; and as it had happened to her in Venice, on her arrival from the Holy Land, so now in the capital of Lombardy,—the Duke, the nobility, and the burgesses besieged her with prayers to fix her abode in their midst.

To their entreaties she replied with a gentle but firm decision that she owed to God and to the generous citizens of Brescia to spend the remainder of her life in that city. The Milanese, however, as we shall see, were to be rewarded in God's own time by the possession of one of the most blessed colonies of Angela Merici's daughters,—and to no one more than to St. Charles Borromeo, Milan's glorious archbishop, was the whole Order founded by the Maid of Desenzano more deeply indebted for its prosperity.

No sooner had Sister Angela and her companions returned to Brescia, than the former found it necessary to change her place of abode. She wished to be near the Church of St. Afra, both because it was under the direction of the edifying Canons of St. John Lateran, of which body her spiritual guide, Father Serafino da Bologna, was a member, but because the church itself was a treasure-house filled with the relics of the glorious Christian martyrs of Brescia.[1] Besides, the church of St. Afra was central, and therefore of easy access to Angela's companions, while St. Barnabas was situated near the walls in an out of the way place. Then again the Canons of St. Afra, who celebrated the divine offices with uncommon regularity and splendor, pressed upon Angela's acceptance an apartment quite near the church, thus affording her every facility for gratifying her ardent piety toward the Most Holy Sacrament, as well as her devotion to Brescia's glorious martyrs. Indeed one of Angela's most distinguished followers in modern Italy[2] declares that there was a special providence in this change of abode, inasmuch as the Saint's spiritual children could only reach their mother, in her new resting-place at St. Afra, by passing over a soil impregnated

---

[1] The church of this name which existed in the time of St. Angela, was one of the most ancient in Brescia. It was rebuilt about 1600 without gaining thereby in architectural beauty The old church had been erected on the site of a temple of Saturn, and was known at first as the Church of St. Faustinus *ad Sanguinem*, because, as Salvatori remarks, there St. Faustinus (together with his companion, St. Jovita) and a host of other glorious witnesses, poured forth their blood during the early persecutions. It was also called the "Cemetery of St. Latinus," probably because this saint, the fourth bishop of Brescia, caused the remains of all these holy martyrs to be collected together and entombed there, and chose the place also as that of his own burial. The restored Church of St. Afra, as it is at present, in spite of its architectural blemishes, contains remarkable works of art,—frescoes by Girolamo Rossi, a native of the city, and paintings by the younger Palma, Bassano, Tintoretto, Titian, and Paul Veronese.

[2] The Countess E. Girelli, *Vita di S. Angela Merici, Vergine Bresciana, e del suo santo instituto*, Brescia, 1571. This lady has devoted her life to the establishment of uncloistered Ursuline Communities according to the primitive plan of St. Angela and her immediate companions.

with the blood of martyrs. The very atmosphere of the place inspired with the desire of self-immolation these generous maidens, who were contemplating a manner of life that was in itself a perpetual martyrdom.

Even in our own days, in spite of the anti-christian spirit from which Brescia and its territory have been influenced not a little, this poor room in which Angela dwelt till her death with Barbara Fontana, is a holy spot to which pilgrims from far and near are ever wont to resort. On the place where the Saint breathed her last stands a little altar. There, on the 27th of January, every year, the Holy Sacrifice is offered up; and there, too, the veneration of the people jealously preserves and points out to the stranger-pilgrim the poor wooden benches used by Angela and her band of female apostles. On the walls are a few mediocre paintings which recall the principal actions of her life. But to the eye and heart of one who prizes true heroism for what it is worth, such a spot needs no ornament. Everything there is eloquent of the loftiest aims and the noblest deeds. The sweet odor of Christ clings to the room and its poor furniture, and a secret virtue goes forth from every object, lifting the Christian man or woman who kneels there above earth and its aspirations to God and the things of God.[1]

---

[1] The room itself is about ten feet broad, twenty-five feet long, and thirty-eight feet high. On a tablet in the wall is an inscription of which the following is a translation:
"*In this poor apartment lived and died the illustrious Virgin, Angela Merici. From this place she was wont to send up toward heaven the heart-cries of her ardent charity. Hither were wont to come, to this woman unacquainted with worldly learning, as to a school of heavenly doctrine, the theologians condemned to live in an age when error flooded the land. Here, Angela calling together pious maidens of her own country, built up that holy society which flourishes more gloriously than ever after three centuries of existence, and extends throughout the Church and civil society the blessings of its labors.*"

The Ursuline Convent of Brescia, situated at a short distance from the Church of St. Afra, was suppressed by a decree of the Piedmontese government in 1866. The nuns, however, manage to live on,—a precarious life full of dangers,—within the walls of their monastery, like the flowering shrubs of their native hills beneath the deep snow and bitter cold of winter. The springtide will come for them yet!

Meanwhile Sister Angela's throng of disciples went on increasing. Her narrow room could no longer accommodate them. For there it was she had to instruct them and to perform in common with them those sweet exercises of piety which are the very soul of daily Religious life. The necessity of their uniting together in these acts so essential to the spirit of fervor, was all the more imperious in their case, that they had to live during the remainder of the time separate in their respective homes. They came to the reunions held by Angela, like famished laborers to the common meal, bearing with them in the spiritual refection there received, the strength needful to sustain them amid their arduous duties in the great outside world. Angela's room at St. Afra was like the upper chamber in the house of Mary, the sister of St. Barnabas, and the mother of John Mark, after the ascension of our Lord. There the Apostles and disciples met to celebrate the divine Sacrifice, and to fill up their hearts with that heroic charity which was to inflame and to change the world. This was the centre from which apostolic zeal spread like a conflagration all over Palestine and Syria, kindling in men's souls the love of God and that of the brotherhood, as it swept round the shores of the Mediterranean, till it enveloped the whole of the Roman Empire in its course.

From Angela's cold and narrow room beside St. Afra's, every soul among these pious maidens issued all aflame with the desire to make God known and to have Him served more faithfully by all whom she met with in her own home or in the outside world. Indeed each one of them was like a piece of molten metal from the furnace, placed beneath the paternal roof to enlighten and warm to all generous deeds every person who came in contact with her. How could the little band of Twelve, being what they were, and formed by so admirable a mistress, not increase daily? Even so, it soon became imperative on Angela to find some larger place, which she might transform into a community-room and an oratory for her growing flock.

At this juncture Providence threw in her way a noble widow lady, Elizabeth Prato by name, who gave up to the new Sisterhood a hall in one of her houses, situated on the Cathedral Square (*Plaza del Duomo*).[1] Thenceforward

---

[1] This Oratory in the house of Elizabeth Prato has always been revered by the Ursulines as the cradle of their Order. In course of time, it changed proprietors, and was sadly neglected. In 1621 it was restored by the then master of the house, John Baptist Bianchi, and in 1672, the Italian traveller, Lombardi, visited and described it. There was, above the altar, a wall-painting of the Crucifixion, the Blessed Virgin and St. John standing beneath the cross, with two female saints,—probably St. Mary Magdalene and St. Mary Salome. The interior, just above the entrance door, was also adorned with three other frescoes bearing the date of December the 11th, 1533 On the side walls was represented St. Ursula, bearing a palm-branch, the Assumption of the B. V., St. Afra, dressed in the primitive habit of the Ursulines, exposed to the wild beasts in the Amphitheatre and miraculously spared by these; St. Elizabeth of Hungary, habited like a Tertiary of St. Francis, surrounded by a number of young girls all in the Ursuline dress, some of them are occupied in preparing materials for the loom, while others are seated at table and served by St. Elizabeth. St. Paula and her daughter, St. Eustochium were painted as on the point of being shipwrecked. The Brescian martyr-brothers, St. Faustinus, a priest, and St. Jovita, a deacon, being special favorites of St. Angela, occupied another space on the walls. Above the door, on the outside of the Oratory, St. Angela herself was represented with the following inscription:

BEATA ANGELA MERICI,
BRIXIANARUM VIRGINUM SPECULUM IMMACULATUM,
HUIC PRIMUM SACRAS VIRGINES SÆCULARES
DIVINO INSTINCTU
SAPIENTISSIME INSTITUIT,
PROPRIÆQUE VIRTUTIS FULGENTISSIMIS RADIIS,
HEIC SÆPISSIME COMMORANDO,
ILLUSTRAVIT.
CONRUEBAT INJURIA TEMPORUM ET HOMINUM
HÆC SACRA ÆDICULA,
AT JO. BAPTISTO BLANCUS TANTO NOMINI DE VINCTUS,
EXSTAURAVIT.
MDCXX.

Blessed Angela Merici,
Of Brescian maidens the spotless mirror,

the little society began to assume a consistent shape. Although Angela's chief care seemed to be bestowed on the selection and training of young girls, who, free from the ties of earthly love, and unencumbered with the formed habits of a more advanced age, could give themselves wholly to the apostleship of education and charity,—there was another class of pious women whom the Foundress labored to attach to her order,—noble widows of spotless fame and known influence. These were to be, in the beginning, the moderating and protecting force in the Order. For an aggregation of young women bound together, principally, by the pursuit of a common purpose, and living in their own families surrounded by the ordinary seductions and distractions of the world, there was need of the eye, the hand, and the heart of motherly ladies whose virtues made them models and safe guides, and whose ripe experience and worldly rank gave them undisputed authority.

In truth, when we consider attentively not only the aim which Angela Merici had set to herself, but the means by which she endeavored to reach it,—we are compelled to ask

---

Here first impelled by Divine grace,
Trained and founded, with consummate wisdom,
A body of consecrated maidens destined to live in the world.
And while tarrying here frequently with them,
She enlightened them
With the resplendent rays of her own virtue.
This little Oratory,
Fallen into decay by the effect of time and neglect of men,
Was entirely restored
By John Baptist Bianchi, the devoted servant of so great
A saint.

After the year 1672, the Oratory thus restored by the enlightened piety of Bianchi, fell into less pious hands, and became an ordinary apartment, applied to secular and household purposes. The wall-paintings disappeared one by one, the fresco of the Crucifixion having alone been spared. Even this disappeared about 1732, while the room was tenanted by a woman named Semenzi, who had the whole place white-washed,—the workmen, contrary to her instructions, bedaubing with lime the remaining fresco.

ourselves whether the circumstances of Italian religious and social life were not such as to render an organization like that which she set on foot most timely and most needful? From the mode of living pursued by Cajetan of Tiene and the early Theatines, by St. Philip Neri and his Oratorians, as well as by Angela Merici and her companions, one might conclude that Italy was in a fearfully disorganized condition, that together with the disorders begotten of a whole century of incessant warfare, there were other perverting influences actively at work, in Italian homes and Italian society,—finding their way to the minds and hearts of all classes, unsettling in souls the faith which had been the guide and consolation of preceding centuries,—and disposing the men and women of the 16th to rebel against God, against His Church, and against all that had till then been held as a venerable authority in Christendom.

Indeed, about this same date, 1533-34, the revolt headed by Martin Luther had not only separated England from the Holy See, arrayed the peoples and princes of Germany in two hostile camps, filled with bloodshed and anarchy some of the fairest portions of that country, but made of Switzerland and France houses divided against themselves, and created in Upper and Central Italy many bitter elements of religious and political dissension. The most glorious institutions of the ages of Italian freedom, and overflowing prosperity,—the monastic orders and their creations,—were denounced as the work of Satan and the bane of Christendom. That Virginal Life, which since the days of Christ and His Mother, had been so devoted to the best interests of God on earth,—the spiritual welfare and temporal comfort of the people,—and so marvellously fruitful in creations of holiness, beauty, enlightenment, and education,—was held up by unblushing apostate monks and shameless priests as contrary to the law of God and of nature.

It became the wise providence of Him, who is ever watchful over His Church and her children, to call holy men and women to live the life of the most austere ascetics in the midst of the world, to raise up in the midst of cities and in the bosom of families, maidens consecrated to God, and wedded to all the sublime charities of the most fervent monastic orders. Have you, dear reader, ever remarked the wonderful art with which Nature repairs the disasters, and heals the wounds of the tree or the plant, and instinctively arms it with a sure defence against the sudden and unforeseen changes of weather and temperature? Here is one of those favorite flowers called hyacinths. Just as it was about to blossom, an accident injured the flower spike, so that it bent over and threatened to break. Just then one of the spear-like leaves turned away from its straight upward position to support, as with a parent's arm, the drooping spike and its opening flowerets. And so it continued to support it, till the vital sap had repaired the injury and restored the needed strength. But no sooner was the spike able to resume and maintain, unaided, its erect position, than the friendly leaflet withdrew and returned to its previous upright form.

We know when the bark has been torn from a portion of the tree-trunk, how all the currents of the vital sap hasten to flow to the wound and deposit the necessary fibrin, rapidly covering over the raw wound, and forming a new coating of bark to protect the injured part from the inclemency of the atmosphere or the inroads of hurtful insects. Is it not even so that Nature's hidden virtue heals the wounds in the human frame? But in that supernatural organism called the Church, the Mystic Body of Christ, informed as it ever is by the indwelling Creator Spirit, is there not a divine virtue which is ever at work to repair the decay of the human and perishable elements in the immortal frame? is there not a hidden current of overflowing vital energy which an infallible instinct directs toward the part which is wounded or weakened in the battle with the powers of darkness?

When the storm has torn from the lordly oak one of its branches, will not the tree hasten to put forth another, and on the same side, to enable the stately tree to maintain its proper balance and withstand the assaults of future tempests? How admirably are all those analogies verified in the life of Christ's Church during the eighteen centuries of her stormy existence!

Even so, in the Italy of the early sixteenth century, when the very existence of monastic life was imperilled, when the Virginal Life in the cloister or in the priesthood, or even as it had ever been honored in the Christian family-home, was declared to be contrary to the revealed will of God,—the Church spontaneously produced such aggregations of holy men and women as the Society of Jesus, as the Theatines and Oratorians, as the Ursulines in Venetia, and the reformed Carmelites of St. Teresa and St. John of the Cross in Spain. It was like armies of virginal souls preaching by the examples of their spotless and most useful lives, the necessity and the divinity of the institutions which rampant heresy assailed, just as when a conflagration has swept over the face of a country destroying wheat-fields, pastures, and forests in its course, the ever-present and all-sufficient energy of Nature hastens to cover up the black ruin with her beautiful vesture of green grass, and flowering shrub, and shooting sapling,— the new life budding and blossoming fast on the footprints of death!

We can, therefore, see, about the date of November, 1533,

Brescia, desolated by unparalleled calamities,[1] and still threatened alternately by the hostile armies of France and Spain, bestowing her chief care on making Religion flourish in her ruined churches and monasteries, in encouraging Angela Merici and her companions to make the most generous piety live once more in every home, and in placing the children of both sexes in the hands of such women as the early Ursulines, and such men as St. Jerome Emiliani and his associates.

Home-life, with its supernatural piety and virtues, with its Christian methods of education, and with the high and comforting hopes which a living faith inspires,—such was the pure source of a renewed national greatness that these devoted men and women aimed at creating or deepening in their native land. Brescia,—and the same can be said in a very great measure of the other cities of Upper Italy,—was at the time too poor and too uncertain of the future, to think of founding large and costly monastic establishments. And the spiritual straits were as distressing as the public and private poverty was great. The Spirit of God, who used such instruments as Angela Merici, Jerome Emiliani, and Cajetano de Tiene to renovate the face of the earth, impelled them to work in the homes of the needy populations, to raise the voice of teaching in the busiest marts of commerce, to display the shining examples of unearthly abnegation along the crowded thoroughfares,—so that every current of

---

[1] Before the destruction wrought by the French in 1512, Brescia, according to a contemporary historian, Robert de la Mark, " was one of the most powerful, of the best fortified, and of the most opulent cities (republics) in all Italy. Nine millions of francs in money were taken away from the hapless city by its French captors,—a sum which was immense for the time. Indeed, we are assured by another contemporary historian, a Frenchman also (*Historie composeé par le* LOYAL SERVITEUR *des faits, gestes, triomphes et, prouesses du bon Chevalier sans peur et sans reproche le gentil Seigneur de Bayard*), that the soldiers of Bayard and Gaston de Foy returned to France with such a rich booty that they abandoned the service, to live on their ill-gotten wealth.

the national life might be thus purified and hallowed by their influence.

In preceding ages, men and women who wished to save themselves from the evil examples of the half-pagan society amid which they were born, fled to the sandy desert or to the most inaccessible mountain-solitudes. At the beginning of the 16th century, the Divine Spirit led His apostles not into the wilderness, but into the very midst of the battle-field where good and evil were struggling for victory.

The citizens of Brescia felt how seasonable, how providential was the appearance in their midst,—in their homes, their schools, and their hospitals,—of a band of maidens formed on the angelic model of the Venerable Maid of Desenzano, and watched over and directed by matrons of the highest rank and the most unquestioned virtue. Clergy and people saw the hand of God in the beginnings of this Society.

Let us now see what induced Angela to bestow on it the name of St. Ursula; and what were the first grand lineaments of the organization.

CHAPTER XII.

WHY ANGELA CALLED HER SISTERHOOD "THE COMPANY OF ST. URSULA."

WHILE Angela and her twelve first companions are forming themselves to the practical duties of their calling by meditating together assiduously in the Oratory of Elizabeth Prato, on the life of Christ and His Virgin Mother,—it will not be amiss to examine what motives led the holy Foundress to bestow on the association created by her the denomination of "The company of St. Ursula."

The popular legends recounting the romantic life of this holy Virgin-Martyr and her companions, vary in many particulars, while agreeing in the main historical facts accepted by the Church and embodied in her liturgy and in the authorized record of the Roman Breviary. The traditions differing from each other in Germany and in Italy, do not affect these great substantial facts relating to the existence, the heroic virtues, and the glorious witness of the virgin band. "These traditions, with their sweet devotional perfume, are like the undergrowth of our southern forests, lovely and graceful plants that spring up beneath the shade of the great trees, and creep up their trunks, hanging their wreaths of bright foliage and brilliant flowers from every branch,—the most beautiful ornament of the forest, but not the forest itself. The heart and imagination of man, even in the most cultivated societies, will produce these flowers of fancy, and wreathe them around his holiest beliefs."[1]

The simple facts of this history are: That about the year 382, when Flavius Clemens Maximus, commander of the Roman armies in Great Britain, usurped the imperial title, and crossed over into Gaul, followed by an army of Celts from that island, he expelled from Armorica the original inhabitants, and divided the land among his British soldiers. Anxious to provide for these colonists wives of their own race, he obtained from Dionoc, prince of Cornwall, that the latter should give his daughter, Ursula, in marriage to Conan, the commander of the British soldiers in the imperial service, and send with her a sufficient number of other maidens to become the partners of the new lords of Armorica, thenceforward named Little Britain or Britanny. The vessels which contained the British princess and her maiden companions, were driven by a storm on the coast of Germany and up the Rhine. There the vessels were captured by the pagan inhabitants and brought to Cologne. The prize was a tempting one for the barbarians, who contended for their possession. Ursula, however, exhorted her companions to die rather than submit to the shameful lot which their heathen captors reserved for them. Their resistance caused the entire band to be massacred as well in hatred of the Christian faith as in the defence of their virginity. Their place of sepulture was shown at Cologne from the fifth century to the present day,—attesting that their number was considerable, without stating it precisely.

The heroic manner in which these stranger maidens defended their own honor against the assaults of the rude pagan soldiery, and their invincible courage in bearing witness to

---

[1] "Heroic Women of the Bible and the Church," ch. xxiv., p. 248.

the Christian faith, rendered their name forever famous among the Germanic populations,—especially after the conversion of the latter to Christianity. They became the ideal type of Christian maidenhood, the protectors of all who choose to lead in the world the Virginal Life, while Ursula, who was their leader and instructress, was everywhere looked up to as the patron saint of all who devoted themselves to the education of young girls.

The legends which became current about these martyrs of Cologne during the middle ages, related, moreover, that this virgin train ascended the Rhine to Basel, crossed the Alps by the Stelvio or the Brenner Pass, visited Venice, Verona, and the principal cities of Upper Italy, and after performing their pilgrimage to Rome returned by the same road to Germany. It is on their arrival at Cologne, that they are are made to fall into the hands of the Huns who massacre them.

Thus at a very early period, the fame of these British Virgin-Martyrs was as popular in Upper Italy as it was along the banks of the Rhine. The cities of the Venetian territory, especially, claimed them as the special patrons of maidenhood and of all institutions devoted to the training of youth. Hence it is that we find, in the year 1490, just when Angela Merici was in her sixteenth year,—the city of Venice founding an establishment for the education of female orphans, and bestowing on it the name of "the School of St. Ursula," (*Scuola di Sant Orsola*). Now it so happened that one of the most distinguished painters to whom the Great Republic gave birth, Victor Carpaccio, was called, at this same date, to decorate the chapel of this institution with subjects worthy of Christian Venice, and representing the history of St. Ursula. Alas, the school of St. Ursula has long ceased to be devoted to its original purpose, and, like so many other creations of the enlightened republican piety of the Queenly City, it has been allowed to fall into irreparable decay. Still, some at least of the master-pieces of Carpaccio have been preserved to posterity, and are now found in the great museum known as the Accademia.

If Angela, either on her passage through Venice in 1524, or during her stay in the city at any other period, had visited the school of St. Ursula, she might have seen Carpaccio's masterly works on the walls where he had painted them. The artist was, like the Brothers Bellini, inspired by a lively faith and a sincere piety which elevated and hallowed his genius. "The richness of fancy,"—says Mrs. Jameson,— "the lively dramatic feeling, the originality and naïveté with which the story is told, render this series one of the most interesting of early Venetian art. Zanetti says that he used to go to the chapel of St. Ursula and conceal himself, to observe the effects which those pictures produced on the minds of the people as expressed in their countenances. 'I myself,' he adds, 'could hardly turn away my eyes from that charming figure of the saint, where, asleep on her maiden couch,—all grace, purity, and innocence,—she seems, by the expression on her beautiful features to be visited by dreams from Paradise.'"[1] In truth Angela needed not to visit Venice or the school of St. Ursula, to become acquainted with the story of the Virgin-Martyr and her companions, or to find that story told, and well told, by loving artistic hands in other sanctuaries throughout Venetia and Lombardy.

The great theological school of the Sorbonne, in Paris, had

---

[1] "Sacred and Legendary Art," vol. 2, p. 514. The picture mentioned by Zanetti is that numbered as 533 in the Accademia. It is the Dream of St. Ursula, in which she is bidden to visit the shrines of the holy martyrs in Rome. Those who have admired the exquisite grace of Raphael in one of his first paintings, "The Marriage of the Blessed Virgin," will find that he is surpassed by Carpaccio in every picture of this magnificent series.

early adopted St. Ursula as the special protectress of its professors and students. How could Upper Italy, with its vivid local traditions, fail to be beforehand with the capital of France? So, everywhere, the glorious Princess who shed her blood in Cologne, was the accepted model and protectress of all who strove to lead the Virginal Life in their own homes or who devoted their existence to educate children of their own sex.

We can now see how natural it was for Angela Merici to choose St. Ursula as a patron for her Sisterhood. They were to live in the midst of the world, offering their examples as a corrective to the vices of the age, and giving their services to the two-fold cause of education and charity. Who could better plead for their interests in Heaven than the Celtic Princess and her sainted band of virgins? Had not Italy been ravaged again and again by hordes more pitiless than Goth, or Vandal, or Hun? Had they not still possession of her fairest provinces, and was not their sway paramount over all?

Indeed about this same time, 1533-34, more than one biographer of our saint places a miraculous vision in which Angela beheld St. Ursula herself with her companions urging the immediate organization of a religious order, and promising the foundress their special advocacy and protection.

This fact,—though not vouched for by any recorded and authentic declaration of Angela, or of her immediate companions, seems to be indirectly attested by the artistic monuments left in Brescia and Desenzano by such of her contemporaries as Il Moretto and Romanino. In their paintings Angela is represented as kneeling before Ursula, who presents her with a standard, while behind and around Ursula the host of palm-bearing virgins smile approval and encouragement. This became, throughout Italy, the received way in which artists transmitted to posterity Angela's motive in naming her order.

Another vision occurring in this same year, and pressing more urgently still on Angela the formal and canonical establishment of her society, is related by the same historians.[1] This extraordinary event,—which seems strangely at variance with our saint's child-like obedience to the Divine Voice and its habitual guidance, happened in this way. One night while Sister Angela was occupied in her usual exercise of meditation, an angel suddenly stood before her in a threatening attitude. She fell prostrate on the ground, filled with a terror which she could not control. Recovering from her fright and lifting up her eyes, she beheld our Lord Himself standing before her. He reproved her for her lack of courage in pushing forward an undertaking so conducive to the spiritual welfare of His people; and she, filled with equal confusion and sorrow, besought His merciful forgiveness, promising an immediate compliance with His wishes.

This last vision is here mentioned, because all the latest historians of the Ursuline Order have recorded it. Without vouching for its having happened, especially with the circumstances above related, we deem it due to the reader not to pass it over in silence. But whether it occurred or not, it is certain that during the year 1535, Angela manifested uncommon activity in preparing her companions, the local Church-authorities, and the public, for a formal inauguration of "The Company of St. Ursula."

She was too humble, too sincere a lover of holy obedience, not to submit all her plans, as she matured them, and every step she purposed taking toward their execution, to her di-

---

[1] Among others, *Histoire de l' Ordre de Ste. Ursula*, Paris and Orleans, 1776, vol. 1., page 57.

rector, and through him to the episcopal approbation. And so the month of November came, when she had settled, with the consent of those who held for her God's place on earth, to bind herself and her twelve associates by the solemn obligations of their religious profession.

The 25th day of November, 1535, is a date ever memorable in the great family of St. Angela Merici. It is the feast of St. Catherine of Alexandria, Virgin and Martyr,— one of the many women who shone by their superior learning in the world-renowned schools of the Egyptian capital. St. Catherine had shared with St. Ursula the honor of being the patron-saint and protectress of the great universities of Christendom. Was it because both of these saints represented the union of heroic maidenly purity with superior knowledge, that Angela chose the name of the one as that by which her Company should be known through all time, and the feast of the other as the most propitious day for its inauguration? Is there a divine instinct in the founders of Religious Orders, which compels them to build better than they know? And does not the spiritual edifice grow to a degree of supernatural beauty and strength, all unconscious the while of the Hand which guides the builder?

On the morning, then, of November the 25th, 1535, Angela with her chosen Twelve began the day by assisting at early Mass in her favorite church of St. Afra, and receiving in Christ's divinest Gift here below the pledge of that eternal possession with which He rewards the souls who give themselves wholly to Him and to promoting His interests. Then proceeding, intoxicated with a holy joy, to their Oratory on the Cathedral Square, they fulfilled, in presence of the proper authorities, and their invited friends, the solemn formalities required for the canonical institution of the Company of St. Ursula.[1] After pronouncing their vows, all subscribed an act by which they bound themselves to each other and to a full observance of the rules of the Company.

But the Spirit who presided over that pious assemblage and these touching formalities, moved others among the

---

[1] Let us compare what thus took place in Brescia, on November 25th, 1535, with what had occurred in Paris on August 15, 1534. One of the most God-like men of the many who glorified God and His Church in the 16th century, the Blessed Peter Favre, thus relates, in his own private diary, the first inauguration of the "Company of Jesus:"—" In this same year, 1534, in August, on the feast of the Assumption of the Holy Virgin, we, all of us having come to the same resolution, and made the Spiritual exercises,—Master Francis (Xavier) had not done this yet, though he had the same resolution as ourselves,—went to the chapel of Notre Dame (de Montmartre), near Paris, and each made a vow to go at the time fixed to Jerusalem, and to place ourselves when we returned in the hands of the Pope; and to leave, after a certain interval, our kinsfolk and our nets, and keep nothing but the money necessary for the journey. At this first meeting were present Ignatius, Master Francis (Xavier), myself, Bobadilla, Laynez, Salmeron, Simon (Rodriguez), and M. John (Cordure). Le Jay had not come to Paris, and Paschase (Bronet) had not yet been gained. The two following years we all returned on the same day to the same place to renew our resolve, and each time we felt greatly strengthened."

The holy place in which the Company of Jesus thus had birth, was a crypt beneath the Church. Peter Favre, the only priest among them, celebrated Mass. Before giving them communion, he turned toward them with the Blessed Sacrament. Each in a firm voice recited the vows of chastity, poverty, obedience to the Pope, and a vow to go to Palestine to convert the infidels. They promised, moreover, not to accept any money for their sacerdotal ministrations. Then they received the Divine Gift,—the Almighty Giver flooding their souls with such joy and blissful fervor, that to the end of their lives they could not recall the memory of that day without feeling their souls lifted upward by a great wave of spiritual rapture. "When I think of that time," says Father Genelli, "I seem to behold the entire scene, to share the hopes and great designs of that little band, to see through the thickening gloom of the intervening years light from Heaven descending, glorifying the obscure crypt and filling those souls with a thrill of triumph. In that moment, so full of mighty promise for the coming years, these men must have known that God was with them, that His Spirit was fitting them to achieve lofty deeds and glorious victories in the midst of a generation whose hearts had lost all generous warmth, and who were buried in the apathy of absorbing self-love. Never till that day did so small a band of soldiers set forth bent on conquering a world; never were true hearts inspired by a higher courage."

The rest of the day was passed near a spring in the fields, whose waters, tradition said, had been stained by the blood of the martyred St. Denis. There they broke their fast, while feasting their souls on the sweet manna of brotherly love. . . Oh, how like to each other are the works of the Spirit of Christ in Paris and at Brescia!

maidens of Brescia then and there to cast their lot with Angela. So that, ere they quitted the Oratory on that memorable morning, fifteen others had joined the Twelve, raising their number to twenty-eight in all. Who can tell the joy of Angela Merici on that day which crowned the long labors, the long waiting and suffering of a life now in its sixty-first year?

There was for the Foundress and her companions, one special reason for choosing the Feast of St. Catherine as the day of the formal inauguration of their company, a reason which we should distinctly point out here. The great Maiden-Scholar and Martyr of Alexandria, had lived in the bosom of her own family, professing before the whole world that she was the bride of Him who had died on the cross to redeem our souls, and choosing to die a most fearful death rather than violate the faith which she had pledged to Him. Hence is it that Christian Art, embodying the constant tradition of preceding ages, represents St. Catherine, when received into Heaven, after her triumph over the persecutor's fury, as receiving from Christ Himself the ring, the symbol of eternal fidelity and unfailing love.

Now,—as we shall be able to convince ourselves, when analyzing the constitutions given to the early Ursulines by St. Angela,—every one of the twenty-eight whose names were registered as her companions on November 25, 1535, was a maiden and purposed to be the ever-faithful bride of the Crucified. It was this dignity of Spouse of Christ, which was the goal of these young hearts' ambition. This conception of their spiritual aims, was to be fundamental for every one of them. To a life of utter devotion to Christ and His dearest interests, as the natural sequence of their divine espousals, these young girls had been carefully trained by Angela; and they in their turn, living up to this sacred ideal, in the midst of the world, were to educate the young girls entrusted to them, training such of them as the Spirit of God moved to adopt the Virginal Life, to become in due time, the faithful, devoted, self-sacrificing brides of the Lamb.

The Virginal Life in its most perfect purity, the exalted rank of Spouse of Christ, with the absolute devotion to His honor and interests imposed by such a dignity,—this was the central notion in the mind of Angela, the generating principle of her Institution.

And yet, during the first stage of the Ursuline Order, the Foundress would not impose the emission of any vow whatever, even a vow of celibacy, as an absolute condition of membership. While leaving to time, to the Spirit who guided her companions, and to the Director of their conscience, to determine whether such vows were necessary, and when they should be made, Angela insisted on the most perfect practice of the virtues themselves. Not only would she not have them, during this first period,—when they were on trial beneath the eyes of all Brescia and all Upper Italy—subject to the seclusion of a cloistered life, or to the obligation of living together in a community; but she would have them, on the contrary, remain beneath the paternal roof as a living and most eloquent refutation of the calumnies of the German Reformers, and the most eloquent exhortation as well to the practice of the most heroic Christian virtues. They were to demonstrate daily and hourly by their conduct that Christian maidens and Christian women of all classes, may lead a life of prayerful retirement and penitential austerity, while seeking and seizing every opportunity to practice charity and benefit the neighbor.

They were bound, by the rules their Saintly Parent gave them, to find out the persons of their own sex who were in need of spiritual consolation, or suffering from illness or poverty. They were to use all industry and prudence in instructing the ignorant, especially in the knowledge of the truths and duties of religion. But, above all, they were to draw to themselves the little children, those of their own sex in particular. The training and education of these little ones was to be their principal labor, to which all their other labors were to be subordinated. But the novices and younger members of the Order were to avoid carefully the acquaintance of all persons of ill or doubtful repute. The reclaiming of these was to be the work of others.

In other respects Angela opened as widely as possible the doors to the admission of all who were deserving,—whether they were rich or poor, learned or unlearned, of high or of low degree; she excluded no postulant who brought to the company a virginal soul, a sound judgment, any one who was well principled, constant in her purpose, single-minded and single-hearted.

As to their dress it was to be of woollen texture, modest both in its color and its make, with a black veil of the same material, and cloak for inclement weather. Thus apparelled, the members of the Sisterhood would be able to attend to their holy avocations in the most public places or indoors without creating surprise or calling forth comment. Angela herself continued to wear to the end of her life the dark blue habit by which she was so well known,—and the close resemblance to it of that worn by her associates only served to conciliate respect and popularity.

The members of the Company were to cultivate toward each other the most active charity,—all, no matter how distinguished otherwise by rank or by wealth, laboring to support themselves by their own manual labor, in imitation of **Christ and His Apostles**,—and all contributing promptly and generously to aid such among them as were suffering from extreme poverty or illness. Indeed they showed the most tender care of their sick and dying Sisters, as well as a pious zeal in decently burying their dead and seeing to it that the souls of their departed dear ones were not forgotten in the Holy Sacrifice and in the good works performed by the living.

Toward their parents, their nearest relations, or such as held toward the Sisters the place of father and mother in the home, Angela was careful to inculcate the greatest and most loving reverence. It was a chief object of her wise solicitude to secure the hearty co-operation of the heads of families and households in forwarding the great work she had in hand, and in fostering among their children or dependents the pursuit of holiness and the accomplishment of the sacred labors of charity and teaching.

As we said above, the noblest and most influential men and women in Brescia took an active part in forwarding the establishment of the Company of St. Ursula, and in protecting it from all obstacles during its early stages. Outside of Brescia, in Milan, Cremona and Bergamo, as well as in Desenzano, Salò, and Verona, the most powerful personages and the most distinguished for enlightened piety, sympathized heartily with the Foundress and her work, and were waiting impatiently to see the goodly tree of the Company so speedily attain to its full growth that it might extend its off-shoots to their own neighborhood.

The new Sisterhood, as we have also said, was called by Angela, "the Company of St. Ursula," just as at the same time the glorious spiritual militia organized by St. Ignatius Loyola was by him denominated "the Company of Jesus." There was, both in the mind of the Holy Maid of Desenzano and in that of the heroic Spanish soldier, a military conception. Angela wanted her associates to form in the midst of secular life, a band of Maidens, like Ursula and her followers, holding aloft the banner of the Virginal Life, and becoming the fruitful spiritual parents of the young of their own sex and the loving nurses and handmaids of Christ's poor and afflicted wherever they were found. Ignatius, on the other hand, called his associates to become the Companions of the Lord Jesus, the Great Captain of Salvation, in subjecting the whole earth to the knowledge, the love, and the service of the Father and King of Ages. Angela never concealed her purpose of placing her Companions as the defenders and promoters of the Catholic faith, the Catholic life and institutions, in every city and in every household into which the doctrines and practices of Luther and Calvin were then sought to be introduced throughout Italy. It is, indeed, a well-known historical fact, that Calvin not only visited Margaret of Navarre and made of her court a centre from which he propagated his tenets, but that he visited her sister Renée, Duchess of Ferrara, in order to confirm the latter in her attachment to the new Reformation. Besides more than one of the village-communities in the valleys of Upper Italy had embraced or favored the Reformed doctrines,—while in the great cities themselves, like Venice, such apostates as Bernardine Ochino, the General of the Franciscans, were laboring stealthily under the monastic garb or the priest's cassock, to pervert the minds of their unsuspecting fellow-citizens.

Indeed, there were thus two hostile armies, standing face to face in the homes and cities of Northern and Central Italy, —the army of the disguised enemies of the Catholic Church and its distinctive institutions,—and another army, composed of the Company of St. Ursula, the little band called the Company of Jesus, and St. Cajetano de Tiene's more numerous cohort of Theatines. The latter,—the Catholic army,— strove, and strove effectually, to counteract the manœuvres of the former, to fill all minds, homes, and hearts with the light of the Christian faith and the beauty of holiness, and thus was stopped the progress of Protestantism in Italy.

But let us look more attentively at this first organization of the Company of St. Ursula. Angela, for the purpose she had in view, divided the city of Brescia into "districts." The novices and accepted young maidens of each district were under the immediate care and instruction of a Mistress, who was always a person of superior virtue, zeal, and practical knowledge of things spiritual. To her came for instruction and guidance all the younger novices and members residing within the districts; and on her it was incumbent to visit, once at least within each fortnight, all who were subject to her, in their own houses. Each district had also another officer named Directress,—a widow-lady of at least 50 years of age, of spotless reputation, high social rank, and of known prudence and wisdom. These were to represent the Foundress, to bestow on their respective charge all the watchful care and tenderness of the truest motherly love, never losing sight of any of the young souls committed to them, warding off from them every danger, cultivating in them every quality of heart and mind, encouraging them to aim higher and higher every day, and shining before them on the road of perfection with the steady glow of their own holiness. To each Governess was assigned an Advisor,— who was to be her assistant and executive, taking note of everything that required attention and remedy, and referring it to the Directress. These Advisors or Counselors were also called by the Saint *Collonnelli,*—a military designation from which is derived our own word colonel.[1] Thus every district had its own government, Matrons, Counselors,

---

[1] The Italian *collonnello,*—from *collonna,* a column,—was a title given in the 16th century to the leader or commander of a column of soldiers.

Mistresses, Members, and Novices,—all moving forward in the regular performance of their assigned duties,—these superior officers referring to Angela herself at all times for special direction whenever there was need of it, and all, at stated intervals, meeting her in council to confer with her upon the advancement and welfare of the Company.

The Foundress, experienced as she was in the ways of the world and the things of God, was also careful to secure for her associates protectors and defenders among the most illustrious citizens of Brescia. Of course snch men as Pentagoli, Augustine Gallo, and Antonio dei Romani, could never fail to befriend Angela and her daughters to their utmost. Nevertheless, she used these old and trusty friends to procure the powerful support and protection of other men of the world, who should, at any moment, be ready to defend the nascent society and its members from the insults, the slanders, or the injustice of wrong-doers.

There is no exaggeration, therefore, in saying, that not only all Brescia, but all Lombardy and Venetia, felt deeply interested in the experiment tried with such singular success by the Holy Maid of Desenzano. We know that at the very time, on that November morning, 1535, Angela and her band of twelve were receiving Holy Communion in the Church of St. Afra, and thus preparing to bind themselves to each other by solemn promise later in the forenoon, Ignatius Loyola was scrambling, way-worn, sore-footed, fainting, and sick, across the Appennines from Genoa to Bologna, and thence to Venice, there to await the arrival from Paris of his nine first companions. It is a tale that moves to the loftiest sympathy the soul of the Christian reader,—this of the noble Spanish Cavalier and his chosen followers coming to Venice on foot across the continent, through fatigues and dangers which might discourage the bravest spirit and break down the most robust, and then, after vainly waiting for a passage to Palestine over seas infested by the pitiless Mohammedan, offering their lives to the Vicar of Christ, receiving holy orders beneath the shadow of St. Mark's, and then spreading over Northern and Central Italy, with hearts all aflame and tongues of living fire, to kindle in all who heard them the love of the Holy Name, the deep regret for sin committed, and the heroic resolve to lead godly lives.[1]

---

[1] Stewart Rose ("Ignatius Loyola and the Early Jesuits") thus describes the voyage of Ignatius from Valencia to Venice: "When Ignatius left the house of his friend Martin Perez, where he had lodged in Valencia many days, to embark for Italy, the sea was infested by pirates; Barbarossa had driven Muley Hassan from Tunis, and swept the Mediterranean with a fleet of 100 galleys, plundering both by sea and land. He did not fall in with the vessel which bore Ignatius; that danger was averted by another; it was caught in a violent storm, the helm carried away, the mast broken. . . At last they reached the port of Genoa; but he was not yet safe. In crossing the Appennines to Bologna, he lost his way, and found himself, after much scrambling and climbing, on the brink of a precipice, where he could neither advance, nor without difficulty, return. He had to crawl on hands and knees up steep rocks, which overhung a torrent far below, holding on by ledges of rock, or by herbs growing in the crevices. He said afterwards that he had never been in greater danger; his escape seemed to him a miracle. He arrived sick at Bologna. The winter was advancing, the rains had set in, the roads were flooded, and when at last the weather mended and he had reached the town, as he entered it his foot slipped in passing a bridge, and he fell into a moat. He rose bruised, wet through, and covered with mud. All along the streets the boys shouted at him; he asked alms but nothing was given to him; he would have perished of hunger and cold but for the Spanish College, which took him in and sheltered him kindly until he had recovered strength. Then after a week he set off for Venice." This was in the beginning of December. Not before January 6, 1537, did his nine companions from Paris join him in Venice. Theirs had been a long, exhausting, and most perilous journey,—doubly perilous, because they had to pass through Lutheran Switzerland and Germany, while a new and terrible war was breaking out between Francis I. and Charles V. In Venice "they resided in the Hospital of the Incurables and that of St. John and St. Paul. There they all taught the truths of their religion, attended the sick, helped the dying, and followed the dead. . . These men of consummate learning and rare gifts, some of them highly born, thought no office too humble for them. They washed and lifted in their arms men suffering from loathsome diseases; watched them by night, consoled, and showed them how to make sufferings and misfortune a privilege and a joy." No wonder that "this great charity edified all who saw it; the Senators and chief men of the Republic often went to look at their apostolic work, and many shed tears of emotion at the sight."

Little knew those who looked upon the pale, emaciated, love-lit countenances of the poor strangers, as they sped, two by two, through the cities and hamlets of the beauteous but desolated land, lisping divinest exhortation in the unfamiliar Italian idiom,—that these poor priests would soon swell to a mighty host of apostles covering both hemispheres with their cohorts, and thrilling astonished Christendom with their God-like labors and sufferings. On what lowly but divinely fashioned foundations was to grow that Company of Jesus, the undying object of so much hate, and such atrocious misrepresentation, but the object too of worldwide love and enlightened admiration!

Without instituting comparisons which might startle the imperfectly informed reader, though more than acceptable to the conscientious student of history,—we may say this much, that Ignatius himself was but vaguely conscious in 1536, of the mighty growth to which his Company was destined, and could not have foreseen all the varied labors which his sons were destined to embrace in their zeal for the glory of God. Still less did Angela Merici forecast the permanent forms which the Church, within half a century after her death, was to bestow on the original mode of life and the inspired rules bequeathed to the Company of St. Ursula as Brescia beheld it at its birth. Both founders "builded better than they knew."

At any rate, while the pulpits of "the Hundred Cities of Italy" resounded with an eloquence that rekindled on every side the expiring flame of faith and piety,—people flocked from the countryside and all the neighboring cities to Brescia, to be edified by the eloquent lives of Angela and her companions. Their pulpit was in the family-home, in the schoolroom, in the hospital, in the darkened hovel of poverty, and by the bed of suffering,—in the divinely-appointed sphere of woman's loving, devoted, and irresistible influence. They toiled away, that lowly maiden band, making themselves most worthy of God, their supreme Love, and most careful of the interests of the souls dear to Him, leaving to Him and to His Providence over the Church—to grant an increase to their numbers, and a blessing to their labors, and such form as might please His wisdom to their little Company.

And so that Company went on, purifying, gladdening, enlightening all homes and hearts in Brescia,—like the streamlets descending through the Alpine valleys above the old Celtic city, which fertilize and brighten every home-field on their way, till they pour, at length, their united waters into some one of Northern Italy's majestic lakes, or thence flow onward to join some one of its lordly rivers, as these roll onward to the Adriatic, blessing the teeming plains and adorning the populous cities on their way.

And is it not a strange coincidence, that, while we are describing the beginnings, in Italy, of these two great religious societies,—the members of both should be compelled by the prevailing anti-Catholic Revolution in that same Italy, to live, throughout the length and breadth of that land,— as lived their parents from 1535 to 1540? The Countess E. Girelli, the author of one of the best lives of St. Angela,[1] tells us how she has labored in Northern Italy, to maintain or to restore the suppressed Ursuline communities by inducing them to live in their homes according to the form of the primitive Company. Thus, though driven from their homes, and despoiled of all their property, the daughters of St. Angela are able to do God's work as they may, blessed of Him in their labors, and blessed as well by the people who more than ever need their example and their womanly

---

[1] These Ursulines thus living in the world are known as the PIOUS UNION.

charity. Even so is it with the Sons of St. Ignatius. They, too, are forced to place themselves at the command of the bishops, and labor as labored Francis Xavier, and Peter Favre, and Ignatius himself. And so God's work is carried on, despite the adverse powers which would seem to sweep away the laborers and to destroy the harvest. The Radical tidal wave which is sweeping over Europe, and which threatens the whole civilized world, may "suppress" every religious institution, and disperse mercilessly the members of all religious communities. But if the spirit of Angela Merici and Ignatius Loyola still animates their persecuted children, the apostleship of edification and education will be carried on quietly, obscurely, but most fruitfully despite the persecutor's utmost vigilance. Achab and Jezabel had fancied that their ubiquitous emissaries had exterminated the schools of the Prophet throughout Israel. They had driven even Elias to seek an asylum and a morsel of bread from the starving widow of Sarephta, in the land of the idolaters. But Elias was doomed not to die, while Achab was to perish on the spot where he had shed the blood of the innocent Naboth, there the dogs were to lick up his guilty blood, while a still more terrible fate awaited his wicked queen, as the great prophet had foretold.

CHAPTER XIII.

ANGELA'S WORK—THE CONSTITUTIONS OF THE COMPANY OF ST. URSULA.

Those who habitually approached the saint during this important period of her life, are unanimous in attesting that her assiduity in prayer and her customary austerities were increased to an incredible degree. She was more than ever anxious to obtain light from on high in order to frame for her Company such constitutions and rules as should secure unity and stability, while leaving free scope to the modifications required by the future necessities of time and place. More even than her advanced age, her increasing bodily infirmities warned her to give definite shape to her handiwork. Although she not only read Italian authors, but was well versed in Latin literature, in all that pertained to the Scriptures and their most authorized commentators, in particular, she had never accustomed herself to write. She was born while the art of printing was in its infancy and before skill in penmanship had ceased to be the science of the few. She therefore called to her assistance a Notary of Brescia, Gabriel Cozzano by name, a man held in high estimation for his learning, integrity, and solid virtue,—one in whom she could repose the most implicit trust; and to him she dictated the constitutions which were to be submitted, first to the approbation of the diocesan authority, and then to the supreme judgment of the Holy See. She consulted on every point, which came under consideration, the most enlightened and experienced of her own associates, as well as her trusted spiritual guides, and the devoted lay friends who had sustained and protected her during her long years of trials and discouraging delays. When the matter submitted to these for deliberation had been determined in her own mind, she had recourse to prayer,—pushing her holy vigils far into the night, beseeching the Divine Majesty for special guidance during Holy Mass and communion, and prolonging before the altar her pleadings with the Master, till the interior Voice had told her that her supplication was heard.

Cozzano, who wrote under her direction, after protracted communications with the source of heavenly light, says of the primitive Ursuline Rule as drawn up by him beneath the eye of the Foundress: "In this work there is nothing which belongs to me, except the trifling merit of having expressed in writing, as faithfully as I could, her own (Angela's) sentiments... She alone, divinely inspired as she was, is the Foundress of this great edifice; but, in a letter prefatory to the Rules, she humbly expressed the wish that I should not mention her name."[1]

If we compare the method followed in Brescia by the Foundress of the Ursulines with that afterward pursued in Rome by St. Ignatius in drawing up the constitutions of his Company, we cannot help being impressed by the fact, that

---

[1] *Non vi ho niente del mio, eccetto un pochetto de scriver fidelmente, quanto potei, li suoi sentementi. Ella sola divinamente inspirata è stata la Foundatrice de tanta opera, ma in una epistola prœmiale alle Regole, volle per umilta, che io tacessi il suo nome.*

These words are taken from a published pamphlet of Cozzano's, in which he explains the Bull of Paul III., *Regimini universalis ecclesiæ*, approving the work of St. Angela.

the same preternatural wisdom presided over the deliberations of both the one and the other. It is fashionable among modern liberal non-Catholic writers to say of Ignatius that he was an enthusiast,—sincere, indeed, in his convictions, and acting up to them as he best knew how, but that he was, nevertheless, nothing but an enthusiast, and as such subject to the most dangerous illusions. Such,—to name one among many,—is the repeated assertion of the fascinating but most untrustworthy Macaulay.

Now, if we look into authentic history and read on the testimony of the most venerable and enlightened witnesses,—what method Ignatius scrupulously followed in framing his Constitutions, we are struck by two things; the incredible patience with which at every step and on seemingly minor details, this most reasonable of saints balanced long and seriously the motives for and against every prescription and rule as it came in order,—and the superhuman fervor with which he sought the aid of the divine light.

"In framing the Constitutions which were to regulate his society through all time,"—says Mr. Stewart Rose,—"Loyola proceeded with the utmost circumspection and humility, preparing himself before he wrote by prayer and meditation; then, imitating the holy Pope Leo, he placed what he had written upon the altar, and offered his plans to God in the Sacrifice of the Mass. He deliberated on every point with extreme patience and caution. A fragment of the journal kept by him, which escaped the flames when he burned all his other papers, a short time before he died, refers to the question he long weighed,—whether the churches and sacristies of the houses of the Professed should be able to acquire property. He considered this point forty days; he wrote down eight reasons on one side and fifteen on the other, laying the whole as usual before God. . . On one point he deliberated ten days, and after deciding, passed four more in prayer. He consulted the other Fathers on everything, but usually not till he had well considered the matter himself, and come to some decision; and it was a common practice of his to write down the reasons for and against in parallel columns. He withdrew sometimes from all other business to carry on this work. When he was in his room, Benedetto Palmia, a novice, was placed at the door that he might not be interrupted. He had read with great attention the rules of other Religious Orders, and employed Polanco to make extracts from them. But while he wrote his own, no books were near him, except the Scriptures and the "Imitation." Perhaps Cardinal Lega knew this when he said that the art by which the Society of Jesus had been so aptly and admirably formed, was divine, not human, and that Ignatius had built it up rather by inspiration than by skill."[1]

At any rate, both Angela and Ignatius showed in the childlike simplicity with which they submitted every word they wrote or dictated to the judgment of the Church,—that God was with them, and that they sought HIM alone in the crowning work of their lives. No sooner had Angela completed her sketch of the Constitutions, than she hastened to submit it to Francis Cornaro, Cardinal-bishop of Brescia, and through him to the authority of the Holy See. From Rome, where all such things are weighed with the slow deliberation of a wisdom derived from the experience of ages, no approbation came till several years after the death of the Foundress. In Brescia, however, Cardinal Cornaro, who derived such consolation from the labors of Angela and her companions, at once committed the examination of the precious document to his Vicar-General, Lorenzo Muzio. The latter would not change an iota in what he knew to be the work of

---

[1] "Ignatius Loyola and the Early Jesuits," pp. 240-41, 2nd ed.

a saint and believed to be dictated by the Holy Spirit. So an official decree was issued on August 8th, 1536, bestowing on the Constitutions and Company of St. Ursula the canonical approval of the Ordinary in terms of the highest commendation.

It was a happy day for Angela, who felt assured that the supreme judgment of the Vicar of Christ would, in God's good time, be added to that of the Bishop of Brescia. And so, the vision of Brudazzo, in which, forty years before, the Maid of Desenzano had beheld that glorious company of virgins descending and ascending amid a throng of angels and the chanting of heavenly harmonies, had at length received its complete realization. The command then imposed on her to establish in Brescia a like company of virgin souls devoted to God and His Church, was fulfilled in spite of interminable delays and obstacles ever-recurring and seemingly insurmountable.

During the ensuing Autumn and Winter the holy Foundress busied herself in explaining to her subordinates every point of the Rule thus sanctioned by the ecclesiastical superiors, and in impressing on the minds of all the spirit of absolute devotion to the Divine Majesty and most perfect self-renouncement which underlay the letter of the Constitutions. It was her wish that every one of those who elected to adopt this Rule as their law of life, should do so understandingly, freely, and lovingly. The allegiance pledged to its observance was not to be a divided allegiance: the pledge was to come from a heart that wholly belonged to God.

So far the Company which she had created looked up to her as a parent whose sway all acknowledged and obeyed with unquestioning submission and grateful love. No one, in their estimation, could ever, so long as she lived, take her place at the head of their little company of apostles. No one had so deep a horror of the Reformed doctrines which were daily gaining ground in Upper Italy, thanks to the constantly renewed quarrels between the King of France and the Emperor,—and to the undisguised and unholy policy of Francis I., who encouraged the Lutherans, throughout the Empire, to refuse all settlement of their religious difficulties, while he subsidized the Turkish sovereign to invade the dominions of Austria and ravage the coasts of Spain and Italy. Angela instinctively and intuitively felt the danger which threatened faith in her native land, and knew that God demanded of herself and her daughters to combat the spread of the new errors in every home in Brescia.

But she believed herself incapable of governing the Company and of directing its fresh energies to the best advantage. She was therefore anxious to place in younger and firmer hands the charge which she had borne hitherto. And, as the Rule prescribed that an election should be held as soon as possible after the canonical approbation of the diocesan authority had been obtained, Angela was impatient to see this done, and thereby to secure the legal establishment of her Order. Imperative reasons, however, compelled her to put off, from month to month, the holding of the first general Chapter till the spring of 1537.

They met in her poor room at St. Afra's on the 18th of March. A Notary Public was called in to draw up in legal form the minutes of the proceedings, so that everything should be done with blameless regularity. Angela, it is said, spent the whole of the preceding night in prayer, and was even favored by another apparition of St. Ursula, who took on herself the protection of the new Company, assured the Foundress of God's especial favor, and of the perpetuity of her work, and left the great motherly heart all flooded with unspeakable consolation. The Notary counted 59 persons present in the crowded room, and 17 were reckoned as being unavoidably absent, thus raising, on this first authentic roll of the Company of St. Ursula, the total number of members entitled to vote, to 76 in all.

The choice of a Superior-General was the first thing in order, and, as the authentic record of the meeting testifies, Angela was elected instantly and unanimously, she alone combating the wisdom of such a choice by every argument she could think of.[1] She prayed, she besought them with the greatest earnestness to reconsider their vote, and to remember her own manifold unworthiness and incapacity. And as they persisted in their determination, she alleged, as a reason which must strike and convince them all, her advanced age and increasing bodily infirmities, which precluded her from attending to the duties of so important an office, especially when there was need of sovereign wisdom and indefatigable activity. She had to yield; for nothing could move the members present to make another choice. Only at their venerated Mother's urgent solicitation, they consented not to press upon her the title of Foundress, nor to have it inserted in the records of the Order. God alone, she thought, was to be considered as the originator of their choice band of maiden champions of His cause.

They next proceeded to elect Mistresses for the different wards of the city, and Lady-Directresses. These latter were only four in number for the present, the Lady Lucretia, widow of Count Hector Lodrone, the Lady Ginevra (Genevieve), widow of Alexandro Luzzago, the Lady Ursula, widow of Jeromè Gavardo, and the Lady Maria, widow of Antonio Avvogadro. To thèse was added, as supernumerary, the Lady Lucretia, widow of Paul Luzzago; she, however, did

---
[1] Salvatori, whom we follow here as elsewhere.

not long continue to occupy this place in the Company. The number of Lady-Directresses was soon increased to eight, as the Foundress saw that the rapid increase of the Company demanded a corresponding increase in the number of these important functionaries. So, to the first four names were added those of the Lady Veronica Buzzi, Joanna Monte, Elizabeth Prato, Leonella Pedezocca, and Catherine Meia. To each of these was assigned the care of one of the eight districts of Brescia. The Countess Lodrone became Angela's chief assistant, her right hand in governing the Sisterhood, and was appointed by her in her last illness Vicar, with power to govern in her stead till her successor had been duly elected. As we shall see, Lucretia Lodrone was chosen to fill Angela's place.

No sooner was the Company thus definitely organized, than the Superior-General deemed it incumbent on her to provide for the spiritual direction of its members priests alike pre-eminent for their spotless life, their knowledge of theology, and their experience in guiding souls. It is so necessary, in a great religious body, to make sure that one spirit shall control the consciences of all, and point their united efforts in the same road toward self-sanctification and the service of others! Fortunately for Angela and her Ursulines, they found two such men in Brescia ready and willing to bestow their enlightened zeal in forwarding the best interests of the new Order. These were Father Paul of Cremona, a member of the Order of Canons Regular of St. John Lateran, and Father Chrysanthus, a member of the Venetian Congregation of St. George-in-Alga and a Canon of the Church of San Pietro in Oliveto, at Brescia. To these may be added a noble Brescian, Father Francis Cabrini, whose family took their title from the neighboring domain of Alfianello. This last saintly priest, himself the founder of a religious Congregation,[1] was not, however, associated with the two preceding in their ministrations toward St. Angela and her first companions. Not before 1556 did he become the spiritual guide of the Ursulines of Brescia; but his zeal and devotion to them were such as to cause his memory to live among them by the side of their first venerated directors.

One other name merits a special mention here by the side of Angela herself, with whom she was singularly united in holy friendship and ardent zeal for the progress of the Company. This noble lady's name is Girolama Buschi. Even in the world Girolama lived the life of a saint, and threw herself with her whole heart and with all the influence of her high position into the good work of co-operating with Angela's female friends and admirers in Brescia,—such as the Countess Lodrone and Elizabeth Prato,—lending them her countenance and active aid in their labors in the hospitals, and in their successful efforts to educate the rising generation. She was a true child of God, this magnanimous daughter of Brescia, and she walked with no faltering or tardy step in the road of self-sacrifice. Angela owed to her not a little of the rapid progress which the Ursulines made, both in the well organized labors which gained them so wide a popularity, and in the heroic virtues which won them the admiration of their most intimate friends and watchful observers among the clergy and laity.[2] Girolama herself became an Ursuline, and died in the odor of sanctity in 1545, yearning to be united in Heaven to her dear Mother Angela, and there to pray for the growth of the Company.

We must not pass away from this portion of our subject

---

[1] The Congregation of Regular Clerks of Santa Maria della Pace, in Brescia, united in 1611 to the Congregation of St. Philip Neri.

[2] In the rare manuscript called *Brescia Beata* is a biography of the distinguished lady, from the pen of its author, F. Benjamin Zacchi, an Augustinian monk.

without bestowing on the written Constitutions of the Order which Angela Merici founded, such notice as may enable the reader to grasp their aim and scope. The Constitutions themselves are given in their entirety elsewhere.[1] Being the work of our Saint, it is proper that the reader should be able to judge of this production, not by unsatisfactory extracts, but from a faithful translation of the document itself, as it comes to us from the very best authority.

As to the purpose which the Holy Foundress had in view, we can best gather it from the lips of the Sovereign Pontiffs, who, from the 16th to the 19th century, have uttered their solemn judgment on St. Angela and her Institute.

We quote in the first place the words of Pius IX. In the year 1861, just when only a narrow strip of territory was left to him around the walls of Rome, and when the rest of Italy was overrun by the destroying hosts of Radicalism, the Holy Father felt instinctively that the future of Christian Italy must depend on the education given to the young girls. They would be the mothers of the coming generation; and on them would depend whether their sons and daughters would be the disciples of a godless materialism and an anti-christian socialism, or the fervent disciples of the Faith which had made Italy the light and envy of the world.

The Pontiff knew that Angela had been the first Apostle of Female Education in modern times, and that the Order founded by her had devoted its entire energies to creating Christian mothers for Christian homes, true Christian women for the edification of all classes of modern society. He therefore bethought him, beleaguered as he was by the advancing tide of the Revolution, that one of the most effica-

---

[1] Chap.

cious means of saving the faith and the future of Christendom, was to glorify in the person of St. Angela the devotion to the task of educating youth,—female youth, especially. Hence a solemn decree of July 11, 1861, making the celebration of the office of St. Angela obligatory on the universal Church, and eulogizing her in the following terms:

"Angelic in her life as well as in her person, St. Angela Merici, while upon earth, like a lily blooming among thorns, shed all around her a wonderful sweetness. This maiden, entering joyously from her youth on the road of perfection, reached so high an eminence, that, a few years after her decease, St. Charles Borromeo openly declared that she was in every way worthy of being herself placed among the saints by the Holy See. After having visited with feelings of the deepest piety the holy places in Palestine, she came to Rome to venerate the tombs of the Apostles Peter and Paul. There she felt herself moved to promote the education of young girls, well knowing that these, surrounded as they were by the spreading errors of Calvin and Luther, would be in peril of losing the flower of their virginal life, choked as it must be by the thorny growth of heresy. She therefore established in Brescia a new Sisterhood of religious maidens under the patronage and name of St. Ursula, Virgin and Martyr: and to their care she entrusted the young daughters of poor as well as rich families, to have them taught the elementary doctrines of our holy faith, to train them to lead a life of virtue and purity, and to initiate them into all the arts and industries which befit their sex.

"From the labors of this Company Angela reaped a plentiful harvest of good to the advantage both of the Church and of civil society; and so plentiful was the grace bestowed on the Company from on high, that it spread all over the world, and that our Lord manifested to His servant, the Foundress, a short time before her death, that it would last forever.

"In these latter and baneful times, when wicked men use every means to ruin both the Church and civil society, and in order the better to effect their purpose, endeavor to corrupt the souls of women, of young girls especially, so that from the perverted mind of mothers the poison of error should flow more deeply into those of their children;—petitions have come to our Holy Father Pope Pius IX., from several Cardinals and many other Prelates throughout the world, beseeching him instantly to extend to the whole Church the office and Mass of St. Angela Merici, Foundress of the Company of St. Ursula,—to the end that, by her help and merits, our Lord may be pleased to preserve the female sex from stain of impurity and taint of error, and that, baffling the designs of His enemies, He may grant to His Church uninterrupted peace."

So, then, it was in Rome, while visiting the tombs of the Holy Apostles Peter and Paul, during the Jubilee, 1525, that,—according to Pius IX., Angela "felt herself moved to promote the education of young girls, well knowing that these, surrounded as they were by the spreading heresies of Luther and Calvin, would be in peril," cherishing as they did the purpose of leading the Virginal Life in the midst of the world, "of losing the beautiful flower of their purity, choked as it must be by the thorny growth of heretical practices."

With these maidens, thus saved from the blight of the spreading contagion, and enrolled in the Company of St. Ursula, she set about caring for the "young daughters of poor as well as of rich families, teaching them the elements of Christian doctrine, training them to a life of virtue and innocence, and initiating them into all the arts and industries of their sex."

Thus the Ursulines, from 1540 to 1545,—the year in which their Institute was first approved by Paul III.,—were doing in Brescia what the Jesuits were doing in Rome, what St. Francis Xavier did in India, catechizing little children, saving the little ones of the flock, and through them, saving their parents, but saving the little ones at any rate, by teaching them to know and to follow Christ. This is why Paul III. is said to have uttered the remarkable words put on record by the Annalists of the Ursuline Order, and addressed, on the very day when he approved the Constitutions of St. Angela, to Ignatius Loyola: "Lo! we have given you sisters!"

When St. Charles Borromeo, Archbishop of Milan, was sent by the Holy See as Visitor Apostolic to examine into the actual condition of the Company of St. Ursula, some forty years after the death of the Foundress, his soul was filled with joy at seeing the good the Sisterhood was effecting in the great work of education, not only in Brescia and Cremona, but in the surrounding territories.

"Among the manifold consolations and spiritual joys, granted to me during this visitation,"—he writes to them in 1581,—"not the least was to find your devoted Company making such solid progress in the ways of God,—to find among you so many persons whose lives are a true imitation of the Blessed Ursula and her companions. . . This is why I have felt no weariness amid the various heavy labors of this visitation." . . Elsewhere, addressing the nuns of St. Paul in Milan: "It must be to us a cause of deep confusion to see some souls,—I have known such,—who, like the Sisterhood of St. Ursula, are so truly pious, so athirst for the things of God, so fervent in receiving the Holy Communion, so averse to all worldly pleasures, so wrapped up in the sweet solitude of their own spirit; so mortified, humble, and little in their own esteem; and withal ever content and resigned to the Divine will! Albeit they live in the world, they display in it virtues which cloistered nuns might imitate to advantage."

On the other hand, the bull of canonization of St. Angela (1807), affirms, in speaking of the miraculous vision of Brudazzo, that in it the Maid of Desenzano "heard the voice of our Lord commanding her to establish in Brescia a select company of maidens." . . . And further on: God from heaven called her to the labor of procuring by manifold and wonderful means the eternal salvation of the neighbor and of bestowing on him many other advantages. He at first moved her to found a Company of Maidens under the name and patronage of St. Ursula, for the purpose of promoting and propagating the pious and Christian education of young girls. And this Company—continues Pius VII.—"like the rose in springtide gladdens the Church by the sweet odor of its virtues, acquiring in the present age, as it will with the Divine Aid in the future, rich and glorious merits by instructing the youth of its own sex."

The Church and her Pontiffs have thus declared that Angela's purpose in founding her society was the Christian training of children of her own sex. The preternatural wisdom shown in organizing the Company of St. Ursula, in framing for it Constitutions so admirably fitted to its twofold aim of living an uncloistered life of absolute purity and all-embracing charity, and of winning the respect and love of all Christian families,—tended only to promote the essential object of EDUCATION, thoroughly pious and Catholic education.

No word is said in the Constitutions drawn up by St. Angela of this great design, for which she and her companions and daughters through all time were the chosen instruments. But these Constitutions, as well as the two admirable documents which she dictated on her death-bed, are to be read in the light of this providential design. When we thus study them, we understand how marvelously fitted they are to form a body of mistresses able to meet all the educational needs of any age or country, and able as well to survive what would appear radical and ruinous changes in the organization of any other religious body.

The holy Foundress would have her Company, as she first organized it and gave it laws and rules, form as it were a component part of the civil society in which she lived, with its roots at every hearth-stone,—so that its own divine and heavenly life should embrace and penetrate the whole framework of the busy world around it, and pour into all minds, hearts, and homes, the saving and sanctifying influences of supernatural faith, teaching, piety, and example. We remember how a Maryland farmer once explained to us long ago how the wild mulberry tree took such a wonderful hold of its native earth, pushing its sturdy and countless roots far and wide, so as to extend beneath the houses of an entire village, or to cover with their hidden network several neighboring fields. Ah, but sweeter far, and far more precious than the mulberry, were the fruits borne by the tree of St. Angela's Sisterhood wherever it took root; and fairer and more glorious than all the richest silks of the East is the glorious soul-vesture which her daughters,—devoting themselves, like the silk-worm to one purpose in life and death,— weave for the female youth of Christendom!

She was but an instrument in the hand of the Divine Workman, that Holy Maid of Desenzano; and, like Moses, she built the Ark and its temporary surroundings as the Divine Voice dictated. Moses knew that a more glorious and permanent structure would one day replace the precious wood, the gold, and the gems employed in building the

Holy of Holies. David continued the work of Moses, and Solomon executed the designs of David, erecting to the one true and living God a temple in which a nation might worship. But the Ark of Moses was the very soul of Solomon's Temple.

So was it with Angela. She knew that her Company was to last forever. She gave to its beginnings that organic form which was in the most perfect keeping with the spirit and the needs of her country and age,—infusing into that first form the soul of those characteristic virtues, of that heaven-sent wisdom, which were to pass with the name of Ursuline into every transformation and change rendered afterward necessary by the circumstances of time and place, and approved and directed by the Spirit of God in the Church.

Thus, with a marvelous adaptability, the parent Sisterhood allowed its off-shoots to be transplanted to Milan by St. Charles Borromeo, and there subjected to the restraints of cloistered life without losing any portion of its spirit, of its vitality, or of its attachment to the Brescian Company,—although the members of this persisted in rejecting every modification not imposed by the extreme necessity of obedience to lawful authority. From Milan the cloistered communities spread to other parts of Europe, accepting with each new abode such change as lawful authority imposed. They were swarms from the primitive hive, building their own wheresoever they settled, in garden or in wilderness, in strict conformity with their surroundings,—with the soil and the climate,—but everywhere making sweetest honey, although every swarm was an independent community in itself—dependent only on His direction and guidance, who ruleth all things with the resistless might of the Infinite Creator, who ordereth all things with the loving gentleness of the best of Parents.

CHAPTER XXIV.

THE LAST LABORS AND TRIALS—MOST BEAUTIFUL COUNSELS— THE STRONG WOMAN SETTING HER HOUSE IN ORDER.

THE approbation given to the Ursuline Institute by Cardinal Cornaro, bishop of Brescia, could only permit of its extension within the limits of that prelate's jurisdiction. In order to see the Company called to labor outside the diocese of Brescia, it was necessary to obtain the official approbation of the Holy See. At no period in the history of the Church, since the era of Constantine, was it more difficult to have the Sovereign Pontiff's sanction for the establishment of a new religious order. And, as we have seen, the Company of St. Ursula seemed, at first sight, to deviate widely from the traditional and consecrated forms of monastic life and rule, especially with regard to women. As an innovation, therefore, upon what had since the thirteenth century, been universally regarded as essential to the constitution of female Religious Orders,—the year of grace 1536 was singularly unfavorable towards its acceptance in Rome. The schism just consummated with such ruthless atrocity in England, and the successful progress of the Reformation in Germany and Switzerland, compelled Churchmen in Italy to be on their guard against innovations. It had required all the authority and influence of St. Cajetan of Tiene and of Cardinal

Caraffa (afterward Pope Paul IV.) to obtain a formal approbation of the Theatine Institute, well and widely known as its founder and members were throughout Italy for their zeal in the service of the Church, the purity of their lives, and the purity of their doctrine, as well.

When, in 1538-39, Ignatius Loyola and his companions presented themselves to Paul III., giving him, all Rome, and all Italy, proof of their uncommon learning, their sound orthodoxy, their holy life, and most fruitful zeal, it required more than one delay, and the removal of more than one formidable obstacle to get from the admiring Pope a first preliminary approbation of the new institute as the Company of Jesus, even though they only demanded to be looked upon as simple priests living in community and under a rule, like the Theatines, and not as monks, like the Dominicans, Franciscans, Benedictines, or Cistercians.

The form drawn up by St. Ignatius was presented to the Pope by Cardinal Contarini on Sept. 3, 1539 Paul III., after carefully reading this form and the accompanying documents, exclaimed: "The finger of God is here!" Nevertheless, he would not dispense with the usual examinations prescribed in such weighty matters, and committed the petition of Ignatius and the abridged form of the proposed Company to a commission of three Cardinals. "But one of them,"—says Stewart Rose—"was Bartolomeo Giudiccioni, of Lucca, whose opinion was entirely hostile to Religious Orders; and he would not even take patience to read the papers sent him; *for*, said he, *all Orders become relaxed, and then do more harm to the Church than they did good in the beginning.*" Giudiccioni was a redoubtable opponent, for he was an excellent theologian, a distinguished poet, possessing great abilities, and so highly venerated for his holy life, that when he died, Paul III. exclaimed: *My successor is dead*. His horror at the disorders into which many of the monks and nuns had fallen, made him desire, not reform, but suppression; he wished all orders abolished but four, which he would remodel and place under strict governance. To allow a new Order, was, to his mind, an idea not even deserving to be discussed. He would not waste a thought on the scheme of Ignatius; and the weight of his judgment carried with it that of the two Cardinals conjoined with him.[1]

Such then was the disposition of the most eminent men in Rome, of those with whom rested the practical decision of the weightiest concerns of Church government. To be sure, Cardinal Giudiccioni was brought to change his opinion about the Company of Jesus by something which very much resembled a miracle. None the less can we see, from the above passage, how opposed the best and most influential men in the Church then were to the establishment of new Religious Orders.

This was one cause of Angela's disappointment in not seeing her work sanctioned by the supreme authority in the Church. There were others which stood even more in the way. Charles V., now the undisputed master of Italy, as well as of Spain and the Netherlands, and Emperor of Germany as well, was again at war with the restless king of France. While (1535) the Emperor had been chastising the Mohammedan pirates of Tunis and liberating from the most cruel bondage 22,000 Christian slaves, the Most Christian King was consummating an alliance with Solyman II., of Constantinople, and inducing him to send an army to invade Hungary and a powerful fleet to ravage the coasts of Italy, himself the while pouring his armies into Lombardy

---

[1] "Ignatius Loyola and the Early Jesuits," pp. 213-214.

and uniting his galleys with those of the Turks. Returning triumphant from Tunis, Charles V., at the head of 7,000 choice troops, proceeded to Rome, where he did his best to overawe the Pope and his Cardinals, and deported himself as if he were in reality the head of the Church as well as the arbiter of Europe. But the Pope, who was the Supreme Pastor and Father of all Christians, was anxiously casting about for some scheme of mediation, some plan by which he might pacify the two warring sovereigns, and thus avert from Italy and from the Church the manifold calamities of invasion by land and by sea, the sacrilegious ravages of the Turkish fleets let loose to prey upon both shores of the Peninsula, superadded to the butcheries of Henry VIII. in England, and the sanguinary dissensions which marked in Germany the progress of the Reformers.

And so Paul III., in his 71st year, and burdened by grief and care, had to undertake a long voyage by land to meet Francis and Charles at Nice, and there endeavor to bring about a reconciliation (1538). Then again the Holy Father was endeavoring to remove all obstacles,—and these were many and seemingly insurmountable,—to the speedy assembly of an œcumenical council, in which, he flattered himself, the German Reformers could be brought to terms and induced to return to the bosom of Catholic unity.

Such were a few of the many obvious reasons why Angela Merici's petition was not immediately complied with, and why the last years of the laborious life of trial and expectancy were somewhat clouded with this supreme hope deferred.

Nor was this the only or the greatest trial which Angela had to endure after the establishment of her Company. Just as both Theatines and Jesuits,—because they had not adopted the distinctive dress and forms of the old Regular

Orders,—were assailed by long, bitter, and most unmerited opposition; even so was the Ursuline Sisterhood in Brescia reviled by many, because the members were not distinguished by the customary religious habit, nor bound by the usual vows of poverty, chastity, and obedience, or compelled to live together in community. Even before the formal establishment and official recognition of the Company, the rigorous formalists had sneered loudly enough at Angela and her attempts to conciliate the freedom of a secular life beneath the paternal roof, with the practice of the austere virtues and difficult duties of the Religious state. The sneers reached her ears, but moved her not. Remonstrances also came; but were set aside with that gentle and courteous firmness which ever won her the respect and affection of those whose opinion she had to reject. Even though it had not been given to the humble Foundress to witness the rapid increase of the Company and the immense good it was doing in the diocese of Brescia, she was too deeply convinced of its being the work of God to be affected by mockery, reproach, remonstrance, or unworthy aspersion. So, wholly intent on forming her daughters to all manner of godliness, of so filling their souls with an absorbing devotion to the Divine Majesty that they should deem no sacrifice great enough to glorify and serve Him,—she allowed the idle murmurings of the few discontented outsiders to pass by her with the same indifference with which she heard the rain-drops pattering on the window-panes of her lowly home at St. Afra.

The whole machinery of her government worked so smoothly, the entire Ursuline Family was so knit together by the motherly love and watchful tenderness which she and the Lady Directresses displayed in their management,—that all serious-minded ecclesiastics as well as laymen could not help saying, "The hand of God is here!"

Of course, the constant application demanded by the care of so large a body of young women dispersed over an entire city, an entire diocese, did not induce Angela, though long past her sixtieth year, to mitigate the uniform austerity or her own private life, or to abridge her long prayerful vigils. The Holy Spirit had said to the Israelites through Moses[1] what the Master repeated to the enemy of all holiness and self-denial:[2] "Not in bread alone doth man live, but in every word that proceedeth from the mouth of God." The manna of the Old Law was but a figure of that of the New, in which the Giver bestows Himself in His gift. But the near communion with that covered and veiled Presence, only prepares the believer for the unclouded contemplation and the blissful possession of the Divine and Infinite Reality. How can we, who firmly believe in these most consoling facts of our Holy Faith, wonder that men and women so forget themselves and all their bodily needs, while conversing in prayer, with HIM, or prostrate in adoration at His feet in holy communion, as to need no other sustenance than that of His near and blissful Presence? Of how many saints do we not read, that they could live for weeks and months on the sole Eucharistic Bread? Moses,—so the Scripture affirms,—conversed forty days on the mountain-top with the Lord, and felt no bodily hunger the while. And Elias, the mighty prophet, journeyed forty days amid the fearful solitudes of Southern Palestine, sustained by the single cake of bread the Angel had brought him. We read of one of Angela's own contemporaries,—whose holy life shed its splendors on Rome:—"When our Father was dead, we proceeded to embalm him as well as we could, . . . and this caused greater wonder and edification; for his stomach and

---

[1] Deuteronomy, viii. 3. [2] Matth. iv., 4.

abdomen were empty and shriveled up, whence his physicians judged his abstinence to have been great in former times, and his fortitude also, since in so much weakness he went about his laborious duties with such constant serenity. When they examined the liver, they found three small stones, which testified how true was what the good old man Diego d'Eguia said, that certainly for a long time past our Father was kept in life by a miracle. I, at least, cannot guess how, with a liver so diseased, he could have lived in a natural way, if God our Lord had not provided for this organic disease, and kept him in life while he was necessary to our Society!"[1]

Yes,—to see God face to face, to love and possess Him securely, and to sound forth His praises in one eternal heart-song, this is the food of the Blessed above, the true life of the everlasting Kingdom. And why should not those who here below solely seek Him and His justice,—as the flower seeks the pure air and the sunlight, not have such a sweet and protracted foretaste of the eternal fruition, that they seem to be raised above the need of bodily sustenance?

Even so, most actively devoted to every duty of her high office to every detail of her administration, did Mother Angela,—as she was then called,—live on through these closing years of her life. Nothing could persuade her to give her attenuated body rest, or to abridge her long meditations. But there were many among her daughters who knew well from what well-spring she drew the waters of life which strengthened and intoxicated her, or enabled her to go forward without fainting or faltering to the Mountain of God, where alone she could rest.

About the beginning of Spring, in the year 1539, however,

---

[1] Father Polanco's letter recounting the death of St. Ignatius Loyola,—quoted by Stewart Rose.

a low fever seized upon the weakened and aged frame. She struggled in vain against the lassitude and sense of oppression it caused. Her accustomed manner of seeking sleep, by siting on a low bench and leaning back against the bare wall, no longer reposed or refreshed her. She had been forced, of late, to seek the luxury of lying down on a poor pallet;—she would have none other. But she was at length induced to accept a bed. The consulting physicians, knowing the purity of her blood and her habitual abstemiousness and austerity, did not think, at first, that the feverish symptoms threatened anything serious. She, apparently, knew better.

True mother as she was, in her absorbing love for her charge and her all-embracing forethought, she did not want the direction of the Company to remain for a single hour in the hands of such as she now was, sick and prostrated by utter debility. She forthwith summoned to her bedside the Lady-Directresses and her secretary, Gabriel Cozzano, and bade the latter draw up an act appointing as her Vicar in the government of the Company, the Countess Lucretia Lodrone. The choice was one which gave universal satisfaction, and the Lady Catherine Meia was immediately named by the Saint and elected by those present to fill the new Vicar's vacant place among the eight Lady-Directresses. Thus relieved from the burthen of immediate care, Angela was able to dictate to her secretary, Gabriel Cozzano, two of the most touching and pregnant documents ever bequeathed to a Religious Order, by its founder. One of these is a series of half-counsels, half-injunctions addressed to the Lady-Counselors (*Avvisatrici.*), whom Angela to the end designated as *Collonelli*;—because they were, in her thought, to be, each in her own district, the leaders and advisers of the Ursulines therein residing, under the control of the Lady-Directresses. This most important document we shall give presently. The other is addressed, as a kind of spiritual last will and testament, to the Vicar and the Lady Directresses; and this shall be given in its place, after we have told of the Saint's death and burial. For, according to the most reliable authority, it was only after the funeral that Cozzano read this testament to the ladies for whom it was destined.

In the uncertainty regarding the precise date when Angela felt her end approaching,—or rather, was assured of it by a special warning from on high,[1]—we may be nearest to the truth in assuming that with the beginning of January, 1540, it became apparent that she could not last much longer.

Unwilling to wait till the last day and the latest hour to give her daughters the solemn instructions demanded by her very peculiar,—and, as it appeared to many, precarious,—position, she called the Lady-Counselors or *Colonelli* to her poor room at St. Afra, and, when the first greetings and inquiries were over, she desired Cozzano to read in her name the precious instructions, destined to remain for all time the living and eloquent expression of her motherly tenderness, provident care, and superhuman wisdom toward those who glory in being her children.

"SISTER ANGELA, unworthy handmaid of Christ Jesus, to her beloved Daughters and Sisters, the Lady-Counselors (*Colonelli*) of the Company of St. Ursula.

"May the strength and true comfort of the Holy Ghost be with all of you, that you may thereby be enabled to bear and execute manfully and faithfully the task which you have undertaken,—and may also look forward to the great reward which God hath prepared for you.

"Let each one of you earnestly apply herself within her own

---

[1] Doneda positively asserts that St. Angela knew of the day of her death by revelation. This knowledge is not inconsistent with the facts related by other historians. There is only confusion in placing them.

district, to be both faithful and pains-taking for the welfare of her Maiden charge, all of whom have been committed to your care, as to that of guardians, watchful shepherds, and efficient ministers. Hence it is that you have a great need of continual prayer, in order to obtain from God that He may enlighten you, direct you, and show you clearly what it is incumbent on you to do, for love of Him, toward the fulfillment of your trust,—a trust than which none can be more exalted, since it consists in being the guardians of those who are affianced to the Most High God. Hence also arises the reason for your conceiving a lofty esteem for them; for in proportion to your respect for their quality will be the love you bear them; and the more you will love them, the greater will be your care and watchfulness. Thus will it become an impossible thing for you not to bear about you, night and day, the image of each one of them, as if it were attached to your breast, imprinted on your very heart; for such is the effect of true love. Far from being averse to such a task, you should, on the contrary, give God most heart-felt thanks for your being of the number of those whom He chooses for the burthen of government and the keeping of His dear treasures. This is both a great favor, and a most enviable lot, if you would only learn to prize it! Nor must you lose heart if you think that you have neither the knowledge nor the practical wisdom required by so special a government as ours. Place your hope and firm trust in God; He will surely help you in every difficulty. Be instant in praying to Him, in humbling yourselves before His Almightiness; for most assuredly, since He hath trusted this undertaking to you, so will He give you strength to carry it out, provided only that you fail Him not. Do your duty, therefore, go about your active functions, be full of trust, of courage, of high hope, send up your heart-cry to God in your need;

and doubt not but you will see Him do great things for you, while you will aim at doing all things for the praise and glory of His Infinite Majesty, and for the spiritual welfare of the souls dear to Him.

"Among the other duties, which you have to accomplish with the aid of God's grace,—I entreat you all and beseech you by the Passion of Christ and that of His Blessed Mother, to do your best to put in practice these few Advices which I trust to you to carry out after my death. They will at least help to remind you somewhat of my intentions and wishes. Thereby, too, I shall know if you take pleasure in doing me a grateful thing: for you are well aware that, presently, I shall enjoy a fuller life than I did while among you, and that I shall see more clearly and value more accurately and gratefully the good deeds I shall always behold you performing; and that I shall have both a greater will and a greater ability to assist you, and to do you service in every emergency.

"*First Advice.*—I therefore remind you above all things, Daughters and Sisters mine in the blood of Christ Jesus, to bestow your utmost effort with the help of our Lord, in penetrating yourselves with this deep and humble conviction, that you are not worthy to be Superiors and Officers, but hold yourselves as the poor servants and handmaids of your Sisters; considering the while that you are more benefited by the services you render them, than they are by your government of them; for God might have provided them with more efficient instruments of His loving care than you know yourselves to be. His Fatherly mercy deigns to use you for your own greater good, that you may acquire a larger store of merits in the sight of His infinite liberality, and thus furnish Him a motive for bestowing a fitting reward. Lay to heart the lessons taught by our dear

Lord during His life on earth, where he labored as a servant, obeying His Eternal Father down to His dying day. Therefore did He say, '*Which is greater, he that sitteth at table or he that serveth?*' (St. Luke xxii. 27). Which means 'I have been with you as one who was the servant of his brothers, not as one who received service from them.' And St. Gregory the Great, Pope as he was, always styled himself 'the servant of the servants of God.' He so discharged his office as superior and Supreme Pontiff, that in his heart he esteemed himself the least of all men, really the servant of all God's servants, bearing constantly in mind the words of the Gospel: *He that is greater among you, let him become as the younger.* (Ibid. 26.) In like manner must you, for the very reason that you know you are placed over others, esteem yourselves as their inferiors. For this very reason God will raise you up in proportion to your self-abasement. Therefore, too, is it that all true servants of God will never fail to abase themselves in their own heart, and to trample under foot and destroy all feelings of self-esteem and the natural yearning to be extolled by others. They set their hearts on the solid delight arising from the true glory and unfading honor which they expect from the Master,—relying on his own words, *He that shall humble himself, shall be exalted.* (St. Matth. xxiii. 12.)

"*Second Injunction.*—Be affable and courteous toward your dear Daughters, and endeavor to show yourselves and to be solely animated by the love of our Lord, as well as by the purest zeal for the souls dear to Him, whenever you admonish them, or give them advice, when you would persuade them to strive after some good, or to avoid some spiritual danger. You will effect more by loving words, and a courteous manner, than by bitterness, or sharp reprehension, which should never be used but in extreme necessity, and with a prudent regard to the place and time, as well as to the disposition of the person addressed. True charity, which aims in all things to honor God and to be useful to souls, knows how to teach this practical discernment;—it impels the heart to be, according to the necessities of time and place, now affable and courteous, now sharp and stinging, with a proper measure in gentleness or reproof, as need may be. Whenever you see a weak soul, timid, and disposed to lose hope and heart, comfort her, give her courage, open up to her the bright vision of God's infinite mercies, and enable that shrinking heart to open itself wide to the sweet influences of consolation. On the other hand, when you meet with a presumptuous soul, who follows the dictates of a lax conscience, without much fear or compunction,—then must you fill her with salutary terror, with a just apprehension of the rigorous judgments of the Most High, with a sense of the dreadfully contagious nature of sin, with a great fear of the pitfalls which beset the sinner's path, and a dread of the awful uncertainties of this mortal life,—recalling ever to mind the inspired warning· *Blessed is the man that is always fearful; but he that is hardened in mind shall fall into evil.* (Prov. xxviii. 14).

"*Third Injunction.*—Be subject to the head Mothers, whom I leave in my place, for this is but right. Wherefore, whatsoever you do, do it in obedience to them, and not as following the bent of your own will. In obeying them you obey me; in obeying me, you obey Christ Jesus Himself, who, in His boundless condescension hath chosen me to be, in life and in death, the Mother of this glorious Company,—albeit on my part I was most unworthy; and who, moreover, after choosing me, bestowed on me the grace to govern it in accordance with His holy will.

"Should it so happen that you find any just cause for opposing or censuring these Superiors, do it with great delicacy and reverence. And if they should not yield to your representations, bear the disappointment patiently, convinced that simple justice demands of you to love your Mothers when they are good; and when they chance to be otherwise and differ with you, then must you bear with them; be careful never to give way to murmuring, or complaint, or to speak ill of them to any one, above all to your Daughters. On the contrary, maintain the honor and reverence due to your Mothers, considering that it is God's command, that we should honor not only our fathers and mothers according to the flesh, but still more so our Spiritual Parents. Thus will you succeed in always raising them high in your own esteem and respect, but more so still in that of your own dear inferiors. When you are blessed with good Superiors, bethink you that you do not deserve to have them; and when they are not what they ought to be, reflect that they might be still worse. When in your heart you feel sure of having some reason to be dissatisfied with them, you can without scruple speak of it, under the seal of secrecy, to some pious and trustworthy person. When, however, you clearly see that there is any danger to the souls or honor of your Daughters, you must on no account remain passive, or indifferent, or afraid to offend others by your interference. In all these things proceed advisedly and with due deliberation.

"*Fourth Admonition.*—You must show solicitude and watchfulness in taking cognizance of all that relates to the conduct of your Daughters, and inform yourselves of their spiritual and temporal needs. Provide for their wants to the best of your power, in order to throw as little of such burden as possible on the shoulders of the Lady Directresses. If, however, it be not in your power to provide the needful, have recourse, and that without delay, to the head Mothers, and expose to them fearlessly the wants of your little flocks. Should they be slow to act on your representations, speak to them again and again. And on this point I bid you to be importunate and exacting. For, should any soul in your charge be lost through your neglect, God will call you to a strict account for it on the Day of Judgment. Wherefore, you must know and hold for certain, that He will never fail to provide you with all that is necessary both for body and soul,—if you are careful to do your part well. Whence too, since it is God who has established this Company, even so will He never forsake it, in accordance with the words of Scripture: *I have not seen the just forsaken, nor his seed seeking bread.* (Ps. xxvi. 25).

"*Fifth Admonition.*—Be pleased to go often (according as you have time and convenience), especially on Feast Days, to visit your dear Daughters and Sisters, and to greet them in all kindness, to see how they are, to comfort them, and to encourage them to persevere in the manner of life they have chosen, to excite to a desire of the heavenly joys and possessions, to look longingly forward to the joyous feasts and unspeakable delights of the City of God, to its blissful and everlasting triumphs, and to tear themselves away from the love of this pitiful and treacherous world, where no one can find either true rest or contentment, but only empty delusions, bitter labor, and everything miserable and paltry. Put them in mind of their obligation to lead at home lives regulated by good sense, and distinguished by prudence and modesty. Let them be well-mannered and temperate in all things. Let them take food, and drink, not for the pleasure of the appetite, but simply to sustain nature, and enable themselves to do God's work. Let them be moderate also in their sleep, giving to it the time required by necessity; and so in laughter, let it be decorous and subdued; in hearing others discourse, let them never listen to anything that is not modest, and proper, and to the purpose; and so in their own discourse, let their conversation be instructive and courteous, not harsh or rude, but gentle and peace-loving and charitable. Tell them, that it is my wish, wherever they happen to be, that they should give good example, charming all by the sweet odor of their virtues, showing obedience and submission to all who have authority over them, and zealous to promote good feeling and peace everywhere. Above all, let them be humble and affable, and let holy charity regulate their whole bearing, their every action and word, and let them bear everything patiently; for with these two virtues,—charity and patience,—one is sure to crush the head of the enemy lying in wait for souls.

"And when you visit them, I bid you, in my name, to greet them and take them by the hand. Tell them also that my desire is that they should maintain great union and mutual harmony, all of them bending their wills to the one purpose of standing together obedient to the Rule; that the one thing most important of all for them, is to cherish the honor of Christ Jesus, to whom they have promised both their maidenhood and themselves; and so they must place their hopes and their love in God alone, and in no living creature. Give these dear ones comfort and courage, and let them be of good cheer! For you may also give them these glad tidings, which I announce to them from Christ and our Blessed Lady,—that they have great cause to exult and make holiday in their hearts, inasmuch as in Heaven for all and each of them in particular is prepared a new crown of glory and bliss,—provided only that they keep themselves firm and immovable in their holy purpose, and strenuously observe our Rule. Of this assured prospect let nothing make them doubt, no matter what may be their trouble or difficulty; for all these little miseries will soon vanish from their path, and be succeeded by serenity and joy; and, then again, the little we may have to endure in this life is as nothing in comparison to the wealth of happiness stored up in Paradise.

"Besides, let them hold this too for most certain, that they shall never be forsaken in their necessities. God will provide for them in a wonderful way. Let them never lose heart or hope. How many Nobles, Queens, and other exalted personages are there not, who in spite of all their treasures and powers, are not able to find any sweet comfort in the hour of their most extreme need. And yet their poorest dependents can enjoy abundant consolation and cheer! . . .

"Assure them, moreover, of this,—that I shall, by and by, be more truly living, than I was when their eyes beheld me in the body, and that soon I shall see them and know them better, and be better able to help them, inasmuch as I shall be always in their midst with Him who is my Love, who is the Love of all of us. Wherefore, as they believe all this, let nothing damp their courage or dim their hope. Thus must you enlarge upon the promises made to your Sisters, resting in the assurance that the realities will more than correspond to their expectations,—and this do ye particularly in favor of such as you may find desponding, wavering, or pusillanimous.

"Tell them that they must wish to see me, not on earth, but in Heaven, where our Love is. Let them place their hopes on high, not on the things of earth. Let Christ Jesus be their only treasure; since the object of their affection must be sought for, not here below, but in the highest Heaven, where He thrones at the right hand of His Father. Hence the Apostle said: *If you be risen with Christ, seek the things that are above: where Christ is sitting at the right hand of God.* (Coloss. iii. 1.)

"*Sixth Injunction.*—You must so live and demean yourselves, that your conduct shall be a mirror for your dear Daughters. Whatever, then, you would have them do, that do yourselves first. What weight can your reprehensions or admonitions have, if the fault you would correct is but too apparent in your own conduct? How can you counsel or persuade them to the practice of virtues, which you evidently lack yourselves? At least must you, to make up your deficiency, begin to work in earnest with your Sisters. Let your conduct, therefore, be such as may move and encourage them in the pursuit of virtue. Nor must you fail to shape your lives so as to conform with them in all praise-worthy and virtuous actions befitting your profession and within your power, especially in your outward bearing, in the practices of frequent Confession and Communion, and other such good works. It is but right and proper that Mothers should be models and mirrors to their Daughters,—particularly in blameless life, and modest carriage, as in all other things which regard exterior life.

"*Seventh Reminder.*—Bear in mind that it is your duty to protect and rescue your lambs from wolf and thief,—that is from two classes of pestilential persons, namely,—fair-speeched worldlings and hypocritical religious, on the one hand, and heretics on the other. In the first place, regarding your intercourse with the worldly-minded,—be especially averse to any kind of familiarity with young men, or indeed with men of every age, no matter how spiritual-minded they may be. For too great a familiarity with even the spiritual-minded, leads to anything but to spirituality. You must not allow them to keep up any acquaintance, so far as you can, with women who lead an aimless life, with such as show themselves averse to purity, or who are fond of gossiping about frivolous things, or enjoy nothing but worldly amusements. See to it, also, that no Confessor, or Religious, shall cause them to make little of any of their holy resolutions,— of their customs of fasting, or their settled purpose of keeping their virginity inviolate, or their attachment to this holy Rule of ours, divinely prepared for us; or of any other such things. For there are many persons who, under some specious pretense of seeking a higher good, will turn away the mind of poor young girls from following up their own virtuous inspirations and resolves. Now, as to guarding your charge from the contagion of heretical opinions, whenever you learn that such a preacher or other public personage has the reputation of entertaining heretical opinions, or that they preach novelties in contradiction to the settled doctrines of the Church, or in opposition to what we have been teaching you,—then must you take means to prevent your Daughters from hearing such doctrines. For it not unfrequently happens that certain little seeds of doubt cast into the mind, become so deeply rooted there that they can scarcely be plucked out. With all such persons you must have no familiar dealings. Leave these men to go their own road; and, while abstaining from judging any one rashly, be prudent in guarding your own souls from evil. For it is better to follow the beaten path where you apprehend no danger, than to expose yourselves to pitfalls on a road untried. Follow ever the broad highway of the Church's teaching and practice, laid out and perfected by the hands of so many saints under the direction of the Holy Spirit.

"Live yourselves a new life. As to the doctrines which

originate in our day, or which may arise hereafter, let them pass by like clouds borne along by the winds; they do not concern you. Meanwhile, pray, and make others pray, that God may not forsake His Church; but that it may please Him to reform her as best beseemeth Him, and as He shall judge more conducive to our good, to His own greater honor and glory. Indeed, in these times, so pregnant with danger and with moral pestilence, you can find no better refuge than at the feet of Christ Jesus. If He directs and teaches you, you shall be well taught indeed, as the prophet says: *Blessed is the man whom Thou shalt instruct, O Lord, and shalt teach him out of Thy law!* (Ps. xciii. 12.) Humble yourselves beneath His mighty hand, and you shall find the light and joy mentioned by the same Prophet: *Enlighten my eyes that I may never sleep in death.* (Ps. xii. 4.)

"*Eighth Reminder.*—Show an equal love to all your dear Daughters, nor must you permit yourselves to show partiality to any in preference to the others. For all are what God made them, and you know not what glorious use He may yet make of them. How can you tell but those very persons who seem to be of little account, or even utterly worthless, are not about to become the most generous and the most acceptable to His Divine Majesty? Besides, to whom has it been given to read the hearts and penetrate the secret thoughts of His creatures? Take them all to your heart, therefore, and bear with them all tenderly; for you have not been appointed to judge God's handmaidens. He alone knoweth what His own purpose is: He can from the stones of the street create children worthy of Himself. As for you, do what your office enjoins: correct your dear ones lovingly, charitably, when you see them falling through human infirmity. Thus will you continue to prune the vine committed to you by our

Lord; leaving the result to Him, who will bide His own time to do wonders for you.

"*Last Reminder.*—The last word of prayer which I address to you, and which I could write with my own blood, is that you continue to be bound together in so sweet and loving a union that all have but one heart and one will. Yes,—let the bond of charity so draw you to each other, that you may prize and esteem each other, help each other, and support each other in Christ Jesus. If you are earnest in your endeavor to be thus united, doubt not but our Lord God shall be in the midst of you. You shall have as your protectors our Blessed Lady, the Apostles, the entire company of blessed men and women, with the Angels, the whole Heavenly City, and the whole order of this Universe. For such is the eternal law of our Creator, that all those who labor unitedly for His honor, shall prosper in everything, that their efforts shall be crowned with success, inasmuch as they have with them God and all His creation. You may thus admire the wonderful effects of union and harmony of wills.

"Wherefore you must desire it, seek it, cherish it, and hold it fast with all your might. I assure you, that if you thus stand together with united hearts, you shall be like a mighty rock or tower, impregnable against all the ill fortune, the persecutions, and the Satanic assaults of the future. This, moreover, I assure you of,—that every grace you may ask of God shall be infallibly granted to you, and that I shall be always in your midst, assisting you to obtain the object of your prayers.

"Exhort and encourage your dear ones, therefore, to carry out the undertaking we have begun; and in so doing, cheer each other with the assurance that all things shall most certainly turn out for you as I now say. Beside the immense and priceless grace which my love as well as your own, will grant you when death is nearest,—for true friendship is best known in the extremity of need,—hold this also for certain, that in that hour especially you shall know me to be a true friend to you.

"And now I leave you. Be comforted, and have a lively faith and hope. I wish you to be blessed, In the name of the Father, and of the Son, and of the Holy Ghost. Amen."

CHAPTER XV.

THE GATES AJAR—LOVE STRONG IN DEATH—THE PILGRIM AT REST.

VERY few death-bed scenes in the history of the holy founders of religous orders approach in touching solemnity and deep interest to that presented in the poor narrow room at St. Afra's, where lay, near the end of her long pilgrimage, the parent of the most numerous and wide-spread order of women in the Church—the first of their sex specially devoted to the great apostleship of education. The only change allowed in the poor and scant furniture of this lowly dwelling—which Angela was allowed to occupy by charity—was the little bed rendered necessary by the exigencies of her long illness, the rush-pallet introduced as a first modification of the sufferer's austerity in the beginning of her sickness, and now probably used as a luxury by the faithful Barbara Fontana, and the crowded wooden benches on which sat the sorrowing daughters of this great Mother of saints and missionary nuns.

One may easily picture to one's self the pious emotions of the lady-counselors who had been from the beginning among the most tried and trusted helpmates of the foundress in spreading and strengthening her institute. It is not unlikely, too—although no mention is made of the fact by Father Salvatori,—that the lady-directresses were also present; for the admirable advices and directions contained in the RICORDI are more precious than gold or the choicest pearls to all who are charged with the government of others. Gabriel Cozzano himself, identified as he was with the labors, the fears, the hopes, the successes, and the joys of Angela and her company, could not help drinking in every one of the inspired lessons, which his own ear had first heard from the lips of his saintly friend, and which his own hand had put in writing for the benefit of all after ages.

We must not forget amid what disheartening prospects Angela beheld her little company as the shadows of death were gathering around herself. Of the wars—the insane, fratricidal, and ruinous wars—between the two greatest princes of Christendom, which broke out with renewed fury at this time, like the sudden eruption of a volcano's long pent-up fires, we need say nothing. All Brescia—all upper Italy indeed—was in an agony of the most terrible expectancy. From the horrors of war, however, Angela most probably knew, in the prophetic light vouchsafed her so abundantly as the eternal day drew near, that Brescia and her dear ones would be safe. But there were other—less apparent and more formidable—perils for the members of her company, of which she had a vivid consciousness. The nascent Ursulines were to be assailed, both from within and from without, by the same enemies and the same dangers, which went so near, —at the very same time, too—wrecking the Society of Jesus under Claudio Acquaviva. But nearer to Angela, around her very home, in the public squares and streets of Brescia, within her monasteries as within the homes of her patricians, numerous enemies were lurking, who were lying in wait for the faith of her daughters, and most anxious to overturn from its foundations the edifice of virginal life and missionary zeal which the Maid of Desenzano had been instrumental in raising. In 1540 nearly one half the population of Brescia either belonged to the Protestant faith or was disposed to adopt it! And the dying saint, from her death-bed near the watch-towers of the ancient Celtic city, could see the new doctrines spreading over Lombardy, Venetia, and Piedmont, like the resistless waters of the Po and Adige, swollen by the wintry streams from her own native hills, inundating and devastating Italy's fairest and most fruitful regions.

One half of Brescia Protestant! What a light this simple fact throws on the fervent admonitions addressed to the lady-counselors to protect their young flock of maidens from this rising flood of heresy and the consequent heretical hatred of the virginal life and all that bore the semblance of monastic institutions! Surely, even in this nineteenth century, and in every land under the heavens, it is daily becoming more and more a matter of vital importance to guard the young from these "little seeds of doubt cast into the mind, and becoming so deeply rooted there, that they can be plucked up only with the utmost difficulty." Surely, in these days of independent thought and scorn of all religious authority, even young children will understand how much wiser it is "to follow the beaten path where no danger can be apprehended, instead of the untried road among pitfalls and precipices"! And how timely is the advice to "follow ever the broad highway of the Church's teaching and practice, in which so many saints walk before us"!

What strikes one as most precious in these reminders of a dying saint and foundress are the beautiful and most practical lessons on the lofty esteem in which they should hold their own institute and the virginal life which is its immediate purpose and the mainspring of its efficiency; the absolute trust to be reposed in the Divine aid, and the no less absolute humility and self-denial which must be characteristic of their service toward the Divine Majesty; and then the unlimited and unwearied charity with which they must cultivate the happiness and spiritual interests of their flocks of devoted maiden souls.

One is apt—in a self-seeking and sensual age, amid a society where the sweet ties of parental love and filial duty are daily and hourly growing weaker, and becoming, like obsolete statutes, things of the past, lifeless and without any practical virtue—to fancy that of all places in which the counterpart of the home affections ought to prevail, monasteries are the last; and that nowhere would one be less disposed to seek for the perfection of parental piety than in the bosom of a cloistered or even an uncloistered nun. Yet here we have the practical injunction of the sweetest, the most delicate, and the most self-sacrificing motherly tenderness inculcated and enjoined by the holy Maid of Desenzano; and we may be sure that the Ursulines who have inherited her spirit never could have covered both hemispheres with their teeming houses, did not that angelic motherly love still govern the breasts of the sisterhood and influence the souls of their countless pupils.

It is, however, of that motherly tenderness so necessary in the heart of the superiors of a monastery, and so much needed by their inferiors, that we wish to speak here. In no family or household in the world outside of the cloister do the inmates need and crave such kindness, such loving care, such unvarying patience and gentleness, a tenderness so deep and true and exhaustless, as they do within the cloister itself. If superiors who read this will only remember their own need in the past, and the vain yearnings for a true mother's heart to lean upon, and the unsatisfied want of the true maternal instincts ever inseparable from patience, gentleness, and devotion!

Listen rather to that wonderful woman—whose life seems to have been one continuous and successful effort to stifle all the dearest sentiments of her sex and to crush within her heart all the most sacred family affections—listen rather to that heart, as, like a fountain unsealed, it pours forth as with a mighty rush of water the tide of its hallowed womanly charity.

The trust committed to these lady-counselors is to be " the guardians of maidens who are affianced to the Most High God. . . . It will become impossible for you not to bear about with you, night and day, the image of each one of them, as if it were bound to your bosom or imprinted on your very heart. . . . Penetrate yourselves with this deep conviction, that you are not worthy to be placed over others; but rather you should deem yourselves the poor servants and handmaidens of your sisters. . . . Be gentle and courteous. . . . You will effect more by loving words and gentle courtesy than by bitterness and sharp reproof, which should never be used except in extremity. Whenever you see a weak and timid soul, . . . comfort her, give her courage, . . . open up to her the bright vision of God's mercies, and enable that sensitive and shrinking heart to open all its avenues to the sweet influence of consolation. . . ."

Angela left her daughters uncloistered, scattered throughout their homes in the city; some of them were but poor seamstresses, or servant-girls toiling hard for their masters, and sanctifying their respective households by the example of a pure life and a generous piety. The lady-counselors are to make themselves thoroughly acquainted with *the most needy*, whether spiritually or otherwise—with those, more especially still, whose great need puts the life of body or soul in peril. That need must be supplied instantly. Where the counselors are helpless to provide, they must apply forthwith to those above them. "On this point I bid you to be importunate and exacting," says the great motherly heart. "Should any soul in your charge be lost through your neglect, God will call you to a strict account for it on the Day of Judgment. . . . For, hold for certain that He will never fail to provide you with all that is necessary to both souls and bodies."

As to the young maidens themselves, who are members of the Order, or postulants on trial, no matter how highly or lowly born, "Tell them," the dying parent says, "that it is my wish, wherever they happen to be, to give good example, charming all whom they meet by the sweet odor of their virtues, showing obedience to all who have authority over them, and zealous to promote good feeling and peace among their friends." It is on record that these early disciples of Angela Merici were perfect models of all the filial virtues in the homes where they continued to reside. The noble Brescian families, as well as those of the burgess class, who gave their darlings to the company of St. Ursula, were amply rewarded by the untold blessings which these, in return, brought to the paternal fireside. The Company spread and took such deep root in Brescia and its territory only because every man, woman, and child within it had daily and hourly experience of the beautiful lives and heavenly virtues of these modest followers of the Maid of Desenzano.

"Tell them also," their venerable Mother says, "that the one thing important above all others is to cherish the honor of Christ Jesus, to whom they have promised both their maidenhood and themselves. On Him alone must they build their hopes and place their affections. . . . Let them take comfort and courage ! . . . For you may impart to them these glad tidings, which I bring them from Christ Himself and our Blessed Lady—that they have good cause to exult and to make holiday in their hearts, inasmuch as in Heaven for all and each is prepared a new crown of glory and bliss—provided only that they remain immovably firm in their holy purpose, and strenuously observe our holy rule. . . . Assure them moreover of this—that I shall presently be more truly living than when they saw me in the body, and that soon I shall see them and know them better, and be more able to help. For then I shall be in their very midst with Him who is not only my Love, but the Love of all of you. . . ."

When Secretary Cozzano came to the last "Reminder," Angela sat up in her bed, not only that she might catch every word more distinctly, but that she might so remember this concluding paragraph as to repeat it to her daughters when the Secretary had finished. The feelings which the lady-counselors labored to restrain, as every portion of the touching paper was read to them, became uncontrollable toward the close. It might well seem to them as if they stood at the gate of Heaven, with its portals ajar, ready to receive their worshiped Mother, and the light from within streaming out on them. So divinely did she speak of their dignity, their duties, their assured reward, and the promise given to the foundress, that the company should "ever be like an unshaken rock, and a tower which no enemy could ever possess;" while, beside the continual presence and aid of Christ in their midst, His love and the motherly care of Angela herself should be more particularly shown to each of them in her dying hour.

They had to restrain their tears when Cozzano had concluded. For Angela, summoning all her remaining strength, and uttering every word with glowing face and a tongue on fire with the charity of the other life on which she was entering, spoke so firmly and so fervently, that she seemed to pour her own soul into theirs.

One, in reading of such a scene, is reminded of the two

great prophets of Israel at its darkest hour—Elias ascending to Heaven in a chariot of living flame, and Elisæus gathering up his master's cloak with the inheritance of his God-like spirit, and gazing upward at the receding figure of the divine man, while he bethought him of the Israel of Achab and Jezabel, God-forsaken and plunged in the most fearful idolatry.

The daughters of St. Angela present at her death-bed could not help feeling that their parent spoke in God's own name ; that their calling was indeed from God ; that the great institution they were laboring to complete was truly the work of the Most High ; and that the promises so explicitly and so solemnly made and reiterated by the dying saint would be realized both with regard to the permanence of the company of St. Ursula, and with regard to the special assistance guaranteed in life and death to its faithful members.

Everything was supernatural in this interview between Angela and the lady-counselors. Not that the sweet and holy emotions of natural love and gratitude found no vent there, but that the tears which were shed and the grief felt and expressed at parting with one who had been most truly the mother of their souls, was so tempered and brightened by the almost heavenly atmosphere of that poor bare sick-room, and by the sensible nearness to the blessed company of the everlasting city, that earth was forgotten in the light of Heaven, and filial sorrow swallowed up in the great flood of joy and hope which lifted upward all their hearts.

It would appear that the energy with which Angela spoke while repeating the last "Reminder" and the motherly benediction on her dear ones was such that she seemed to them to be, for the moment at least, restored to her former strength. Both directresses and counselors went away from St. Afra's with the hope that a life so precious would be spared to them yet awhile. Such was also the impression produced on the attendant physician, Dr. Gardoni. Among the citizens of Brescia, however, there was produced by the rumor of the saint's danger a feeling akin to consternation. They had been so long familiar with the modest and gentle presence, had so often experienced the benefit of Angela's wise and heavenly counsels, had found her so true and helpful a friend in their sore need, so safe a confidant and guide in their troubles and doubts, and the families of high and low had been so often blessed by the holy influences which she and her daughters brought with them in their visitations, that to lose her now was to lose the common parent of poor and rich alike.

As we have already seen, from the very first beginning of Angela's stay in Brescia (1516) the reputation of her sanctity and wisdom was such that her advice was eagerly sought by persons of every class. She thenceforth became the spiritual guide of all persons who aspired to a life of greater perfection—to the young and old of her own sex particularly. The long years which elapsed, and the dreadful misfortunes and vicissitudes which befell Brescia in the interval and up to 1540, instead of diminishing her influence over minds and hearts, had only endeared her more with every successive year to the entire city, and had only served to increase the universal veneration felt toward her.

We have said "universal veneration," for even those who were led astray by the doctrines of Luther and Calvin were so convinced of Angela's superior merit and extraordinary virtue, that they approached her as they approached, in the church outside of Brescia, such men as Cardinals Contarini, Pole, Caraffa, de Tiene, and such saints as Philip Neri and Ignatius Loyola. The historians of that age inform us of the repeated attempts to enlist, under the pretext of reforming the Church, such great men as these in the unholy rebellion which made reform a by-word of scorn and derision.

Even at the present day, in spite of the fearful inroads made by radicalism and impiety among the inhabitants of Upper Italy, the entire city and territory of Brescia are yearly moved by the return of the anniversary of Angela Merici's death, city and country pouring forth their population around her tomb in St. Afra. But we are anticipating.

During the whole period of her illness her lowly abode near that venerable church was beset daily by anxious visitors.[1] Two in particular are mentioned by Father Salvatori—the Cavalier James Chizzola and Signor Thomas Gavardi. Both had, as they afterward testified, been much benefited by her counsels and direction ; they now came to seek a last advice from one whom they believed to be led by the Spirit of God. Sitting up in her bed, as her two noble friends besought this last favor from her, she first addressed herself to Chizzola, seting forth, with an eloquence and cogency of argument which he had never before witnessed in her exhortations the duties of the true Christian man. Her very fervor, however, exhausted her, and when she turned to Gavardi she could only say, with an air and an accent that stamped every word on his soul forever after, *Whatever you would wish at your dying hour to have done in health, that do now while you may!*

There were others besides the two gentlemen present who heard these words and were deeply moved by them. More than one took them to heart and began to lead a truly Christian life. They were repeated abroad in the city, and fell, like the dew from heaven on the parched earth, on many a needy soul, sinking deep into generous hearts, and helping to reform the course of more than one erring life, or to spur to

---

[1] *Della vita di S. Angela Merici, vergine Bresciana*, E. Girelli, pp. 169-171.

nobler effort and higher aims those already on the right road.

How long an interval elapsed between Angela's last conference with the lady-counselors and her death, has not been explicitly stated by her biographers. The *testament*, addressed to the lady-directresses, had been, according to some writers, intrusted to the Countess Lodrone, as soon as the latter had accepted the charge of Mother Vicar. This testament was to be communicated to the proper persons only after Angela's death. As to Angela herself—without repelling from her door or her bedside the friends and acquaintances who came to see her for the last time, or to hear her loved voice once more, or without refusing to receive such of her daughters as yearned for a last interview with their mother—she intimated her desire that the members of the Company should not quit their post of duty to satisfy even these cravings of a grateful love. But she allowed free access to all other persons, mindful to the last of the golden rule of true piety and Christian charity, that one may leave God's presence in prayer to find Him equally present in the needy souls who seek one's aid. So, ardently as she wished to devote to communion with Him alone the brief interval that separated her from the Judgment, she continued to be in death what she had ever been in life—the ever-ready and most patient counselor of those who sought her guidance.

But one can scarcely form a conception of the holy fire which filled her heart and served to chasten still more, amid her bodily ills, the pure soul which had been chastened by more than half a century of suffering and voluntary crucifixion. With that sovereign reverence for her virginal body which the Christian doctrine and practice inculcate, she would allow no hand to touch it save her own as she prepared it for its supreme repose in the sepulchre. It is said that on the eve of her death, dismissing even Barbara Fontana from her room, and shielding herself from every mortal eye, she so prepared and decked herself, that it only needed her poor Franciscan habit to be ready for her place in St. Afra. And there she lies at this day, as she had laved and vested to meet the Heavenly Bridegroom.[1]

It would appear that some anxious visitor knocked at the closed door while Angela was thus decking herself for death's bridals, and when admitted expressed surprise to find her able to leave her bed. When Barbara Fontana returned with such of her sisters and Angela's lady friends as were admitted with the former, they too could scarcely help chiding the brave-hearted sufferer for what they considered an act of imprudence or even foolhardiness. But she had been so well accustomed through life to rise above every bodily weakness, that even in death she seemed to make the sinking flesh do the will of the spirit.

She told them, however, that death was at hand, and with an air and in a tone that dispelled all doubt and hesitation. It was time to administer the last sacraments and divinest consolations of religion. So Extreme Unction washed away every vestige of soil contracted by these unwearied feet in their many pilgrimages, every stain which might have remained on her hands, even when breaking daily and hourly the bread of charity to God's poor, or while binding up the inveterate wounds of others. And into the temple of her virginal body, thus anointed anew for the coming of its Lord, Christ Himself came in His last gift to mortal man, Holy Viaticum, the bread of the traveler about to cross the boundary between this vale of tears and the land of the living.

To Catholics who believe in the Divine Reality of this great central sacrament, the veiled presence consoling, cheering,

---

[1] Salvatori, p. 119.

and fixing our hearts on GOD during this life of faith and trial, it scarcely needs to be told with what transports the saints and all holy souls approach the mercy-seat on our altars during their pilgrimage here below. But when the end has come, when faith is about to give place to the clear vision of God, souls like Angela Merici, who had made of prayer and contemplation their daily bread, who had knelt before our tabernacles as if the treasure these contained were visible in its divine form to them, must see with a keener sense as they stand within the first beams of the coming brightness. To those who have lived a life of sensual enjoyment, in conformity with the instincts of the natural man, the clear-sightedness vouchsafed to "the pure of heart" while still in the body is a thing absolutely incomprehensible. But when these pure hearts, cleansed from the very last alloy of earth, gaze, at the very verge of eternity, on the face of their Emmanuel, their hidden God, through the thin and wasted shreds of their mortality—as one beholds the face of the rising sun through the veil of the morning—are they not filled with ecstatic joy, as every instant brings the unclouded form of the luminary more distinctly before the eye?

"Writers say"—such are the words of Father Salvatori—"that at the approach of the Holy Viaticum she appeared transformed as with the beauty of Paradise; and that as soon as she had received it she folded her arms as in a transport of love, breaking forth into the most tender expressions of devotion. After having thus entertained for a long time her divine guest, like one intoxicated with holy love, she summoned around her all the members of her company, and addressed them a moving discourse on charity, obedience, humility, the faithful observance of the rule, the wariness with which they should guard the treasure of their virginity, and the love and holy fear of the Most High God, till they all broke forth into uncontrollable weeping. Then, loving mother that she was, she blessed them, and took leave of them, saying that on earth they should not meet again, but giving them all a rendezvous in Heaven. 'Having thus fulfilled every duty, and feeling that her Beloved was now approaching fast, she bade them fetch her habit of a Tertiary of St. Francis, and put it on herself. Then, as the tradition has it, she arose from her bed, and lay down on the rush-mat. Thus extended on the floor, she forgot everything earthly, and, like one in ecstasy, she gave no further sign of seeing or hearing what passed around her. Only her eyes, peaceful and shining with a preternatural light, remained fixed on Heaven, while she was heard from time to time to utter, amid her ardent sighs, the sweet name of JESUS. Presently, with her face overspread with unearthly joy, she broke forth into the dying words of Christ on the cross: *In manus tuas commendo spiritum meum.*[1] She thereupon bowed her head on her chest, closed her eyes, and the blessed spirit went peacefully forth from its tenement on the 27th day of January, 1540. It was a Tuesday, about six o'clock of the afternoon. . . ."

Thus closed a life marked by obscure toil and suffering; by constant striving, in the face of ever-recurring obstacles, after the accomplishment of a mighty enterprise divinely foreshown, and rendered seemingly impossible of execution by the imperious necessity of adverse circumstances. But, while yielding to the misfortunes of the times, the brave and faithful spirit continued to hope against hope itself, schooling her own mind and heart to the acquisition of supernatural wisdom and the practice of the most heroic virtues, leading the life of an anchorite in the midst of a crowded city, the

---

[1] "Into Thy hands I commend my spirit" (St. Luke xxiii. 46).

visible providence of the poor and afflicted, the guide of all classes and both sexes in the road of Christian perfection, the teacher of prelates and priests, the trusted counselor of princes, a reformer who shone by the unearthly splendor of her own heroic generosity and self-denial in the age of a false and calamitous Reformation—a great missionary, though but a poor, single-handed girl, in the midst of a population demoralized by such a fatal succession of wars as the world had not seen since the age of Attila, and in comparison with which the wars of the First Napoleon were only a thunder-shower in a summer sky.

No: not merely a missionary, and working single-handed to reform an age more unfortunate than guilty, and to restore the bright days of early Gospel faith and enlightened piety among a people blessed above all others by the lavish hand of nature and nature's God; but who were the victims of domestic political passions which they neither shared nor could control, and of the most unholy foreign ambitions begotten by the very sight of their most beautiful country. Angela Merici was an apostle, the first of a class of apostolic women sent to educate the youth of their own sex at the beginning of an era hostile to all the divine teachings of Christianity, and thereby to save the society of the future just as the floodgates of Socialism and Communism were about to let loose on Christendom that deluge of error which threatened the foundations of the family home and of all social life.

In the pictures at Brescia and elsewhere in Upper Italy, painted too in the sixteenth century, the vision in which St. Ursula and her band of virgin martyrs appeared to the Maid of Desenzano, is so represented that Angela, kneeling, receives a standard from Ursula's hand, while around the kneeling figure are a numerous train of followers. If we may look upon the three centuries and a half which have now elapsed since that lowly death-bed scene in Brescia as embodying the realization of Angela's vision or dream, we cannot help being struck by the fact that, while the company founded by the Maid of Desenzano was the first established for educating female youth, other holy women, following her example, have founded similar societies, each at present vieing with the Company of St. Ursula in numbers, zeal, and efficiency.

None the less to that sweet and heavenly form lying low in death beneath the shadows of St. Afra's Church is due the leadership among this glorious band of apostolic women, educators of youth, and destined to be, in the hand of God's Church, the most successful agents for saving society and the moral world.

CHAPTER XVI.

A SAINT'S TESTAMENT AND LEGACIES—A PEOPLE'S GRATITUDE AND VENERATION — INCORRUPTION LASTING THROUGH CENTURIES.

IN some biographies of St. Angela the reading of the testament intrusted to Mother Lucretia Lodrone is deferred till the conclusion of the last solemn obsequies, which only took place several weeks after her decease. They also separate the testament itself from its proper place in the narrative, and oblige the reader to seek for it in an appendix. Assuredly, one so wise as Lucretia Lodrone, and who knew so intimately the intentions of her saintly friend, could have deemed no time so opportune for the reading of the document as that immediately following her own and her sisters' bereavement, and no place so suggestive of heroic resolutions and generous sentiments as the room in which lay all that was mortal of their worshiped parent.

We can, therefore, assist in spirit at this meeting in the death-chamber of the nine women to whom Angela Merici had given, while she was still among the living, the grave responsibility of continuing her own divinely-appointed work, and of imparting a final and perfect shape to an institution from which Christendom was to derive such abundant and lasting benefit.

Here is this last will and testament, translated as closely as the sense would permit from the original presented to the Roman tribunals during the process of Angela's canonization, and transcribed faithfully by Father Salvatori:

"*Testament drawn up by St. Angela during her last illness, and addressed to the Lady-Directresses of the Company.*

"SISTER ANGELA, unworthy servant of Christ Jesus, to my Lady the Countess Lucretia, Head Mother of the Company of St. Ursula, and to the other Directresses and Mothers, the noble matrons Lady Genevieve di Luciagi, Lady Maria di Avogadri, Lady Veronica di Bucci, Lady Ursula di Gavardi, Lady Jean di Monti, Lady Isabella da Prato, Lady Lionella di Pedeciocchi, Lady Caterina di Mei. May the everlasting blessing of the Almighty God, Father, Son, and Holy Ghost, be upon you all! Amen.

"As it has pleased God, Sisters mine most dear to my heart in the blood of Christ Jesus, and Mothers worthy of all honor, to choose in His eternal counsels from out this vain world many persons, virgins especially, to form this Company of ours, and as it hath also been His pleasure, in the immensity of His goodness, to select me to co-operate with Him in this great work, without considering how incapable and unworthy a servant I was; even so hath He deigned, as is the wont of that same goodness, to bestow on me the necessary graces and gifts enabling me to govern in accordance with His will and to provide for the manifold needs of my charge—particularly hath He vouchsafed the grace of directing and maintaining them in the manner of life to which they have been called. But among these gifts and needful provisions made for me by the Almighty, you are one of the most precious: you who have been found worthy to be the true-hearted mothers of so noble a family, a family placed in your hands that you may cherish and care for its members as if they were your own proper children—indeed, to show them a greater love, if such be possible. And here I wish you to consider most attentively how great a favor and high an honor God hath vouchsafed to do you, by making you the parents of so many virgins, and by placing in your hands and committing to your faithful care these souls affianced to Himself. What reason have you not to thank the Divine Majesty, and to beseech Him that just as He hath been pleased to place you at the head of this great flock, even so it may please Him to grant you the wisdom and strength necessary toward fulfilling your charge with honor to Him, and with perfect fidelity to your own obligations? It behooves you, therefore, to come to a generous and firm determination to accomplish most perfectly His holy will; to accept with a living and firm faith the task imposed on you by His love; and, come what may, to persevere to the end in your glorious labor. Above all things, I pray and beseech you by the Passion and Blood of Christ, to take to heart with all earnestness the execution of these few dying injunctions, which you may see written down here one after the other. I am now leaving this life, and put you in my place, so that these counsels of mine shall be like bequests made to you, my heirs, which, being the expression of my last will, I leave to you to execute faithfully.

"First, and principally, therefore, beloved Mothers and dear Sisters in Christ, endeavor with the help of God to conceive and cherish in your hearts the purpose of taking on you this charge and its cares for the sole love of God and the pure zeal for the salvation of souls. Thereby the whole course of your labors and government will be like a tree planted and rooted in this twofold love, incapable of bearing any but the sweetest and most healthful fruit. Our Lord hath said it: *A good tree cannot bring forth evil fruit* (St. Matt. 7 : 18); that is, the soul and will aflame with charity and directed by it, can only bring forth good and holy deeds. This also is the reason why St. Augustine says, *Ama, et fac quod vis;* ' Only love, and then do what you will ;' as if he said, Only fill your soul with that supernatural love and charity, and you cannot help doing well; or as if he said more openly, Perfect charity cannot sin.

"*Second Bequest.* I next beseech you to bear not only in your mind, but graven on your heart, all your daughters, and each one of them in particular; not their names merely, but their quality, their natural disposition—all that concerns each one, in a word. Nor will this be difficult if you love them truly. For it is the nature of true motherly love among persons of the world, that if a parent had a thousand sons and daughters, she would have all and each of them perfectly present to her mind and heart. This is the law of love. And experience proves that the more children one has, the greater grows for each the parent's loving care. How much more so, in the spiritual order, can and should Mothers such as you manifest a like love of their dear ones. Supernatural love is incomparably stronger than that of nature. Wherefore, dearest Mothers, if you only love these dear daughters of ours with a lively and heartfelt love, it will become impossible for you not to have their images deeply imprinted on both heart and memory.

"*Third Bequest.* In the third place, I ask of you as a favor to attract and direct these dear ones with the gentle and loving hand of motherly tenderness, instead of treating them haughtily and rudely; under every circumstance be gentle and courteous to them. Listen to the Master, saying : *Learn of Me, because I am meek and humble of heart* (St. Matt. 11 : 29). Of the Almighty Creator and Ruler it is also said, that He *ordereth all things sweetly;* and the Master says of Himself : *My yoke is sweet, and My burthen light*

(Ibid. 30). Thus it behooves you to employ the utmost gentleness. Above all, take care never to use compulsion. God hath made us all free-willed, and to no one's free-will doth He do violence. He leads them to obey Him by show of reason, by inviting motives, and by gentle persuasion. Thus, doth He say in the Apocalypse: *I counsel thee to buy of Me gold fire-tried, that thou mayest be made rich* (3 : 18). 'I counsel thee,' He says; not 'I compel thee.' On this point, however, I do not wish to be understood as blaming reproof unqualifiedly; for both reprehension and sharp correction may be required in certain circumstances, and prove useful at times to certain persons. Only, in order to make them useful and seasonable, one should be moved by charity and by zeal for the spiritual welfare of souls.

"*Fourth Bequest.* You must be desirous and zealous to see your daughters clad with the beautiful vesture of innocence, and adorned with all manner of virtues, that so they may find grace in the eyes of Christ Jesus, their Spouse. More particularly, still, must you see to it that they do Him perfect and chaste service by every act of theirs, by their modest and gentle bearing, by their reserve and prudence, their patience and charity. One sees mothers in the world bestow so much care and earnestness in dressing and adorning their daughters, to make these pleasing to their suitors; and the more these earthly lovers are elevated in rank, the more pains do such parents take in adorning their dear ones, suiting the artificial graces with which they set forth their charms to the personal taste of him whom they want to win. Indeed, these mothers seem to make their happiness consist in having daughters worthy of such courtly suitors, and place their hope on the friendship and favor these will show them for love of their daughters. Wherefore, bethink you how much more zealous you ought to be concerning the spiritual loveliness of these maidens of yours, who are lifted up to the heavenly rank of affianced brides of the eternal Son of the Most High God! Oh, what honor and dignity are yours to be thus the rulers and Mothers of these brides of the King of kings, and to stand in the relation of parents to the Son of God, drawing His favors down on yourselves through your daughters! Yes, most happy will it be for you if you show yourselves prompt and eager to feel and assert this new and singular rank bestowed on you.

"*Fifth Bequest.* In the fifth place, when it happens that you have kindly admonished three, or at most four times, any one of your subjects, without finding in her any disposition to obey, then let her alone, and send to her neither Counselor nor other visitors. For this neglect may induce the poor culprit to conceive regret for her obstinacy, as well as a more fervent desire to remain and persevere in the Company. One reason why God banished Adam from the earthly paradise was that his isolation should force him to acknowledge his fault and do penance for it. Should any one of the maidens thus left to herself desire to return and manifest sorrow for her fault, you must receive her on the condition that she shall ask pardon of all of you, as well as of her own Counselor, and let her, in expiation, fast one Friday on bread and water.

"*Sixth Bequest.* In the sixth place, when you find a young person so vain of her personal appearance as to have great difficulty in laying aside her pretty head-dress or other trifling ornaments, this should make you conceive but a feeble hope of her persevering in such a life as ours. For if she is unable to make such trifling sacrifices as these, how can she be expected to have strength for far greater? However, there is need of discernment in such cases. For it may happen that a soul who thus yields to her inclination in some trifling matter, will afterwards in all other difficulties show superior generosity.

"*Seventh Bequest.* Seventhly, you must endeavor to assemble the Counselors (*colonnelli*) once or twice a month, and consult with them, examining with great care the details of your administration, especially what the Counselors may lay before you with regard to the conduct of your daughters, to their circumstances, their bodily and spiritual necessities, so that you may provide for all as the Holy Spirit shall direct you.

"*Eighth Bequest.* You must also be careful to call your daughters together from time to time, in such place as you may deem best or most convenient, and there, when you have at hand a proper person, give them the benefit of a short sermon or exhortation. Their meeting each other thus, will enable them to greet each other like true sisters, to converse about their spiritual concerns, to exchange congratulations or consolations, as the case may be, and thus to go back home greatly delighted.

"*Ninth Bequest.* You should know that, had it not been both useful and proper for our Company to possess any source of revenues, our Lord would not have begun to provide us with them. Wherefore I advise you to be in this matter good, prudent, and true Mothers, employing these revenues for the welfare and increase of the Company, in conformity with the dictates of your motherly love and prudence. On this point I wish you not to seek counsel from outsiders. Do what is needful among yourselves alone, being directed by your charity and the light of the Holy Spirit, aiming in all your measures to procure the spiritual benefit and advancement of your daughters—not only for the purpose of inciting the existing members of the Company to a greater love of their vocation and to a stricter obligation to be perfect, but also to attract to you a fresh accession of numbers. For the charitable use of wealth, that which is acceptable to God, consists in bestowing pecuniary aid and showing real kindness whereby so doing souls can be saved from sin or dangerous habits, or induced to practise virtue or to contract good habits, or again to seek a higher degree of spiritual advancement. Thereby the almsgiver in a manner forces the recipients to act in a certain manner and in a given direction, as it pleaseth him : just as we see a young girl in the world who consents to receive presents from another contract the obligation of so pleasing that person that she may no longer say him nay. In like manner, neither more nor less, presents and alms well bestowed attract and impel the recipients to the practice of virtue, and bind them to persist therein. Keep to these well-tried methods, and they shall not lead you astray.

"*Tenth Bequest.* I entreat you from the bottom of my heart to keep an anxious and watchful eye on all these subordinate guardians of the holy flock I intrust to your keeping. Be careful that no discord or uncharitableness shall grow up among them ; be especially so to preserve them from every breath and taint of heresy in this pestilential age. Remember that the devil never slumbers, but evermore seeks our ruin under a thousand disguises. Wherefore keep a strict watch, and take particular pains to maintain among your flock union and harmony of wills, as we read of Christians in the primitive Church, that *the multitude of believers had but one heart and one soul* (Acts 4 : 32). Such must you endeavor to make the union between yourselves and your daughters. For the more united you are the more will Christ be with you, fulfilling the office of Father and Good Shepherd. Indeed, you can have no surer mark by which you may know if the Company has the grace of God, than in this mutual love and close union of its members. Christ Himself hath said it : *By this shall all men know that you are My disciples, if you have love one for another* (St. John 13 : 35). So, then, mutual love and union of wills are an infallible sign that the road we follow is the good road—that which leads to God! Wherefore, dear Sisters and Mothers, be watchful here. The enemy will cover his snares with the fair appearance of good. So, as soon as you perceive the first sign of mischief, hasten at once to guard against it with all the energy God may give you. Do not allow the baneful seed of disunion to take root for one moment among you; it would injure your credit in the city as well as beyond it. Disunion in every corporate body means dissolution and death. Our Saviour hath said it: *Every kingdom divided against itself shall be made desolate* (St. Matt. 12 : 25).

"*Last Bequest.* In conclusion, make it your highest care that the ordinances made for you, especially all the prescriptions of our Rule, shall be scrupulously obeyed. Should the lapse of time or other circumstances render it necessary to make new ordinances, or to change in aught your manner of doing things, make the change warily and with the aid of wise counsel. Let your main resource in all emergencies be to go to the feet of Christ Jesus. There superiors and subjects must unite in fervent prayer to Him. For, most certainly, He will be in the midst of you; He will enlighten you and teach you—true and kind Master as He is—what it behooves you to do. Of this be firmly assured, that this Rule of ours comes immediately from His hand, and that He will not forsake this Company so long as this world lasts; for if He has had the chief share in establishing it, who can ever overthrow it? Trust to Him; doubt not; and believe with an unwavering faith that this shall be as I say. I know what I am saying to you: Blessed are those who really lose their own mind on this matter.

"If you are faithful to act in this way in these and similar circumstances, under the direction of the Holy Spirit and in conformity with the need and gravity of the times, I bid you to rejoice and to be brave of heart. Lo, great is the reward prepared for you; and where the daughters will be there shall be the Mothers. Be comforted and doubt not! We should wish to see you in our midst in Heaven, even as our common Love will have it; and who may withstand Him? His light and the sweet splendor of His truth shall surround you in the hour of death, and shall deliver you from the hand of the enemy. So, then, persevere joyously and faithfully in the work you have undertaken. Beware, beware, I say, of yielding to tepidity. Every promise which I make you shall be fulfilled with overflowing measure. Now I am about to depart; and you must, within the interval, do what you have to do. I embrace you all and give to all the kiss of peace, beseeching God to bless you, *In the name of the Father, and of the Son, and of the Holy Ghost. Amen.*"

The Company of St. Ursula over which Lucretia Lodrone now found herself placed numbered one hundred and sixty members. Their field of labor, so far, did not extend beyond Brescia and its suburbs. Within these limits their virtues and services were familiar to every household. The death of their parent was, therefore, a subject of general regret and admiration : of regret for the loss of one who had long been revered as a public benefactress and a shining model of the highest Christian perfection; of admiration, because all the circumstances of her saintly death only served to bring before the mind of the Brescians these supernatural qualities of purity, charity, forgetfulness of self, unbounded devotion to the good of others, of masculine courage and endurance in a weak and aged woman, of extraordinary knowledge and far-seeing prudence both in the things of God and the concerns of every-day life : in a word, of angelic goodness and almost divine wisdom in one who had lived and died a poor Tertiary Sister of St. Francis.

They knew instinctively—as indeed all true Christians do—this good people of Brescia, what constitutes true sanctity ; they had seen more than one saint in their midst or in their near neighborhood during Angela's lifetime. All the declamations or insidious calumnies of the emissaries and adepts of Calvinism had not yet succeeded in persuading them that the Church of Italy was not fertile in saintly men and women. And a quarter of a century's intimate acquaintance with Angela Merici's person, with her comings and her goings, and with every detail of her labor among the sick, the poor, and the young, every feature of her obscure life of prayer, poverty, and self-denial, had only convinced them beyond all possibility of doubt or error, that the Maid of Desenzano was most truly A SAINT.

And, now that the angelic spirit had gone to join its kindred hosts on high, there was nothing to prevent the thousands of town and country who cherished her name from paying the lifeless remains the honors due to a saint. The emaciated frame, clad in the poor brown Franciscan habit, lay on the rush-pallet where she had breathed her last. The sweet, modest face, beautiful all through life, but most beautiful in death, seemed still to wear the ecstatic smile with which the Holy Name and the last sacred words were uttered. And, although the eyes were closed, one could fancy that they looked upward toward the eternal hills over which the true day-dawn was breaking, and that a faint reflection of its splendors rested on the calm and pallid features.

She had, with her own hands, decked herself for the long sleep in expectation of the Resurrection Day. Her daughters had not even to cross her hands on the virginal bosom : they had been meekly folded there when the last prayer was uttered ; they only had to close the eyelids. There she lay, from the first moment of her repose, as she has lain ever since in her tomb at St. Afra's, no matter how costly the structure and its ornaments, in her brown Franciscan habit, with her pilgrim's staff by her side.

The pilgrimage was over at length ; the weary feet would travel no more. With what transports of mingled sorrow and joy did Lucretia Lodrone and her companions kneel in succession to kiss these feet which had trodden the hill-sides of Bethlehem, the streets of Jerusalem, the ascent to Calvary, the precincts of the Holy Sepulchre, and all the footprints of the Saviour in and around the Holy City ! These poor, cold, motionless feet had, like those of the Master, been unwearied in seeking out the stray sheep of His flock and bringing them back to the fold, or in marking out for souls athirst of perfection the steep and rugged paths that lead to sanctity.

And while the daughters of Angela Merici were thus satisfying their own instinctive feelings of veneration for the departed, others were thronging to the well-known door to kiss these same feet and gaze upon the transformed features of their benefactress, their counselor, their guide. Prelates, priests, monks, nobles, burgesses, tradesmen and laborers, ladies of the most exalted rank, and the poor seamstresses and servants whom Angela was wont to console, to cheer, to teach, and to guide toward all good—they came streaming in all day and all night, day after day, and night after night—city-folk and country-folk—from Milan and Bergamo and Verona, from Angela's own home in Desenzano and from Salo, which loved to claim the holy maid as half her own ; it was pitiful to see the poor and the lowly surging around that door and that inanimate body—the sacred tabernacle of a saintly soul ; it was glorious to see the heartfelt homage of prince and priest, of the exalted in rank and learning and fame, kneeling by that poor rush-pallet to honor God's goodness, wisdom, and power in His greatest master-work— A SAINT.

The affluence was so great from the very first announcement of Angela's death, that, to prevent accident, to afford an easy access to the ever-increasing throng, as well as to show proper respect to the departed, the body had to be removed to the adjoining Church of St. Afra in the evening of the 28th. This removal was effected in the most solemn manner, amid an immense concourse, the ladies putting on mourning as if for one of their nearest and dearest, the entire clergy and gentry of Brescia joining in the cortége. Brief as was the space which separated the death-chamber from the main portal of St. Afra's, the crowd was so dense that those who bore the corpse, and the Sisterhood who surrounded and followed it, could only move through the surging mass with extreme difficulty. Yet there was no disorder ; there was only an intense desire to cast one look on the face of the saintly dead, or to touch even the hem of the poor Franciscan habit. And while the solemn chants of the church ascended to Heaven, with them mingled the sobs of the multitude, the fervent blessings on the BLESSED departed and her sorrowing daughters, and the prayers and loud cries of praise which come so warm from the generous Italian heart. No earthly prince or potentate could command or expect to receive such a spontaneous and fervent homage of the deepest and holiest affections of the human soul, offered by the united voices of a whole people.

In the venerable and beautiful church which Angela had loved so well in life every altar beheld the Adorable Sacrifice offered up for the repose of her soul. The Augustinian Canons, whom Angela had so deeply trusted, paid to her remains and her memory every mark of respect, of veneration even. The voice of the multitude inside and outside of the sacred edifice ceased not to call her Saint (*Beata*); bishops and priests who had long known her echoed the popular voice with heart and lips. The emotion of the dense crowd who filled the church was a something indescribable. It lifted one's soul to God, and inspired every heart with heroic resolutions. The touch of Elisæus' holy remains recalled to life the dead man cast hurriedly into his sepulchre by terrified friends; why should not the near presence of yonder virginal body, reminding the worshiper of sixty-five years of unsullied purity, of heroic deeds of self-denial, self-sacrifice, and widespread beneficence, not warm into newness of life the tepid bystanders? How could all these men and women, of whatever degree, not feel their hearts beat with more generous pulsations as they remembered how much that lowly Maid of Desenzano had accomplished, single-handed, for God and themselves, and how aimless and barren their own lives had been?

And so, when the Divine Victim had been offered up, where she had so often worshiped, they bore her remains to the crypt or lower church, known in the city as "the most holy place," because there were buried the glorious martyrs who, like St. Afra herself, had died in Brescia to bear their witness to Christ.

The entombment, however, was not allowed to be completed according to the prescribed legal form. The chapter of the Cathedral Church claimed the privilege of possessing Angela's precious remains, because she was the foundress of an Order, and as such ought by right to be buried in the principal church of the diocese. The clergy of St. Afra, which was Angela's parish church, had an undoubted canonical right to give her a resting-place within their own precincts. And then the Minor Observants of St. Francis could urge in their own favor the fact that Angela was a Franciscan, recognized as such while living, and in death wearing the honored habit of their founder.

To the superficial reader it may appear an unseemly strife —this arising for the possession of the remains of a poor religious. But the Church has ever held in such honor the bodies not only of her saints, but of all her children. St. Paul affirms that the Christian's body is the temple of the Holy Ghost :[1] if this be true of all the baptized faithful, how much more true of these heroic souls who, following generously the promptings of the Holy Spirit, lay down their lives in glorious witness to the divinity of their faith, or demonstrate that divinity by a long life of God-like abnegation and self-sacrifice ! Hence the extraordinary care with which the bodies of the early martyrs were buried in some secret place where the Holy Sacrifice could be daily offered on their tombs. Hence, when persecution had ceased, and men were called on not to die as witnesses of the Gospel truth, but to live in perfect conformity with its teachings and its Divine Ideal, the reverence with which all those who died in odor of sanctity were buried near the sanctuary, and, when their holiness had been solemnly recognized by the Church, the splendor with which their shrines were ornamented. And all this because, in the truest sense of the word, these holy bodies had been in life the temples of the Holy Ghost. Church vied with church, city with city, nation with nation, for the possession of these sacred treasures, which were to all

---

[1] " Know you not that your members are the temple of the Holy Ghost, who is in you, whom you have from God; and [that, therefore] you are not your own ?" (1 Cor. 6 : 19)

who approached them in God's house a perpetual exhortation to sanctity and Christ-like generosity.

Angela had, indeed, obtained in 1532 a brief from the supreme authorities in Rome, authorizing her to choose the place of her burial. It does not appear, however, that she had in her last moments either produced the brief or expressed any definite wish about its application. When, therefore, it was found and produced, it failed to settle the dispute. So that a delay of thirty days occurred, and during this interval the body remained unburied in the crypt of St. Afra's, exposed on a simple bier to the view and veneration of the faithful. It was, doubtless, a providential delay. It afforded pious pilgrims—and their numbers were countless— the opportunity of gratifying their devotion by coming from far and near to gaze upon that heavenly face, to kiss the feet of the great benefactress of the people, and to touch the hem of her Franciscan robes, as if they knew that a virtue went forth from them. It was a species of popular canonization, the voice of the people being here, in the true sense, the voice of God. The whole of Lombardy and Venetia seemed moved by one mighty impulse to pay this thirty days' homage to the dead Franciscan Tertiary, herself the foundress of a great religious family whose future no one then could forecast.

And this judgment of the popular mind and heart was shared by the high-born, the learned, and the clergy. Indeed, it was the fact of her having been in her lifetime universally regarded as a saint that had given rise to the edifying contestation about her place of burial.

During the first week that the holy remains thus reposed in the crypt of St. Afra's, keeping company with the glorious martyr-band buried there, the city was startled and awestricken at beholding a preternatural brightness in mid-air above the sacred edifice : there it continued during three whole days and nights, shining like a beacon-light to guide the multitude to the spot where Angela Merici lay unburied![1]

But there was given to the sorely tried and tempted populations of Upper Italy a still greater sign than this radiance in the heavens. Throughout these thirty days that the body lay exposed to the air, in this low, damp, underground place, although no precautions had been taken to protect it from the air, and there could have been entertained no thought of embalming it, the flesh remained without the least sign of corruption, sweet-smelling, fresh-colored, flexible, and elastic,[2] bearing to all external appearance every sign of a living body. Not only was there about it nothing redolent of putrefaction, but an aromatic fragrance seemed to emanate from it and to fill the whole crypt.

This interval also, Father Salvatori assures us, afforded the pious artists of Brescia ample time to take plaster casts of the saint's features, or to paint her as she lay in the calm majesty of death. Thus, many of Angela's noble Brescian friends were enable to obtain admirable likenesses of their venerated spiritual guide.[3]

Nor, reflecting on the extraordinary state of incorruption in which the body of the saint was found at the end of these thirty days, must we imagine either that it could be accounted for by the state of the atmosphere, or that it ceased

---

[1] F. Salvatori, p. 125.   [2] F. Salvatori, *ibid.*

[3] The two celebrated Brescian painters, of whom we have already spoken so favorably, Moretto and his pupil Romanini, were kept busy at this work in the crypt of St. Afra's. To them we are indebted for the only authentic portraits of Angela Merici, as she lay thus in life-like death. There is not one of Moretto's beautiful works that does not bear some trace of the Christian ideal, which the conversation of such a woman while living and the contemplation of her angelic features in death, were so apt to create in the artist's mind. From such conversation and contemplation did Giotto, and Fra Angelico, and Fra Bartolomeo draw the ideal forms which charm and captivate us in their immortal works.

when the final ceremonies of sepulture had been performed and dust was returned to its native dust. As we have said, the crypt was underground, and very damp; while the crowds of pilgrims who poured in continually increased both the heat of the place and its dampness, and could only serve to hasten the progress of putrefaction. Incorruptible, however, the virginal flesh of the Maid of Desenzano continued to remain for more than a century and a half after the inhumation. Faino, the historian of St. Angela, who speaks of what he had seen with his own eyes, affirms that it was free from corruption in 1672.[1] Bonifazio Bagata reaffirmed the same fact eight years later,[2] adding that the same extraordinary fragrance which filled the crypt of St. Afra's before the solemn ceremony of entombment was still sensible when the remains were uncovered.

So, after the thirty days of patient investigation, the ecclesiastical judge gave his decision, and the Canons-Regular of St. Afra were authorized to bury the body of Angela Merici where it had been so long lying, in the very place which Angela's own heart had chosen to rest forever. Of course, the good Fathers were overjoyed to possess all that remained of one whom they had known so long and so well, and had learned to revere as a saint from the very beginning. They made immediate preparations for the funeral solemnities, their Superior, Father John Francis Saramondi, setting artists to work—Moretto and his scholars, most probably—to design a tomb in every way worthy of so great a servant of God, and worthy as well of Brescian gratitude and piety. As is the wont in Italy, accurate representations of the monument, with its mosaics and sculptures, were forthwith painted

---

[1] Bernardo Faino, a native of Brescia, Superior-General of the Brescian Congregation, in his "Life of St. Angèla," published in Bologna in 1672.
[2] *Admiranda Orbis Christiani*, fol., Venice, 1680.

for the day of entombment, the erection of the real tomb itself in its costly materials being left to the near future. Among the devoted friends and admirers of Angela, beside Moretto and his scholars, there were poets also, and they too would add their tribute of praise to the works of architect, sculptor, and painter. Foremost among these was Gabriel Cozzano, whose intimate intercourse with the saint during the last years of his life had made him love her with a filial love full of infinite reverence. Another was Father Valeriano, of Bergamo, one of the Canons-Regular of St. Afra; and a third was a no less devoted and grateful admirer of the saint—the Doctor Zanetti, of Brescia.[1]

---

[1] The Latin verses written for this occasion were afterward engraved on the slab of black marble which covered the tomb. They are given by all the biographers of the saint, and for this reason they are reproduced here:

1 Angela virtutum varia redimita corona
   Hic jacet, extremo restituenda die.
Spiritus æthereas penetravit fervidus arces,
   Et summo ingenuus astitit ille Deo,
Illa hæc est Virgo, quæ morum regula viva
   Illustrem erexit virginitate chorum.
Brixia, crede mihi, sacrum venerare sepulchrum:
   Nil non Sancta, Deo proxima, Virgo potest.

Behold, deck'd with her varied virtues' crown,
Here Angela awaits the resurrection morn;
The while her spirit 'mid the angelic throng
Resplendent shines before God's awful throne.
She is that Maid whose heavenly purity
Drew Brescia's maids to that angelic band,
To suff'ring consecrate and innocence.
Ah, Brescia! fear not thou to venerate
Her tomb who, near High God, still pleads for thee.

2 Proposita Martyr, Virgo actibus, ore Magistra:
   Sic tribus aureolis, Angela, dives ovas.
Angela, nuper eras morum vitæque Magistra:
   Nunc patriæ Tutrix Præsidiumque veni.

No one can read these tributes, as well as the authentic narratives of all that took place immediately after her death and during the interval between her funeral obsequies and the final entombment, without feeling convinced that the popular conscience proclaimed her a saint, and that the popular heart with a resistless impulse paid her the veneration due to a saint.

This sentiment only grew with each succeeding year, and was intensified by the miraculous favors which were wrought through her intercession by Him who delights in honoring

---

>A martyr in desire, in life a spotless maid,
>By words and shining acts our teacher thou,
>Angelic woman ! Thus a triple crown
>On high thou bear'st. Angel of earth, thy deeds
>A pillar of fire before us shone. 'Mid Heaven's bliss
>Be still the guardian angel of thy native land.

3 ANGELA viva fui, nunc Angela mortua dicor :
>Sum tamen angelicis Angela juncta choris.
>Vos qui me nostis, exemplo vivite nostro :
>Sic facile ut docui mortua adhuc doceo.

>ANGELA they named me living ; dead, Angela still
>They call me, though now mix'd with the angel choirs.
>O you who loved me ! I would have you live
>E'en as you saw me ! so might my life with you
>A speaking mirror be to loving eyes.

4 Conditur hoc tumulo cui nomen et insuper omnis
>Vita superis æquiparanda choris.
>Angela divisa est tria per loca : Corpus in urna,
>Spiritus in Cœlo, nomen in ore virum.

This last is from an anonymous pen:

>Within this tomb lies one whose name and life
>Made her most angelic on earth appear.
>Angela our treasure now divided is :
>This urn her virgin body keeps ; her soul
>Shines 'mong the blessèd ; and her name
>Is on men's lips where'er they worship God-like deeds.

after their death the great servants whose life was devoted to the promotion of His glory.

One display of the divine power, in connection with Angela's tomb, must be related here, because in this instance God vindicated the outraged honor of the Maid of Desenzano.[1] A priest belonging to the noble family of Rossi had come, some time in 1571, to visit the crypt of St. Afra and to admire the tomb of Angela Merici. He was accompanied by a theological student, also of noble birth, but whose name is not mentioned by any biographer of our saint, probably through respect for the young man's relatives. He was perfectly familiar with the popular veneration toward Angela; he had witnessed the heartfelt piety with which the faithful, after worshiping the Blessed Sacrament on the principal altar, came to kneel and pray before the shrine of their fellow-citizen and benefactress. He could not help being acquainted with the leading facts in Angela's history, and with the priceless services rendered to Brescia by herself and the Order she had founded. Yet, standing before her shrine, he examined the decorations and inscriptions with the irreverent mind of a sceptic and a scoffer. He was one of those shallow young men who think they are giving proof of superior knowledge and judgment, when they rise above the belief of the unlettered crowd, and who deem it a merit to sneer where others worship and adore. Most likely our sciolist thought that Signor de Rossi was, like himself, too enlightened to pray to Angela Merici. So, after gazing, half-amused, at the simple-hearted men and women who knelt, wrapped in devotion, before the tomb of the saint, and critically reading such verses as we have just quoted, the young divine turned to his companion with a smile. "God only

---

[1] This fact is related at length by F. Salvatori, p. 128.

knows," said he, "whether she merits all this praise." The words were scarcely uttered when two fearful explosions as loud as thunder-claps, seemed to issue from the shrine itself, and people started in terror to their feet, as if they felt the church falling about their ears. One of the Canons who happened to be occupied within the choir in the upper church ran down to see what terrible accident had occurred. The imprudent young scoffer, however, did not wait for any further signs of the divine displeasure, for he, at least, needed no explanation of this prodigy. Falling on his knees he besought aloud God's forgiveness, and that of God's great servant whom he had dared to asperse. His shallow scepticism was changed into sincere veneration, and, let us hope, he lived to be a better and a wiser man.

The shrine, with its architectural and artistic decorations, remained in the state in which they had been completed till the year 1580, when the renovation fever seized upon the good Fathers of St. Afra. After disfiguring the upper church in conformity with what they deemed the rules of classical art, they resolved to repair or to disfigure the crypt also. The remains of Angela, as well as the relics of the ancient Brescian martyrs, were taken from their place of rest while the work of restoration proceeded. The good Canons wished to erect new shrines more in keeping with the piety of the people and more worthy of the sacred treasures they were to contain. An appeal was made in particular to the Ursulines of Brescia, and a modest sum, proportioned to the means of a poor and growing community, but sufficient for the purpose in an age when money was scarce and artists and workmen still labored for the love of God and His saints, was placed in the hands of the Canons.

On the north side of the large chapel dedicated to St. Calocer the builders constructed a monumental tomb of white marble, of good design for the age, adorned with sculpture and painting. On the pediment was inscribed in gold letters the following distich :

Conditur hoc vere tumulo Angela : quid ni ?
Terram terra tegit ; spiritus astra tenet,[1]

The tablet bearing this inscription is supported by two angels kneeling with their faces bent reverently toward the tomb beneath. The shrine proper, placed within the thickness of the wall, was ornamented externally by Moretto's beautiful painting, in which the entire figure of the saint was shown in profile, as she lay on her death-bed. When it became necessary to show the body of the saint, this ornamental painting opened out on hinges, and from the thickness of the wall was drawn forth a metallic chest containing the precious remains. On removing the lid, these were seen enclosed in crystal. In recent times—since the canonization in 1807, most likely—a more convenient disposition of these relics has been adopted. The body is placed in a shrine beneath the altar, raised a few feet above the floor, and surrounded by a crystal frame longer than the body, which thus permits the latter to be seen by the pilgrim.

A living writer who visited Brescia in 1867 [2] thus speaks of the present condition of St. Angela's tomb and remains :

"On the very evening that I arrived in Brescia I went to see the saint's body in St. Afra's. I expected to find nothing but a skeleton, or a waxen figure covering the bones. But what was my surprise to see the original features preserved

---

[1] "Within this tomb Angela lies truly buried : why not ?
Earth here covers what of her was earthly ; her soul dwells in Heaven."

Or : Believe this tomb doth ANGELA contain ;
For here dust covers dust ; her soul with Christ doth reign.

[2] L'Abbé Richaudeau.

entire during three hundred and twenty-seven years! It is of course very much shrivelled; but putrefaction has not touched it. The skin is entire; the chin, the lower lip, the forehead, have scarcely lost anything of their first form. The cheeks are flattened, but not very much so. The upper-lip has shrunk and exposes the teeth, of which not one is missing. The eyes are sunken from the evaporation of the liquid parts of the sockets; but these are not empty. The eyelids are closed and joined. The nose has suffered most; it is very flat. The general color of the face is very pale, approaching a yellowish rather than a leaden color. The whole figure has none of the repulsive features of a corpse; quite otherwise—my companion and myself thought its appearance pleasing, apart from the flattened shape of the nose.

"On our return to the monastery (Ursuline), the Lady Superior showed us a plaster cast of St. Angela's features, made soon after her death, as well as an engraving which showed how she looked in life. The resemblance is so striking, that any one who had seen St. Angela living could not fail to recognize her features as they appear at this day in her shrine. The right hand has been taken away; the left, placed on her pilgrim's staff, shows five fingers extremely emaciated, the skin barely covering the bones.

"In what state is the rest of the body, covered with the brown habit and bound at the waist with the white cord of St. Francis? Doneda, who wrote at the beginning of the present century, says that the precious remains were disjointed by the frequent shocks it received while being taken out from the wall in its casket to be exposed to the veneration of the faithful. He adds that the body is now but a skeleton. He is certainly mistaken, so far as this assertion regards the face and the left hand, as well as the left foot which is in the possession of the Ursulines of Brescia, and which is still surrounded by the dried flesh. . . .

"I afterward visited the chamber in which Angela lived and died. It has been preserved in the state in which she left it, without one additional ornament, save a few engravings that recall the principal incidents of her life. The walls are just in the state in which she beheld them. At the end of the room is an alcove or recess where her bed was. Now it contains an altar, within which is her first coffin. On the wall, opposite to the window, is an inscription in gilt letters, setting forth that—

"In this poor chamber the most eminent theologians and enlightened churchmen were wont to consult St. Angela, and went away astonished at the knowledge communicated by her."

CHAPTER XVII.

VENERATION PAID TO ANGELA MERICI—MIRACULOUS FAVORS IN ANSWER TO THE POPULAR TRUST IN HER INTERCESSION—WHY HER SOLEMN BEATIFICATION AND CANONIZATION WERE SO LONG DELAYED.

WE have seen how spontaneous and universal was the impulse which moved the popular heart in Brescia and its territory to show the dead Maid of Desenzano the veneration due only to such as live and die in "the odor of sanctity." This last expression is too familiar to Catholic readers to need any explanation here. The life of every one of us diffuses within our homes and the social sphere in which we move the good or ill odor of our virtues or our vices. Elias and Elisæus, living among the mountain solitudes of Carmel, in the evil days of Jezabel's ascendancy in Israel, and of the general apostasy of God's people, had sent their fame far and wide through the northern tribes—like the fragrance of Carmel itself when the spring-tide breezes from the Mediterranean waft the united perfumes of all its flowers inward all over the land. And just as in mountainous or Alpine regions the lowland cattle, after their long winter, become wild with impatience to be led into their familiar upland pastures as soon as the winds bring them down the scent of fresh grass and spring flowers,[1] even so, and more particularly after

---
[1] It is customary in Switzerland, as it is in Tyrol, to lead the herds and flocks to the

long seasons of religious aridity and disturbance, are the souls of all who believe in the true God drawn irresistibly to those men and women whose virtues and supernatural lives convince all who approach them that the Spirit of God is in them, and works through them. It needed no stupendous miracle performed by any one of these devoted servants of the Most High to make all who closely observed their lives to exclaim, "Now, by this I know that thou art a man of God!" (3 Kings 17:24.) Even before Eliseus had obtained by his prayers that his kind but childless hosts at Sunam should be gladdened by the presence of a son, they had discovered the holiness of the man. The "Great Lady" who was to have such signal proof of the prophet's power might well say to her husband: "I perceive that this is a holy man of God, who often passeth by us" (4 King s4:9). Was it the sole wisdom of Debbora that made "the children of Israel go up to her for all judgment," as "she sat under a palm-tree ... in Mount Ephraim"? Was not Debbora's wisdom only one effect of her sanctity—a supernatural gift of the Holy Ghost, like the extraordinary learning of Angela Merici, which made her poor chamber of St. Afra's the oracle of priests and laymen alike, of the most learned and the most

---

uplands—high up near the glaciers and everlasting snows—as soon as these Alpine pastures are covered with the first verdure of spring. There, as is well known, the flocks and their guardians remain till the end of summer. It is a most curious spectacle to watch the motions of the cattle as the day approaches when they are to be led to their grassy paradise among the hills. They refuse to eat, and manifest their impatience to set out by their frequent lowing, their restlessness, and by turning toward the familiar upland road. When, at length, they are allowed to set out, nothing can exceed the joyous alacrity with which they hasten toward their goal. They are drawn to the green and flowery slopes of their favorite "Alps" just as the bee is infallibly directed to the far-off garden or meadow where it can load itself with sweets and then return to the hive. The spiritual and the physical order, the soul-world unseen, and this beautiful earth we live on, are full of the most marvelous and striking analogies—of lessons of living light to eyes that can see—because they are the work of the one Almighty hand, planned by the same all-wise Mind.

exalted? Wisdom alone, the mere gift of extraordinary science in man or woman, apart from the merited fame of true sanctity, may attract the curious or the ambitious learner. But who will think of opening his conscience, of laying bare the deep sores of his heart, or of begging spiritual guidance for future needs from the worldly *savant* or scientist? It is to Samuel, the man of prayer from his infancy, the Nazarite from his birth, not to Saul, taller by head and shoulders than the multitude of his brethren and superior in wisdom as he was in stature, that the people of Israel say in their sore distress: "Cease not to cry to the Lord our God for us, that He may save us out of the hand of the Philistines" (1 Kings 7:8).

Yes; a holy man or woman, no matter how poor and mean their exterior, no matter how carefully they conceal themselves and the place of their abode from the public gaze, is like a vessel filled with a most exquisite and penetrating perfume. You may hide it away in the remotest and darkest recess of your house; but its fragrance will spread around in spite of your pains to conceal it. The Spirit of God in man and woman will betray His presence and His gifts, despite every precaution which humility may take to hide them. "The sweet odor of Christ" will go abroad, and will spread far and near. For a true saint of God is God's master-work here below; and the priceless and incomparable gifts with which He endows an Angela Merici in Brescia, a Teresa in Avila, or a Francis Xavier among the heathens of India and Japan, are only the "sweet odor" of a goodness all divine, which draws the souls of men heavenward.

And just as high and low were thus drawn to the poor and narrow room of Angela beneath the shadow of St. Afra's and while Angela was still among the living, even so when Angela was laid to her rest in the crypt of St. Afra's, among the tombs of kindred saints, the Christian people could no more be restrained from flocking to her grave, and bestowing on the sweet recumbent figure of the holy pilgrim their heartfelt testimonies of veneration, of love, of gratitude, than the swollen waters of the neighboring Adige could be made to flow back to their source in the Tyrolean mountains.

The people—and when we say the people, we mean all classes of the population, and churchmen as well as laymen—began at once, ere Angela had been laid in her tomb, to bestow on her the appellation of "Saint." A quarter of a century after her death, a great Italian saint and bishop, St. Charles Borromeo, declared openly his conviction that she was worthy of the honors of canonization. He only gave utterance to the universal sentiment throughout Upper Italy—the sentiment of the clergy, of the higher and most enlightened portion of the community, as well as the feeling, deep and heartfelt, of the masses.

It was to be expected that Desenzano, the native town of Angela Merici, where her angelic life and heroic virtues, in childhood, girlhood, and womanhood, had ever been household topics of edification, would not be backward in paying homage to the memory of one so inexpressibly dear to the inhabitants. The municipality was not slow, very soon after the death of Angela, in choosing their saintly townswoman as their special patron and protectress in Heaven. In 1587 her picture was placed in the principal church among those of the saints.[1] And in 1608, as the miraculous favors ob-

---

[1] To restrain within due limits the popular feeling toward persons dead "in order of sanctity," wise regulations forbidding certain acts of public veneration were enacted by Popes Clement VIII. (1592-1605) and Paul V. (1605-1621); and these, again, were rendered still more stringent by Urban VIII., who in 1625 decreed that no such honor as those mentioned above in the case of Desenzano, should be paid to any person whatever, who had not been solemnly beatified or canonized. The Church in her wisdom forbids that the titles of "saint" or "blessed" or "venerable" be applied to any person till the Apostolic See has first bestowed it officially, and after due examination.

tained by her intercession increased the devotion felt toward her by the citizens, a chapel was set apart in the same church and called after her name, to which were attached a special chaplain and a guardian salaried by the grateful inhabitants of "Desenzano-on-the-Lake." Remembering, moreover, the two miraculous visions sent to "the Holy Maid," as they loved to call her, near the town, they built on the farm owned by the Merici family, and on the spot pointed out by tradition as the scene of one of those apparitions, a little oratory, which became forthwith a favorite resort of pilgrims, and where pious priests loved to come and offer up the Adorable Sacrifice.

With the spread of the Ursuline Order to the cities of Lombardy and Venetia, the veneration for their foundress was also extended in proportion. The virtues and services of the daughters could not fail to conciliate reverence and affection for their saintly Mother; and so, throughout the rest of Italy, through every country of Continental Europe, through Canada, where the venerable Mary of the Incarnation and her Sisters were the first apostles of female education, and through more than one country of Spanish and Portuguese America, the name of Angela Merici was always mentioned with that mingled love and respect with which the faithful regard the saints. Pictures, statues, medallions, and engravings of the Holy Maid of Desenzano became common, expressing everywhere the sentiments with which she was regarded. Gregory XV., in a bull issued on the 9th of February, 1621, in favor of the Ursulines of Tulle, in France, mentions, without censuring it, the custom followed in their monastery of "honoring by a special devotion St. Augustine, St. Ursula, and their own blessed Angela." Archbishops and bishops in their respective dioceses authorized or approved the custom of celebrating her feast with a public office—in some instances with a whole octave—enjoining a strict fast on the vigil of the feast, and marking the solemnities of the latter by a public procession, in which Angela's picture was borne along. These were honors reserved to canonized saints, and in tolerating or sanctioning them the bishops themselves were carried away by the current of an enlightened public opinion anticipating the solemn judgment of the Holy See.

Indeed, this instinct of popular piety, which is so sure in discerning true holiness of life from its hollow semblance, had been, from the very beginning of Christianity, one of the chief grounds on which the Church based her judgment about the sanctity of the illustrious dead. During the ages of persecution, the people as well as the clergy watched carefully the remains of the martyrs, preserved a record of their acts, and honored and perpetuated their memory by erecting over their burial-place churches or chapels, called, most appropriately, "Memories" of the martyrs. This was the testimony of the Christian people to the heroic souls who had so gloriously "witnessed," by shedding their blood to the divinity of Christ Himself and of His religion. When persecution ceased, the heroic sanctity of such men as St. Basil and St. Chrysostom, St. Augustine and St. Martin, was as well proven to those whom they evangelized and edified, whom they fed by the bread of their lofty teachings and induced to practise what they taught by the eloquent persuasion of their own saintly examples—was as easy, as familiar, and general a theme of popular opinion, as the martyrdom of St. Cyprian or St. Irenæus or St. Polycarp. And, when these great fatherly souls and lights of God's people had gone to their reward, their tombs were visited and their memory cherished with a veneration as great and a gratitude as undying as those shown to the martyred dead.

Still, while allowing all due weight to popular sentiment on facts which were open to the judgment of all, the Church never ceased to exercise the wisest discernment in the supreme sanction she gave—as was her exclusive right—to all devotional practices in honor of persons of reputed sanctity.

This prudent discernment was not only practised in Rome, where a body of "notaries," or official recorders, collected and arrayed in the most authentic form all that pertained to the life and death of the holy martyrs and confessors, but in every episcopal centre throughout the entire Church. We have one remarkable instance of it in the precautions taken and the instructions issued by St. Cyprian—destined himself to bear a glorious witness to Christ. He commanded, as may be seen in his 37th and 79th epistles, that correct lists should be kept of all those who had suffered for the faith, and that these, together with the most precise information relating to their trial and execution, should be sent to himself.

These precautions, instead of diminishing, increased with every succeeding age and with the growth of the Church, the central authority in Rome gradually reserving to its own tribunals the task of examining and sifting the testimony sent to it concerning all persons to whom attached the fame of sanctity. Pope Urban VIII. (1623-44) gave to the pontifical legislation on this weighty matter its present complete and permanent forms; and the entire proceedings used in the long and patient investigation of all claims to the supreme degrees of heroic virtue presupposed by true sanctity were most admirably explained by a Pope of the last century, Benedict XIV. (1740-58).

During the half-century succeeding the death of St. Angela, however, the bishops of Italy and other Catholic countries followed the custom hitherto prevailing in their respective dioceses, and sanctioned or permitted the demonstrations of private and public devotion toward the Foundress of the Ursulines—all which, of course, was done without prejudice to the rights of the Holy See, which is alone the seat of infallibility. In some houses of the Company, as in that of Treviso, for instance, the name of Angela was introduced into the prayer *Confiteor* ("I confess to Almighty God, etc.") after the names of Saints Peter and Paul. This was authorized by custom in Upper Italy, and was a usual mode of honoring the patron-saints of parishes, religious communities, dioceses, and guilds. Not only were wax-tapers lighted in honor of the "Blessed" Angela, as she was generally called, but lamps were kept perpetually burning in her honor. In France, where, during the first half of the seventeenth century, the Ursuline communities spread with a marvelous rapidity, a complete "office," with appropriate hymns, lessons, and anthems, was composed and recited in the Ursuline monasteries. They went further, and drew up forms of prayer for every day in the week, with special litanies reciting the virtues and glorious actions of the saint.

Nay, in Rome itself the Ursuline monastery, in 1718, celebrated an eight-day festival in honor of Angela, whose panegyric was daily pronounced from the pulpit to a crowded church, and the church itself hung with paintings from the hand of the best artists, representing the saint and the principal incidents of her life and death. What is most to the point is the fact that the reigning Pope, Clement XI., honored these solemnities with his presence, thereby indirectly sanctioning the public veneration thus paid to the Holy Maid of Desenzano.

This *cultus* (worshipful veneration) paid to St. Angela in advance of the sovereign judgment of the Vicar of Christ received an uninterrupted, though indirect, sanction from the Holy See up to the beginning of the judicial process instituted at Rome for her solemn beatification, in 1763. It will be well worth the reader's while to glance at the main facts on which this long sanction is founded.

In the year 1617 Cardinal de Sourdis, Archbishop of Bordeaux, induced the colony of Ursulines which he had introduced from Italy to adopt the rules of cloistered nuns. This change involved some serious modifications in the Rule established by St. Angela, as well as additional observances, among which was the keeping of a strict fast on the vigil of Angela's feast (27th January), and the receiving of Holy Communion on the feast itself. Every one of these prescriptions, as well as the Ursuline Rule thus modified, was approved and rendered obligatory on the Congregation of Bordeaux by a decree of Paul V., dated February 3d, 1618; they were further confirmed by Clement IX., on October 12th, 1667, who extended the Rule thus sanctioned, with the devotional practices in honor of the foundress, to all the Ursuline monasteries of Germany. All this was made obligatory on the monastery just founded in Rome by Innocent XI., in 1688. Last, but not least, the great canonist and theologian, Benedict XIV. himself, on May 22d, 1753, confirmed this same Rule with its observances, after a most careful revision, and made them obligatory on all monasteries of the Ursuline Order for all time.[1]

The decrees of Pope Urban VIII., however, enact that no judicial proceedings shall be instituted by the Roman tribunals for the beatification of any person till the fiftieth year after the death of such person. This, we know, was deviated from in the case of St. Alphonsus Liguori; and, again, quite recently in the case of Pope Pius IX., a deviation was asked for and refused.

Now, with respect to St. Angela, the first judicial steps

---

[1] Father Salvatori, pp. 134, 135.

were taken by the municipality of Brescia in 1560, and a commission was appointed to make inquiries and collect documentary evidence. In 1568 the Bishop (Bollano) of Brescia commissioned John Baptist Nazari, a notary-public and resident of the city, to obtain the sworn testimony of the persons who had intimately known Angela Merici. Among these were Antonio dei Romani, Augustine Gallo, Bertolino Boscolo, and James Chizzola—our old acquaintances, nearly all of them. From the evidence thus collected Nazari drew the materials of his Life of Angela Merici—the first published biography of the saint. In 1572 the town-council of Brescia besought St. Charles Borromeo to use his influence with the Roman authorities for "the introduction of Angela's cause;" but as he did or could do nothing, they again renewed their instances in 1581, when the holy archbishop was in Brescia, as Visitor Apostolic. Rome was in no hurry then as now; and a century nearly elapsed before anything could be done. In 1674 the French Ursulines began to move in the matter, the monastery of Dijon taking the lead and sending to Rome a commissioner with the funds necessary to pay all the costs of the proceedings. He tried in vain, however, if he tried at all; and, although the good nuns made persistent attempts to have the cause opened in 1674, 1682, and in 1692, their perseverance proved unavailing.[1]

The time chosen by the French Ursulines to urge these proceedings on the Roman tribunals was most unfortunate. To be sure, the daughters of Angela Merici and the promoters, under them, of the beatification of their parent, must have been roused to renewed zeal by the canonization, on April 12th, 1671, among others, of St. Gaetan de Tiene, St. Francis Borgia, and St. Rose of Lima (born 1586; died 1617). But

---

[1] Salvatori, pp. 138, 139.

the question of the *regalia*, or royal rights over the revenues of benefices, had already been raised by the French Parliament in 1668, and assumed such a formidable aspect all through the succeeding years, that God's providence alone saved the Church of France from being hurried into both schism and heresy, as the Church of England was by Henry VIII. Pope Innocent XI., who ascended the pontifical throne in August, 1676, was one of the purest, the most learned, and the most fearless rulers ever given to Christ's flock. He did not create the terrible storm which assailed the Church and lasted all through his pontificate. It was the work of the French king's intolerable arrogance, abetted as he was by his Jansenistic lawyers and parliament, and but very mildly contradicted by the majority of his bishops. In 1682 was issued that famous and fatal "Declaration of the Gallican Church" which a royal decree made obligatory on all teaching bodies, and which became thenceforward a kind of national creed, till monarchy, creed, parliament, and hierarchy went down, ingulfed in the tidal wave of the French Revolution. There is no need, therefore, of supposing for a moment that the Roman tribunals were guilty of unaccountable supineness during these calamitous years (1676-89) when the French ambassador at the head of an armed force braved and insulted the Pope in his own capital, and all the energy and patience of Roman statesmen, jurists, and theologians were taxed to the utmost to solve the mighty and perplexed questions pressed on their attention by the king, the bishops, and the parliaments of France.[1]

The favorable opinion entertained of the Ursulines and their foundress by Benedict XIV., as we have seen above,

---

[1] See the biographies of Innocent XI., and of his immediate predecessors and successors, in Artaud's "Lives of the Popes," vol. ii.

and the tacit approbation given by him to the *cultus* of the latter, encouraged the Order to prosecute her cause more zealously than ever under that pontiff's successor, Clement XIII. (1758–69). The cause, thanks to the energy of the then superior of the Ursuline Monastery in Rome, was formally opened in 1763. All the evidence pertaining to Angela Merici's life and death, to the honors paid her by the faithful, to the heroic virtues practised by her, and the miracles performed through her intercession, was scrupulously and unceasingly sifted year after year till April 30th, 1768, when Clement XIII., by a solemn judgment, sanctioned the *cultus* paid to the Holy Maid of Desenzano, and confirmed as rightful the appellation of "Blessed" bestowed on her from the hour of her death by the public voice.

The "beatification" of a holy personage, however, only permits the breviary office and the mass appointed by the congregation of Rites to be recited within a religious order, or within the limits of a diocese, etc.; whereas, in the solemn ceremony of canonization, the Vicar of Christ pronounces his judgment *ex-cathedra*, addresses his sentence to the entire church, and extends to the whole flock of Christ the *cultus* hitherto paid in a private or limited manner to the saint.

When the certainty of the approaching beatification became known in Brescia, it caused a deep joy among the now numerous but still fervent company who claimed her as parent, and clung with undying devotion to the place of their birth and the shrine which contained her remains.

One may not unreasonably regret that they were moved by their piety to give her a more splendid tomb, and to disturb the virginal body from its repose, especially as it had already been disturbed during the reparations of 1580. The appearance of the remains, preserved as they had been till then from the corruption of the grave, could not fail of being injured by this second removal. The miraculous preservation of the body and the sweet fragrance which continued to cling to it were enough of themselves to make the lowliest of sepulchres venerable and lovely to the Christian heart. All these removals—made without due care, perhaps—shook and dislocated the frail texture of the dried flesh; and there ensued deterioration and disfigurement.

"In 1774," says Father Salvatori, "a casket of more beautiful shape and material was made, adorned with carving and gold, and in this, reposing on cloth of the most precious texture, was placed the body of the saint, protected further by plates of crystal. Now, while taking it out of the old casket and replacing with a new the old Franciscan habit, they found it still incorrupt in several parts. The head was still covered with the skin, as in life; the hair was entire; and in the right socket the eyeball was full, showing the pupil with its natural black color, and the eyelids open, but slightly shrunken. The left leg, in its full length, was covered with the skin, as well as the chest, the parts about the heart being perfectly preserved, and not at all displaced. The rest of the body was but a skeleton; and on one finger was a ring of lead, on which were engraved the words *Jesus Christus*. After expelling from these sacred remains the humidity which clung to them, and replacing the old Franciscan habit with a new one of silk of the same shape and color, the Ursulines laid them reverently in the new casket and restored this to its proper position in the old tomb.

"Two years later, however, it was resolved to transfer the remains to the drier atmosphere of the upper church. So, the Pontifical rescript (July 1st, 1776) authorizing this change having been obtained, they set about preparing a beautiful tomb of white marble adorned with gilt bronze, situated above the altar of St. Latinus, and immediately beneath the picture of that saint. They also constructed another shrine, of the exact size of the old one, and richly decorated. Everything being ready, on the 4th of April, 1777, the Bishop of Brescia, John Nani, accompanied by a select number of ecclesiastics, noblemen, and Ursulines, went to the lower church and took out the casket, which was then carried in solemn procession by priests to the upper church, and placed on a table richly draped. A delay of a few days was granted to the Ursulines, from among whom the bishop chose a few to cleanse the sacred body and to reclothe it with the former habit. A distinguished professor of anatomy, with trusty witnesses, was present the while, the professor seeing to it that each bone was replaced in its proper position, and all the proceedings being carefully attested.

"When the Ursulines had thus satisfied their filial piety, the church was magnificently draped, and on April 12th the bishop headed a solemn procession, and the new casket, borne on the shoulders of priests, was deposited in the new shrine, where it is at present venerated. Then clergy and people united in the celebration of a most joyous festival."[1]

One can scarcely recall these dates, and the triumphant festivities of the Ursulines throughout the world, in France and Rome particularly, without remembering at the same time the calamities under which the Society of Jesus lay crushed, and to all appearance annihilated forever. During the month of November, 1775, while the Roman Ursulines were laboring to obtain the necessary authorization for the solemn translation of the remains of their foundress to a more splendid monument in the upper church of St. Afra, Lawrence Ricci, the Superior-General of the suppressed Company of Jesus, was dying, a prisoner and heart-broken, within the

---

[1] Salvatori, pp. 139, 140.

Castle of St. Angelo, in Rome. With his dying breath, in presence of his Judge, veiled in the Holy Viaticum, and in the hearing of more than one exalted personage, the dying man—as pure-minded, great-souled, and devoted a priest as had ever sat in the place of St. Ignatius Loyola—protested that the Society governed by him, and suppressed amid circumstances of such odious barbarity and barefaced injustice, was guiltless of the crimes charged against it by the royal conspirators of the Houses of Bourbon and Braganza, and by their Jansenistic and anti-Catholic abettors and agents.

It was a strange contrast—that of the two great teaching orders, founded almost the same year, by saintly personages so much alike in wisdom unacquired in the schools, in austerity of life, loftiness of purpose, and deep appreciation of the needs of their country and age : the one providentially exalted, praised, fostered, and flourishing more and more daily ; while the other, which on one day counted an army of 30,000 apostles of the heathen and preceptors of youth, was on the next utterly swept from the face of both hemispheres ; the one celebrating the beatification of its glorious parent amid the transports of the millions who looked up to her daughters with such deep gratitude and trustfulness, while the head of the other was dying, imprisoned like the worst of convicted criminals, and those who still loved to call him "Father" pining, themselves, amid the dungeons of Portugal and Spain, or condemned to hold down their heads beneath the intolerable load of calumny all-powerful iniquity compelled them to bear. Not forever were they to bear or forbear. The sacrifice which combined kings and conspiring statesmen wrung from the helplessness of one Pontiff was to be compensated by the fearless magnanimity of another, who had also drunk deep of the cup of persecution held to his lips by despotic hands.

But from November, 1775, to August 7th, 1814, how assiduously were both Ursulines and dispersed Jesuits to labor for the one great cause so unspeakably dear to the heart of the Church—the cause of female education! The sons of St. Ignatius, in their accepted exile and obscurity, and while cherishing the fond hope that the resurrection-dawn would soon come again for their suppressed Company, worked untiringly to provide educators for the young generation of the nineteenth century; they gave, as Sisters and auxiliaries to the Ursulines, the daughters of Sophie Madeleine Barat and Julie Billiart, without mentioning others!

And so the two immediate successors of the sorely-tried Clement XIV., Pius VI. and Pius VII., might well make it a labor of love, in the midst of the unceasing persecutions which assailed them, in their turn, to encourage the Roman tribunals in forwarding the canonization of the Blessed Angela Merici.

A decree of Pius VI., dated July 16th, 1777, declared that the virtues practised by the Maid of Desenzano were heroic, each in its kind. Meanwhile, the Congregation of Rites was diligently inquiring into the authenticity and nature of the miracles attributed to her; for, in this matter of miracles, the Holy See demands the most absolute and overwhelming certainty, as a condition toward canonization. As we shall see in the next chapter, God was pleased at this very juncture to glorify His lowly handmaiden before men, and in a most troublous age, by working at her intercession miracles most solemnly attested.

At length, on the 27th January, 1790, Angela's two-hundred-and-sixteenth birthday, Pius VI., after offering up the Holy Sacrifice in the chapel of the Ursuline Monastery in Rome, promulgated the decree which declared the miracles authentic, and authorized the final proceedings toward canonization. Two months later, on the 29th of March, he addressed to the assembled cardinals the memorable allocution in which he deplores the anti-Christian revolution taking place in France. A few years afterward Pius himself was to be carried away by force from Rome and Italy, to die in a French prison at Valence; while during the intervening years the Ursulines of France were to be driven from their monasteries by the revolutionary storm, and more than one of them was to glorify her Mother Angela and the faith of her fathers by laying down her head on the scaffold or perishing amid the horrors of the Terrorist prisons.

And thus was the Company of St. Ursula tried by blood and fire, and prepared for the memorable 24th of May, 1807, when the voice of the lamb-like but heroic Pius VII. proclaimed her sanctity in St. Peter's, uniting with her in these supreme honors of canonization the French peasant-girl St. Coletta or Nicoletta Boillet (1380–1447), who reformed the Poor Clares of France; the noble Hyacintha Mariscotti (1588–1643), of Viterbo; St. Francis Caracciolo (1563–1603), a native of the Abruzzi, and the founder of the Minor Clerks Regular; and St. Benedict Filadelf, a man of negro parentage (1526–1589), and the light of Messina, his native city, and of all Sicily in his day. How like to each other were the three saintly women thus united in the veneration of the Church, one may know who reads their most edifying lives.

Six years afterward, Pius VII. himself was dragged from Rome by the soldiers of the French Emperor, and subjected to the long trials of which the world has heard the details with equal pity and indignation.

Thus the Ursuline communities, amid their mingled joys and sorrows, hopes and fears, could exult in the honor bestowed on the name of Angela Merici, and invoke her name with increased fervor and confidence, while addressing themselves to the arduous labors of a new era and looking forward anxiously to the pregnant and threatening future. They, like their sisters in Valenciennes,[1] might lose even their lives for the faith; but they now could believe with unbounded trustfulness the divine promise that they were not to perish, while such pure and generous blood as theirs could only impart to the wide-branching Ursuline tree a new vitality and fruitfulness.

---

[1] "On the 17th and 23d October, 1794, eleven Ursulines belonging to the Monastery of Valenciennes sealed their apostleship of teaching by martyrdom. On the eve of their execution they were so happy as to receive Holy Communion from a priest, who was their fellow-prisoner and soon became their fellow-martyr. They were allowed to celebrate their Last Supper together, saying to each other that on the morrow they would celebrate it in Paradise. All who beheld them thus shed tears of admiration. . . . They cut each other's hair (to be ready for the guillotine), issued from prison with their hands bound behind their backs, . . . and went to the scaffold chanting the *Te Deum*. . . ."—*Rohrbacher*, "*Hist. of the Church.*"

CHAPTER XVIII.

MIRACLES, AND VIRTUES AS MARVELOUS AS MIRACLES.

WHEN the Son of God had come down to teach and to save the world, He, concealed as His infinite majesty was beneath the lowliness of our human nature, did not ask of His countrymen to believe in Himself and His mission on the simple ground that He asserted Himself to be the long-expected Redeemer. His first disciples; after the miracle of Cana in Galilee, "believed in Him," because by changing the water into wine He "manifested His glory"—that is, displayed His power as God and Author of nature. When John the Baptist, after the resurrection of the widow's son at Naïm (St. Luke 7), sends two of his own disciples to ask of the Master, "Art thou He that art to come? or look we for another?" He, answering, . . . said to them: "Go and relate to John what you have heard and seen. The blind see, the lame walk, the lepers are made clean, the deaf hear, the dead rise again, to the poor the Gospel is preached." To the Jews who persisted in closing their ears to the divinity of His teaching, He solemnly said: "I speak to you, and you believe not; the works that I do in the name of My Father, they give testimony of Me. . . . If I do not the works of My Father, believe Me not. But if I do, though you will not believe Me, BELIEVE THE WORKS."[1]

---

[1] St. John 10: 25, 37, 38.

Nor was this divine miracle-working power to cease with Him: it was to remain throughout all future time, with His apostles and their successors in the Church, as the seal of their mission and the convincing proof of that Church's sanctity. He said, in His very last discourse to them before His ascension: "These signs shall follow them that believe: in My name they shall cast out devils; they shall speak with new tongues; they shall take up serpents, and if they shall drink any deadly thing, it shall not hurt them; they shall lay their hands upon the sick, and they shall recover." [1]

When, therefore, St. Peter, in fulfillment of the Master's promise, had performed in the most conspicuous and frequented entrance to the Temple a stupendous miracle, he said to the astonished crowd of Jews: "Ye men of Israel, why wonder you at this? or why look you upon us, as if by our strength or power we had made this man to walk?" [2]

It is impossible to resist the evidence of our senses when we see a man at one moment a helpless cripple who has never walked in his life, and behold him the next moment standing upright before our eyes, walking, sound in every limb, and praising God for the sudden change. There is another sense, too, whose evidence goes irresistibly with that of the eye—that divine light of reason in the soul which tells us, when such a cure has been thus made *in the name of God* or *of His Christ*, that the calling on that name is a challenge to His power and goodness, and that the cure which follows is as surely the work of His right hand as was the creation of the world in the beginning. Your Liberal, your atheist, your modern scientist and materialist, could no sooner see that cripple suddenly cured by the invocation of

---

[1] St. Mark 16: 17, 18.   [2] Acts 3: 12.

the Holy Name than all the voices of his soul would call on him to kneel and worship Jesus as the true living God.

Priests and children of the Catholic Church and heirs to all Christ's promises, we believe in miracles to-day, as did our fathers before us since the days of the apostles, since Peter and John stood in the Beautiful Gate. Our fathers have seen miracles age after age, and year after year; and they have borne their witness to the fact that God in their midst still continued to be glorified in His saints, and to glorify them by using them as the instruments of His power and fatherly mercy. Nor can we Christians of the nineteenth century believe that the hand of God is shortened; for He multiplies on every side the prodigies of His power to convince an unbelieving and devil-ridden generation that there is still a God who is the Judge of the whole earth.

We give the following miracles in the order in which they are given by Father Salvatori, who followed himself the acts of canonization, and the order followed by the Sacred Congregation of Rites:

1. *Angela Filippini in* 1777. This lady was the wife of Pietro Ravelli, a notary and well-known citizen of Brescia. She was a long and patient sufferer. Her illness began by a great sense of lassitude in every member, accompanied with acute muscular pain, and soon followed by the appearance of livid spots, now in one part of her body and now in another. Her teeth grew black, her gums became swollen and emitted frequently a fetid and bloody matter, while she experienced extreme difficulty of breathing, great wakefulness, a burning fever, and convulsions. All these symptoms became intensified when she reached her sixty-seventh year. Besides, her arms, chest, and stomach were covered with small tumors, which caused excruciating pain. In October, 1776, two sores more painful than all the others broke out on her lower

limbs, and these soon became ulcerated. After some time, however, the ulcer on the left leg was closed, but that on the right increased in size and malignancy. . . . The issue from these sores was of the most offensive nature; but a cessation of it only threw the poor sufferer into deadly spasms. Under these circumstances, Dr. Charles Tebaldi, her physician, and a man of great repute, declared that these symptoms were those of a virulent scurvy which had poisoned the entire system. He advised the lady to have recourse merely to applications of soothing vegetable poultices which would keep the ulcers open. And in this advice he was sustained by the surgeon. During the five months which intervened between his advice and the lady's miraculous cure, the ulcers only grew more frightful, so that no hope of a change for the better remained.

Just then the approaching solemnities of the translation of the remains of St. Angela gave a great impulse to the popular devotion in Brescia. There was to be a Triduum or three days' public prayers immediately following the translation, and a friend of Madame Ravelli's strongly urged her to have recourse to the saint. So, on the 10th of April, 1777, the translation occurring on the 12th, the poor sufferer began to pray fervently to the Blessed Angela. But her suffering only seemed to increase with every prayer she offered up. She was not discouraged, nevertheless. Indeed, she seemed to have from the first moment a firm confidence that she would be healed. On the 13th day of April—that is, the first day of the solemn Triduum—she had herself taken, in spite of her bodily torture, to the neighboring Church of St. Zeno, where she made her confession and received Holy Communion in honor of the saint, thereby hoping to incline the latter to favor her suit, and to render herself more worthy of the grace she solicited. Her efforts apparently did but aggravate the ulcers and increase in proportion her agony of suffering. Still, this very increase only inspired the patient with a firmer trust in Angela's intercession. The morning of the 15th April dawned; it was the last day of the Triduum. She asked to be taken to the Church of St. Afra; and no one could find heart to dissuade her from her purpose. So, leaning on her husband and her maid, she dragged herself along with indescribable pain, and stopped not till she was before the tomb of the saint. Nothing could prevent her from kneeling down to hear the Mass which was beginning; and having heard a first without much difficulty, she remained kneeling during a second and a third, praying the while with extraordinary fervor. The last Mass being over, she arose of herself and without either assistance or pain, and, feeling no longer the presence of anything like swelling in her limbs, she hastened homeward without the slightest assistance, to see what had become of the ulcer. The poultices fell away of themselves, leaving the entire limb perfectly sound, no trace remaining of the dreadful ulcer but that the lips of the scar which marked its place were not yet quite closed.

"Thereupon," says Salvatori, "she applied to the wound an image of the saint, beseeching her most earnestly not to leave incomplete the merciful work of her perfect cure. Nor was the prayer unheard; for, withdrawing soon afterward the image, the cure was seen to be perfect in the fullest sense. It were out of place," continues the historian, "to paint the astonishment, the joy, the deep devotional feeling, not only of the lady herself, but of her household and of the entire city. The reader will easily understand them, and allow me to pass to the other miracles which I must mention."

2. The second miracle occurred in the great City Hospital of Brescia. The person who was this time the subject of

God's infinite goodness and the motherly solicitude of Blessed Angela, was a girl by name Maria d'Acquafredda, a member of a "Conservatory" or training-school for nurses attached to the hospital. She was in her twenty-seventh year, and in a very poor state of health, when, on the 20th of February, 1779, she was struck with apoplexy. She fell senseless to the ground, her right side paralyzed, her teeth so firmly set that it was with extreme difficulty a few spoonfuls of liquid were introduced. Eight entire days of the most energetic and skilful treatment only served to make the patient recover a little consciousness, leaving her, however, quite speechless. The paralyzed members remained insensible to the action of lancet or fire. This state of lethargic prostration lasted till the end of May, when the rector of the parish and the attendant physicians judged it necessary that the sufferer should receive the last sacraments. As the 31st of May was the day on which the Blessed Angela's feast was always celebrated in Brescia, the poor, dying girl, collecting all she could of her remaining strength and impaired senses, besought by signs her attendants to invoke in her favor the intercession of the saint. This suggestion had first come from one of the girl's companions, Maria Faustina, who bent all her efforts to excite in her friend the most unlimited confidence in the Blessed Angela's prayers. A present of olive-oil was therefore sent to St. Afra's to be used in the lamps kept burning before the shrine, and from the lamps themselves a little oil was taken back to the hospital. While the sufferer was exhorted to lift her heart to God and to pray fervently to His glorious servant present near Himself in Heaven, the infirmarian took a feather, dipped it in the oil, and anointed therewith the mouth. At the very first touch of the oil the jaws opened freely, and the infirmarian proceeded to touch in like manner the teeth and tongue and side. In an instant Maria d'Acquafredda recovered her speech, and felt that her paralyzed limbs had recovered their sensibility. She rose forthwith from her bed, and began to move through the room as if in the full possession of health and vigor, exclaiming the while, "I am cured! I am cured!" Maria Faustina, like one beside herself, and scarcely able to believe her own senses, ran about the hospital telling everybody of the miracle. The Superior and her companions came hurrying in to the sick-room to see with their own eyes what had taken place, and remained overwhelmed by the sudden and total change. In the afternoon the happy girl in whom it had been wrought anointed herself once more with the oil, supped with the community, and on the next day went about her usual occupations as if she had not been ailing for a single hour. More than that, not a trace of the chronic affection from which she had been suffering before her paralytic stroke remained with her recovered health. She felt she had a new lease of life, and lost no time in going to the tomb of her benefactress, and showing in the most public manner her gratitude and veneration.

3. Following the narrative of Father Salvatori, as well as the order in which these miracles were examined and reported by the Congregation of Rites, we come to another cure not a little like the preceding, which took place in Verona in 1778. Maria Angela Comini, a professed nun of the Monastery of St. John the Evangelist *della Beverara*, in Verona, began, when in her twenty-fourth year, to be afflicted with a pain in the chest and left side, which prevented her from lying down, or from resting on her left side. On the 13th of October, 1777, she found, on attempting to leave her bed, that she had lost the use of her left leg. Then, in spite of the medical aid called in, she lost the use of the right arm and hand, besides experiencing an intense pain in her head, a

partial paralysis of the organs of speech, and extreme difficulty in breathing. The symptoms went on increasing till at length the whole left side was paralyzed and void of all sensibility. The first appearance of these paralytic symptoms was accompanied with a violent fever, which, with slight intermissions, lasted nine whole months, and had all the symptoms of an acute inflammation. During this long interval the patient was bled thirty times, and every other remedy known to the ripest science of the day was employed in vain. She complained of excruciating pain in her chest, which frequently deprived her of consciousness, and the purulent discharges noted by the physicians convinced them that there was an internal tumor in the chest. For six entire months she lived on a little broth—so little, indeed, that it was a matter of wonder how she could live at all, with want of nourishment and her sleepless nights and unceasing agony. "It was not," says, in his sworn testimony, the physician in charge, "so much apoplexy that we feared she was coming to; but what caused us most apprehension was the pain in the chest, which had brought her to death's-door: no medicament could be introduced by the mouth for forty days before the cure, as she had not the power to swallow anything; nor during this interval did her extreme debility allow us to think of bloodletting." Indeed, the sufferer had more than once received the sacraments of the dying, as her attendants believed that her last hour was come. Such was the condition of Sister Mary Angela on July 13th, 1778, nine months after her first attack of apoplexy. Then it came into the mind of Sister Teresa Fortunata Gamba to make the patient have recourse to the Blessed Angela. A relic of the saint was forthwith placed near her bed on a table between lighted tapers, and a novena of prayers was at once begun. From that moment a slight improvement was noticeable, and this became more so still on the next day, the confidence and fervor of the sick nun increasing with this sensible change for the better. On the third day, carried away by her fervent faith in the powerful intercession of Blessed Angela, she besought her in the most touching tones to obtain her perfect cure, saying to the saint that a perfect restoration of her strength and health within the next twenty-four hours would prove to every one that the change was a true miracle, due to God, the author of every blessing. This was on the 15th; and on the 16th, in less than twenty-four hours after putting up her fervent petition, Sister Mary Angela stood before the entire community, completely cured of every ailment! She dressed herself without any assistance, and went to announce to one of the Sisterhood what God and Blessed Angela had done for her. Not a trace was left of her former ills. And her physicians, overcome by the surprise of a change so sudden, affirmed that it was a double miracle, and testified to this effect in the juridical proceedings instituted by the local authorities.

These are the three miracles examined with such conscientious care by the Roman tribunals; all the documentary evidence relating thereto being of the most authentic kind, and a single imperfect link sufficing to cause the judges to set aside inexorably proofs which would be accepted as convincing by any judge or jury among us or outside of Rome. As the reader may perceive on perusing carefully the above narratives, the miraculous cures were most public, most sudden, and most perfect. The patient in each case was reduced to such extremity, that all human skill was of no avail, and the physicians themselves had to confess their utter powerlessness to effect a change for the better or to arrest the fatal course of the disorder. Then came the sudden and perfect change, for which no remedy, no agency, other than the almighty power of the Creator, could account. Here there is no possibility of delusion or of the intervention of any cause, natural or preternatural, save that of the sole Lord of life and death, and of the pleading with Him in Heaven of the great motherly heart which had ever been on earth the ready friend of all kind of human suffering.

Other miracles, through every century which has elapsed since the death of the Holy Maid of Desenzano, have attested, both in Italy and all over the world, the efficacy of her intercession. It would be pleasant to present them here for the edification of the reader, were it not that our limited space warns us to reserve for matters which may not be omitted our remaining chapters.

But as miracles such as these described are the test of real personal holiness, and constitute the assurance of a saintly personage's power with the all-powerful Creator and all-merciful Dispenser of graces, even so are the heroic virtues practised by Christian man or woman the very substance and soul of that holiness of life of which miracles are the seal.

Not less carefully, patiently, and thoroughly do the tribunals appointed by the Holy See examine into and scrutinize every detail of the public and private life of those who die in the odor of sanctity, and for whom the honors of canonization are claimed. As to the life which we have been describing—though our delineations be never so imperfect—yet must we have failed to grasp ourselves and to convey to our readers the distinctive traits of Angela Merici's heroic figure, or she must stand before the mind's eye as different in her own beautiful womanly character from other saintly women, as John the Baptist was from the prophets and saints who preceded him, and as St. John the Evangelist was from his fellows in the College of Apostles. But, no matter in what sphere the saints move during their lifetime, and no matter what may be their sex, their avocation, or the personal gifts and endowments which they may bring with them to their calling, the virtues and qualities which go toward making up true, perfect, heroic—supernaturally heroic—manhood and womanhood, are substantially the same in all.

"Very various are the saints," says Cardinal Newman;[1] "their very variety is a token of God's workmanship; but however various and whatever was their special line of duty, they have been heroes in it: they have attained such noble self-command, they have so crucified the flesh, they have so renounced the world; they are so meek, so gentle, so tender-hearted, so merciful, so sweet, so cheerful, so full of prayer, so diligent, so forgetful of injuries, they have sustained such great and continued pains, they have persevered in such vast labors, they have made such valiant confessions, they have wrought such abundant miracles, they have been blessed with such strange successes, that they have set up a standard before us of truth, of magnanimity, of holiness, of love. They are not always our examples, we are not always bound to follow them; not more than we are bound to obey literally some of our Lord's precepts, such as turning the cheek, or giving away the coat; not more than we can follow the course of the sun, moon, or stars in the heavens; but though not always our examples, they are always our standard of right and good; they are raised up to be monuments and lessons, they remind us of God, they introduce us into the unseen world, they teach us what Christ loves, they track out for us the way which leads heavenward. They are to us who see them, what wealth, notoriety, rank, and name are to the multitude of men who live in darkness—objects of our veneration and our homage."

---

[1] "Discourses to Mixed Congregations," p. 94, Eng. ed.

And here it is that the divine truth and beauty of the Catholic teaching and practice shine forth so transcendently. For truth is, to our minds, but the knowledge of beings and their relations toward each other : it is like the light, at the close of the darkest night, dawning upon earth and sky and making them and all that they contain visible to the eye. And beauty is the resplendent creation of truth, just as color is the creation of light. Now because the Catholic doctrine is divine it enables the mind of man to take in not only the relations which bind nature to its Author, but more especially the essential ties which bind the natural man to his Maker, the natural virtues which merely as man he has to practise in order to fulfill the idea of manhood stamped on the souls of the entire race by the hand which made them. And these virtues are exalted to a sublime, inconceivable, and divine ideal in the Person of our supernatural model, God made man for our imitation.

The perfect Christian man is man with all that is good and great in his moral nature exalted to the dignity of adopted child of God, and so living in that divine rank as to verify the saying of the old Roman pagans about their Christian contemporaries : *Christianus alter Christus,* " every Christian in another Christ," as if every son born of the blood of Calvary reflected in his conduct the divine virtues of Jesus Christ. The ordinary good and serious-minded Christian man is he who with his whole heart strives to be Christ-like in thought, and word, and deed ; the saint is the man or the woman who is truly and in a sublime degree Christ-like in their interior and their exterior life, in mind and heart and conduct.

As to Angela Merici, we may here quote appositely to our purpose the pen-portrait drawn of her by John Baptist Nazari, her earliest biographer, and the man to whom was committed to draw up a juridical and authentic summary of her life and virtues, from the sworn testimony of those who had known her longest and best in Brescia. "In her," he says, "one could discover no unworthy affection, because she was a stranger to ambition, vainglory, and anger. Her sole delight was in humility, in the quiet, contemplative life fostered by religious rule. In this manner of life, as in the pathway marked out by our Lord, she practised fasting, long vigils, and prayer, so that, like a true religious, she was always firm in her faith, humble in her conversation, modest and exemplary in her dress, unwearied in her nightly vigils, fervent in all her prayers, most patient in ill-fortune, most devout in receiving the sacramants, and ever most ready to practise all the good works of a Christian."

The Heroic Manner in which St. Angela practised all the Moral Virtues.

To begin with those virtues which are enjoined by the law of nature written on the hearts of all men, as with what is easiest and most accessible to our good-will, let us give a glance at the four principal of these—the Cardinal Virtues, as they are termed, because they are the very foundation of a true moral excellence in every man and woman deserving of the name. These are the fundamental virtues on which the heathen philosophers of old made all manly goodness and greatness to hinge, and on which they made the existence of all human society to depend. They are Prudence, Justice, Temperance, and Fortitude.

If prudence, in the sense in which its nature and attributes are usually understood by theologians, be considered as the habitual disposition toward choosing the highest and holiest end, and employing the means best suited to its attainment;

we can see that virtue shine forth in Angela's conduct from her childhood to her latest day. Under the impulse of the Divine Spirit, when yet in every sense a child, her whole soul seemed fixed on striving after the highest good—after that supreme holiness of life of which she heard in the Lives of the Saints. And she pursued this supernatural ideal constantly ever afterward, while allowing herself to be governed by the wise counsels of her parents; just as, arrived almost at womanhood, she submitted unmurmuringly to the restraints which her uncle Biancosi advised her to put upon her yearning after solitude. All through life, while pursuing with inflexible firmness the course of rigorous ascetical practices she deemed necessary for her own sanctification, she nevertheless was always found ready at a moment's notice to give up her loved solitude, the sweets of prayer and contemplation, and her penitential austerities, to minister to the good of others. She was admired and revered almost as much for her reserve, her discretion, her tact, her exceeding wisdom in counseling all sorts of persons, as she was for her devotion to the poor, the suffering, the ignorant, or for that spotless purity of life and exalted spirit of prayer which seemed to make her on earth a blessed soul enjoying the beatific vision. But our readers will take in our meaning better by comparing, on this head, the words and actions of other saints with those of Angela. Take, for instance, the prudence so necessary to the saints in moderating bodily austerities, when these are no longer necessary toward the repression of the sensual appetites, or the making the body most docile to all the workings of the Spirit. Hear what is said of St. Ignatius Loyola.

"He had learned by his own experience the true principles of that asceticism which perfects the moral nature without ruining the body, which carefully avoids all imperfect and false direction in the spiritual career, and which never allows the sentiment of feeling to predominate at the expense of reason and understanding. He used to say that in the first days of conversion men ought to lead a more severe life ; but from the time that the soul has come to a state of greater purity from its stains, exterior mortification should be somewhat diminished. We will cite here one example. He alowed St. Francis Borgia at the beginning of his conversion, and while he was still Viceroy of Catalonia, to follow the impulse which led him to penitential austerities; but when he considered that he had done enough, and that he seemed to attach too much importance to practices of this kind, he interposed his authority and regulated the practice of his spiritual exercises. *As I consider in our Lord,* Ignatius writes to him, *that certain spiritual and corporal exercises are necessary at one time, and not so at another time, and that after having been useful to us they are not so useful in the sequel, I wish to say to you, in the presence of the Divine Majesty, that which presents itself to my mind with regard to this matter. . . . First, as to what concerns the time you have prescribed to yourself for these interior and exterior practices of prayer and penance, I think the one half of them might be retrenched. For if in proportion as our thoughts are carried away either by our own evil inclinations or by the devil to vain and unlawful things, and if again in proportion as we feel ourselves to be the more disposed to be attached to these unlawful things, we ought to multiply our practices of penance, so as to overcome our propensities, each one according to his disposition, or according to the variety of his thoughts and temptations, that the will may take no pleasure in them nor consent to them ; so, on the contrary, as these (evil) thoughts are put to flight and give place to holy inspirations, it is our duty to give entrance to such inspirations into our mind, and to open wide to them the gates of our soul. And, therefore, as you have no longer* need of so much defensive armor to repel the enemy, I think in our Lord that you will do better to employ the half of that time in the government of your estates, and in spiritual conferences and studies; for in the future acquired science will be more necessary to you and more useful than infused knowledge. But, at the same time, endeavor to keep your soul in peace and repose, and ready to receive all the workings of our Lord in it. . . .

"In the second place, with regard to fasting and abstinence, I think that it is better for the glory of our Lord to preserve and strengthen the stomach and other powers of nature, than it is to debilitate them; for, when we have the fixed resolution rather to die than of deliberate purpose to commit the least offence against the Divine Majesty, and when we are not attacked by any particular temptation from the devil, the world, or the flesh, exterior mortification is no longer necessary. Now I am convinced that you are in this disposition of which I have been speaking, and that you are free from temptations; I desire, therefore, that you will fully master this thought—that the soul and the body are the gift of God, our Master and Creator, and that you will have to give Him a strict account of both, and that for His sake you ought not to enfeeble your bodily nature, because if you take away its strength the spiritual nature cannot act any longer with the same energy. . . . We ought so much more to love the body, and to wish it well, the more it obeys and serves the soul; and the soul in its turn finds in this obedience and assistance of the body increased strength and energy to serve and glorify God our Master and Creator.

"As to the third point, namely, the chastisements which you inflict upon your body: I would avoid, for our Lord's sake, to spill even the least drop of blood. If hitherto the Divine Majesty has given you, as I am convinced He has, a particular grace and attraction to this practice, . . . I do not hesi-

tate to affirm, . . . that it is better for the future to leave off these things, and, instead of trying to draw a little blood, to seek to unite yourself more closely with the Lord of all, asking of Him more precious gifts, as, for example, the grace to shed a fountain of tears, or, at least, some few drops, whether it be for your own sins or for those of others, or whether it be in contemplating the mysteries of our Lord Jesus Christ in this life or in the next, or in considering or loving the divine perfections. And these tears will be the more precious and meritorius as the thoughts and meditations which make them flow shall be more elevated. And although in these several objects the third is in itself more perfect than the second, and the second than the first, nevertheless that is the best for each individual in which the Lord our God the more abundantly communicates Himself to him, and bestows on him a greater abundance of His holy gifts and spiritual graces, for He knows and sees what is the most advantageous to him, and shows him the way which he ought to keep, for He knows all things. But in order that we may discover this by His grace, it is very useful to prove and try many ways, so that all may choose the one which is the safest and the best for us in this life, and the most conducive to life eternal. Now among these gifts I reckon those which it is not in our power to be possessed of at our will, but which are simply bestowed upon us by the Giver of all good, such as are those which have a more immediate relation with His Divine Majesty, namely, actual faith, hope, and charity—spiritual peace and joy, interior consolations, elevation of soul, divine impulses and lights, together with all other spiritual impressions and joys, having always regard to the due subordination between these gifts, and manifesting all respect and humble obedience to our Holy Mother the Church and to those who are appointed rulers and doctors in it. . . . I do not mean to say that we ought to seek these gifts simply for the pleasure they cause us; still, all our thoughts, words, and actions, which without them are cold, confused, and disorderly, would, through them become, to the greater glory of God, fervent, enlightened, and just. And when the body finds that it is in peril through its excessive exertions, the best thing to be done is to seek for these gifts by spiritual acts and other exercises taken in moderation. It will then come to pass that not only will the soul be in a sound state, but there will be a sound mind dwelling in a sound body, and the whole man will be the more healthy and better disposed for the service of God."[1]

It is impossible to read this extract, so pregnant with heavenly prudenc, without remembering the wise practical rules for self-direction and the methods of governing others contained in St. Angela's "Reminders" and "Spiritual Testament," as well as those interspersed here and there in her Constitutions. One is reminded, both in perusing what she has written and in reviewing the actions of her life, of the beautiful figure of *Prudence* sculptured by Giovanni Pisano on the Baptistery of Florence. She is represented as having a double head: the one is that of a young woman, whose face is toward the earth with its temptations and its cares, while in one hand she holds up a serpent, as if to warn off some assailant; the other face is masculine and bearded, with the eyes fixed on the Eternal Hills. The head is surrounded with a halo—the attribute of supernatural sanctity. Such was the prudence of Angela with its twofold aspect, the soft, delicate, shrinking womanly nature ever using the wisdom of the serpent in dealing with a world full of deceit and danger; while, on the other hand, she ever kept the eye of her soul turned heavenward, planting her foot from early girlhood resolutely on the

---

[1] Genelli, "Life of St. Ignatius Loyola," Meyrick's translation from the French.

royal road of self-sacrifice, and persisting in it with indomitable courage. But this already brings us to the virtue of Fortitude.

Of Temperance, in the case of Angela Merici, we need say but little. If by the word we understand the virtue which teaches us to moderate and keep in subjection not merely our unruly bodily appetites, but the passions and movements of the soul itself, we are forthwith reminded not only of the heroic generosity with which our saint subdued every evil inclination and kept in subjection these passions, which cause so much sin and misery, but was to the end of her life the perfect mirror of abstinence as she was of purity and gentleness.

The natural virtue of Justice, as moralists explain it, consists in our rendering to the full whatever we owe to God, to the neighbor, and to ourselves. Her whole life was one uninterrupted effort to repay the Divine Goodness for all its gifts—with what supreme purity of intention, we know now, after reading the preceding chapters. Nor did she separate devotion to the good of the neighbor from her devotion to the glory of the Creator. The Company of St. Ursula, with its far-reaching services, proves abundantly how she paid to her kind the debt of her love. Nor did she forget to be just to herself—loving herself, so far as she might, as God loved her, and working till her last hour to make herself worthy of Him, by decking her soul with the ornaments of most perfect righteousness.

As it belongs to Prudence to see and to choose the road which leads to the highest moral perfection, and by it to the Most High God, so does it pertain to Fortitude to persevere in it in spite of all obstacles, dangers, and difficulties. As we have shown, the way of Christian holiness is the companionship with Christ in labor and suffering—to the garden, the pillar, and the cross. The Maid of Desenzano never, so far as human evidence can attest it, separated herself from His blessed side, whose whole life, as St. Bonaventure expresses it, "was a cross and a martyrdom."

The heroic temper which buoyed up Angela in her formed purpose of founding the Company of St. Ursula never forsook her for a day amid the disheartening delays and constantly occurring difficulties of well-nigh forty years. And this she knew how to breathe into others. How she gave courage and energy to her companions, when after the loss of her eyesight they wished to return to Venice and give up their journey to the Holy Land! And again, during the fearful perils of the storm at sea, how the strength which filled her own soul was communicated to all on board, enabling officers, crew, and passengers to work with a will in keeping the ship afloat, while trusting themselves unreservedly to God's keeping!

The fact is, that all these sweet womanly virtues which graced Angela's life and character, and these sterner qualities which gave her such invincible strength "to bear and to forbear," were sustained, vivified, elevated, and perfected by the supernatural virtues of Faith, Hope, and Charity, which are the fruits in the soul of the indwelling Spirit of God. Hers was the faith which, all through life, enabled the eye of her soul to behold God near her, as if the veil of mortality had been withdrawn. "Blessed are the clean of heart: for they shall see God!" The perfect faith which the Holy Ghost, the Spirit of our adoption, bestows on willing souls, is that firm belief, instinct with charity and buoyed up by yearning hope, that He who is the Infinite God is as present to us as the atmosphere we breathe and the light that fills it by day —that He is present within us in our heart of hearts, prompting its every aim and aspiration, its every affection, its deeds of self-sacrifice and divinest generosity. Let any one read the "Meditation on Divine Love" in the spiritual exercises of St. Ignatius Loyola, spelling to himself slowly and patiently the characters and syllables of that most divine of human conceptions, and he will know what is the Faith—the illuminated eye of the soul—and what the Charity which accompanies true faith as necessarily as the warmth of the sun's rays is poured out with his light. Oh that our hearts could see as do those of the saints!—that our life were as full of unceasing activity for God and the neighbor as His life is unceasingly devoted to our souls' welfare!—that, like St. Ignatius and St. Angela Merici, our heart was so purified from all earthly affections, and the eye of our soul so unclouded as to see in all that is fair and good and perfect here below but the reflection of His beauty and goodness and illimitable perfection—the streams descending from the ocean of all being and perfection, up which our souls may reascend to the Primal Source of life and love and joy eternal! On this one absorbing vision of the One infinitely true and fair and good and lovable beyond all present thought, such pure souls as Angela's are set from the dawn of reason. As to St. Agnes, the little Roman maiden, so beautiful in the exquisite simplicity of her childlike character, so heavenly in the angelic light in which she beheld her Betrothed and the magnificences of the invisible world—so to Angela Merici there was One ever present who drew her eyes and her heart all to Himself, and left no room in her soul for other love.

CHAPTER XIX.

ST. ANGELA'S CONSTITUTIONS.

WE may fitly pause in spirit before the shrine of St. Angela Merici in the Church of St. Afra, and, while kneeling with the pilgrims from every land to look upon her venerable remains, and to adore that God whose glory shines forth so wonderfully in His saints, cast our eyes upon the Constitutions which she has left behind, as upon the worthiest monument which could be placed beside her tomb.

These Constitutions divinely given to her, as she herself hints repeatedly in her last instructions to her dear ones, were the mould in which were cast and formed these primitive Ursulines of Brescia, Cremona, and Milan, who so won the admiration and reverence of all Upper Italy during the last half of the sixteenth century, that France, the Low Countries, and all Germany were fain to possess them. What though the outward form changed with the new countries in which they were called to labor, and with the imperious necessities of the altered times and the increased labors they had to assume? The apostolic spirit breathed by St. Angela into the Company of St. Ursula as trained and constituted by her, the mighty educational purpose which lay at the foundation of her institute, and the heroic virtues to which she had formed her daughters and which result necessarily from that formation—all passed into the congregated Ursulines of

Milan, and from them into the glorious monasteries of Aix and Lyons, of Bordeaux and Paris. The spirit of St. Angela so lived in the hundreds of Ursuline establishments which flourished in France and the Netherlands, in Italy and Germany, before the calamitous events of the French Revolution and the Napoleonic Empire, that the dry-rot of tepidity or worldliness never touched these nurseries of true Christian womanhood.

Nor have all the storms which have assailed, in these same countries, the impoverished and persecuted Ursuline monasteries during the present century impaired in aught either the admirable fervor of these devoted teachers of youth, or the culture which they bestow on their precious charge. In New York, as in New Orleans and Quebec, as in Paris and Brussels, as in Bordeaux and Vienna and Rome, the Virginal Life of the daughters of Angela Merici sheds the same heavenly fragrance all over the land, and bears the same undying fruits for Christian homes and public society.

The study of these Constitutions, therefore, the principal literary work bequeathed to us by St. Angela, is of deep interest to the statesman as well as the churchman—to every class of enlightened readers, indeed.

Travelers through Italy who have paused in Assisi to visit the shrine of St. Francis will remember the beautiful little Church of "the Portiuncula," preserved, like a casket of gems, within the splendid temple erected above and around it by the faith and piety of generations. The lowly little Oratory of the Portiuncula was the first possession ever bestowed on the seraphic saint and his followers—the first spot which they might call their own to worship God in without let or hindrance. When afterwards arose that stupendous structure on which Christian artists lovingly lavished, century after century, the tribute of their genius, they had no thought of disturbing the primitive chapel in which the sweet saint loved to refresh his soul in prayer. They covered it, on the contrary, with artistic gems, the love-offerings of the Christian heart to the cradle of a mighty religious Order.

Even so will the Ursulines of our day, no matter what may be the congregation which claims their filial homage, cherish this first cradle of their Order, and preserve it intact with infinite reverence, while never ceasing to be grateful to God for the more perfect Constitutions given to them, respectively, by the Vicar of Christ on earth.

IN THE NAME OF THE MOST HOLY TRINITY.

The Rule of the Company of St. Ursula of Brescia.

As it hath pleased God, my beloved daughters and sisters, to draw you out of the darkness of this miserable world, and to unite you in the service of His Divine Majesty, you are bound to return Him endless thanksgiving for having bestowed on you after so special a manner this singular favor. For how many exalted personages are there not—empresses, queens, duchesses, and the like—who, in view of their own greater glory and happiness, would be glad to be your humble handmaidens, considering how much more noble and enviable your condition is? Wherefore, dear sisters, I exhort, or rather, I beseech you, who have been chosen to be most truly the chaste spouses of the Son of God, to consider how great, how unheard-of, and how admirable is the dignity thus conferred on you; and then to endeavor by every means within your power to remain ever worthy of the title by which you are called. Seek to find and follow every path that can lead you infallibly to this happy result, and in this path persevere to the end. For no good beginning avails that is not crowned by perseverance. These persons alone can save themselves without difficulty who are willing to profit by all the necessary ways and means. For there is but little difference in saying to one's self, *I am resolved to serve God no longer*, and in making up one's mind to reject the means and neglect the rules which can alone help one to remain faithful in God's service.

Hence the greater is the need which we have, dear sisters, to be watchful in this matter, that we are the more called upon to be so by the sublime dignity of our rank of affianced brides to the Son of God, and destined queens of His kingdom. Wherefore, also, the greater need of wariness and prudence, that what we have engaged ourselves to accomplish is of infinite importance. We must bear in mind that we shall meet on our path all manner of formidable obstacles. We are surrounded with dangers and snares. Our bodily appetites and senses are not dead. And there are our sworn enemies, "the world, the flesh, and the devil;" the last raging and roving around us, seeking by every artifice to surprise and devour us. Let not this, however, terrify us, dear sisters. If in all future time you are resolved to live as becomes those who are in very truth the brides of the Redeemer, and to keep this Rule as the way by which you have to walk and in which all is ordained for your good, I firmly trust and hope in the Divine Goodness that we shall not only overcome all difficulties and dangers, but that our victory shall be attended with such honor and joy, that our little day of life shall seem to be all consolation, that grief and sadness shall be changed into sweetness and exultation : every thorny and stony path shall become flowery, smooth, pleasant, and filled with golden splendors.[1] There the angels and the heavenly choirs shall keep us company so long as we lead like them an angelic life.

---

[1] Le strade spinose, erte, e sassosi faransi a noi floride, piane, gioconde, e di finissimo oro coperte.

Let us then, dearest sisters, all together take this rule to our hearts, coming as it does to us from the hand of God. Let the careful observance thereof be to you what the arms of Judith were, enabling her to cut off the head of Holofernes. We too shall cut down our enemy the devil, and gloriously enter Heaven, triumphing there to the joy of both Heaven and earth.

Wherefore, with the aid of God's grace, open your ears and your heart to these precepts.

CHAPTER I.—HOW POSTULANTS ARE TO BE ADMITTED.

LET every one who desires to be received into this Company bear in mind, above all things, that she must be a virgin. Then, having moreover the firm purpose of serving God in our way of life, she must come to us cheerfully and of her own free-will. Thirdly, she must not be one who has bound herself to enter any monastery, or who was disappointed by a human lover. Fourthly, if she has a father, a mother, or other superiors, she must begin by obtaining their permission. The lady-directresses of the Company may, if needful, see the latter and speak to them, whenever without a legitimate reason they should chance to oppose their charge in their wish to take on themselves the yoke of our holy obedience. Fifthly, the postulant must have attained the age at least of twelve years, before asking to be received; she must be fifteen before receiving the habit, and being admitted to the chapter; and she must be from eighteen to twenty when the time comes for her receiving the veil and having her name inscribed on the Company's register. Let those who are under age remember that they can only be admitted among us for the purpose of being trained to our way of life.

CHAPTER II.—THE HABIT WORN IN THE COMPANY.

BE it also borne in mind that the dress worn by us should be becoming and simple, such as maidenly modesty demands. Each one must wear her dress covering the entire figure, and over it let her wear a linen veil of good texture, but by no means transparent like cambric. Of this same quality should be the other stuffs. The garments should be of woollen cloth, or serge, and of a dark color. [Let them also wear a long leathern cincture as a badge both of exterior and interior mortification, and of perfect chastity; and it is hereby declared that the habit proper to the virgins of this Company consists in the veil of linen and the leathern cincture. This habit shall be forfeited by any one of the members who for disobedience to the superiors, or for any other reason, shall be dismissed from the Company; and any one who would refuse to lay the habit aside after dismission would incur the penalty of excommunication, as it has been decreed by the illustrious and most Reverend Charles (Borromeo) Cardinal of St. Prasede, Visitor Apostolic, and at present a canonized saint.] Their slippers, sandals, and shoes shall be black, simple, and of becoming shape. Their underclothing must have no embroideries; they must not, finally, wear any of the fashionable vanities in vogue, which might leave a stain on their own conscience, be a cause of scandal to the neighbor, or appear to be in opposition with virginal modesty.

CHAPTER III.—THE MANNER OF LIVING IN THE WORLD.

THEY must, moreover, bear in mind : firstly, to have nothing to do with women of ill-repute; secondly, that they must never consent to receive messages from any man or woman, particularly secret messages; thirdly, that they are not to go to weddings, balls, carousals, and other such spectacles where worldlings have their pleasure ; fourthly, that, for many reasons, they are to avoid standing on balconies, beneath doorways, or in the streets ; fifthly, that in passing through the public highways they should have their eyes cast down, their garments modestly closed and gathered up ; they should go on their way quickly without loitering or stopping here and there, or standing still to admire anything whatever ; for in all places they may find manifold danger, and hidden snares of the enemy ; sixthly, whenever their mothers or other persons placed above them in the world would expose them to any such dangers, or prevent them from fasting, praying, going to confession, or any other such good work, they are to lay the matter before the lady-directresses of the Company, who will provide a remedy.

CHAPTER IV.—ON FASTING.

They are also to remember that each one ought and must practise fasting from bodily aliment, as a thing that is necessary and as a means for practising spiritual abstinence, by which all mental vices and errors are extirpated. We are evidently called on to do so by the example of all holy persons and by the whole tenor of Christ's life, which is for us the sole way leading to Heaven. This also is what the Church our mother sounds in the ears of all her children, saying to God (in the Preface for Lent) : " Thou who by bodily fasting dost repress vice, lift up the soul, and bestow both virtue and its reward." [1] Just as gluttony was the source of all our woe, even so is it befitting that abstinence become the origin and means of all our spiritual weal and increase. Hence, we exhort every one of you to observe as a special

---

[1] *Qui corporali jejunio vitia comprimis, mentem elevas, virtutem largiris et premia.*

fasting day each of the following days throughout the year, over and above the fasts prescribed by our Holy Mother the Church.

1. We must fast during the whole of Advent.

2. We must fast three days each week, beginning with the Wednesday following the second Sunday after the Epiphany.

3. We must fast, beginning with the week following the octave of Easter, three days in each week, namely, Wednesday, Friday, and Saturday.

4. We must fast on the three Rogation Days, or the three days immediately preceding the feast of the Ascension, during which the Church chants the Litanies in solemn procession to obtain the divine assistance for the Christian people.

5. We must fast and persevere in prayer, every day after the Ascension to the coming down of the Holy Ghost—that is, "the Easter in May"—beseeching the fulfillment of Christ's magnificent promises to His elect and to all who are intent on good works.

Inasmuch, however, as nothing is here demanded that is not in accordance with reason and discretion, let no one undertake the above fasts without the advice of the spiritual father, and of the lady-directresses of this Company, to whom it belongs to modify the number of these fasts as necessity may demand.

CHAPTER V.—ON PRAYER.

BEAR also in mind that each one of you should be diligen in, what regards prayer, both mental and vocal ; for prayer goes always hand in hand with fasting, even as the Scripture saith : " Prayer is good with fasting ;"[1] and hence we read in the Gospel of Anna, the daughter of Phanuel, that she

---

[1] Tobias xii. 8.

"departed not from the Temple, by fasting, and prayers serving night and day;"[1] and as by fasting one mortifies one's bodily appetites and senses, even so by prayer one obtains from God the real gift of spiritual life. Wherefore, considering our constant need of the divine assistance, we should apply mind and heart to the task of praying without intermission. We also, and by all means, recommend the frequent use of vocal prayer, which, by making us collect our senses, disposes the soul to mental prayer. Let every one of you, then, recite daily at least the Office of the Blessed Virgin Mary and the seven Penitential Psalms, with attention and fervor; since, in reciting the Office, we converse with our Lord. Those who do not know how to recite the Office should learn from those who do. As to such as cannot read, let them recite daily, at the hour of Matins, thirty-three times the Lord's Prayer and the Hail Mary in honor of the thirty-three years of our Lord's mortal life. At Prime let them say the same seven times, to obtain the seven gifts of the Holy Ghost; and so at each of the other hours—Tierce, Sext, None, Vespers, and Complin. And in order both to afford matter for mental prayer, and to open some sort of a way to it, we exhort every one of you to lift her soul to God every day and to exercise herself in this manner of praying, saying, in the secret of her heart, the following or some other such form of prayer:

"O Lord! shed thy light on the dark places of my heart, and grant me the grace rather to die than ever offend Thy Divine Majesty. Give stability, O Lord! to my affections and sentiments, so that they may cause me to commit no transgression, nor to take my eyes away from the light of Thy countenance, which is the sweet comfort of every afflict-

---

[1] St. Luke ii. 37.

ed soul. Oh, with what bitterness I feel, as I look into my own heart, how I should blush to lift my eyes to Thee, knowing as I do that I deserve to be buried in hell! Besides, when I consider the errors of my ways, my spiritual deformity, my baseness, the monstrous perversity of my actions, the fearful fancies and figures that haunt my imagination, I am compelled night and day, whether I walk or stand, work or reflect, to cry out to Heaven, and to implore Thee, O my God! to pity me and grant me time to do penance.

"Vouchsafe, therefore, O Lord! to pardon all my sins, all my faults—everything in which I have offended Thee since my baptism. Vouchsafe also, O Lord! to forgive the sins of my father and mother, of my relatives and friends, and of all mankind. I beseech Thee to do so by Thy most sacred Passion, by Thy precious Blood shed for the love of us, by Thy Holy Name of Jesus, which I beg all earth and Heaven, all the choirs of angels and archangels, to bless and praise eternally.

"I am heartily sorry, O Lord! to have begun so late to serve Thy Divine Majesty. Wretch that I am, I have never, up to this moment, shed so much as one drop of my blood for love of Thee; I have cared so little to be obedient to Thy law, that the most trifling misfortune would fill me with bitterness, loving Thee so little as I did.

"My God, I grieve and feel my heart wrung with pain at seeing all these unhappy creatures of Thine, who are so blind as not to know Thee, who have no care of being made sharers in the merits of Thy sacred Passion. Most willingly would I, were it in my power, give my life to have the veil removed from their eyes.

"Wherefore, O my Lord and my God, Thou who art my life and my hope! I beseech Thee to take this unworthy and unclean heart of mine, and to cleanse and chasten it in the furnace of Thy love. I beg Thee, O Lord! to take from me all self-will, which, infected and blinded by sin, is unable to distinguish good from evil. Accept, then, O Lord! every thought and word and action of mine—everything, indeed, whether interior or exterior, that belongs to me. I place all here at the feet of Thy Divine Majesty, entreating Thee not to reject it, all unworthy as my offering may be."

CHAPTER VI.—ON HEARING MASS DAILY.

LET every one go to Mass daily, and hear at least one with all modesty and devotion. In this adorable Sacrifice are contained in the most wonderful way all the merits of the Passion of our dear Lord. The greater the attention, the faith, the contrition of the assistants, the greater must be the share they have in these blessed merits, and the deeper the consolation derived therefrom. Thus you may communicate spiritually. However, you must not loiter too long in the church. If you are moved to make a longer prayer, go and shut yourself up in your room, and there pray as the Spirit of God and your own conscience shall dictate to you.

CHAPTER VII.—ON CONFESSION.

YOU are exhorted to go frequently to confession, in order there to receive the remedy needful to the wounds of our souls. Let every one present herself to the priest, as she would to God, our Eternal Judge; and there, grieving with heartfelt sorrow and a firm purpose of renouncing everything sinful, let her confess her sins and ask pardon therefor. Let her kneel before her confessor with the reverence expected from persons of solid piety. Besides, you must not forget that a particular place or church must be designated in which all must meet on the first Friday of each month, and there receive communion from the spiritual father. Moreover, we exhort each of you to confess and receive communion in her own parish church on the great feasts of the year.

CHAPTER VIII.—ON OBEDIENCE.

WE exhort each of you to observe holy obedience, which is the only and true renouncement of one's own will. Obedience grounded in charity is, in the soul of man, like a great light, in whose brightness all his works are made good and acceptable. To have this light, let every one of you, first of all, observe the Divine Precepts; for it is written: "They are accursed who decline from Thy commandments."[1] Next, we must obey the commandments of our Holy Mother the Church, of whom the Truth hath said: "He that heareth you, heareth Me; and he that despiseth you, despiseth Me."[2] In the third place, you must obey your own bishop and pastor, your spiritual father, the lady-directresses and other superiors of the Company. In the fourth place, you must obey your parents and the other persons placed above you at home, of whom we advise you to ask pardon once a week in sign of your obedience and of the love you bear them. Fifthly, you must obey the laws and ordinances of the civil magistrates. There is, besides, obedience due to our interior inspirations, when on the judgment and approbation of the spiritual father we know them to be from the Spirit of God.

To resume: we are bound to obey God for love of Him, and, following the injunction of the Apostle, we should be subject " to every human creature for God's sake,"[3] where what is commanded is not opposed to the divine honor, to our own, or to our eternal salvation.

---
[1] Ps. cxviii. 21.   [2] St. Luke x. 16.   [3] 1 Peter ii. 13

CHAPTER IX.—ON VIRGINITY.

EACH one must be careful to preserve holy virginity ; and this, not because our Rule binds any one to make a vow of virginity, but because every one should form the firm purpose of keeping her virginal treasure entire for God. For virginity is so highly prized, that she is called the sister of the angels, the conqueror of all sensual appetites, the queen of virtues, and the mistress of all spiritual treasures. Whence it behooveth every one of you so to conduct herself in all things, that she be conscious of doing nothing toward herself or in presence of others that might seem unbecoming a bride of the Most High God. Therefore, above all things, let her keep her heart pure, and her conscience free from every evil thought, from every shadow of envy, ill-will, dissension, rash judgment—in a word, from every sinful emotion and desire. On the contrary, let her be joyous, filled with charity, faith, and trust in God.

In conversing with the neighbor, let us be sensible and modest, observing the counsel of the Apostle : " Let your modesty be known to all men :"[1] thereby every action and word of ours shall be decorous and well-timed. We must not pronounce lightly the name of God ; nor use expressions like an oath, but simply say " No, no ;" " Yes, yes," even as our Lord taught us ; nor give haughty answers ; nor do what we are asked with ill grace ; nor keep up anger ; nor murmur ; nor ever relate what we saw that was evil ; nor, in fine, must we ever be seen doing an action, or making so much as a gesture, that could be deemed unseemly, especially in one who glories in being Christ's handmaiden. Let all our words and actions and movements be such as to edify and teach those who know us intimately, proceeding always

---

[1] Philippians iv. 5.

from a heart inflamed with charity. Furthermore, each one of us should be disposed to die rather than ever consent to soil what is her sacred joy and her treasure.

CHAPTER X.—ON POVERTY.

WE exhort every one of you to embrace poverty, not merely that which rids us of all love of temporal wealth, but above all that poverty of our spirit, by which the soul puts away from herself, all attachment to and hope of created and transitory things, indeed, all love of one's self; placing all her treasures in God, and esteeming herself, without God, poor in all things, and herself a mere nothing; while, possessed of God, she possesses all things. This is what the Gospel says: "Blessed are the poor in spirit!"[1] For this purpose, let each one set herself about divesting herself of all things, and placing all her wealth, her love, her delight, not in dress, or in eating and drinking, or in her parents and relatives, or in herself or her personal foresight and wisdom; but in God alone, and in His fatherly and infinitely wise providence. This is why our Lord hath said: "Seek ye, therefore, first the kingdom of God and His justice, and all these things shall be added unto you."[2] Again He saith: "Be not solicitous for your life, what you shall eat, nor for your body, what you shall put on.... For your Father knoweth that you have need of all these things."[3]

CHAPTER XI.—ON THE GOVERNMENT AND OFFICERS OF THE COMPANY.

JUST as the Council of Trent has enjoined on all bishops to have a care of those who lead the virginal life and live under the regular discipline of monasteries; even so are

---
[1] St. Matthew v. 3. [2] *Ibid.*, vi. 33. [3] *Ibid.*, 25, 33.

bishops and pastors bound to have no less care of those who lead the virginal life and have resolved to lead it forever while remaining within their own homes. Indeed, a greater care would seem to be needful to the latter, whose perils are greater and more numerous. Therefore it is that the Company of Virgins who combat under the standard and name of St. Ursula, recognizing and obeying as their father, pastor, and superior the present Bishop of Brescia, and every one of his lawful successors, submit themselves to his obedience, and recommend themselves to his fatherly and pastoral care.

CHAPTER XII.—OF THE FATHER OF THE ENTIRE COMPANY.

AND because the care of so large a diocese would not permit the bishop to occupy himself with all the concerns of our Company, in the measure which would be necessary to maintain and advance its prosperity, it is indispensable that he should have a vicar placed over it, whom all should accept as their Father, and as the superior placed over them by the bishop, and selected to fill the latter's place—a man to whom all must render the obedience which is due to him.

As it belongs to the episcopal office to select this Father and to place him over the whole Company of St. Ursula, as his own vicar, so is it his privilege to confirm him, or to change him at his own discretion, when he shall know this to be expedient or more useful to the Company.

This Father will have charge of all that regards the advancement of the Company, making it his duty to remove every obstacle which may present itself in the general government thereof, or arise from the conduct of some individual subjects, and having recourse to the episcopal authority whenever it is necessary.

The ladies who are charged with the government of the

Company may not convene a general congregation without the said Father being present thereat, or without his formal permission and approval; wherefore, all the acts of such congregation in which the said Father would not be present, or which would be held without his consent, are to be considered as null and void.

The maidens who ask to be admitted into the Company must be first examined and approved by the Father; and should any one be admitted without such examination and approbation, she is in no wise to be considered to be admitted, till she has been by him examined and approved.

CHAPTER XIII.—ON THE SUBSTITUTE.

IT is proper that there should be given to the spiritual father, as a substitute and coadjutor, some other priest. For, because of the increase of members and the extension of the Company, it would become a very difficult matter for a single priest to suffice for all the demands upon him, while, on the other hand, the first Father happening to fail or to be absent, it would be needful to have another used to the spiritual government of the Company and taking a hearty interest in its welfare.

This substitute shall only have, in what regards the Company, such powers as the bishop may give him, and shall only act under the direction of the Father of the Company.

On the two feast days which we particularly celebrate, those, namely, of St. Catherine and St. Agnes, the solemnity must be honored by the presence of the bishop, and timely invitation must be sent him, so as to allow him to be with us in good season. This must be more particularly observed when on either of these feasts any of our sisters are, through greater devotion and a desire of higher perfection, to make a public vow of virginity. We here declare that such vows, although made in public, are not intended to be other than simple vows. If on these feast days the bishop cannot be present, the Father of the Company will do what is needful.

CHAPTER XIV.—ON THE MOTHER OF THE WHOLE COMPANY.

There shall be one Mother and Superior of the whole Company, whose office shall be for life, and who shall be chosen by the two thirds of the members convened for the election, in the presence of the bishop, or, at least, in that of the Father of the Company, and the person thus chosen shall have no authority till she has been confirmed therein by the bishop.

For this election of the Mother shall be convened all the Lady-Directresses, and all the Mistresses, the Counselors (*Avvisatrici*), with all the sisters who have been received into the Company; and the assembled electors shall be expressly admonished to select the member most distinguished for her edifying life, one of exemplary conduct, and tried by long years in the practice of all the virtues; so that she may possess over all the moral authority necessary toward directing and leading them to that perfection of life which should be the aim of all, and toward maintaining therein so many souls, the servants and brides of our Lord. Above all, let this person be known as a woman of eminent charity and tenderness toward the young members of this Company, so that in all their needs she may prove herself one who with a ready motherly heart can help and comfort them.

When they are assembled to elect the Mother, let each one have with her a paper on which is written the name of her chosen candidate, and this she shall place, folded, in a box prepared for that purpose in the room.

If a person with the above qualities can be found among the maiden sisters of the Company, she ought to be preferred to a widow, inasmuch as the former belongs to a higher condition, to that indeed of those over whom she has to be placed as Mother. In such a person, too, it is more likely to find a deeper love and tenderness for the Company, whose child she is and on whose milk she has been fed. Nor is it unlikely that in her shall shine forth with greater lustre all the virtues necessary to such a Mother, and in the practice of which a maiden sister had always lived.

When, however, because of immature years or other reasons, a proper person cannot be found among the maiden sisters, let a widow be chosen on whom God hath bestowed more abundantly than on the others the gifts above enumerated.

The Mother should hold her office till death, unless her great age or serious infirmities should disable her, or that, for some other cause connected with the greater good of the Company, the bishop should deem it expedient to have another chosen.

Although in choosing the Mother greater regard should be had to maturity of spirit and tried constancy in virtue than to ripe years; nevertheless, it seems becoming that she should not be under forty years of age when elected, and that she should have been ten years a member of the Company, if a maiden sister, or, if she be a widow, she must have moreover filled the office of vicar during ten years.

CHAPTER XV.—THE MOTHER VICAR.

IN order that the body of the Company should never on any occasion remain without a head to rule and govern it, it is of great importance that a vicar should be given to the

Mother, to hold the latter's place when absent, and to aid her in every emergency.

In the vicar should be found, let us say it briefly, the requirements and qualities demanded by such an office, which are none other than those which we have mentioned as necessary to the Mother herself.

The Mother Vicar shall be elected with the formalities prescribed for that of the Mother, and must, like her, be confirmed by the bishop.

Although the Vicar fills the Mother's place during her absence, she may not in her absence introduce any innovation, or change anything decreed by the Mother. Her duty shall simply be to execute the Mother's ordinances or such measures as are prescribed by the Rule or otherwise decreed.

On all occasions she shall hold the first place after the Mother, whose vicar she is.

When the Mother is present, the Vicar's authority shall not differ in any way from that of the other assistants; in the absence of the Mother, she shall possess just the measure of authority granted to her by the Mother, on whom, while she lives, the Vicar has to depend in everything.

When the Mother dies, the government passes into the hands of the vicar till the election of a new Mother, when the vicar's office ends. To the vicar belongs to perform all that is needful for the burial of the dead Mother as well as for the election of a new Mother, according to the ordinances of the Company.

She can not lawfully, either during the lifetime of the Mother, or during the interval between her death and the election of a successor, admit either to the chapter or into the body of the Company any maiden-sister, even though the assistants and the lady-directresses should consent to her doing so. And what is here said of admissions must be also understood of dismissions from the Company. This must be reserved to the Mother to whose office it properly belongs; and we hereby declare that all admissions or dismissions occurring during the absence or death of the Mother are absolutely null.

The vicar shall make no outlay that is not usual or demanded by urgent necessity during such absence or death.

Although the office of the vicar and of the assistants expires with the creation of a new Mother, the vicar can be continued in her charge, should the general congregation judge this expedient in view of the divine glory, and the utility of the Company.

CHAPTER XVI.—THE ASSISTANTS.

ALTHOUGH it has been settled that there shall be but one Mother Superior of the whole Company, in conformity with the wise opinion which prefers the government of the one to that of the many; nevertheless, taking into consideration the great needs of all these servants of Christ our Lord, exposed as they are to manifold and various perils of soul and body; and considering also that the unaided strength of a single person cannot provide for so great a family without the risk of harm or disorder among her charge—we deem it necessary to give to the Mother four other ladies as her assistants, with whom she can confer and consult concerning all the affairs and needs of the entire Company, or which may relate to any one of its subjects.

Let the Mother Superior hold no deliberation on matters of any importance relating either to the common welfare or the good of individuals, without the advice and consent of the majority of her assistants or of at least two of them—and this in order that the deliberations should be conducted with more light, more prudence, more aid from the Holy Spirit, to the greater glory of our Lord, and the increase of peace and progress of the Company, as well as the riper benefits for all its subjects. For it is a thing on which all men have agreed, that the eyes of two persons see more than those of one.

The qualities required in the assistants, as is evident from the nature of their office, should resemble those demanded of the Mother Superior herself. They shall be chosen by the same electors and in the same form as the Mother; immediately after her, and with the approbation of the bishop.

What was said above of the Mother Superior must also be said of them; they should be riper in mind and virtue than in years. Nevertheless, for very just reasons, no one should be elected to the office of assistant, who has not passed her thirtieth year; and if they are maiden sisters, they must have had ten years of membership in the Company; and if widows, they must have spent five years in governing the Company.

Their office is not for life, but expires with the Mother, with whom they were elected. They may be confirmed in their charge at the election of a new Mother; and should any one of them die before the Mother, another person is to be chosen in her stead by the Mother, the remaining assistants, the lady-directresses, the mistresses, and counselors, in presence of the Father and with his consent.

The office of the assistants consists in affording as much help as possible to the Mother. Let them meet once in the week to consult together on such affairs as have to be dispatched to provide for all the pressing needs of the Company at large or of particular members. Hence they must not call together the lady-directresses save when this can be done without inconvenience, and when some grave and urgent necessity occurs to which they are not equal.

One of the assistants shall be selected to take the Mother's place in keeping the moneys of the Company, as well as a full account of receipts and payments. She must carry out with diligence and charity whatever shall be determined by the assistants in council or what shall be ordered by the Mother. To fill such a charge as this, the person selected must be one who, in the judgment of all, shall have displayed equal ability and experience in treating business matters as well as in her own household management.

What has been said about the Mother should be reaffirmed of the assistants and of all persons fit to govern the Company; when subjects are found among the maiden-sisters distinguished for prudence, charity, and other shining virtues, they are always to be preferred to ladies who are not of maidenly condition, and that for the reasons already enumerated.

CHAPTER XVII.—ON THE LADY-DIRECTRESSES.

CONSIDERING the large number (ever increasing through the blessing of our Lord) of His servants and spouses, and hoping for a still larger increase, and for the purpose of securing to them better government with greater security and provision against every need, let there be elected also eight ladies, distinguished for their practical judgment, their prudence, and other ripe virtues, more even than for their advanced age, to each of whom one district of the eight into which the city has been divided shall be made over that she may have a special and loving care of the sister maidens living in that district, which should also be her own place of residence. Below shall be found the rules and methods to be followed by each in governing her little flock.

These lady-directresses are to be elected and confirmed in

the manner prescribed for the assistants and for the Mother; and when any one of them is taken away by death or otherwise, let another be chosen in her place by the Mother, the assistants, the lady-directresses, and all the others who meet to elect the assistants.

To these lady-directresses it will belong to make known all the needs both of the Company in general, and of their own charge in particular. No one of them, however, may busy herself with the concerns of another lady-directress's charge —unless she be impelled to do so by informing such lady-directress of what relates to persons subject to the latter, and in order to enable her to provide a proper remedy. Should the latter, however, neglect to do so, then the matter can be laid before the Mother and her assistants, that they may see to it in their wisdom.

No postulant shall be presented by any person to the Father or to the Mother of the Company, either to receive the habit, or to be accepted and admitted into the Company, or to make the vows, unless such postulant shall have been first examined by the lady-directress of the district in which such postulant lives. Moreover, the mistress who in this same district is like the executive of the lady-directress, should also beforehand have had information about such postulant. Furthermore, the Mother Superior herself of the whole Company may not accept or present for acceptation to her council of government any maiden whatever, without following the order prescribed here; and this, in order that everything may be done with greater regularity and uniformity, and that these maidens may be well known and carefully examined, who are to be accepted or who are preparing to be accepted in the future.

Whenever it happens that one of the lady-directresses is chosen to be assistant to the Mother, another directress is to be elected in her place, who shall replace the new assistant in her charge over the maiden-sisters.

What has been said of the proper age of the assistants applies equally to the lady-directresses.

CHAPTER XVIII.—THE OFFICE OF THE LADY-DIRECTRESSES.

THE ladies should inform themselves minutely about the maiden-sisters intrusted to their care. Let them know the name of each, with that of her abode and family; let them be acquainted with the rank and condition of each, with their habits, their conduct, and their conversation both inside and outside their homes.

Let them see to it that the sisters are most diligent in putting into practice all the prescriptions of the Rule as taught them by the mistresses. This they can make sure of by making the former give an account from time to time of the lessons taught them by the latter. With those in particular whom they suspect of carelessness, of tepidity, or of little liking for spiritual things, or who are exposed to some great danger, they must exercise a more diligent watchfulness.

Let them also know who is the confessor appointed for each, and endeavor to ascertain whether the sisters are punctual in receiving the sacraments of Penance and Eucharist on the days prescribed, if they are constant in going to the same confessor, or if they like to change. Let them try especially to know if the sisters are in need of help either for their bodily or for their spiritual wants.

And, although our chief concern should be about the soul, nevertheless it is a duty of charity to bestow also help on the body—especially when sickness or poverty has reduced any of the maiden-sisters to real want. For, then, it should be seen to that bodily want become not a danger for the soul itself.

This motherly care must increase whenever any one belonging to their charge is drawing near her last hour ; then, two sisters, judged the most able to assist the sufferer in her extreme need, should be sent to remain with her.

When any sister dies, her lady-directress should provide for all that is necessary toward her funeral service and burial, notifying the spiritual father and the Mother Superior, that these also may do their duty.

They shall have the greatest care of the novices, making the mistresses and counselors visit them, and seeking by every means to obtain a detailed knowledge of their habits and way of living ; so that when the time comes for admitting these to the chapter or unto the Company, the ladies may be able to give certain and truthful information concerning them to the other directresses.

Every directress should call to her the mistress and counselor at least every fortnight, in order to consult about the wants of the maiden-sisters of their district.

Let them be also careful to assemble all the sisters of their district at the time appointed, inquiring into and providing for the need of each ; let them make a note of the necessities which present themselves and endeavor to meet them ; and if they cannot do so, let them expose them in the general congregation.

Should any one of the sisters be guilty of disobedience, or misbehave in any other way, her lady-directress must impose on her some salutary penance, which, being in conformity with the delinquent's disposition, may, with the help of God, bring about amendment.

Above all things, let each lady-directress love all the maiden-sisters of her charge with that true charity which comes from the heart, and which is due to those who are the chosen brides and dear children of Christ Himself, endeavoring to take them all to her heart with a true motherly affection; not looking down on them as persons beneath her own rank, but seeing in them God Himself, for whose sake she has undertaken to care for them.

CHAPTER XIX.—OF THE MISTRESSES.

BESIDES the directresses, it is necessary that there should be eight other persons—mistresses, as it were, who, under the direction of these ladies, shall deal more familiarly and frequently with the maiden-sisters of each district, comforting these assiduously with loving care, and, whenever there is need, correcting them with that charity and respect which the Spirit of Christ requires. Whenever they meet with that obstinacy and incorrigibleness which renders correction unavailing, they must lay the case before the lady-directress, relating what they have themselves done in the way of reproof, and then the directress will apply the proper remedy.

As to the mistresses, their endeavor must be to manifest their great solicitude for the maiden-sisters of their charge, by taking pains to become acquainted with the natural disposition of each one, her inclinations and habits. Let them observe how they behave both in the bosom of their families and outside of their homes; and for that purpose let them pay the sisters frequent visits, and that unexpectedly.

Let these mistresses be ordinarily chosen from the maiden class, and persons of such ripe judgment, exemplary life, and proved virtue, that they can be unhesitatingly intrusted with the formation and direction in spiritual life of so many servants of our Lord. They should be adorned with such shining virtues, that any lack of authority due to their youth might be compensated by the esteem and respect in which they are held by all.

These mistresses shall be elected and confirmed in the same manner as the lady-directresses; and to each directress it will belong to designate the mistress who, in her judgment, is the best fitted for her district : each mistress, in order to qualify herself for the efficient discharge of her important functions, being careful to observe the following rules, to read them often, and then bear them easily in mind, when an opportunity occurs to apply them :

The office of a mistress shall be—as the name itself indicates—to train the maiden-sisters placed under her care. The first means for so training these must be the mistress's own exemplary life, in which ought to be mirrored forth the life to be led by all the maiden-sisterhood of St. Ursula.

She must often call around her these maiden-sisters, and exhort them with loving words dictated by true charity to be earnest in acquiring the spiritual perfection which is necessary to their calling, to use unhesitatingly all the means at their command, to avoid everything that might be an obstacle on the road to holiness, and to bend all their energies toward a most faithful observance of our rules.

When the time appointed for a congregation (or general meeting of all the sisters) of each district, the mistress shall give them the following " Reminders :"

1. Let them be mindful to fulfill carefully and lovingly God's holy commandments and those of His Church, showing thereby openly the reverence and awe which they entertain toward the Divine Majesty. For—and they must not forget it—if it be incumbent on all true Christians to observe both the law of God and that of His Church, how much more so are our sisters obliged thereunto ?

2. In urging upon them the faithful observance of the Divine Law, we intend also to remind them more particularly of the precept enjoining reverence and obedience toward those

whom they call "Fathers" and "Mothers," both of the body and of the soul—and indeed toward all superiors. One who carefully remembers and diligently fulfills the latter precept of reverence and obedience toward parents and superiors, will be all the more likely to fulfill the former; indeed, it will help toward fulfilling all the others.

3. Inasmuch as it is most proper that one who professes to be the bride and servant of Christ should be the faithful imitator of all the virtues of the Divine Bridegroom; and because among the manifold virtues which adorned His life, charity, humility, meekness, and gentleness shone forth with a special lustre; therefore is it becoming that the mistresses should, in these general assemblies, specially impress upon their young charge the necessity of displaying in their home-life these same virtues of charity, patience, humility, and gentleness.

4. They are to be reminded not to cultivate the acquaintance of all sorts of persons. Let them be familiar only with such as lead a pious life like themselves; such persons only can by their intercourse contribute to the good name of our sisters as well as to their real happiness. As to worldly-minded and ill-famed women—they are to be shunned. The sisters must never converse with men without having a companion with them, and without a real neccessity.

5. Those who make profession of the virginal life should ever bear with them the lighted lamp of good works, so as to shed the light of edification on all who see them. They should, therefore, have a care not to give cause of offence to others, as, for instance, one might easily do by being talkative, or by conversing about frivolous or worldly matters— and much more so by backbiting, or by giving ear to detraction. It would be most unedifying to be seen running to the

window, loitering beneath doorways and porticoes, or standing still to gossip in the streets.

6. Let the mistresses confirm those of their charge in their design of remaining maidens, or (for such as have made it) of keeping faithfully their vow of virginity. And let them impress upon the sisters that such virginity should be not merely that of the body, which once lost is lost forever; but that of the soul, toward the preservation of which all the avenues of the senses should be most sacredly guarded.

7. Let their dress be such as becomes their calling and the spiritual perfection which they professedly strive after, and in conformity with our Rule. As they are bound to wear a veil and cloak of non-transparent stuff, so they must avoid these habits of softness and fastidiousness, which constitute no slight danger for maidenly modesty, when they do not tend to ruin it inevitably.

8. Let the sisters receive the sacraments at least once a month, and more frequently if it should be judged proper by the confessor of each. Let them assist punctually at sermons and Scripture-lessons; and learn from them what may greatly help toward their own spiritual advancement.

9. When no lawful impediment prevents them, let them endeavor to hear Mass every morning, making it their care to assist at this Divine Sacrifice with all interior devotion, while edifying by their exterior reverence all those who are present.

10. Let the mistresses recall to them the necessity of busying themselves, each with the approval of her confessor, in some pious work, and particularly in giving CHRISTIAN EDUCATION. Let the sisters be prompt and obedient to the voice of their superiors, and so demean themselves in their special good works, and particularly in teaching, that their pupils shall learn from them virtuous habits as well as the knowledge of their religion.

11. Such of them as are compelled by poverty to leave their own homes and live with others, are to be told that they must not visit outside of their abode without the consent of their confessor and of their lady-directress. Nor must they change their place of residence without the knowledge and consent of the same.

12. They are also to be told that, however praiseworthy a thing it be to make a long stay in the church, nevertheless, when, in the judgment of those who have care of their souls, they have spent in devotion the necessary time, they must go home. It is not becoming that our maiden-sisters should be overmuch abroad; and prolonged absence must inconvenience their household. Let them be careful to derive as much devotion from their staying in the house as they are to edify by their modesty outside of it.

13. It is also to be impressed on them that it is quite opposed to the decencies of their calling to go forth frequently into the streets without any necessity. Wherefore, let them not be seen passing through the city, unless there be a necessity for doing so, or unless they are called by their respective counselors to the general or particular congregations, or to the solemn processions. To such all are to go when not kept at home by necessity. For such necessary absence a respectful and humble excuse is to be given.

14. Although the fasts prescribed by the Rule do not oblige under pain of sin, nevertheless the sisters are to be exhorted to keep them so far as their strength will permit and with the advice of the confessor.

15. They are also to be told that every one must have a fixed confessor, whom they may not change without permission from the spiritual father of the Company.

16. On the last Sunday of each month all are to go to the church of the Company, where the Rules shall be publicly

read. The sisters are to lay these Rules to heart in order to observe them faithfully. In the same Church they are all to receive Holy Communion on the first Friday of the month, unless prevented by some lawful reason, in which case they are to excuse themselves with all humility.

17. They must not go outside of the city without the permission of their lady-directress.

18. The mistresses, besides all this, must take a great care of the novices, and see to it that these are instructed on all the various matters herein mentioned. They are to see the novices frequently for the purpose of becoming thoroughly acquainted with them and with their way of living. Thus, when the time comes for admitting these beginners to the chapter or into the body of the company, the mistresses will be able to give to the ladies charged with the government the full information required.

CHAPTER XX.—OF THE COUNSELORS.

As the mistresses may be prevented by their occupations and sometimes even by their age from visiting as frequently as it would be needful the sister-maidens of their charge, it is necessary that there should be other ladies intrusted with this care. These shall have it as their duty to visit the sisters on the proper occasions, and to observe the proceedings of the latter, informing thereof the respective directresses and mistresses, so that these may the better govern and direct their subjects, or bring them back to the rule whenever they deviate from it.

These ladies shall be called *Counselors*. It will be also their duty to call the sisters of their district whenever their respective mistresses want to see them, or when the lady-directresses want to have them meet together, or, again, when the Mother Superior desires them to assemble in general or particular congregation pursuant to the ordinances.

Their number is to be equal to that of the directresses and mistresses, so that every district shall have its own counselor as it has directress and its mistress. To these the counselors must be subordinated as their ministers, helping them in the matters above-mentioned as well as in others, as occasion shall demand or obedience prescribe. They must be no less ripe in virtue than in years, well known for their blameless conduct, and of about fifty years of age. They may be chosen from among the maiden-sisters or the matrons, from the former in preference, for this and all such offices, because of the higher dignity of the virginal state.

CHAPTER XXI.—OF THE GENERAL CONGREGATION OF THE COMPANY OF ST. URSULA.

THE first thing which may be prudently stated regarding the general congregation, is that to it should be called all persons holding offices in the government thereof, together with all the maiden-sisters who have been admitted into the body of the Company, whether these have bound themselves by the vow of virginity or not.

The general congregation must be convened when it is necessary to elect the Mother of the whole Company, or one of the assistants or one of the lady-directresses.

To the Mother Superior or to the person holding her place, it shall belong to call this congregation and to compel the assistance of the electors. [The place of assembly shall be the Church of the Pietà bestowed on the Company; but this is left to the judgment of the Mother and of the spiritual father of the Company.]

Every one of the electors on entering the place appointed

should make a brief prayer, recommending to God our Lord the business about to be transacted. This done she will take the place assigned to her either on account of the office she holds, or on that of her date of admission to the Company. And this same order is to be observed by all in giving their votes.

The person whose office it shall be to call the congregation together shall also take care that, while those already assembled are waiting for the others, some pious book be read; as well to shut out idleness and to fill up profitably the time of waiting, as to preclude all opportunity for talking, and other such inconveniences.

Let all the electors be fully warned that they must not endeavor directly or indirectly, by their own exertions or by others, to secure the election of this or that person, or the rejection of this or that person. But let them after recommending the matter to God, allow the Spirit of God to suggest His choice as it pleaseth Him, and thus to cause that person to be elected who may best promote the Divine honor and the welfare of the Company. It is not thereby forbidden to the electors that when they are questioned about the qualifications of certain persons, they may not answer truly; but they are to guard against the danger of allowing their own affections to exaggerate unduly the virtues of one person or the imperfections of another.

Let the person whose office it is to preside over the congregation see to it that the place of assembly be suitably prepared and furnished, so that all the electors may be seated according to their rank; and let there be a table with a box or urn in which each elector can deposit her written vote.

Let the spiritual father in the absence of the bishop, as soon as the congregation is opened, recite the prayer appointed for such occasions. The same is to be done in closing the meeting. Only, when some matter of extraordinary importance has to be decided by the congregation, it will be proper to recite the hymn "Veni, Creator," and at the end of the assembly in which the Mother is elected, the "Te Deum laudamus" with an appropriate prayer should be said. If the mother be not chosen, some other prayer will do.

CHAPTER XXII.—OF THE GENERAL CONGREGATION OF THE OFFICERS OF THE COMPANY.

It is most seemly that the governing body should be well ordered, since on its being so depends good order throughout the entire Company. Now, to secure a well ordered and regulated government, five things are to be considered here: the persons to be called to this congregation, the motives which have led to its being convened, the time and the place of meeting, and the forms to be observed in its sessions.

1. The persons whom it is proper to call to this congregation are: the Father and his substitute; the Mother Superior and her four assistants, and the eight lady-directresses with their mistresses and counselors. Moreover, when temporal affairs are to be discussed, the protectors of the Company should also be admitted. The Father substitute can fill the functions of chancellor.

2. The motives for calling this congregation shall be: to decide whether a general congregation should be convened; the choice of some officer whose election regards this congregation—as, for instance, the election of a counselor, or of a protector of the Company; the admission of some of the maiden-sisters to the chapter or the body of the Company, or the dismission of those guilty of misconduct or disobedience; the decision of some matter advantageous to the Company; and, finally, the necessity of meeting some local

need pointed out by the lady-directresses, and which cannot be met in the district meetings.

3. The proper time for assembling shall be : a few days before the time appointed for admitting the maiden-sisters ; a few days before the time appointed for making the voluntary vow of virginity ; the ninth week after the eight successive weekly district meetings held by the lady-directresses.

4. [The place of assembly shall be the house of St. Ursula, which is] the house of the Company, and which the Mother will have prepared for the comfortable accommodation of the members.

5. The form to be observed shall be : When any one of the above motives presents itself for assembling the congregation, the Mother will consult with the spiritual father, fix with him the time and place of meeting, and give notice thereof to all the members of the Congregation. On entering the place of meeting, let each one pray for the success of the matter under deliberation, and then take her appointed place. The lady-directresses shall present a written statement of the needs of their respective districts to the Mother, who will hand them all over to the Spiritual Father. In order that no time be lost, the spiritual father will ask one of the members present to read out of some pious book, the others listening in silence. When one half of the officers called have arrived, the reading is stopped, and the congregation is opened in the following manner :

The spiritual father or his substitute kneels down with all the members present and says the prayer appointed, which is also to be done at the close. The prayer ended, the spiritual father or the substitute, having determined the matters to treat of, and the order in which they are to be proposed, states them successively, each member being allowed to express her opinion freely. The judgment of the majority is to be held as decisive on every matter so proposed. During these deliberations each member should remember two things : first, to give her opinion standing, unless prevented by age or infirmity, and that she may not without permission speak twice on the same subject ; the second is, that when the majority have adopted a contrary decision, she must show neither temper nor displeasure, but acquiesce in the judgment of the majority.

Let every decision arrived at by the congregation be entered on the book of records by the chancellor, in order to secure a better execution of the measures adopted. In the next meeting of the congregation the records will show whether the decisions have or not been carried out faithfully. Wherefore, at the beginning of each congregation, as soon as the opening prayer has been said, the minutes of the former assembly shall be read to ascertain how far the orders of the congregation have been executed, and what other remedy may be judged necessary in the premises.

Each session is to be closed with prayer, and with the spiritual father's blessing.

CHAPTER XXIII.—OF THE DISTRICT ASSEMBLIES OR CONGREGATIONS.

WHAT has been said about the general assemblies of the governing body, applies in a great measure to the order and proceeding to be observed in the district assemblies. The members composing each district congregation are the three superintendents of each, namely, the lady-directress, the mistress, and the counselor, together with all the maiden-sisters already admitted to the chapter or to membership, or presented to the lady-directress for inscription in the district book, or in the list of the counselor. No other person is to be admitted except the Mother Superior and the spiritual father, who have a right to be present at all assemblies.

The motives for calling these district assemblies may be manifold, as are the necessities which may arise. There are, however, three causes of more general occurrence : The first is to ascertain, how the rules of the Company are observed by all the members, as well as the ordinances of the particular congregations. The second, to draw attention to the ordinances of the governing body, and to publish them officially. The third is to provide a remedy for the pressing bodily and spiritual needs of each district.

The ordinary time of meeting shall be fixed by the Mother Superior and the spiritual father, and notified to each lady-directress. The extraordinary occasions shall be whenever the lady-directress finds it expedient to call a meeting in order to provide for some important need, or when some urgent necessity compels her to take such action ; in this case, the meeting must not be held without the previous consent of the Mother Superior and the Spiritual Father.

As to the place of meeting, let it be chosen with a regard to the convenience of the sisters who live farthest off, to the quickness of the deliberations, and to remoteness from the busy haunts of men. The counselor must prepare everything in the place of meeting, seats for all, but special raised seats for the directress and mistress, and one a little lower for herself. The sisters will occupy three rows of benches in front of the directress : on the first row shall be seated the maiden-sisters admitted to membership ; on the second, all those who have entrance into the chapter ; and on the third, the postulants. Some holy image shall also be conveniently placed, before which the sisters on entering can make a short prayer for the success of the deliberation.

As to the manner of proceeding, this is to be observed :

When the meeting has been resolved upon, the directress, mistress, and counselor should confer together, at least three days before the opening of the district congregation, about the needs of their district and the matters to be discussed at the session ; and this, in order that everything should be brought forward, and understood to better purpose, and that the needful measures should be decreed more understandingly. They must next determine the hour of meeting, consulting therefor the convenience of all the members, and appoint as well the most favorable place. The counselor shall be instructed to inform the sisters of all this, bidding them all, in the name of the directress, to be present at the congregation. Each one, on coming into the hall, shall kneel to pray before the sacred image, and then, saluting the others in our Lord, take her appointed place. While they are coming in the mistress shall have a pious book read. When all are assembled, or, at least, one half of them, the list of names is read out, and the absences noted. This done, the opening prayer is recited, and the session begins in this way. First, the lady-governess explains why the congregation has been called ; next, she will ask of each sister how she has been since the last congregation, and how to her knowledge the rules and ordinances have been observed. Then she will beg the mistress to give an account of each of her subjects ; as to how the sisters have read and understood the rules and prescriptions given them, and all that pertains to the discharge of the mistress's office. The counselor shall be required to state ·how far each one of the sisters has faithfully observed the rules and ordinances of the Company ; for the counselors are the guardians to whom the Company commits the keeping of the maiden-sisters of St. Ursula. Their duty is to punish by proportionate penances all carelessness and culpable neglect in keeping the rules, and all acts of disobedience toward the superiors, consulting in their corrections what is due to the edification of the other members.

When any new decision of the congregation of government is to be published in the district assembly, the lady-directress must have it so read and explained that all can understand it. She will ask of all present if they find any difficulty in executing this decision; and should any one of them express unwillingness, the directress must take pains to remove it, advising the dissatisfied person to be satisfied, and leave all in the hands of the superiors. But should she remain obstinate in her opposition, a note is to be taken of her persistency, and the matter is to be referred to the congregation of government for final action.

Whenever it is necessary to make provision in the district assembly for the corporal or spiritual necessities of the maidens, this must be done with all the tact and charity possible. Especially is this indispensable when we have to meet the spiritual needs of any sister; we must have regard to the natural disposition and social rank, and be careful not to embitter her by sharp reproofs, which only drive the guilty to despair and to the commission of more grievous faults. On the other hand, it would not do to correct gently those who bear themselves insolently and contemn the ordinances and rules of the Company. It must also be remembered, that certain faults committed publicly should be visited with public reprehension, as well for the good example due to others, as for the benefit of the offenders themselves. Others, on the contrary, demand to be secretly corrected, for this will benefit them most. In one word, some are improved by public reprehension, while others are greatly helped by secret reproof. The superiors must derive from the light of the Holy Spirit and from true and heartfelt charity the wisdom necesary to procure in these difficulties the advancement of the divine honor and the salvation of the maidens committed to them.

After this, the lady-directress shall recommend to all the faithful execution of the rules and ordinances, and shall endeavor to make them all apply themselves to teaching the Christian doctrine, in which pious occupation all should have greatly at heart to reap abundant fruits. Then, after offering prayer once more, the directress bids them separate in God's name.

On the day after, the three superintendents shall go to report the proceedings to the spiritual father and the Mother Superior.

CHAPTER XXIV.—OF THE PROTECTORS OF THE COMPANY IN THINGS TEMPORAL.

EXPERIENCE has proved that many pressing straits may arise in the Company relating to temporal matters, to which women are powerless to find an issue. This makes it necessary to choose three men, who shall be ever ready to assist us in our needs, when their aid is required either by the whole Company or by some of its members.

The Mother and the ladies who are charged with the government of the Company can propose to the bishop the names of such as they deem most able and willing to bestow the needed help. The choice must be approved and confirmed by him. He may also change these protectors when he knows this to be conducive to the greater good of the Company.

CHAPTER XXV.—OF THE URSULINES THROUGHOUT THE DIOCESE OF BRESCIA.

"GOD is not a respecter of persons,"[1] but bestows His grace on all with open-handed liberality, illuminating their

---
[1] Acts x. : 34.

minds with the light of His Holy Spirit, in order that they may see and use the means necessary to the salvation and conducive to the perfection of their souls. There are many persons who are illustrious in the sight of their fellow-men, who are poor and mean in His eyes; others, on the contrary, who are of little or no account in the eyes of men, are great and glorious in the sight of the Divine Goodness. It is not to be wondered at, if He hath inspired with the desire of serving Him in this holy Company of ours many devout persons beyond the walls of Brescia, and living in the hamlets and domains belonging to this diocese. Surely, such persons must not be frustrated in their pious purpose. They shall have admittance among the members of this Company, and shall be made sharers in the good works and merits proper to it.

These sisters shall be as much under the fatherly and pastoral care of the bishop as those within the city; and they shall acknowledge and reverence as their father and superior the priest looked up to by the entire Company as its Father, and given to it by the bishop as his own vicar.

Although it is necessary that the sisterhood throughout the country places should have officers and superiors like the city sisters, nevertheless it seems best for the welfare and unity of the whole body that the officers of the country sisterhood should be subordinated to those of the city, and that no decree or ordinance shall be made by the former, confining themselves to execute and enforce only such ordinances as shall proceed from the persons forming the government within the city.

They shall acknowledge the Mother of the whole Company as theirs also, and her assistants and the lady-directresses as their superiors, endeavoring in all things to show them reverence and obedience by executing their ordinances, admonitions, and commands.

As they are to be occasionally visited every year by the Father in the discharge of his office, or by the Father substitute, when the former is lawfully prevented from visiting them, they must pay him all due respect and obedience, as to their acknowledged superior and the vicar placed by the bishop over the entire Company.

[They may not choose at will their own confessor; but must confess themselves to him alone who has been selected for them by the Father or his substitute, and that in order to secure among us all greater uniformity and oneness of spirit in the service of the Divine Majesty.]

All the superiors, namely, the substitute, lady-directresses, mistresses, and counselors, or at least some one of their number, shall be obliged once a year, on the feast of Pentecost, to come to Brescia, and present themselves to the spiritual father and the Mother Superior; and that, both because by so coming they strengthen the union which should exist between the city sisters and their own subjects, and because this visit enables them to give an account to their superiors of the sisters committed to their care, to expose the wants of the latter, and to return strengthened by the advice and the needful aid of the former. It is not hereby intended to make this journey obligatory to such as live at a great distance or who could not come to the city without great inconvenience to themselves. The circumstances are left to the judgment of their spiritual father, who may dispense them from the obligation of this annual visit, while providing in some other way to make them fulfill the object of this injunction.

Let every one of these substitute superiors use all the opportunities in her power to have recourse to the city superiors when the needs of her subjects require it. For the city superiors, having more experience and practice in such matters, will be better able to extend to them the required aid.

Let them know that all the rules, customs and ceremonies in use among the superiors and members of the city sisterhood should be, as far as possible, observed by the sisterhood outside of Brescia.

The substitute directresses and the spiritual fathers duly appointed for the sisterhood outside the walls must know that they cannot, without permission, accept or admit into the Company any postulant.

In electing their officers the sisterhood outside of Brescia must observe the form prescribed above for the Company inside the city; such officers are not to be elected without the knowledge and permission of the Father of the Company."

From beside the shrine of St. Angela and this monumental work in which her spirit still lives, we can now glance rapidly at the wonderful spectacle presented by the history of the Order which she founded. It can only be a rapid survey, however, enabling the reader to grasp, in the marvelous destinies of the Ursulines, the purpose of the obscure, penitential, and laborious life we have been sketching so far.

PART II.

THE URSULINES.

CHAPTER XX.

THEIR VARIED FORTUNES IN ITALY—PRIMITIVE CONGREGATION OF BRESCIA—HOW THEY FARED IN MILAN—URSULINES OF VENICE, PARMA, PIACENZA, FOLIGNO, AND ROME.

As we have already seen, the Institute of St. Angela was not approved by the Holy See till 1545, whereas she died in January, 1540. Meanwhile, the Company she had founded was, and that almost immediately after Angela's death, assailed by more than one fierce storm. True, the Company grew and spread in spite of the fury of the blast; but it is none the less true that its violence was such as to threaten the Ursulines with total destruction.

One formidable objection, which prevailed at a later period, was urged against the uncloistered condition of the sisterhood. But this was discussed and pressed by outsiders, principally by canonists and members of the existing religious Orders; within the Company itself it found no favor, and was, therefore, comparatively harmless, for the moment at least. The other objection, though based on a matter of mere secondary importance, was well-nigh fatal to the young sisterhood, because it found many advocates and abettors among themselves. This objection regarded the question as to whether or not the Ursulines should all wear one form of religious habit. The holy foundress had merely prescribed the wearing of a sober and modest dress which should sufficiently distinguish the members of the Company and render them easily recognizable to each other and to the people in whose behalf they labored. As they were destined to live in the bosom of their own families, she did not care to attract to their persons or their attire more attention than was needful for the great purpose they had in view.

At any rate, scarcely had her remains been laid to rest in the crypt of St. Afra's, when some fault-finding lay friends, abetted by some clergymen, began to press on the Countess Lodrone and her assistants the propriety of wearing a uniform—a dress of black with a white kerchief, and a chord similar to that worn by the Tertiaries of St. Francis. The Augustinian Fathers, in particular, urged the use of a chord or cincture. From the Countess and four of her assistants this proposition or suggestion met with favor. But the other four assistants, together with the Countess Luzzago, opposed a most determined resistance to this innovation, and were ably supported by Gabriel Cozzano, who drew up an eloquent memoir against the proposed change.

Nevertheless, on December 11th, 1545, a decree was issued by the Superior-General enjoining on all the members to wear a cincture, as a badge of their unworldly vocation. The Countess Luzzago and her followers were excluded from the Company; but the Vicar-General, Ferretti, to whom they appealed, decided in their favor and against the innovation.

Meanwhile, the bull of approbation of Paul III. was published in Brescia; and soon afterward, in answer to a petition from the Countess Lodrone, the Pope sent a brief granting an indulgence to all religious women who dressed in black and wore the Augustinian leathern girdle. This contained no injunction to the Countess Lodrone and the other opponents; and the question was only settled in 1546 by a papal commission. It decreed the wearing of a black flowing robe, with the black cincture of leather as worn by the Augustinian nuns.

These bickerings were most unfortunate, and were the very thing against which the dying foundress had warned her family in her pathetic adjurations in favor of charity and harmony of thought and feeling.

No sooner had the bull of approbation been published, than Desenzano and Salò petitioned the Mother-General for colonies of Ursulines. It was but natural that Angela Merici's birthplace, as well as the dear home of her mother, should be first among the localities privileged to possess houses of the Order. That of Salò has long ago ceased to exist —probably since the first French invasion. The community of Desenzano seems to have shared the fate of the Ursulines of Brescia, remaining faithful to the primitive rule and blessing the thrifty little town by its manifold holy influences and pious labors, till suppressed by Bonaparte.

We shall listen to what their successors write from "Desenzano-on-the-Lake," February 8th, 1877:

"Dearest mothers and sisters," they write to all the houses of the Order, "we invite you to rest a few moments by our side beneath the lovely sky of Italy—of that Italy so dear to every Ursuline. You will find here but a poor and lowly offshoot of the great family founded by St. Angela. Our monastery dates from 1841. It began very modestly, three choir sisters and one lay sister forming the new community under the guidance of a venerable Ursuline, who had been one of the victims of the revolutionary suppression. At the present date we reckon twenty-two members in our house. . . .

We all work hard from morning till night; and this is our sole happiness, together with the charity which binds us to each other. The house itself is anything but spacious. Still, we are proud and happy to live in it. Is not the soil around us impregnated with the sweat of our first Mother? Is not the air we breathe all fragrant with the perfume of her virtues? We have a well-kept orchard, divided by a large alley, and in this we take our accustomed exercise. We regret that our boarding-school cannot be separated from the dwelling of the community. We are also without spring-water, bathing-place, or infirmary. At this very moment one of our boarders is sick, and we have to give up to her the school-room of our youngest pupils, while they have to be taught in one of our own cells. And of these the number is so limited, that four nuns have to occupy the same room. Nevertheless, albeit we may glory in our poverty, we are still the spoiled children of Providence. For, although we have no infirmary, as we were just saying, we should also add that during the last six years we have not known sickness. Our last death was in 1870."

The yearly pension paid this poor community while under the Austrian Government ceased as soon as they passed beneath the rule of the Piedmontese. They were allowed, however, to retain possession of their little monastery; but were compelled to send their sisters all the way to Turin to be examined and certificated as teachers!

We now return to Brescia.

It was well that the Company of St. Ursula was severely tried in its native spot, and cordially approved by all who beheld its members at their divine work in the schools they had founded, in the hospitals where their helpful charity and angelic modesty shone like sunbeams, and in the families which boasted the presence and possession of maidens so devoted, so heroic, so powerful for good. The peculiar features of their religious life, and their devotion to training the young especially, challenged attentive observation and elicited not a little unjust criticism during the first twenty-five years after the death of the foundress. But the closer, the more thorough, and the more conscientious the observation of men, even the most prejudiced, the more enthusiastic and unanimous was the praise called forth by virtues and services beyond all praise.

Angela had not been anxious to see her sisterhood extend itself beyond the walls of Brescia, and particularly beyond the limits of the diocese bearing that name, during her own lifetime. Her chief solicitude aimed at so moulding her daughters to an exalted esteem for their own calling, to a generous devotion to its duties, and the fervent practice of the great fundamental virtues of the virginal life, that they should remain immovably faithful in the divine service, whether in the noise and bustle of the most public place and occupation, or in the privacy and seclusion of their homes.

Meanwhile the neighboring cities and dioceses were desirous to share in the precious fruits produced in Brescia and its territory by the new sisterhood.

One of St. Jerome Emiliani's early disciples, a Brescian called John Scotti, was the first to obtain a colony of Ursulines. He, encouraged by the Bishop of Cremona, Nicolas Sfondrati, afterward Pope Gregory XIV., brought with him in triumph to the city so dear to Angela a few of her daughters; and Cremona soon rejoiced in seeing this first offshoot of the goodly tree take root in its soil and grow up and bear most sweet and salutary fruit. This happened in the year 1565.[1]

But Milan, where St. Angela's name was scarcely less pop-

---

[1] Salvatori, pp. 59, 60.

ular than in Cremona, had also been impatiently waiting for a colony of Ursulines. The capital of Lombardy was at that time blessed in the possession of a prelate held by all Christendom to be, in modern ages, the model of all those who have charge of souls—St. Charles Borromeo. Man of God as he was before and above all things, he had a keen instinctive sense of the spiritual needs of the popular masses ; and no sooner had he heard of the new sisterhood established in Brescia, than he felt that they were destined of God to preserve the rising generation from vice and error, to instruct the children in all religious knowledge and saintly deeds, while winning the souls of the parents to God and the love of all good, by the silent persuasion of their own pure and devoted lives.

Twelve Brescian Ursulines came to Milan in 1566, and in pursuance of the plan formed by the archbishop, they were lodged in a spacious dwelling, where they might open schools for their pupils, and attend to their usual avocations. The sisters began immediately to visit the different wards of the great city, seeking out the children and taking every means to teach them all that was suited to their age and condition. Besides, a no less zeal was displayed in drawing to themselves young girls, whom they instructed and formed to all the duties of Christian life as well as to the higher virtues of evangelical perfection. To older women, to wives and mothers, indeed to all the adult persons of their own sex, they held out an invitation to meet weekly in the community house and hear lectures on religious and spiritual topics most interesting and useful to all. Thus while the little colony continued to live together in the dwelling bestowed on them by the generous archbishop, they permitted the new members recruited from all classes of the Milanese population, to live in the bosom of their own families, precisely as did their

Brescian sisters. On certain days all met together in the "House of St. Ursula," where they were instructed and comforted by their local superior, and where the saintly archbishop himself would often come to address them and to pour into their souls the spirit of heroic generosity and self-sacrifice which filled his own to overflowing.

How could the daughters of St. Angela, living so near him, hearing every day and hour the praise of his saintly deeds and Christ-like goodness, and blessed, moreover, with the special care bestowed on themselves, not look up to such a man and such a bishop, as to the living oracle of the Divine Master? So when, in his addresses to them about religious perfection and the beauty of holiness, he came to express his wish to see them live together in homes which would give them the joys and helps of family and community life, their hearts were won to yield a ready assent. When, next, he exhorted them not to be satisfied with a simple determination, though never so firm, of living a life of poverty, chastity, and obedience, but to bind themselves irrevocably to their Lord and Love by religious vows of the same intent, and uttered publicly in the chapel attached to their residence—they were carried away by the eloquence of one whose tongue seemed touched with a seraph's fire, and whose whole life was the most admirable embodiment of voluntary poverty and self-crucifixion, of angelic purity, and strict obedience to the law of God and the Church. Who that looked upon that face which ever glowed with unearthly light could refuse to follow such a guide up the steepest paths of self-denial and immolation? St. Charles, at the very moment he proposed this change, had much to suffer from more than one community of nuns in his episcopal city who would not be led by him to return to the pristine fervor of their Order; he was therefore all the more anxious to make of the daughters of Angela Merici, apostles of education as they were, models of strict religious observance, to whom all might look up for edifying example. So, in 1572, at the solicitation of the Archbishop of Milan, Pope Gregory XIII. issued a bull, which, after approving and confirming anew the Institute of Angela Merici, authorized the Ursulines to form congregations, to live in communities, and to adopt this modified form everywhere. They are thus known in history as the "Congregated Ursulines," very different from the Cloistered Ursulines. Until then the Ursulines of Milan had taught school outside of their own house in various parts of the city. It now became an object of the archbishop's care to have them teach only within their residence; and, to secure the benefit of their teaching to the different wards of his city, he resolved to establish therein separate Ursuline communities.

Thus this first change—so momentous for the Company—was brought about gently, silently, irresistibly, like the growth and maturing of the harvest through the summer months and by the gentle but mighty agencies of nature. The Cardinal-Archbishop gave a great degree of solemnity to the inauguration of this new form of community life, as well as to the emission of the substantial monastic vows by the sisterhood. St. Angela, from her place of glory near God's throne, could not but contemplate with pleasure this phase in the life of her Company, which foreboded so wonderful an extension to its members, and so incalculable an amount of good to the Christian world.

St. Charles fervently recommended, in 1576, the establishment of these "congregated" Ursuline communities to the bishops of Lombardy assembled in provincial council. The splendid heroism displayed by the sisters during the great plague of that year served as a powerful confirmation to the eulogy bestowed on their fervor and efficiency. It contributed also to increase their reputation throughout Upper Italy, particularly through the Venetian territory, which claimed their glory as its own. So we are prepared to find that Venice, which had retained so precious a recollection of Angela Merici's merit, was among the first cities of Italy to solicit a colony of Ursulines. It is uncertain in what year they were invited to Venice. In 1557, however, the name of the noble patrician widow lady, Donata Falier, is mentioned in connection with the establishment there. She was a woman of extraordinary merit, and may have been the foundress of the Venetian Ursulines. Nor are we informed whether these began or not like those of Milan. Probably the example of St. Charles had some influence in giving to their manner of life the form in which we find it at a later period. Certain it is that the Ursuline monastery in the city of St. Lawrence Justiniani assumed at an early date the exclusive restrictions implied by their title of Noble Nuns—a title which they also bore in the cities of Parma and Foligno. They were also titled canonesses, and wore a white dress with a black veil. They expressly claimed to belong to the religious family of Brescia. Their school, from its very foundation, held and maintained a foremost rank in Venice. Indeed, it would appear that the purpose of its founders was so to bring up the daughters of the nobility in all goodly knowledge and solid virtue, that from them and through them the benefits of Christian education and example might extend downward to the laboring population. The Ursulines always endeavored, by every means within their power, to make their noble and wealthy pupils the apostles of the poor.

Genoa, on the opposite shore of the peninsula, was not behindhand with its ancient rival, Venice.

The spirit of St. Catherine of Genoa seems to have long survived in her native city, producing women remarkable alike for their holy life and intellectual superiority. One of these, Mother Venarcia, who established and governed the first society of Ursulines in Genoa, was so distinguished for heroic virtue, that the senate and magistrates petitioned the Holy See, after her death, to have her cause introduced for beatification. She, like St. Angela, had not been brought up in the schools; still she taught herself so well, that she left behind her four volumes on spiritual life. It is most likely that the example of St. Charles in Milan encouraged the friends of popular and religious education in Genoa to introduce and favor the Institute of St. Angela. The first Ursuline establishment there dates from 1573. Mother Venarcia governed it during sixty years.

From Milan, Cremona, and Genoa the sweet odor of the Company of St. Ursula, which St. Charles Borromeo called "the Tree of Life," in recommending the love of it to its members, spread southward to Central Italy. In 1595 Ranuccio Farnese I., Duke of Parma, called the Ursulines to educate the daughters of the nobility in his states.

It was, however, but a onesided view of the education needed by his country and age. The Ursulines might have done for Parma what they were even then doing for Milan and Brescia, and what they were preparing to do so effectually in France—they might have educated and elevated the children of the people, while bestowing especial care on the daughters of the highest families.

So Ranuccio I. was content to create a house of Ursulines in Parma, in which forty, and only forty, noble maidens could embrace the Institute of St. Angela, and devote themselves to education. The duke took it on himself to legislate for this establishment, modifying according to his caprice the rule of the holy foundress, forbidding the Ursulines to acknowledge any other protectors than himself and his successors, removing them in things spiritual from the jurisdiction of the bishop and placing them under the direction of the Jesuits, prescribing to them the very form and color of their religious costume—a white tunic and veil with a long flowing mantle of blue. It was as if one should take a shoot from the sacred fig-tree of India, and plant it in a hothouse, carefully lopping off every one of the air-roots by which this glory of Indian vegetation ever seeks to extend itself over the adjacent soil and bless the earth around with its grateful shade and wholesome fruit!

The good nuns were so edifying and so useful, nevertheless, that Piacenza wished to have a monastery of the same kind, and two members of the sisterhood were sent to be the directresses of this new establishment. The benefits resulting to both Parma and Piacenza from institutions aiming principally at female education, were so great, in spite of the unwise restrictions of their founders, that the fame of the Ursulines extended into Umbria. A maiden lady, known as Paula of Foligno, from her native city, became with Cardinal Baronius instrumental in creating a most flourishing establishment at Foligno in 1599. The same fundamental limitations unfortunately prevailed there too. A few of the sisters—all of whom were noble—lived with Paula in community; the others continued to make their homes with their parents.

The Ursulines of Rome itself date from the same period. There were two distinct congregations of them, the first of which was composed of uncloistered sisters, like those of Brescia. Strange to say, the foundresses were both noble young French women, who had, like Angela Merici in 1525, been brought separately and providentially to Rome, the one on her way to Jerusalem, the other for the Jubilee of 1600. One, Frances de Montjoux, arrived there in March, 1598, and was induced by Clement VIII. to fix her abode there, instead of going to

Palestine. The other, Frances de Gourcy, was a kindred spirit; and both were drawn to each other by that mighty spiritual attraction begotten of sanctity. They had both heard of the immense good done by the Ursulines in Upper Italy, and resolved to become themselves daughters of St. Angela. They purchased a house, and, with the approbation of the reigning Pope, opened classes. Other generous souls like their own were not slow to unite with them, and their community, as well as the numbers of their pupils, grew apace.

They had begun to teach in 1600, calling themselves Ursulines, and following the Rule of St. Angela. A few years later the Church of St. Rufina and St. Secunda was given to them by Paul V. (1605-21), and this first Congregation of Roman Ursulines, called, after their church, "the Congregation of St. Rufina and St. Secunda," has subsisted down to our own times.

The other congregation, of cloistered Ursulines, dates from 1684, and was an offshoot of the Belgian congregation, itself a prolific branch of that of Bordeaux. The Duchess of Modena, Laura Martinozzi, a niece of Cardinal Mazarin, and her daughter, Mary of Modena, Queen to James II. of England, were the instruments by which this second establishment was brought about. The Duchess of Modena during her stay in the Low Countries had many opportunities of admiring the saintly fervor and practical wisdom of the Ursulines of Mons and Brussels. Indeed, the Ursuline monastery of that capital was a creation of the mother house of Mons. She studied the sisters in their home life, their schools, their constitutions; she gathered the most reliable information about their labors in the other cities of Flanders, and resolved, on her return to Rome, to found in the capital of the Christian world a monastery governed by the same rules and directed by some of the admirable women who were such a blessing to the Flemish populations.

Her petition to Innocent XI. was sustained by Cardinal Howard, the English ambassador in Rome. The Pope took a warm personal interest in the matter, convinced himself that the proposed constitutions were those approved for Bordeaux in 1618 by Paul V., and on March 24th, 1684, he issued the bull instituting the Roman establishment.

No sooner was this communicated to the Duchess of Modena at Brussels, than she set out for Rome with six professed nuns, during the month of September, arriving in Rome on the 12th of November. On their arrival they were all hospitably received in the convent of St. Catherine of Sienna at Monte-Magnanapoli, where they remained perforce till the 13th of May following, when they moved to hired lodgings, and opened a school. The delay was inevitable. The journey from Brussels had cost the Duchess of Modena her life, and the Ursulines were solely dependent on her bounty for their present subsistence and future prospects. Her sudden death left them unprovided for in the midst of the great city; and, like all people who come to do in any place what others should or could have done, the little colony of Flemish nuns met with but scanty sympathy and little or no support from the Romans on their first arrival. Their generous benefactress had put in their hands a sum of 7000 Roman crowns ($7000), but this would barely suffice to procure them suitable accommodation for the present, leaving them totally unprovided for in the future. Such was one of the chief grounds of opposition that their establishment met with at the beginning. They began courageously, nevertheless, drawing from their poverty and the efforts made to prevent their obtaining a foothold in Rome the assurance that their work was God's work, and that He would not forsake them.

They were not disappointed. After considerable delays, the testamentary dispositions of the Duchess of Modena became known; and one of them was a legacy of 15,000 crowns to her dear Ursulines. Besides this, the dying princess had so warmly recommended them to the Queen of England, that the latter added a considerable sum to her mother's provision. Timely as was this liberality, it had come too late for a portion of the little Ursuline colony. Three of them had returned to Brussels.

The three remaining nuns, however, lost no time in securing a more commodious habitation in the Via Vittoria, beneath the shadow of the Pincian Hill; and in this house, annexed to, which was a little chapel, they settled down to hard work on April 27th, 1688. The ceremony of the canonical inauguration of this first monastery of cloistered Ursulines in Rome took place four days afterward, on the 1st of May, the great Innocent XI. confirming by a new brief the bull issued for their establishment in 1684, and permitting the Ursulines of Brussels and Mons to send auxiliaries to their Roman sisters. This they did without delay.

But during the long four years of trial, opposition, and painful suspense which the three Ursulines who remained in Rome had to endure after the death of the Duchess of Modena, they did not allow any discouragement to interrupt for a moment their labor of teaching, or to damp the ardor with which they gave themselves up to their pupils. They had their boarding-school for the daughters of the nobility, as well as their free day-schools for the children of the people. To both of these they gave great developments after their installation in the *Via Vittoria*. They needed now no other recommendation to families of all classes; for all had learned to revere and bless and love them. "They may be held up as a model to all the monasteries of Rome!" exclaimed

Clement XI. (1700-21). Nor did their light grow dim as the eighteenth century held on its course, destroying faith in men's souls, making of scepticism implanted in the minds of each rising generation the fatal germ of the intellectual, moral, and social convulsions which are now running their course as fatally as the avalanche let loose from Alpine summits upon the doomed hamlets of the adjacent valleys.

The revolutionary armies of Napoléon Bonaparte found the Ursulines of Rome in 1796 so dear to the Roman people, that they dared not molest them in their holy avocations. Nor in 1809, when Napoleon's unholy policy suppressed all the monasteries of the capital of Christendom, did the sacrilegious invader drive the Ursulines from their schools and their home. He was satisfied with abolishing the cloister, behind which the educators of Roman womanhood concealed the austerity and simplicity of their private life. The despot had hoped that these devoted women would at once return to the enjoyment of the worldly honors and pleasures which they had freely renounced. The world, however, only saw with admiration that the uncloistered daughters of St. Angela clung more lovingly than ever to their desecrated home, their class-rooms, and their over-rich poverty. Not one Ursuline forsook her post.

The fatal seeds of error and systematic moral corruption which the First Napoleon, his armeis, and his officials scattered broadcast over Rome and all Italy, from 1796 to 1815, were cultivated with too intelligent and persevering a husbandry not to cast deep roots in the soil after the expulsion of the French. Italian revolutionists had learned too many good lessons from French Jacobinism, and had too much intellect of their own not to improve on their master's methods. When God's inscrutable providence permitted another Bonaparte to exercise over Rome his baneful protectorate, and over Italy the influence of his revolutionary sympathies, the Italian mind was ready to discard all teaching that spoke of religion, and to destroy all teachers who would make the youth of Italy look with love or reverence on the religious glories of their fatherland.

One of the first acts of the Piedmontese masters of Rome was, on January 1st, 1871, to abolish the yearly rent of one thousand crowns granted to the devoted Ursulines in favor of their schools by Benedict XIV. On the 5th of April following the good nuns were compelled to yield to the new Roman municipality all the classes of their day-scholars, which were thus handed over to the teaching of the Garibaldian evangelists. It was in vain that the nuns tried, by opening classes for their day-scholars in a portion of the boarding-school, to afford a portion of their attached pupils an opportunity of continuing their education. Within a few weeks these classes were forcibly given up to the municipal officers. Even the portion of the monastery occupied as a novitiate had to be surrendered to men who would be satisfied by nothing less than by starving and crowding out the poor defenceless nuns into the street.

Then they were informed that, in order to be authorized to teach, they must adopt in every point the programme and method prescribed by the government, and pass an examination before receiving a diploma of capacity. To all this, in the hope of being allowed to break never so little of the bread of life to the children of Rome, the Ursulines submitted with heroic fortitude. The government, however, merely wished to weary their patience and force them to leave the monastery altogether. In November the monastery itself was declared government property, and a miserable pension or pittance was assigned to each member of the community. . . . And to fill their cup of bitterness to overflowing, they were commanded to hold themselves in readiness to leave the monastery at any moment. The courageous superior meanwhile appealed to the civil courts, and, wonderful to relate, the courts decided in favor of the Ursulines! This judgment was given on September 29th, 1874.

The Italian Government, nevertheless, only half obeyed the decision of the law courts. The nuns were peremptorily commanded to give up one half of their monastery and garden to an Orpheonic society favored by the authorities. On the 31st day of May, 1876, the commissioners and workmen came to make the necessary changes, or rather to create as much disorder as possible in the house—for they knew, as all Romans know, that the 31st of May was, in Italy, the solemn Feast of St. Angela! They were shamed into a little delay, however, and consented to wait till the next day.

Do we wonder that the venerable superior, Mary-Margaret Eutizi, sank beneath this last cruel act of antichristian and cowardly oppression, after having battled heroically, though an octogenarian, with the unfeeling spoiler for more than five years.

And so the poor Ursulines of Rome, compelled to teach school in the narrow cells allotted to their sadly diminished number, still continue the work of God. The tale they could unfold is only one—and that far from being the most heart-rending—among thousands upon thousands throughout the length and breadth of the once Catholic Italy.

There are a few other Ursuline schools scattered through the Peninsula which endeavor to maintain a precarious existence in spite of the determined hostility of the government: at Calvi and Stroncone, in the diocese of Terni; at Sesto-Calende, Cannobio, Galliate, Omegna, Miasino, and Saluzzo in Piedmont and Lombardy; at Benevento in Southern Italy, and in other places, where the Catholic populations still foster and protect, as best they may, the loved teachers of their children, till it please an overruling Providence to give rest to the land from the earthquake and the storm.

The reader naturally will ask, What was the fate of the Congregation of Brescia amid these extraordinary vicissitudes? The changes introduced into the Rule and manner of living of the Ursulines throughout Italy were powerless to induce the Congregation of Brescia to modify the Constitutions received from their holy foundress, approved by the Holy See, and slightly modified by St. Charles Borromeo as Commissary Apostolic. The early associates of St. Angela had been so thoroughly trained by that great mistress of Christian perfection, their souls had been moulded by her gentle, firm, and skillful hand into a form of such persistent goodness, that both priests and people found no symptom of degeneracy when the first generation of Ursulines died out and were succeeded by a second and a third of equal virtue and even more skilled usefulness. Thus this admirable sisterhood, in the land which was its birthplace as well as that of Angela Merici, continued to be consistent with themselves amid the religious struggles and political convulsions of the age, as constant in their edifying purity, as deep and inexhaustible in the resources of their manifold devotedness, as the waters of the Lake of Garda around Desenzano and Salò; their firmness in resisting and repelling all innovation was as calm and unmoved as the mountains which encircle the beauteous lake itself; and the fruits of their apostleship in training youth and guarding the ancestral faith of their people were as plentiful and as perennial as the golden harvests of Lombardy and Venetia.

In 1581, during the official visitation made by St. Charles Borromeo, the Brescian Congregation numbered four hundred sisters. Down to the invasion of Upper Italy by the

French revolutionary armies under Bonaparte in 1796, the Congregation of Brescia continued to exist in the conditions in which St. Angela had left it, and which St. Charles Borromeo had approved. The conqueror suppressed an Order which taught the female youth of Italy to live according to the Gospel of Christ; for the Jacobinism of the revolution would have no Gospel but its own godless creed, and no charity exercised toward the poor, the sick of body, and the infirm of spirit, but that of an equality, a liberty, a fraternity, as hollow, bitter, and deadly to the taste as the fruits

> "which grew
> Near the bituminous lake where Sodom flamed."

The property of the Ursulines—the sacred patrimony of the poor, and the sweet nursery of the little ones of Christ's flock—was ruthlessly seized by the Corsican, and never again restored to its former uses. In 1827, when Italy and Europe began to recover from the chronic disasters of the Napoleonic wars and the long intoxication of revolutionary doctrines, the Bishop of Brescia, who had found the few surviving Ursulines busy at work amid the social ruin, like a few sickly bees clustering around the fragments of their once swarming hive, induced the devoted women to give up living in the bosom of their families and to adopt the seclusion of the cloister. With the self-sacrificing docility which had ever characterized the daughters of St. Angela in their dealings with episcopal authority, the greater number of the Brescian Ursulines yielded to the counsels of the good Bishop Gabriele-Maria Nava; but there were many to whom the restraints of the cloister were impossible or unacceptable, and who yearned only for the liberty of following out their vocation in the footsteps of their holy foundress. These continued to live unmolested, and respected by all, in the bosom of their own families, devoting themselves unobtrusively, unmurmuringly, and hopefully to such duties and labors as they were permitted to fulfill. The aged, who remembered how numerous and blessedly active the uncloistered bands of Ursulines had been in city and country, before the Jacobin soldiery had poured across the Alps to blight and to destroy, beheld with regret the disappearance from the streets of Brescia of the well-known habit. And the men and women whom the long cycle of revolutionary storms had bound more firmly to the faith and customs of Catholic Italy were frequent and loud in their wishes to see the habit of St. Angela once more worn by the daughters of the noblest and the wealthiest, and gracing their homes with the virtues it was ever sure to bring. The poor and the laboring classes especially needed the familiar and ever-welcome presence of the modest veiled figures of the *Umiliate*—" the little sisters" whose heart understood so well the wants of the poorest and the pangs of the suffering, and whose hand had been to their fathers before them the hand of God ever extended to succor—gentle, merciful, and patient. And so Brescia, while surrounding with its sympathy and reverence the cloistered community founded by Bishop Nava, could not help cherishing with a grateful pity and a hopeful expectancy the scattered and drooping remnants of their own once numerous and worshiped Company of St. Ursula.

Nor were all these hopes doomed to disappointment. When, following up the work began by French Jacobinism, the Piedmontese Government let loose on Upper Italy—indeed, on the entire peninsula—the well-organized and disciplined armies of antichristian radicals and revolutionists, who are fast obliterating the glorious civilization of the Catholic ages, it became an imperative necessity to preserve the homes and the children of all classes, of the laboring poor in particular, against the active and most intelligent propagandism of the secret societies. Cloistered communities of Ursulines and other religious women could, where by some miracle they were tolerated, receive and educate the daughters of the highborn and the rich. But it needed the presence in the home and in the school-room of such women as were Angela Merici and her companions, to show by a God-like life, by the divinest charity and devotedness, that there was still a God upon earth, and that He had care of the poor and the suffering ; to demonstrate to the victims of unbelief and rampant Socialism, that Christian virtue was still a living force in the world, and that heroic self-sacrifice was ready to save society by the cross.

Pius IX., with that Heaven-sent instinct which attaches to the office of the Supreme Shepherd of souls, encouraged or created everywhere he could associations aiming to train the young to Christian life. Hence the promptness with which, in July, 1861, when the greater part of Upper and Central Italy was overrun by the fanatical apostles of Mazzini, followed and abetted everywhere by the colporteurs of the Evangelical Alliance and the Bible Societies, he issued a decree authorizing the Church in every land to celebrate the feast of St. Angela Merici as it was in Italy, and bestowing on this great apostle of female education and on her daughters, throughout the world, the generous meed of praise so well merited by centuries of fruitful toil. The terms in which the Holy Father spoke of Angela and her Institute—of their priceless services in the past, of their adaptation to the sore need of the present age, and of the divine promise that they should last through all future time—thrilled the souls of the Ursulines everywhere, but more especially those of the uncloistered remnant of the venerable Congregation of Brescia. This decree signed by Cardinal Patrizi, but speaking in the name of the Vicar of Christ, solemnly stated a fact unmentioned by any historian of St. Angela—that it was in Rome, while visiting in 1525 the tombs of the holy Apostles, "she felt herself moved to promote the education of young girls, well knowing that these, surrounded as they were by the spreading heresies of Luther and Calvin, were, like the opening flower among thorns, in imminent peril of losing their virginal blossom."

But now that errors far more deadly than those of the sixteenth century were poisoning the homes, the minds, and the hearts of all Italy—of all Christendom indeed—this voice from Rome was like the breath of inspiration for all who, like Angela and her early associates, thirsted to be to the modern world the apostles of education, and to shed the light of their teaching and example around the hearthstone of every Christian home. In Brescia, desolated by the invasion of triumphant radicalism, the few remaining uncloistered Ursulines were recalled to a new life, as by the tones of the resurrection trump. The Countess Girelli and her sister immediately set to work, with the countenance of the local superiors, to reorganize the primitive sisterhood as Angela conceived it, and as required by the social needs of our day. The two ladies soon saw themselves surrounded by a numerous body of young women animated by the spirit of St. Ursula. Steadily and rapidly these numbers went on increasing, to the intense delight of the Brescian Catholics. Donna Girelli began with twelve, just as St. Angela began in 1535. On the 4th of April, 1864, the first regular assembly was held. In 1866, Girolamo de' Verzeri, Bishop of Brescia, gave these new and welcome auxiliaries canonical institution, enjoining them to keep the primitive Rule inviolate. On the 29th of July that same year, he received the religious profession of the members of the restored Company—the very day on which Pius IX. beheld the statue of St. Angela Merici solemnly placed in St. Peter's among those of the other founders of religious Orders.

There was thus great joy in Brescia, both in the cloistered community of St. Ursula, who saw their own hands strengthened by this providential accession of numbers, and among the fervent followers of the Countess Girelli, who soon counted five hundred sisters within the single diocese of Bishop Verzeri! From Rome came again in 1867, through the Cardinal Prefect of the Congregation of the Council other eloquent words of commendation and encouragement warm from the fatherly heart of Pius IX. "Your fervent Company of maidens," such were some of the words, "having for its object to secure in the midst of secular life the sanctification of both mistresses and pupils, is to us a great comfort. May it please our Lord, through the intercession of St. Angela Merici, who has deserved so well of your city and who is the protectress of your Company, to make the latter become like the mustard-seed of the Gospel, growing to the stature of a great tree, in which the birds of the air shall build their nests!"

We may well trust, now that he is near St. Angela in Heaven, that Pius the Beloved will obtain by his prayers that the "mustard-seed" shall live and grow and increase mightily through the long wintry years of Italy's sore trial.

CHAPTER XXI.

THE URSULINES IN FRANCE—CONGREGATIONS OF AIX, BORDEAUX, PARIS, LYONS, AND TOULOUSE.

IN 1572, the year in which the bull of Gregory XIII. approved and confirmed anew the Institute of St. Angela, and sanctioned the changes made in it at Milan by St. Charles Borromeo, was born at Avignon, in France, a child destined to exercise immense influence on the destiny of the Company of St. Ursula. This was Frances de Bermond. She was a child of extraordinary promise, given for a brief space in her early girlhood to the enjoyment of the admiration and homage which her birth and precocious talents inspired, and then suddenly and wholly devoting her life to God and the good of souls. Urged on by the advice and examples of a saintly aunt, Frances made a vow of virginity and gave up her whole time to the instruction of poor children, winning to the cause of Christian education her former playmates, with whom she formed a society wholly consecrated to the God-like work of caring for the children of the poor. They were all of noble birth, these French maidens. Without, perhaps, having heard of Angela Merici and her Brescian companions, Frances de Bermond and her mates followed precisely the same road as Angela. As, however, the French maiden was born a century later than the Maid of Desenzano, she found the printing-press in full operation everywhere, furnishing books, at an incomparably lower price, to all classes of the community, and thus stimulating the children of all classes to acquire the elements of secular knowledge. These highborn ladies of Avignon had all, like Frances herself, shared in the enormously increased facilities of learning, and they were inspired to open schools in their native city, in which the children of the poor and the laboring classes were taught not only the elements of the Christian doctrine, but the elements as well of human letters.

The entire city, astonished at first, and amused by the resolution taken so suddenly by young ladies so gifted and so petted, did not hesitate to admire and applaud when it became evident that this devotion to a great and sorely needed work was not a passing caprice, but a serious purpose conscientiously formed and carried out with quiet but constant earnestness. It so happened, too, that a saintly French priest, the venerable Cæsar de Bus, had just founded a society of priests on the model of the Institute of St. Angela ("Fathers of the Christian Doctrine"), and having for its aim to bestow on the children of the lower classes the inestimable boon of a truly Christian education. Father de Bus was neither slow nor lukewarm in encouraging the labors of Frances de Bermond and her little band of apostles. The Archbishop of Avignon also, who was delighted with the zeal of these new teachers and with the blessed fruits it produced, obtained from Pope Clement VIII. (1592-1605) a formal approbation of the nascent society.

So far, Frances de Bermond and her associates had no connection with the Company of St. Ursula, and probably no certain knowledge of its existence or purpose. By a providential train of circumstances, the life and work of St. Angela was soon made known to the devoted girl. A young lady of Avignon of about the same age as Frances, and self-consecrated like her to the virginal life, received from her spiritual director, the Bishop of Carpentras, a copy of the Rule of St. Angela, as approved and modified by St. Charles Borromeo for the Ursulines of Milan. This was no sooner communicated to Frances de Bermond and her fellow-laborers, together with an account of St. Angela and the Society founded by her, than the fervent Avignonese maidens unanimously resolved to become the spiritual daughters of so great a parent.

Miss de Masan de Vaucluse, who had been instrumental in making the work of St. Angela known to Frances de Bermond, was now enabled to complete what she had so happily begun, and bestowed on her new friend a house of her own in the little town of L'Isle, some twenty miles to the southeast of Avignon, and noted for its industry as well as its picturesque situation.

This first house of the Ursuline Order in France was the hive from which swarms of holy women were to go forth to almost every part of France—indeed, to every Catholic country of Europe, except Italy. To be sure, these swarms, as they settled and housed themselves and began to ply their indefatigable industries in this or that province, had, by the imperious necessity of circumstances, to modify the conditions of their existence—just as bees in the gigantic forests of Brazil build their homes and lay up their sweet stores of honey in a manner that differs much from the hives they construct in our gardens; and just as the European sparrow, lately introduced into America, when forced or induced to nestle in our woods, will cease to confine himself to the eaves of our dwellings, but build in the tree-tops like the singing birds which he persecutes and puts to flight. Still, under these altered conditions of climate, country, and habitation, bees are bees and sparrows are sparrows the whole world over.

St. Charles Borromeo, in inducing his Ursulines to live together in community and to bind themselves by the simple vows of religious life, did not purpose to establish what canonists call a strict inclosure, or a cloister attended with the rigorous and inviolable seclusion known among the old monastic orders of women. The Ursulines were primarily intended as an active Order—as one to occupy itself principally with teaching. So, while living within their own houses, the Milanese Ursulines were wont to busy themselves continually both in teaching little girls and in giving religious instruction to adult persons of their own sex. The new house at L'Isle copied faithfully those of Milan.

Soon, as the limited field of activity afforded in that town became like the garden of God under the cunning husbandry of Mother de Bermond and her sisterhood, other places along the Rhône and its affluents began to covet the happiness of the people around Vaucluse.[1] Aix was the first city of Southern France to solicit a colony of sisters from Mother de Bermond. This was in 1600. Another colony was sent to Marseilles in 1603. Indeed, all Provence seemed anxious to have its daughters trained by such exemplary and accomplished mistresses. The centre of government of the French Congregation, as established by Frances de Bermond, was at Aix, the capital of Provence. Avignon itself, "the City of the Popes," and at that time still belonging to the Holy See, seems to have followed the example of Aix and Marseilles, instead of honoring itself and the noble maidens who were born in it, by being the first to claim their services. At any rate, in 1605, after the death of Clement VIII., the Cardinal-Archbishop of Bordeaux, Francis de Sourdis, happening to pass through it on his way to the Conclave, made the ac-

---

[1] The Valley and Fountain of Vauclue, immortalized by Petrarch are in themselves most wonderful and beautiful. The whole country abounds in sublime scenery.

quaintance of Mother de Bermond and her daughters. He wished to see them at work in their schools, and was so charmed by what he saw, that he resolved to introduce them into his diocese as soon as he had come back from Rome. The conclave ended, the archbishop, who was a most worthy prelate, stopped at Milan on his homeward journey, in order to visit the tomb of St. Charles Borromeo, to study the institutions of every kind which the Apostle of Lombardy had created for the benefit of religion, and to fire his own soul near the grave of this model priest and pastor with the sacred flame which had enlightened and purified Milan.

It was remarked that the noble pilgrim remained in prayer by the side of the holy archbishop's remains during seven consecutive hours, beseeching God through the intercession of His great servant to grant himself the fullness of the apostolic spirit of devotion and self-sacrifice. De Sourdis, in one of his letters, tells us that his soul received great favors there—among them the determination to copy faithfully the virtues of St. Charles, and the design of establishing in Bordeaux a virginal company of teachers like those in Milan and Brescia.[1] He purposed combining both forms—the life in community and the freedom of remaining with one's family. In 1618, however, he carried out a further resolution of having, together with Ursulines of these two classes, a monastery of cloistered Ursulines subject to all the forms of rigorous monastic life, such as that just established in Paris by the joint action of Mother de Bermond, Madame Acarie, and Madame de Sainte-Beuve.

Cardinal de Sourdis found ready to his hand three of those

---

[1] Salvatori, p. 63. Abbracciò subito il piissimo cardinale la santa ispirazione; e giunto a Bordeaux mise mano all' opera. Fu questo circa il 1606, quando vi stabilì buon numero di Vergini sotta la Regola di nostra santa, colle aggiunte fattevi da S. Carlo; ed alcuna di loro ne unì a vivere congregate in una specie di conservatorio, lasciandone altre sparse per le famiglie.

Christian women so numerous in the France of the sixteenth and seventeenth centuries—women in whose souls ever burned the spirit of St. Louis, St. Vincent de Paul, and St. Jane Frances de Chantal. These were Frances and Mary de Cazères and Jeanne de la Mercerie. The cardinal gave them the Milanese Rule, and sent them to reside in a kind of half-cloistered seclusion at Libourne, some twenty-five miles from Bordeaux, where they prepared themselves with uncommon fervor to receive the religious habit, and to make, at the proper time, the simple vows required by the Rule. They received the habit solemnly on June 24th, 1606, returned to Bordeaux six months later, and on November 30th the Ursuline community was inaugurated with great solemnity, Frances de Cazères being declared superior.

It was, as is well known to students of history, a brief interval of repose for storm-tossed France, torn and desolated by the civil and religious wars of more than half a century. The bitter and protracted strife between Protestants and Catholics, aided and abetted by the evil passions of foreign powers, had roused the tepid into fervor, and disposed the fervent to enthusiasm in all good works that aimed at elevating the intellectual and moral condition of the people. There was among most Catholics in France something akin to aversion toward new monastic orders on the old plan; and, besides, the need of the age and country was instruction for the ignorant, thorough religious education for the young, bodily and spiritual help for the countless hosts of the suffering, and the edifying example of a holy life brought home to every fireside.

It was a Godsend, therefore, the good people of Bordeaux thought, this creation of the Holy Maid of Desenzano, which enabled young women either to live the virginal life of useful devotedness in common, or to bring its bright examples to the family hearth ; to make for a sufficient period a thorough trial of their strength to bear the yoke of religious vows, and then either to return to purely secular avocations, or to bind themselves permanently to follow "the more perfect way."

Frances de Cazères was in Bordeaux what Frances de Bermond was at Aix and L'Isle and Marseilles—the living image of Angela Merici. Between 1606 and 1618—an epoch ever memorable to the great family of monasteries which claim to be the offspring of the Congregation of Bordeaux—Mother de Cazères was called on to found no less than six houses of the Order. Nothing but the lack of well-trained and experienced subjects prevented a further extension in the South and West of France.

The saintly superior, however, must have seen great dangers for the souls of her sisters in their mixing so freely with the joyous and pleasure-loving French society of the epoch. One must naturally conclude this much from the bull of Paul V., of which we shall have to speak presently. The conviction must have forced itself on her practical mind and scrupulous conscience, that the daughters of the upper classes could be more safely and successfully trained to all the accomplishments and virtues necessary to their future career in the world by being secluded with their mistresses during their school years ; that the children of the poorer classes could also be admitted daily to the Ursuline schools without compelling their teachers to leave the seclusion of their religious home ; and that the occupations of the school-room could be made to conform in every essential respect with the strictest requirements of claustral life.

It is affirmed, and on the very best authority, that Mother de Cazères had, in 1608, an ecstatic vision not a little like that of St. Angela at Brudazzo, in which she was shown the wonderful extension of the Congregation of Bordeaux in France and outside of it, the bitter opposition she must expecct in her labors, the transformation of her present establishments into monasteries of cloistered nuns, and the cooperation of the Holy See toward this much-desired end. Her associates, her trusted assistants in the gigantic labors of their first foundation, heard her say and repeat that the divine voice expressly declared : " Thou shalt be the parent of a monastic society, and shalt have to bear more than one cross." Cardinal de Sourdis, himself a man of God, inquired into the truth of this vision ; and having listened attentively to the modest and ingenuous answers of the superior, entertained no doubt of the fact. From that moment both he and Mother de Cazères labored together to draw up such rules as would meet all the requirements of the monastic society which they both contemplated, and which might satisfy the Roman canonists, the committee of cardinals appointed to examine into such weighty matters, and the Holy Father himself.

The cardinal undertook to go himself to Rome. Before setting out, however, he deemed it both wise and just to submit his project and all the proposed changes to the Ursulines themselves. They had not been unprepared for his design, and looking up to him as to another St. Charles, and to their mother superior as to a second St. Angela, they saw, in what both had matured so long and so conscientiously, a providential plan for the exaltation of their own Order and the increase of its usefulness.

The changes proposed by Cardinal de Sourdis and subsequently approved by the Holy See are thus resumed briefly by Father Salvatori :

" They believed it a timely measure to create a third class of cloistered nuns with (solemn) religious vows, as had been done in Paris a few years before (1612). For that purpose, retaining the substance of the Rule of the holy foundress enjoining on the members to consecrate themselves not only to the work of their own sanctification, but also to the sanctification of others, they drew up a new code of rules, embodying whatever was most fitted to their design from the primitive Rule, from those of St. Ignatius Loyola and St. Augustine; they bestowed on the new Constitutions the name of the latter as the greatest, and called the new monastic Order *Ursulines under the Rule of St. Augustine.*"[1]

Paul V., after weighing the considerations presented to him by the Archbishop of Bordeaux, and receiving a cordial commendation from the cardinals appointed to examine into the proposed change, issued, on February 5th, 1618, the bull *In Supremo militantis ecclesiæ solio,* fixing for all time the form of the new Ursuline Congregation of Bordeaux, and regulating with the most minute detail the manner in which the nuns themselves are to live thenceforward, and that in which they are to keep their schools of boarders and day-scholars in conformity with the requirements of a cloistered life.

"We bestow the most earnest care," the Sovereign Pontiff says, "on everything pertaining to the monasteries and other regular establishments, in which devoted women labor to increase the glory of religion and zeal for the service of God; in which wise virgins, impelled by a charitable zeal, apply themselves to secure not only their own salvation but that of others, by taking on themselves the task of educating young girls. Their successful and most fruitful labors therein are a matter of notoriety; while others, drawn by their example to imitate them, and contemning the attractions of a worldly life, desire only to bestow their whole lives on serving

---
[1] Book i. c. 10, p. 63.

God within the seclusion of the cloister, and the discipline of regular observance, and thus be more free beneath the guidance of so holy an institute [manner of life] to gather 'flowers of honor' and 'fruit of riches,'[1] as well as to secure their own everlasting happiness."

This, the pontiff goes on to say, is what has been and is still done by the Ursulines of Bordeaux. "They have founded a society under the banner of St. Ursula, resolved, in imitation of this saint, to preserve their virginity as a thing pleasing to God, taking on themselves, as their proper and peculiar mode of life (*Instituto*) to educate young girls, and to teach them the Christian doctrine. Not long after these beginnings, considering—the Holy Ghost inspiring them the while—how great an obstacle they must find, both toward the preservation of their maidenly purity and the leading a blamelessly religious life, in the familiar intercourse with men, and the private banquetings which French customs countenance in the houses of both women and men, they sought the seclusion of a dwelling of their own, where, in order to shut themselves off from intercourse with men and the better to guard their virginal treasure, they resolved to live a cloistered life under a regular rule. Thither they all betook themselves, and, after two years of probation, they bound themselves by the simple vows of chastity, obedience, poverty, and stability in their calling, according to the will of the Apostolic See. From that time, wearing a habit which is equally becoming to maidenly modesty and the religious profession, they have not ceased till now to devote themselves to the education of young children of their own sex. In their house, as is the wont in colleges, they have established distinct classes, in which their pupils are taught, first of all, the Christian doctrine, enforced by salutary examples and

---
[1] Ecclesiasticus xxiv. 23.

illustrations, thereby preserving these tender minds from their worst bane—the poisonous fruit of heresy. They also train them to abstain from extravagance in dress, to which their sex is so much addicted, teaching them all the arts and industries becoming women of the world ; and, in order to induce the children of the poor and of needy strangers to come to these schools and learn the Christian doctrine, the daughters of St. Ursula teach them the useful accomplishments which may enable them afterward to earn a livelihood. Nor have they less care and devotion on feast days to assemble servant-maids and poor women whose Christian training had been neglected, and to impart to them all the knowledge so sadly needed. The motherly tenderness displayed by them toward the young girls who, with the permission of the cardinal-archbishop, live in a separate part of their religious abode and are educated by them, is most admirable."

Such, then, is the institution, admirable indeed in every way, new to France, suited to the sore needs of its people, called for by the spirit of the age, which Paul V. proceeds to erect into a regular monastic establishment, so constituted and disciplined that it shall fulfill the loftiest aims of Angela Merici and her early associates, take its place in the Church of God by the side of the most venerable creations of the Holy See, and be, by the blessing of Christ's Vicar, endowed with the power to multiply itself and cover all France and all Christendom with its offshoots.

While the Congregation of Bordeaux was thus rapidly advancing through the successive stages which brought it to its final form of completeness, the Ursulines of Paris were passing, but more rapidly, through a similar process of development. The reader will not be sorry to know who were the saintly women who planted in the capital of France an establishment vicing in efficiency and fruitfulness with that of Bordeaux. The bull of Paul V., erecting the Parisian establishment into a monastery of cloistered nuns, was issued June 13th, 1612, while the bull obtained by Cardinal de Sourdis was dated some six years later.

As we are, however, occupied with the only true superiority of which the daughters of Angela Merici are envious—that of zeal in the cause of education and fervor in the pursuit of holiness—we may well pass by whatever relates to chronological questions, and attend solely to one of the most surprising moral phenomena recorded in the history of the Church.

Mother de Bermond, as we have seen, was called upon in 1608 to send some of her sisters to Paris, where an establishment of Ursulines had already been begun. Two of the most illustrious women of that age were the founders of this great nursery of apostolic educators of youth : Barbara Avrillot, widow of Pierre Acarie de Villemor, who founded in France the Reformed Carmelite Order of St. Teresa, became herself a Carmelite nun, and was beatified under the name of Mary of the Incarnation ;[1] and a cousin of Madame Acarie's, also a noble widow lady called Madeleine Lhuillier de Sainte-Beuve. While the former's husband was still living and his worshiped wife was busied in educating her three sons and three daughters, she found time, among the many good works which she and Monsieur Acarie originated and promoted, to introduce and to found the Reformed Carmelites. So great was the number of postulants for admission into the new Order who presented themselves to Madame Acarie, that no place could be found for them in the first house opened, and many who were admitted were unable to endure the privations and austerity of the Carmelite Rule. Nevertheless Madame

---

[1] It was doubtless in her honor that Marie Guyard-Martin, foundress of the Ursulines of Quebec, took the name of "Mary of the Incarnation," under which she is known and has already won the title of "Venerable."

Acarie's motherly solicitude provided for both classes a house in which they could lead a life of religious seclusion while looking forward to a realization of their cherished hopes. She induced them, while thus waiting, to devote their energies to the instruction of children of their sex. The Hôtel Saint-André, a spacious mansion in a Parisian suburb, was selected for the common residence and the central school, and placed under the direction of Nicoletta Le Pelletier, who had founded a like establishment at Pontoise in 1599. The Bishop of Paris, charmed with the great good effected by these young teachers, heartily approved the establishment, and graduated classes of pupils were at once opened, attracting more children than could be accommodated.

At first, and while the school was in its infancy and the number of the teachers inconsiderable, Madame Acarie found in her own resources and the generosity of her friends wherewith to meet all the necessary expenses. But as the work grew on her hands, and its fruits increased beyond her most sanguine expectations, she cast about anxiously for some one of those noble souls, so easily met with on French soil, whose great wealth is far beneath their liberality. She suddenly bethought her of her young and widowed relative, Madeleine de Sainte-Beuve. The latter had been herself divinely moved to undertake some such work. "I cannot refuse to put my hand to this good work," she said in answer to her relative. "We shall together found a community of Ursulines, on one condition, however—that the members shall, as soon as it may be done conveniently, adopt the rules of monastic life."

Madame de Sainte-Beuve lost not a moment. She took lodgings in the neighborhood of the Hôtel Saint-André, and made her design known to her friends and acquaintance. The quick religious instincts of French women of the upper classes enabled them to perceive at a glance what a vast and fruitful field was thus about to be opened to the zeal of the young and the generous-hearted. As if the voice of Madame Acarie and her relative were a trumpet-call summoning the *élite* of French maidenhood to a new apostleship, the daughters of the best Parisian families immediately came forward to join the community of the Hôtel Saint-André! Among them were noble maidens bearing the names of De Marillac, D'Urfé, De Vieuxpont, and D'Ésigny. It was then, when the future of this first great school seemed so promising, that Mother de Bermond was summoned from Marseilles. She was forthwith appointed to govern the new establishment with the title of prioress, and both Madame Acarie and Madame de Sainte-Beuve besought her to enforce among the sisterhood the Ursuline Rule, as borrowed from the Congregation of Milan. Madame de Sainte-Beuve, meanwhile, had sold a portion of her patrimonial estates, and purchased near the Hôtel Saint-André the grounds needful to her design, on which she constructed two additional buildings—one for a boarding-school, and the other for the sisters' dwelling-house. A spacious chapel also arose under the energetic supervision of the foundress; and everything was urged forward with such indefatigable activity, that the chapel was opened for divine service on September 29th, 1610.

Until that day, however, no word had been spoken to Mother de Bermond about the proposed transformation of her Parisian community into a monastery of cloistered nuns. But Madame de Sainte-Beuve had only been waiting for this occasion to lay her design before the prioress and the entire sisterhood. So, after mass, they were all assembled in chapter, and their benefactress exposed her views of monastic life in connection with the mighty work to which they had all put their hands, giving her motives with such eloquence and persuasiveness, that her hearers, the prioress herself setting the example, assented at once to the proposal. Mother de Bermond, as well as her sisters, stipulated expressly that the purpose and spirit of St. Angela's Institute should be preserved in the new Rule, and that, whatever changes should be decreed by the Holy See, the cloistered community should remain a part of the Company of St. Ursula.

In spite of the energy with which Madame de Sainte-Beuve pushed matters forward in Paris and at Rome, the bull *Inter Universa*, converting the Ursuline community of the Hôtel Saint-André into a monastery of cloistered nuns with the Reformed Rule of St. Augustine, was only issued on June 13th, 1612.

The chief point from which the monastery of Paris is made to differ from that of Bordeaux, canonically erected in 1618, is that together with the ordinary religious vows of poverty, chastity, and obedience, there is enjoined an additional obligation of "devoting themselves to the instruction of young girls, making of this occupation their chief end and purpose, ever keeping this before their minds, ordering to this end all and each of their functions and offices, giving to its attainment their whole strength and care, convinced that in so doing they are fulfilling the purpose of their divine calling." [1]

The Ursulines of Aix and its dependencies were not willing to lose the services of Mother de Bermond, and unprepared, as yet, to accept for themselves the great change about to be effected in the Parisian sisterhood. So they hastened to recall one whom they still reverenced as their parent and guide.

---

[1] Elapso probationis tempore professionem emittere, paupertatis, castitatis et obedientiæ votis se adstringere, necnon dictæ puellarum instructioni, eum sibi præcipuum finem et scopum proponentes, id perpetuo cogitantes, ad id omnia et singula munia et officia disponentes, totis viribus et sedulitate animi in id incumbentes, ea demum ratione se divinæ vocationi satisfacere posse credentes. . . .

Madame de Sainte-Beuve was thus left free to accomplish her purpose. On the 11th November, Henri de Gondy, Bishop of Paris—which, by the way, only became an archbishop's see in 1622—the first Ursuline monastery in the capital of France was inaugurated with all the solemn formalities required by the canon law, and in obedience to the bull of Pope Paul V.

The holy woman, who had found in Madame Sainte-Beuve a providential instrument ready to her hand and docile to all the promptings of Christian generosity, never for one moment ceased to watch over the growth of their joint work. It was only about a year after the canonical institution of the Ursulines in their monastery of the Hôtel Saint-André that Barbara Acarie lost her noble husband, and some further time elapsed before the widow entered the Carmelite monastery in which one of her own daughters was superior, and assumed the name, now dear to the Christian world, of Mary of the Incarnation. What she did for her cherished Ursulines, and which should be mentioned in this place, may be best stated in the words of her Italian biographer.

"Fully aware of the great good effected by the religious Ursulines in giving a Christian education to young girls, according to the method of their pious Institute, and how advantageous to the city of Paris it would be to possess at least one monastery of their order, she lost not a moment in laying before a rich and devoted relative her desire, and persuaded her to undertake the foundation of the proposed establishment. Having obtained the promise of her cousin, Blessed Mary forthwith took all the steps necessary toward the execution of their joint enterprise. The requisite authorization was obtained, and the first Ursuline monastery soon arose in Paris.

"The zeal of Blessed Mary did not, however, stop there;

as soon as the sisterhood was established in their home, she would frequently visit them to see that they had everything comfortable and orderly, to make sure that the pupils lacked nothing that was needful, to animate every person within the house to fervor, to the exact observance of the Rule, and inducing the most saintly men of that age to visit and instruct the rising community. Nor did she cease from her care and labor till the monastery was in perfect working order."[1]

We are thus minute in describing the efforts of the noble women who were chiefly instrumental in founding each one of the first great Ursuline nurseries or congregations. The subsequent history of each of these, and of their numerous fruitful offshoots, does not come within our limited scope. That can only be attempted in a history of the Order itself—a task long ago most successfully achieved by others.

This first Parisian monastery, patronized by royalty, and sustained by the nobility, whose daughters it educated and from among whose daughters the sisterhood never ceased to be recruited—blessed too by the popular classes, and fostered by the grateful solicitude of the clergy, had in course of time to multiply itself far and wide. Madame de Sainte-Beuve, privileged to reside within the institution she had founded, died the death of the saints, August 29th, 1630 ; but not before she had seen the eleventh Ursuline monastery established by her own princely liberality.

In 1640 the monastery of Paris sent two of its noblest and most devoted women to join, in Quebec, the little band of three Ursulines from Tours who had landed there a twelvemonth before, led by another heroic widow-lady, who was to give to the religious name of " Mary of the Incarnation" the added consecration of missionary labors and God-like virtues.

---

[1] Page 128 of the Italian Life of B. Mary of the Incarnation, published in Rome in 1791, the year of her solemn beatification, and quoted by Salvatori.

Thus the two congregations of Bordeaux and Paris were to blend in the great monastic school of Quebec their distinctive differences and common spirit of unbounded self-sacrifice. The saintly foundress of the Canadian Ursulines adopted in the Rule which she drew up the fourth vow of the Parisian sisterhood, binding the members to make education their principal aim and chief labor, while imposing on her companions the religious habit of Bordeaux somewhat modified.

Mother de Bermond obeyed without a moment's hesitation the order of her superiors at Aix, recalling her to the field of her own early labors. She made a great sacrifice in obeying; for she heartily desired to live a strictly secluded life, and had been overjoyed by the prospect of seeing the Parisian house elevated to the dignity of a regular monastery. But as she had been only lent, not given, to the sisterhood of Paris, as a mistress and a guide, she deemed herself, very properly, bound to yield prompt and unqualified submission to those who had sent her thither, and who now recalled her.

It was soon seen that they were in this seconding God's merciful designs for the Ursuline Order in Southern and Eastern France. The high-souled woman took the road to Aix, stopping, in those days of bad roads and slow stage-coaches, for a day or two of rest at Lyons. But the truth is, that, servant of God as she was and wholly led by His Spirit, she could not tarry anywhere for a single day without seeing the germ of some holy enterprise suddenly burst forth from the soil beneath her feet, and become, like the tree which shaded the prophet of old, a thing of mature growth within the space of a night's slumber.

It so happened that a wealthy citizen of Lyons, John de Ranquet, charmed with all that he had heard of the Ursulines of Aix and Milan, and alive to the great want of Christian education in his native city, had prepared an establishment for the reception of Ursulines, and had laid aside a fund for their maintenance. More than that, he had encouraged in his two daughters Clémence and Catherine the determination to join the sisterhood the moment they took possession of their abode in Lyons. He no sooner learned that Mother de Bermond was in the city than he called on her, laid his offer at her feet, and obtained her acquiescence. The superiors at Aix sanctioned this acceptance, and Mother de Bermond and her traveling companion took instant possession of the proffered residence, and opened it to their Lyonnese pupils. This was in 1612. During the next six years the good work so grew beneath the hands of these two women, and the number of postulants from among the noblest and best in the community became so great, that the best minds among the Ursulines and the holiest men in Church and State wished to see in Lyons the same transformation effected which had taken place in Paris and Bordeaux. From the infant establishment of Lyons several offshoots were planted in various parts of Eastern France between 1612 and 1620; among others, that of Moulins in 1616, under Perretta de Bermond, a younger sister of Mother de Bermond; that of St. Chamond in 1613, itself the fruitful stem of future monasteries; that of Mâcon in 1615; the great monastery of Clermont-Ferrand in 1616, which in 1621, under the government of Clémence de Ranquet, adopted the changes just introduced among the Ursulines of Lyons.

We omit the long list of others. A bull of Paul V., dated April, 1619, conferred on the monastery of Lyons, and on the establishments to be affiliated to it, the rank and privileges granted in the preceding year to Bordeaux.

Thus Rome was not allowed to be unacquainted with the marvelous strides which the Order of St. Angela was making in France, nor to remain inoperative in seconding the zeal of these apostolic women. In very truth, their appearance in the cities of France, the sudden rise of their schools, and the intellectual and moral revival which was either caused by their influence or invariably seen to attend it, reminds one forcibly of the first spread and growth of Christianity in Syria and Asia Minor.

The Lyonnese sisterhood were neither so prompt nor so unanimous as those of Paris and Bordeaux in consenting to accept the changes proposed by the Archbishop of Lyons and desired by Mother de Bermond. Her example and her persuasive arguments, however, finally won them all over to her wishes. On March 25th, 1620, the monastery was canonically established, and Mother de Bermond, with her three senior sisters, received from the archbishop's hands the religious habit, and pronounced by special dispensation the three solemn vows of their profession.

The saintly foundress, who has been justly called the Angela Merici of France, continued to labor with the same indefatigable zeal and the same humility of heart to the end of her life. She had completed in 1622 an establishment in the little town of Saint-Bonnet, near Lyons. As it so often happens in little towns, the progress of her community was opposed by passions and pretensions out of all proportion with the size of the place itself. Her sweetness, humility, and firmness overcame everything. But the privations endured by the sisterhood and their hard struggle for existence induced the great-souled woman to take up her abode with them. And thus she died in 1628, in her fifty-sixth year, like the night-blooming cereus, as the sun of her life went down, embalming the whole country with the sweet perfume of her sanctity.

It now remains that we should briefly describe the origin of the Congregation of Toulouse, so closely connected with that of Lyons.

As we have seen, the Blessed Cæsar de Bus contributed greatly toward the increase and prosperity of the first French Ursulines under Mother de Bermond. The Congregation of Fathers of the Christian Doctrine, of which this holy priest was the founder, everywhere took an active part in promoting the spread and growth of the Ursuline communities, whose scope was almost identical with their own. Now the right-hand man of Cæsar de Bus, both in founding and in governing his congregation, was Father de Vigier, a native of L'Isle, the very first town of France in which the Ursulines had a regular establishment. One of his sisters, Marguerite de Vigier, was encouraged by him to join the Ursulines, and became a foremost member of the Order in the South of France. After having distinguished herself by her virtue and capacity at Avignon, she was sent to Chabeuil, in Dauphiné, where the success of her school and the influence of her saintly examples were such, that all the Protestant population, with the exception of five families, was won over to the Catholic faith.

Thereupon the Cardinal de Joyeuse, Archbishop of Toulouse, besought Cæsar de Bus to obtain for his episcopal city, which was overrun by Protestants, a colony of Fathers of the Christian Doctrine and an establishment of Ursulines. This was in 1604; and Father de Vigier and his sister Marguerite were forthwith sent to Toulouse to found houses of their respective Orders. Year by year the number of Mother Marguerite's pupils increased, and with them increased in proportion the numbers of postulants for admission into her community. In 1609 Cardinal de Joyeuse's successor in the archiepiscopal see bestowed on the Ursulines the chapel near their convent. In 1610 Mother de Vigier and her companions adopted the resolution to live exclusively within their own residence, although no steps were immediately taken to erect the latter into a monastery. This, however, was merely a question of time. Meanwhile, the many works of charity which the Ursulines had either originated in Toulouse or promoted most zealously seemed doomed to die out after the withdrawal of the sisters into the seclusion of their new life. But many of the ladies who had labored under their guidance among the sick and poor and ignorant, in the hospitals, prisons, and the chapels where female sodalities were wont to be instructed by the Ursulines, now, at the bidding of Mother de Vigier, resolved to continue their wonted merciful labors.

Thus was formed the society of the "Ladies of Mercy of St. Ursula." They were the zealous and invaluable auxiliaries of the Ursulines, and conferred by their pious and enlightened zeal the greatest services on Toulouse and its neighborhood. The members never ceased to look up to Mother de Vigier and her successors as to their mothers and religious superiors. The Holy See looked upon this affiliated society with favor, and Pope Clement X. (1670–76) granted to the members many spiritual privileges.

But the change which had led to the formation of this society was followed in 1615 by the transformation of the convent into a monastery of cloistered nuns. Mother de Vigier herself was prompt to see the necessity or the opportuneness of this change. She had carefully trained her daughters in preparation for it. Her excellent brother was sent to Rome to obtain the bull of erection. On September 8th, 1615, they solemnly received at the hands of the archbishop the consecrated habit of religion, and on the 27th December following they pronounced the solemn vows of their profession.

Something of the southern enthusiasm marked thenceforward the fervent piety of Mother de Vigier and her Ursulines. Their austerities were such that the ecclesiastical superiors were obliged to interfere to moderate them. But they neglected no duty of their calling while thus indulging in a rigor which makes our sensuality or our tepidity shudder. Besides the increased labor imposed on them by their numerous boarders, the good nuns opened five new classes for poor children, and on Sundays and holy days gathered into their halls poor servant-girls and married women sadly in need of instruction, and explained to them the saving truths of the Gospel and the practical duties and virtues of their condition. Theirs was an apostleship which extended its blessings and—we had almost said—its miracles, to all. For the change of life wrought in the women of all classes, and by these in the men, was little short of a miracle.

Of course, other cities were not slow to hear of all this or to seek to share in these blessings; and so, as it happened in Paris, and Bordeaux, and Lyons, here also the Ursuline monasteries had to multiply themselves in order to satisfy the wishes of the surrounding populations.

The Congregation of Toulouse soon covered the whole of the province with its flourishing establishments, none of which—and the same may be said in all truth of the other Ursuline congregations throughout France—knew any decline in their fervor or decrease in their usefulness, till the French Revolution came to involve them all in one common ruin. From that ruin the Congregation of Toulouse was fated never to rise again, as well as those of Tulle, Arles, Dijon, and Dole. The few struggling establishments belonging to the latter cannot obtain further mention in our limited space.

One branch of the stock planted by Mother de Bermond merits, however, a special mention, though never so brief. This was the religious body known as the Ursulines of the Presentation of Avignon, founded in 1623 by Lucretia de Gastineau, and approved as a cloistered monastic establishment by Urban VIII. in 1637. The Presentation Ursulines established monasteries and schools in several cities, and in 1785 sent from Pont-Saint-Esprit a reinforcement of zealous nuns to the long-suffering Parisian community of New Orleans. A second band of sisters under the guidance of Mother Gensoul came out from Marseilles in 1810 ; and in January, 1816, the establishment assumed, as we shall see presently, the title of Ursulines of the Presentation of Our Lady.

CHAPTER XXIII.

OFFSHOOTS OF THE FRENCH URSULINES THROUGHOUT THE GERMAN AND AUSTRIAN EMPIRES, CANADA, THE UNITED STATES, IRELAND, AND ENGLAND

The Congregation of Bordeaux, like its great rival in excellence and apostolic zeal, the Congregation of Paris, was blessed with a truly marvelous fecundity. Many of the monasteries which owed their birth to Frances de Cazères and her associates did indeed, as we saw in the preceding chapter, join the Parisian Congregation; nevertheless, at the time of the French Revolution, over one hundred establishments of education claimed to belong to the Congregation of Bordeaux. Its branches extended to the Low Countries, Germany, Italy, Austria, Hungary, Poland, Bohemia, and Canada. Indeed, in the year 1650 we find sixty-eight monasteries belonging to this flourishing congregation.

With the exception of a few houses, the Ursulines of Germany, Austria, Hungary, and Poland derived their origin from the Congregation of Bordeaux. They rendered everywhere priceless services to religion and society. Of course, wherever the Revolutionary French armies penetrated and maintained a brief sway the Ursuline communities were either dispersed or subjected to many annoyances. Still they managed to remain on the spot, protected by the gratitude and veneration of Christian families. When Napoleon I. fell, and the French domination ceased, they resumed their peaceful avocations. In more recent times the cruel and unwise enactments known as "the May Laws" once more threatened the Ursulines of the new German Empire with total destruction. Even in Catholic Bavaria nothing but the powerful protection of public opinion stood between them and suppression.

To one of these Bavarian houses, that of Landshut, midway between Ratisbon and Munich, conjointly with the Hungarian Ursulines of Oedenburg, the United States are indebted for some of the most promising Ursuline schools—those, namely, of St. Louis and New York.

The Ursuline monastery of Breslau, thanks to that Providence who so kindly proportions spiritual help to the needs of a population, educated daily some fifteen hundred pupils! And their sisters throughout Prussia and Austria-Hungary vied with them in holy zeal and the fervent practise of religious perfection. At Vienna, Prague, Salzburg, Presburg, Gratz, Klagenfurt, Innsbruck, and elsewhere, the Ursuline monasteries were peopled from the beginning by the noblest in worldly rank and in goodness; and, as like ever attracts like, they have continued down to the present day to have for educators of the female youth of all classes the very flower of native womanhood. It is on the Christian women who go forth from the twenty-four great Ursuline schools of Austria-Hungary that good men build their hopes for the society of the future.

So may the Ursulines of the Austrian Empire long continue to be—a blessing to the land which shelters and fosters them! Far otherwise is it with their sisters in Prussia and other parts of the new German Empire. Of course, an anti-Catholic policy which seizes the most shadowy pretexts for wholesale persecution could not long tolerate the existence of such admirable schools as those of Breslau. So, the Ursulines, guilty solely of devoting their lives to the children of rich and poor alike, were informed by the Prussian authorities that they might no longer either teach the poor or live in holy poverty themselves on the land of their birth! They had foreseen their doom and prepared for it, having taken measures to open an academy for German children at Marseilles. They had been commanded to disappear before October 1st, 1878. "The venerable lady superior," writes the Abbé Richaudeau, "passed through Blois on September the 15th, taking with her one of her nuns, who had obtained from the French Government a teacher's diploma after a whole year's preparation. Fifteen Ursulines of Schweidnitz (some sixteen miles to the south-west of Breslau) have betaken themselves to Skalitz, in Bohemia. Their companions remained with the determination to yield only to force. The Ursulines of Düren have been also expelled. The superior, with most of her nuns, has gone to reside at Meersen, near Maestricht, in Holland. Besides, she has sent a little colony to America, where the Ursulines of Toledo, Ohio, offer them hospitality, till such time as the Bishop of Peoria can establish them among the German population of his diocese. They must have sailed from Havre on the 19th of October."

Turn we now to the Ursulines of America.

Quebec, "the walled city of the North," has the honor to possess the most ancient Ursuline establishment in the New World, and with it a school which, for efficiency and the numbers of its pupils, stands second to no female seminary on the Continent. It was founded in 1639 by the venerable Mary of the Incarnation (Marie Guyard-Martin), seconded by a noble widow lady, Marie Magdaleine de la Peltrie. The foundress and her first companions belonged to the monasteries of Tours and Dieppe, and being joined soon afterward by several sisters from Paris, they adopted a Rule combining the excellences both of the Congregation of Bordeaux and of that of Paris, ending, however, by becoming affiliated to the latter.

The history of the great monastery-school of Quebec forms one of the most heroic records in American history.[1] It has fulfilled a most important part in educating the female youth of Canada ; and, being admirable in every way, as the writer from his boyhood has known it to be, he could wish with his whole heart that it would send colonies of its accomplished educators to every part of our vast continent. From Quebec issued in 1697 the Ursuline establishment of Three Rivers, which, with the brightening prospects of the Province itself, is rapidly increasing its labors and numbers.

Almost a century after the arrival in Quebec of Mary of the Incarnation and her companions, Mother Marie Tranchepain, another heroic Frenchwoman, with ten Ursuline companions, sailed from L'Orient for the mouth of the Mississippi, arriving at New Orleans on the 6th of August, 1727. The history of this little band of devoted women is scarcely less romantic than that of their Canadian sisters. They were at the mercy of the "Company of the Mississippi" till its downfall in 1732, and left to face the most exhausting and varied labors without adequate means of sustenance or even decent accommodation. But their uncomplaining heroism only served to endear them to the colonists. Nor was their condition much bettered by the royal administrators during the next thirty years. In a sickly climate, they had to dis-

---

[1] See "Les Ursulines de Québec," 3 vols., Quebec, 1863-64 ; a most interesting work, compiled from the most authentic sources, under the direction, if not by the hand, of Rev. George Lemoine, the resident chaplain. Also "Glimpses of the Monastery : A Brief Sketch of the Ursulines of Quebec," 3 vols., 12mo. Quebec, 1872-75 ; a charming summary of the more voluminous French work.

charge the duties of hospitalers, to take charge of the numerous orphans left by the Natchez massacres and by the exiled Acadians, as well as by successive epidemics, and to keep school for the girls of the colony. In 1762 they passed with Louisiana under Spanish rule; their numbers decreasing so much, that in 1786 they had to receive assistance from the Ursuline Convent of the Presentation in Pont-Saint-Esprit. The retrocession of the colony to France in 1802 alarmed the good nuns, and most of them, to avoid falling under the yoke of the French Republic, took refuge in Havana. This gave rise to the two Ursuline establishments in Cuba. Meanwhile the Presentation Ursulines, who formed the majority in the New Orleans monastery, continued their apostolic labors, caring for the orphans, teaching their large school, and devoting Sundays and holy days to the instruction of colored women.

When Louisiana became, in 1803, a portion of the United States, the apprehensions entertained by the Ursulines about their religious liberty were soon quieted, and a new reinforcement of nuns arriving from France in 1810, the community were able to increase their field of labor. In 1815, during the siege of the city by the English, their schoolrooms became a military hospital, in which the sick and wounded defenders of New Orleans received the most lavish care during three whole months. In 1818 the State Legislature secured by a special act their rights and privileges as a religious body, and about the same time they received from France a most opportune accession of nine postulants. In 1824 they removed their residence to a more remote position.

In December, 1823, three Ursulines from Quebec had come, at the appeal of Bishop Dubourg, to aid their New Orleans sisters in their increase of labor and lack of laborers.

And, as if the venerable Mary of the Incarnation had sent a special blessing with her daughters, from their arrival dates the uninterrupted prosperity enjoyed till 1861. The calamities of the great civil war weighed heavily on the Ursulines of New Orleans, as it did on the city itself and on the entire State. Let us hope that the revival of commercial industry and general prosperity which is slowly dawning on the Southern States will bring to the two Ursuline schools of New Orleans their merited share of well-being and fruitful increase. They deserve it in every way. Despite their own need of laborers, they did not hesitate in 1847 to send a colony to Galveston under the protection of the devoted Bishop Odin ; and in 1852 a second colony settled in San Antonio.

Meanwhile, in 1812, Father Anthony Kohlmann, who was governing as Vicar-General the infant Church of New York, wished to provide for the education of Catholic girls an establishment as like as possible to the college which he had opened for the education of boys. Three Ursulines from the Monastery of Black Rock, near Cork, Christina Fagan, Sara Walsh, and Mary Baldwin, hesitated not to embark for New York, crossing the Atlantic in the most stormy season of the year, and arriving at their destination early in April, 1812. Father Kohlmann procured a residence for them on a spot which is now the corner of Fiftieth Street and Third Avenue. They forthwith opened a school, were incorporated by a special act of the Legislature, and were soon surrounded by a large flock of pupils. No postulants, however, offered themselves to the good ladies, and as this was the only condition on which they would continue their labors, they returned to Ireland in 1815.

Not before 1855 did New York again possess an establishment of Ursulines. This time, at the call of Archbishop Hughes, the Ursulines of St. Louis sent their superior,

Mother Magdalen Stehlin, who had in 1847 headed the little colony of Hungarian nuns from Oedenburg to St. Louis, with ten companions, to found a monastery in the suburb of East Morrisania. They took possession of their new home on the 15th of May, have prospered under God's blessing, and count at the present moment some fifty professed religious, with a proportionate number of novices and postulants, and a flourishing school. Besides, they have established a monastery within the heart of the city, with some eighteen nuns, and a large school.

The return to Ireland in 1815 of the Ursuline colony of New York reminds American readers of the efforts which were made at the same epoch to found an Ursuline monastery in Boston. This project originated with the Rev. John Thayer, himself a native of New England and a convert to the Catholic faith, who had in 1811 taken up his abode in Limerick, and inspired two of his penitents, the Misses Mary and Catherine Ryan, with a fervent wish to be the first apostles of the female youth of Massachusetts. The undertaking was warmly supported by Bishop Cheverus; but Mr. Thayer died in Limerick in February, 1815, and not before the 4th of May, 1817, could the two noble sisters embark for their transatlantic mission. After a year's novitiate in the Ursuline Convent of Three Rivers, they returned to Boston and took up their residence near the cathedral, being joined in September, 1818, by their youngest sister and Catherine Molineux, a young cousin. Not long afterward two native American ladies, Elizabeth Harrison and Catherine Wiseman, gave the little community firm hopes of increase by their timely accession.

These hopes were, however, attended with serious apprehensions and discouragements. The New England Puritans bore a deep aversion to everything which had the semblance of monasticism, and public opinion in Boston was greatly excited by the presence of the Ursuline sisterhood. Then the two foundresses sickened and died, having been preceded in the grave by their cousin. This was in 1823–25. The superior, Mother Mary Joseph, who was the last to be stricken down, appealed from her death-bed for help to the Ursulines of Quebec, who sent them Mother Mary Edmond St. George (Ursula Moffat).

It was evident that the narrow residence of Boston was also unhealthy, and so in 1826 the Ursulines removed to a new monastery in Charlestown, which they called Mount Benedict, in honor of the Right Rev. Benedict Fenwick, who had succeeded Bishop Cheverus in the see of Boston. In this place, doomed to so sad a celebrity, the academy opened by the sisters acquired a great reputation. Unfortunately, in 1831 the evil tongue of a silly girl whom the nuns had refused to retain in the convent, began to spread false reports among the already prejudiced public of Boston. Simultaneously with this, one of the sisters, in a temporary fit of insanity, escaped from the establishment, and her extravagant and incoherent utterances served as a pretext for the most abominable accusations in some of the daily papers. A clergyman of noted ability and great influence inflamed the public mind by his fierce and frequent denunciations; and the ferment grew so rapidly, that on the night of August 11th, 1834, a mob attacked Mount Benedict, broke into the house, barely permitting the nuns and their frightened pupils to dress and escape with their lives. The magistrates and police kept out of the way, while the convent was sacked and burned to the ground. Every attempt to obtain adequate reparation for this outrage, so disgraceful to the manhood of New England, has hitherto failed. The members of the community took refuge in Quebec, and after vain efforts to restore their ruined home, devoted themselves to the labors of their calling in various Ursuline establishments of Canada and the United States. A niece of the foundresses, Catherine Quirk, known in the sisterhood as Sister St. Henry, died in Roxbury on the 18th October following the catastrophe, in consequence of her exposure on the fatal night, and with her eyes fondly turned to the ruins of Mount Benedict, her chosen American home. Of the Ursulines of Charleston, S. C., we shall speak after giving the history of Black Rock Convent.

The more permanent Ursuline establishment of St. Martin's, near Fayetteville, Ohio, was founded in 1845 under the auspices of the present venerable Archbishop Purcell. The Ursuline colony sent to him were from the fruitful monastery of Boulogne-sur-Mer, jointly with that of Beaulieu (Corrèze). When Bishop Purcell first visited Boulogne in 1839, the Ursulines had for chaplain the Rev. Amédée Rappe, for whom he conceived a warm friendship, and who subsequently became Bishop of Cleveland. Bishop Rappe, in his turn, obtained a colony of Ursulines from Boulogne in 1849, and his diocese now possesses four houses of the Order. So blessed indeed have the daughters of St. Angela been in the United States, despite the drawback which a strictly cloistered sisterhood must meet with in the active duties of education, that they count twenty-nine houses within the limits of the Republic.

We have just mentioned the monastery of Boulogne-sur-Mer; and this will remind the reader that we have yet to sketch the rise of the Ursuline schools in Ireland and England, tracing them to their origin in France—the great nursery of apostolic devotion. Just as it had happened for the establishment of the first Ursuline monastery in Paris, where the Blessed Mary of the Incarnation was mainly instrumental in founding both Ursulines and Carmelites, so was it in

Ireland, where Miss Nano Nagle introduced the first Ursulines, and founded the Order of the Presentation, becoming herself a member of the latter.

This excellent lady had been educated in the monastery of St. Ursula in Paris—the cherished creation of Blessed Mother Mary and her cousin, Madame de Sainte-Beuve. In that fervent community she imbibed, together with the best education France could afford, that zeal for the interests of Christ's afflicted Church which was the motive-power of all her conduct after her return to her native land. She left France in 1750, being then in her twenty-second year, impressed with the conviction that God called her to labor for the elevation of the poor classes in her own country. In the pursuit of her purpose she was encouraged by her own family; and, after having kept for some time a school in Dublin, she went to Cork and soon had under her care two schools for boys and five for girls, with good teachers, and a constantly growing crowd of pupils. She thereupon solicited aid from the Ursulines of Paris, but these did not dare to accede to her request. Four Irish ladies, however, animated by Miss Nagle's own spirit, at once entered the Paris novitiate with the determination of becoming in due time the promoters of what they considered to be God's own work in Ireland. Their probationary term ended, after appealing in vain to the Parisian sisterhood for auxiliaries in their enterprise, they set out for Cork, were joined at Dieppe by Mother Margaret Kelly of the Ursuline convent in that city, and entered their own Irish monastery-home on the 18th September, 1771.

Pope Clement XIV. gave this establishment canonical approbation in 1773, and the sisterhood, increasing in numbers, took charge of the schools hitherto directed by Miss Nagle. A few years later the Ursulines removed to the village of

Black Rock, in the immediate neighborhood of the city, where they opened an academy which soon obtained a world-wide reputation. From this monastery swarms have gone forth not only to Waterford, Thurles, and Sligo, but to North and South America. One South American house only, deriving its existence from Black Rock, subsists in Georgetown, Demarara—a lonely outpost on the confines of that great Brazilian world, which Christian zeal and American enterprise have yet to conquer for God and true civilization.

The other establishment claiming its descent from Black Rock is the Ursuline monastery of Valle Crucis, near Columbia, South Carolina. The story its inmates might tell is full of pathetic interest and vicissitude. Just while Sister Catherine Quirk was on her death-bed at Roxbury, in October, 1834, three professed Ursulines and one postulant from Black Rock were crossing the ocean to Charleston. Under the fatherly direction of Bishop England, himself a native of Cork, the little band of missionaries labored strenuously, and not without plentiful fruit among every class of the Carolinian population —among the wives and daughters of the colored portion in particular. Small as was, comparatively, the number of their pupil-boarders, still, belonging as they did to the best families in the Carolinas and Georgia, their influence on returning to their families was necessarily very great ; and, besides, many of the best families in the country became through them converts to the Catholic faith.

In 1844 Bishop Reynolds succeeded to Dr. England in the see of Charleston, and soon afterward " the older members of the community returned to the parent house, and the others withdrew to the diocese of Cincinnati, where they sojourned until the appointment of Bishop Lynch (1858), at whose solicitation they returned and resumed their former position of usefulness in the diocese." [1]

---

[1] The words of Dr. J. J. O'Connell.

"In 1859," says a circular of the sisters, "Bishop Lynch bought a large hotel in Columbia. . . . There was great excitement among the citizens. . . . But the bishop's influence overcame them all. . . . So great was our success, that our academy soon outstripped those belonging to other denominations, and drew to our school the very *élite* of their pupils." And so the good sisters continued to prosper till the gloomy days of 1861. The convent then became a sort of sacred asylum for children and young ladies who were alarmed by the progress of the civil war or driven from their own homes. Although by far the greater number were Protestants, they found in the Ursulines nothing but motherly kindness, generous hospitality, solid instruction, and edifying example. All this—we blush to record it—did not save the inmates from the cruel fate of war.

The establishment was pitilessly pillaged and destroyed by the Federal troops on February 17th, 1865, in spite of the positive promises of protection given by the commanding general, and almost beneath his eyes.[1] Thanks to the self-sacrificing efforts of the devoted bishop, the Ursuline monastery of Columbia, like the other ruined establishments of his diocese, are now recovering from the effects of the civil war.

In England there exist only three Ursuline houses—at Upton, near London; at Croom's Hill, Greenwich; and at Swansea. Those of Upton came from Sittard, in Limburg, in 1851, at the instance of Cardinal Wiseman. Unhappily for the new-comers, the anti-Catholic spirit aroused by the restoration of the hierarchy in England was then at its height in the capital. As the sisters had shown themselves clad in their religious habit while passing through the streets of London, their appearance excited against them the animosity

---

[1] See circular letter of the Ursulines of Valle Crucis, of October 10th, 1878; also Very Rev. Dr. O'Connell's "Catholicity in the Carolinas and Georgia," pp. 211, 269-80.

of the rabble. After opening school in two localities, they found that their prospects did not brighten and that their health began to fail. The cardinal then found a house for them in Oxford; but as after the expiration of the lease of their residence the Ursulines could not obtain a renewal, and no other house would receive them, they had to return to Belgium in 1861. The next year, however, they gladly returned, and took possession of their present abode at Upton, six miles from London, and on the border of Epping Forest. This time they found themselves at home in their own house, the property having been purchased by the cardinal. On July 9th, 1877, their community numbered twenty members, with a wide and rich missionary field to cultivate.

The Ursulines of Upton, as well as the parent establishment of Sittard, belong to a numerous and flourishing branch of the Ursuline Order, planted in 1818 at Thildonck, near Louvain—a community of independent Ursulines, who since adopted the Rule of Bordeaux, and who made themselves so useful in educating the popular classes, that they soon spread all over the Low Countries, and numbered forty houses at the beginning of 1868. This fruitful congregation was originated by Rev. Mr. Lambertz, rector of Thildonck; and most touching and instructive is the history of these forty Ursuline monasteries, who are the living providence of God among the hard-working people of Belgium and Holland.

This keen and practical sense of what is most needed by the popular classes in every Christian land must be the distinctive character of every man or woman, of every body of men or of women, who would be living and efficient helps to religion, to education, to the family home, and to public society in our day and for many a day to come.

This keen sense was characteristic of St. Angela and her daughters in the sixteenth century. They could not have obtained the confidence of all Christian families in France, Italy, Germany, and elsewhere, as the seventeenth century dawned and ran its disturbing course, had their teaching and their lives not supplied a great social need.

The wonderful propagation of Father Lambertz's Ursulines throughout Belgium and Holland shows as well that the spirit and rule of St. Angela, when embodied in women who understand the wants of the people, are as sure to prosper and call down the blessings of God and men, as the fire is sure to spread in July through the dry grasses of our Western prairies beneath a cloudless sky and propelled by a high wind.

To every house of Ursulines into which this book will go, and to every daughter of Angela Merici who happens to read it, the author sends the fervent wish and prayer to God, that every Ursuline community may sanctify the world around it by cherishing the unworldly and self-sacrificing spirit of the Holy Maid of Desenzano, and that every child of hers may lift heavenward the young souls committed to her, by the fervent and constant practice of her Mother's angelic virtues.

EVERY
SUNDAY-SCHOOL
AND
PAROCHIAL LIBRARY

SHOULD CONTAIN

A COPY OF THE "KAATERSKILL EDITION"

OF THE SELECT WORKS OF

WASHINGTON IRVING,

A special edition of which has been specially arranged and issued in **Five Volumes,** strongly and substantially bound in **Half Morocco,** and is now offered at the **exceedingly low price of Eight Dollars net, per set of Five Volumes;** making it one of the most attractive and indispensable additions to the library, while the price is so low that no one should miss such an opportunity to procure a copy in this style of binding when offered at such a low price.

For a list of the works contained in these volumes see other side.

POLLARD & MOSS, Publishers,

WASHINGTON IRVING,

EMBRACING

HIS LIFE, AND THE FOLLOWING VOLUMES OF HIS WORKS, PRINTED FROM THE EARLY AND ORIGINAL ISSUES, COMPLETE AND UNABRIDGED.

"THE SKETCH-BOOK," BY GEOFFREY CRAYON.
"THE ALHAMBRA."
"LEGENDS OF THE CONQUEST OF SPAIN."
"BRACEBRIDGE HALL."
"SALMAGUNDI."
"THE CONQUEST OF GRANADA."
"TALES OF A TRAVELLER."
"KNICKERBOCKER'S HISTORY OF NEW YORK."
"VOYAGES AND DISCOVERIES OF THE COMPANIONS OF COLUMBUS."
A CHRONICLE OF WOLFERT'S ROOST, SLEEPY HOLLOW, AND OTHER MISCELLANIES FROM THE KNICKERBOCKER MAGAZINE.

The above works, UNALTERED and UNABRIDGED, are COMPLETE, and for the convenience of libraries, an edition has been bound up in five volumes, containing all the works enumerated above, strongly bound in half morocco, price only EIGHT DOLLARS NET, per Set. The work is embellished with a fine Steel Portrait of WASHINGTON IRVING, engraved in line expressly for this edition, and

THE LIFE BY

RICHARD HENRY STODDARD.

The Kaaterskill Irving is a library in itself. Nothing can compare with it in its adaptability to every class, and no one should fail to procure such a work that fascinates every sense by its incomparable style.

Its contents cover such a wide range of subjects in every department of literature, that A MASTERPIECE stands forth yet to be excelled in

HISTORY,	Equal to	"*The Conquest of Granada.*"
DISCOVERY AND ADVENTURE,	"	"*The Companions of Columbus.*"
LEGENDARY LORE,	"	"*The Alhambra and Legends of the Conquest of Spain.*"
HUMOR,	"	"*Knickerbocker's History of New York.*"
WIT AND WISDOM,	"	"*Bracebridge Hall and Salmagundi.*"
BELLES LETTRES,	"	"*The Sketch-Book.*"
ROMANCE,	"	"*Tales of a Traveller.*"
ESSAYS,	"	"*The Miscellanies Contributed to the Knickerbocker.*"

While the POETICAL selections scattered throughout the work are gems that illume by their brilliancy a volume in which not a dull page can be found from cover to cover.

For Sunday-School and Parochial Libraries.

An edition of this work has been specially arranged and divided up in Five Volumes, strongly and substantially bound in Half Morocco, and offered at the exceedingly low price of Eight Dollars net, per set of Five Volumes; making it one of the most attractive and indispensable additions to the library that can be made, while the price is so low that no one should fail to procure a copy in this style of binding when offered at such a low price.

It will be sent to any address upon receipt of the price, by the publishers. Address

POLLARD & MOSS, Publishers, 47 John Street, N. Y.

HACKERAY, ICKENS, AND LEVER

The Templeogue Lever is the first attempt to supply a complete uniform edition of

CHARLES LEVER'S WORKS,

and will embrace all of his known works. It will be printed from new type on the best of paper, and each volume will be beautifully illustrated with sixteen full-page chromo-lithographs printed in eight colors in the highest style of lithographic art.

Vol. Two is now ready and will contain

JACK HINTON, THE GUARDSMAN: THE O'DONOGHUE: ROLAND CASHEL.

With sixteen full-page Illustrations, printed in eight colors, in the highest style of lithographic art.

LIST OF ILLUSTRATIONS:

"TIPPERARY JOE," "BOB MAHON'S ELEVATION TO THE SHERIFF,"
"THE DUKE KNIGHTING CORNY DELANY,"
"THE FINALE TO AN EVENING," "BRAVO TORO,"
"AFTER LUNCHEON—THE START,"
"HOW TO WORK A PATENT PUMP,"
"THE GAME AT MONTE," "THE RECKONING," "THE WAGER,"
"ROACHE'S RETURN TO THE O'DONOGHUES' CASTLE,"
"ROACHE'S CONVENIENCY," "MARK DRAWING A CORK,"
"SIR ARCHY HEARS SOMETHING TO HIS ADVANTAGE."

"The author is pre-eminent for his mirth-moving powers, for his acute sense of the ridiculous, for the breadth of his humor, and for his power of dramatic writing, which renders his boldest conceptions with the happiest facility."—*London Athenæum*.

"The intense spirit and frolic of the author's sketches have made him one of the most successful writers of the day."—*London Literary Gazette*.

"There is no dullness in Mr. Lever's dashing, daring, rapid books. They are inimitable. Who can bewitch the world with such noble horsemanship? He has the true spring of Irish humor and Irish shrewdness in him. Mickey Free is as merry and honest a rogue as ever happy fancy invented, and all the secondary bits of life and character in the home country are admirable."—*Blackwood's Magazine*.

The following is a list of prices and styles of binding:

Each volume will contain nearly 600 pages, imperial 8vo, embellished with SIXTEEN *full-page Illustrations, printed in colors.*

Price, per volume, in cloth extra, ornamental designs on cover, in gold and ink, gilt tops, only . . . . $3.
Half morocco, marble edges, ... 5.
Half calf, marble edges, ... 6.
Full morocco, antique pattern, gilt edges, ... 7.

☞ Any volume sold separately and forwarded by mail, postage prepaid, upon receipt of the advertised price by the publishers.

Address, **POLLARD & MOSS, Publishers,**
P. O. Box 1418.   47 John Street, New York.

THE TEMPLEOGUE LEVER!

THE WORKS OF
CHARLES LEVER.
(HARRY LORREQUER).

An entirely new edition, embracing all his known works, including his early contributions to various periodicals and magazines, never before collected; making the only complete and uniform edition of CHARLES LEVER'S Works that has ever been undertaken. Each volume will contain nearly 600 pages, imperial 8vo, and will be embellished with 16 full-page illustrations, printed in eight colors, in the highest style of lithographic art.

THE TEMPLEOGUE LEVER will be printed from new type, on the best of paper, and handsomely bound in English cloth, the covers ornamented with designs in gold and ink, gilt tops. Price, per volume, $3.75. Volume One contains:

HARRY LORREQUER;
CHARLES O'MALLEY, THE IRISH DRAGOON;
PAUL GOSSELETT'S CONFESSIONS.

Embellished with sixteen full-page illustrations, printed in seven colors, in the highest style of lithographic art.

LIST OF ILLUSTRATIONS.

"LORREQUER ON PARADE."
"NICHOLAS ANNOUNCING MISS BETTY O'DOUD'S CARRIAGE."
"MR. O'LEARY CREATING A COMMOTION AT THE 'SALONS DES ETRANGERS.'"
"DR. FINUCANE AND THE GRAY MARE."
"LORREQUER AS POSTILLION."
"ARRIVAL OF THE CHARGE D'AFFAIRES."
"A FLYING SHOT."   "THE RESCUE."
"THE SUNK FENCE."   "THE ELECTION."   "MR. FREE'S SONG."
"THE TABLES TURNED."   "THE ADJUTANT'S AFTER-DINNER RIDE."
"A HUNTING TURNOUT ON THE PENINSULA."
"O'MALLEY FOLLOWING THE CUSTOMS OF THE COUNTRY."
"CAPT. MICKEY FREE RELATING HIS HEROIC DEEDS."

"Lever has had fewer imitators than any other popular novelist. He would be more difficult of imitation than any. Spurious-grotesque copies of Mr. Dickens, mock-cynical copies of Mr. Thackeray, there have been in plenty; but though he is not on the same line with either, Mr. Lever is more difficult of even coarse imitation than the great humorist or the great ethical novelist. His very faults and absurdities would be hard to catch, while the charm of his writings is lent by a quality of mind and tone of spirits not to be simulated."—*Dublin Review.*

The following is a list of prices and styles of binding:

Each volume will contain nearly 600 pages, imperial 8vo, embellished with SIXTEEN *full-page Illustrations, printed in colors.*

Price, per volume, in cloth extra, ornamental designs on cover, in
   gold and ink, gilt tops, only $3.75
Half morocco, marble edges, ... 5.00
Half calf, marble edges, ... 6.00
Full morocco, antique pattern, gilt edges, ... 7.50

☞ Any volume sold separately, and will be sent by mail to any address, upon receipt of the advertised price, by the publishers, postage prepaid. Address,

POLLARD & MOSS, Publishers, 47 John Street, N. Y.